COMPARATIVE STUDY
OF
THE RELIGIONS

COMPARATIVE STUDY OF THE RELIGIONS

By :

C.R. JAIN

BHARATIYA KALA PRAKASHAN

DELHI (INDIA)

First Published : 2004
Revised Edition : 2025

Published by C.P. Gautam *for*
BHARATIYA KALA PRAKASHAN
3480/1, Narang Colony, Tri Nagar, Delhi - 110035
Ph. 011 71522860, Mob.: 9811642997, 8595139625
E-mail : info@bkpbooks.com; sales.bkpbooks@gmail.com
Website: www.bkpbooks.com

ISBN : 978-81-8090-067-9

Laser Type Setting by
A-ONE GRAPHICS

Printed by :
G.S. Offset Printer
Delhi

FOREWORD

The series of lectures now in the reader's hand is the outcome of many years' patient and persistent study of the causes of diversity and difference among the prevailing religions of the world. In presenting them to the enquiring public I have to announce the momentous discovery of a secret language or script that will revolutionize religious belief and change the very complexion of thought. It has, indeed, been long surmised that the divinities setup in at least certain of the Bibles of the world are purely allegorical in nature; but the true import and significancy of the various allegories have remained a profound secret thus for. It is true that scholars have generally sought to identify these divine personifications with certain physical forces and phenomena, *e.g.*, clouds, rain, spirit of vegetation, fire and the like; but the supposition does not satisfy the prying intellect and has failed to command general acquiescence which it should have done if true. Yet it is obvious from the number and nature of the discrepancies alone that are to be found in them that the scriptures of the world could not have been and were not intended to be read historically. The discovery that has now been made will show that the Vedas, the Qur'an, the Zend Avesta and, indeed, all other ancient mythological scriptures are composed in one single language not with standing the outward diversity of the alphabets and tongues in which they are couched. We may call this secret language Pictokrit, to distinguish it from Prakrit, the people's tongue, and from Sanskrit, the language of the learned. The significance of the term Pictokrit lies in the fact that it gives expression to the most sublime of human thought in pictorial form, its special merit being its capacity to embody whole philosophies in a single picture or panel of paintings. Some of the matter dealt with here has already appeared in my earlier work, the Key of Knowledge, and other books. The present work, composed in the form of lectures, sums up the result of the whole investigation, in, small compass, and is sent out in the hope that it will at least stimulate scientific research.

It only remains to be added that these lectures are connected with one another ofter a plan, and should be read in the order in which they are arranged.

C. R. JAIN

CONTENTS

Kaliya, the serpent—King—Krishna— Abel and Cain—all egorical import of the Abraham myth —the symbology of the Patriarchs—two Moses —the Vision of Ezekiel—the relation between spirit and matter—the story of job—the intelligent fire—Ascension of Isaiah— transmigration in judaism

V. (d) **The teaching of the New Testament**—divinity of the soul—the fall—redemption—bondage of sin—means to the end—'works'—Christian Gnosticism—Messianic symbolism—the virgin mother—father, a carpenter—temptation—srucifixion—Golgotha—rending of rocks— the darkening of the sun—rending of the veil of the temple—the opening out of graves—transmigration in the N.T.—'ye shall know the truth and the truth shall make you free'— redemption not a matter of favour or grace— resurrection—why no marriages in resurrection —*raga* and *dvesha*—transmigration accepted by jews—sexlessness of the soul—Sons of God— merit of renunciation—agreement between Biblical text and Jaina Scriptures—Jesus and John, the Baptist—Evanson on John's doings— Life and Intellect—the baptisms of Jesus and John—devotion and *vairagya*—the bride

V. (e) **Islam**—Muhammad's personality—the splitting of the moon—the *swastika* and the crescent moon—Gabriel, the archangel—other angels of the Qur'an—the teaching of Islam—why Muhammad followed the mystical style of secret teaching—Shamsh of Tebrez—Forid-ul-Din Attar and other mystics of Islam—human and animal life in the Qur'an—Muslim acknowledgment of prior revelations—taqdir the lauh-i-mahfuz—transmigration—the Dervishes—

ABBREVIATIONS

ERE	=	The Encyclopredia of Religion and Ethics.
PHB	=	The Permanent History of Bharata-varsha.
SBE	=	The Sacred Books of the East.
SBH	=	The Sacred Books of the Hindus.
SBJ	=	The Sacred Books of the Jainas.
SSP	=	The Six Systems of Indian Philosophy by Max Muller.

CHAPTER - I

GENERAL SURVEY

Comparative Religion is a science. It is that department of rational knowledge which seeks to ascertain the views of different religions to reconcile their teachings to one another, collecting, sorting and interpreting ancient lore to get at the truth. It proceeds upon a policy of criticism that is constructive in its ultimate nature, in so for, at least, as it seeks to find out the element of truth behind every form of belief, though, naturally, a great deal of destructive work is to be performed in the beginning to get rid of the cobwebs of superstition and error adhering to diverse faiths.

The field of enquiry is vast and almost unexplored. Indeed, no one is known to have ever approached the subject in a scientific spirit. There is one well-known work of the fourteenth century, termed *Sarvadarshana Sangraha*, but it is neither scientific in nature nor exhaustive in scope, its author (Madhava Acharya) contenting himself with a general ,discussion of a few abstract points raised by the diverse schools of Indian metaphysics known to him. Haribhadra's *Saddarshanasamuch-chaya*, too, though richer and fuller in many respects than the work referred to, is nevertheless quite inadequate as a basis for comparative religion. For the problem of today is concerned not so much with the metaphysical analysis of discursive thought as with the bringing into a line of systems so diametrically opposed as Jainism, Vedicism, Christianity, Islam, Zoroastrianism and Judaism appear to be. This task, it is superfluous to add, has never been attempted before, though in recent times a few unqualified or half-qualified writers have endleavoured, from highly laudable motives of good will and human love, to establish a somewhat far-fetched harmony between some of these creeds. As embracing all the diversified forms of belief, that is to say, in its entirety, the subject has never been approached hitherto, nor have the root-causes of misunderstanding between different religions been ever laid bare in the history of human thought.

With respect to the manner of comparison also, it has been a favourite method with those who have gone before us to try to reconcile the divers faiths to one another by pointing out and emphasizing a few features of resemhlance —in each one of them and by ignoring and minimising ,all kinds of differences in their teachings, as if they could be disposed of so easily—by merely being ignored. This method does not appeal to me as satisfaotory, for there can be no, true or lasting reconciliation so long as the differences remain unexplained. To arrive at true reconciliation, then, we must analyse these differences themselves to obtain their common unifying principle, if there be one underlying them. We shall have to dive deep beneath the surface of things to understand the very genesis of mythological thought, so to speak. We shall, if successful, be erecting a Temple of Truth, which shall also be a real Temple of Union, that shall be the place of worship for all kinds and classes of men, where differences shall not need to be stifled, but shall actually go to clarify the real fundamental tenets of Truth, and to cement friendship and amity amongst men, all the more closely for their reiteration.

I must not, however, suffer you to remain under the erroneous impression that anything like complete justice can be done to the subject. This is simply out of the question, being precluded by the vastness of the field of enquiry. My difficulty arises as much from want of time, which is entirely inadequate for the task, as from a lack of knowledge and penetration into a very large number of quaint conceptions of mystic and mystifying thought that have been woven into theological dogmas and myths. In the face of these elements of difficulty there is, however, one great feature of reassurance and encouragement, which consists in the important fact that mystic thought has been running on parallel lines in all the different creeds and cults and that an elucidating "key" is nearly always to be found concealed, or is, at least, easily traceable in almost every ancient scripture. The large and varied assortment of mystic conceptions and symbolic thought is, thus, reducible to a definite number of principles, which fully justify us in the formulation, or rather the reformulation and re-construction, of the original systems of religious thought that have lain buried beneath the dust of centuries. Positive assurance, akin to absolute accuracy, is predicated in favour of the results thus reached by nothing less than the direct convergence of the several lines of research—scientific, metaphysical, mystic and hierological on to one single point, namely, the reconstructed Truth. We shall thus be not only laying down the beginnings of a science of comparative Religion to be built upon by our successors, but shall also be raising up a real Temple of Truth and Union which shall be a permanent heritage of mankind for all times and ages,—a lofty spiritual edifice, complete and self-contained in all its departments, though admitting of additional structures to be raised on lines and foundations already laid down. The results of our spade-work here will, I trust, suffice to demonstrate the validity of the method and means recommended.

With respect to the method of reconciliation, you and I who stand in this Hall of Reason must agree that the strictest logic shall be our guide in the elucidation of the different problems as they arise in the course of our investigation. Bias and bigotry are subversive of truth, and fanatical fervour destructive of reason itself. As for private convictions and vague intuitions of individuals, well, we have to leave them out of account if for no other reason than this that they do not tend to lucidity of thought and are, therefore, out of place in scientific research. As said by me elsewhere, if private intuitions of individuals could be relied upon in place of scientifically true conceptions of reason, every lunatic would have acquired the right to fill the chair of philosophy and every morbid subject of hysteria and hallucination to rank as patron of Science. Reason and reason alone must be our guide throughout, at least till such time as a 'reacher is found whose intuitive wisdom can be implicitly relied upon as an unfailing light to guide our steps in the right direction. For the same reason we must leave scriptural text out of consideration, at least in the first instance, for, in addition to being full of matter which is highly incredible and most unacceptable to anyone except those who accept it as part of their faith, the Holy Scriptures of almost all the religions now prevailing in the world as well as of those that flourished in the past are generally self-contradictory and discrepant with one another, so that it is not possible for them to be accepted as truth pure and simple.

What intellectualism signifies, and how it can be speedily developed, will be explained in the next lecture, meanwhile it is clear that no one who has not eliminated all traces of superstition from his mind can be considered qualified to study the truth. If there be anyone present here who declines to abide by the arbitrament of his own unbiased reason, he should not feel aggrieved if his claim to rationalism is non-suited in the supreme court of common sense.

I shall now proceed to briefly describe the tenets and doctrines of the diverse faiths, so as to be able to ascertain their common features of resemblance as well as their points of difference.

Jainism lays down the following seven *tattvas* (essentials or heads of study) :—

(i) *jiva* (spirit),

(ii) *ajiva* (non-spirit),

(iii) *asrava* (influx of matter into spirit),

(iv) *bandha* (bondage),

(v) *samvara* (stoppage of influx),

(iv) *nirjara* (destruction of bondage), and

(vii) *moksha* (salvation).

There are nine *padarathas*, formed by the addition of two other subjects, namely,

(viii) *punya* (merit) and

(ix) *papa* (demerit)

to the seven *tattvas*. The world is enternal and uncreate, and comprises two kinds of substance, namely, spirit, or living substance, and non-spirit, or *ajiva*, which class includes several realities such as matter, space, ether etc. Of these spirit and matter are the two really important substances. Spirit comprises an infinite number of units, or individuals, termed *Jivas* (living beings), and matter (*pudgala*) is atomic. The changing, shifting nature of the universe is due to the functioning of substances and to the interaction between spirit and matter, which is governed by certain well-defined laws. Mundane souls are spirits existing in combination with matter, by whose union the natural attributes of the former are curtailed, in varying degree, according to the type of their fusion and the quantity of matter adhering to each soul. Complete freedom from matter is *moksha* (salvation), which leaves the soul as pure Spirit, and, therefore, without the curtailments imposed upon its attributes by the associations of matter. 'the attributes of pure Spirit include :—

(i) Omniscience,

(ii) Blissfulness,

(iii) Immortality, and

(iv) Infinite Energy.

Accordingly, every freed Soul become Omniscient Ever-Blissful and Immortal, in consequence of separation from matter. For this reason is a Redeemed one termed *paramatman*, (Supreme soul). The *paramatmans* reside at the topmost part of the universe, at a Place termed *Siddha Sila* (the Abode of the Perfect Ones), whence there is no returning into the pain and misery of *samsara* (transmigration). All the rest whose number is infinite remain involved in transmigration and subject to repeated births and deaths. The embodied soul passes through four grades of life, known as *gatis*. These are the *deva, naraka*, *manushya* and *tiryancha gatis*, The first of these is the condition of existence as a resident of heavens; the second, of life in hells; the third signifies human existence, and the fourth embraces all other forms of life, that is birds, beasts, brutes, insects, plants, minerals and the like. There are different grades of conditions and circumstances in each of these four *gatis*, but the main types are only four. The residents of heavens enjoy great felicity and pleasure, though they are not altogether free from, misery and pain; those in hells have for their lot intolerable suffering; man experiences both pleasure and pain, with the latter generally preponderating; and the *tiryancha gati* is also full of misery and pain. Birth and death characterise everyone of these four types of existence, only those who pass out of transmigration enjoy eternal life. But there is no fear of the merit acquired in one life being lost in a succeeding 'rebirth'. The effect of *punya* (virtue) and *papa* (evil) is carried by the soul from life to life and determines the type of reincarnation (*gati*).

Release from transmigration is obtained by the observance of the vows of *ahimsa* (non-injury), truthfulness, non-stealing, continence and indifference to worldly goods, and by the practising of certain ethical rules,—humility, forgiveness and the like,—as well as by mental and physical asceticism, *e.g.*, study, meditation, contemplation and fasting. Put in a nutshell, the path to *Nirvana* consists in the confluence of Right Faith (belief in *tattvas*), Right Knowledge (knowledge of *tattvas*) and Right Conduct (observance of the prescribed rules). This triple Right Path is designed to enable the soul to attain to Godhood which is its own nature potentially. An infinity of Souls have already attained to the divine status by following this Right Path, which, it is insisted upon is the only method of obtaining *nirvana* (the status and glory of Godhood). This method is twofold: (1) less rigid for householders and (2) strictly austere, to be pursued by ascetics and saints. The householder begins with the acquisition of Right Faith and takes to the observance of the vows already described, gradually rising, step by step, through what are technically known as *pratimas*, to the stage of asceticism when he becomes subject to the severer rules laid down for the guidance of saint. The *pratimas* are eleven in number and mark the spiritual progress made by the soul, each succeeding step signifying an additional feature of progress over and above the preceding one. The life of a *sadhu* is one of great severity; he aims at the attainment of pure self-contemplation by completely detaching himself from the world, and by mortifying his lower nature. In this way, by means of penances and fasts, he frees his soul from the undesirable companionship of matter, thereby destroying the dominion of *karma* and transmigration. With its *karmas* destroyed, the Soul becomes Omniscient and Immortal, and is filled with its own *svabhavik* (natural) Bliss, which shall never know deterioration or abating at any time in the future. According to Jainism, the soul must undergo transmigration till *nirvana* be reached. There are certain souls that shall never obtain *nirvana*, though the potency of Godhood is as much a characteristic of their nature as of any other soul. Their *karmas* are of a very malignant type and shall always debar them from the *ratna trai* (triple Jewel) of Right Faith, Right Knowledge and Right Conduct, without which salvation is not to be obtained. As we shall see later, the Jaina standpoint is purely the scientist's point of view and there is, consequently, no room for any gods and goddesses within its scope, though it recognises the being of 24 Teachers in every cycle of time of incalculable duration. These Great Masters are termed *Tirthamkaras*, *i.e.*, Founders of a fordable passage, to take the soul to the other shore beyond the turbulent sea of *samsara* (transmigration). These Great Ones are not incarnations of any god or other greater or lesser divinity ruling in high heaven, but men who perfected themselves by following the very method which they afterwards preached to others.

Vidicism is the expression of human adoration for a certain type of supernatural beings of whom the most notable are three primary deities that are compressible into or reducible to one. These are :—

(1) Surya,the Sun,

(2) Indra and

(3) Agni

Surya is the leader and king in heaven; the other gods follow him and he bestows immortality on them. It is to him that the sacred prayer termed Gayatri is addressed daily by almost all classes of Hindus.

The text of this most sacred prayer reads as follows :—

"Let us meditate on that excellent glory of the divine
Vivifier; may he open our understanding."

Indra is the lord of the thunderbolt, and the leader of the heavenly hosts. His is a unique figure in Hindu mythology. The seducer of a Brahmana's wife, he was made even more handsome by Brahma, who transformed the thousand ugly marks of the resulting disease on his body into so many eyes. The enemy of the god is Vritra,

"Whose demon hosts from age to age
With Indra war unceasing wage;
Who, times unnumbered crushed and slain,
Is ever newly born again,
And evermore renews the strife
In which again he forfeits life."—Dr. Muir.

Indra is a powerful god, and directly after his birth demands,

"Where, mother, dwell those warriors fierce
Whose haughty hearts these bolts must pierce?"

At last a battle is fought between the god and the demon, resulting in the victory of the former.

The third of these most prominent of the Vedic deities is Agni. He is the priest of gods at whose invocation they appear. He is also their mouth, so that the gods are directly nourished and strengthened by the sacrifices offered to him. Agni is represented in pictures as having three legs and seven hands. As a priest, Agni is regarded as 'the divinest among the sages, immediately acquainted with all the forms of worship; the wise director, the successful accomplisher, and the protector or all ceremonies, who enables men to serve their gods in a correct and acceptable manner' (Wilkins' Hindu Mythology).

As said before, these three gods are the most prominent among the Hindu deities of the Vedic age; they are not conceived as limited by the powers of the others, and none of them ranks superior to any other. As a matter of fact, the same epithets are used with reference to them all indiscriminately.

The object of Hindu worship may be gathered from the following verses of DR. MUIR, composed with reference to another of the Vedic gods whose worshipper is promised all that is implied in them :—

"All imperfection" leave behind:
Assume thy ancient frame once more-
Each limb and sense thou hadst before,
From every earthly taint refined.
"And now with heavenly glory bright,
With life intenser, nobler, blest,
With large capacity to taste
A fuller measure of delight."
"In those fair realms of cloudless day,
Where Yama every joy supplies,
And every longing satisfies
Thy bliss shall never know decay."

Zoroastrianism is the ancient religion of Persia, and is now followed by a section of Indian people, the Parsis (=of Persian extraction). The Parsi worship is chiefly devotion to a deity, named Ahura Mazda, who is one of an eternal pair of twins, the other being Angra Mainyu also known as Ahriman.

Of these, Ahura Mazda is the good Spirit and the other, the power of evil. The name Ahura Mazda signifies the All-wise Lord, from Ahura, the Lord, and Mazda, the All-wise. In addition to Ahura Mazda, the Parsis offer adoration to other gods, including the Sun, the Moon and Agni (Fire). The Parsis believe in a resurrection of the dead and in a regeneration of the world, on the destruction of the creation of Ahriman. The soul is regarded as immortal and responsible for its actions. All souls will be furnished with new bodies on resurrection and shall enjoy eternal bliss thereafter. The Parsis display a great deal of reverence, bordering on devotion, for Fire-whence their nickname of fire worshippers. Good Thought, Good Word and Good Deed constitute the ethics of Zoroastrianism. The *Ashem Vohu*, the formula that every Zoroastrian learns by heart, teaches: "Holiness is the best good and happiness; happiness to him who is the Holy One for the sake of the best Holiness" (ERE. Vol. IX. page 648). Amongst the purificatory rites of the Parsis is included the *ghosel*, a washing with *gomez* (cow's urine). The sacrosanct Ahuna Vairya, a sort of holy *mantram* (formula), is recited by the Parsis as a very effective means of repelling evil. It reads as follows :—

> "As the Ahu is to be chosen,
> So (let) the Ratu (be) from every legal fitness,
> A creator of mental goodness,
> And of life's actions done for Mazda;
> And the kingdom (be) to Ahura,
> Whom (the Ahu, or the Ratu) He has appointed as nourisher to the poor."—ERE. 1. 238

This is to be recited not only at the time of ceremonial worship but also in connection with ordinary duties and work. The scriptures of Parsism, which have come down to us only in fragments, also mention Mithra as a deity to be worshipped, but I propose to deal with Mithraism separately in one of the subsequent lectures. It, may, however, be mentioned here that metempsychosis is openly taught in certain of the Parsi Books, *e.g.*, Mihabad (see the Fountainhead of Religion, pp. 156-158).

The bright, all-happy "blissful abode of the Holy Ones" (SBE. XXIII, page 34) is the place where the Residents know neither sickness, nor pain nor death. This seems to correspond to the Siddha Sila of the Jainas, on reaching which sickness and sorrow are parted from for ever, and where the soul enjoys immeasurable happiness, eternal life and all-embracing knowledge.

Judaism is the ancient creed of thee Jews whose god is Jehovah or Jahweh. He is the maker of the universe and also of all things. He made the first pair of human beings, and placed them in the Garden of Eden which he planted, and which contained, among others, a tree of Knowledge of Good and Evil and one of Life. Man disobeyed Jehovah's injunction, and, at the instance of the serpent, ate the fruit of the first named tree. For this he was turned out of the Garden of Eden with his consort, Eve, who was his companion in the transgression and who became his wife thereafter. Death also came to fasten itself on Adam in consequence of the act of disobedience. Adam had at first two sons, Abel and Cain, the former of whom was murdered by the latter, his brother. Cain thereupon became a fugitive and wanderer on the face of the earth. Subsequently, a third son, Seth, the appointed, was born to Adam, and it was Enos, the son of Seth in whose time people began to call on the Lord, or, according to another reading of the text, to call themselves by the name of the Lord (*vide* marginal notes to Genesis iv. 26).

Ever since the transgression Jahweh has been exhorting the people to obedience and has repeatedly sent messages to that effect to Israelites through sundry prophets. The worship of Jehovah, whose most significant name is I AM, consisted in prayer, pslam and sacrifice chiefly. Jehovah describes himself as a jealous god, visiting the iniquity of men into the third and fourth generations of them that hate him. As for future life, metempsychosis was rejected by Exoteric philosophers among the Jews but accepted by the Kabbalists (ERE. VII. 626). In a way, the Jews believed in resurrection and also the advent of a future Messiah who is to establish a new order of things. Their ethical code may be said to be summed up in the following commandments of Jehovah which are said to have been imparted to Moses:—

(1) "Thou shalt have no other God before me.

(2) "Thou shalt not make unto thee any graven image, or any likeness of anything.

(3) "Thou shalt not take the name of the Lord thy God in vain.

(4) "Six days shalt thou labour, but the seventh is the sabbath of the Lord thy God, in it thou shalt not do any work.

(5) "Honour thy father and thy mother.

(6) "Thou shalt not kill

(7) "Thou shalt not commit adultery.

(8) "Thou shalt not steal.

(9) "Thou shalt not bear false witness against thy neighbonr.

(10) "Thou shalt not covet thy neighbour's house, thou shalt not covet thy neighbour's wife, nor his man servant, nor his maid servant, nor his ox, nor his ass, nor anything that is thy neighbour's."

Vedanta is the most famous of all the systems of Hindu metaphysics and pursues the line of thought Known as Idealism. The visible perceptible world, all that the senses reveal, everything that the mind knows, is unreal, unsubstantial and imaginary. The senses are deceptive; we often mistake a rope for a serpent! How, then, can a man in possession of his wits rely upon their revelation. It is a huge illusion that lies stretched before us; a tremendous unending dream is being played on the mystery-stage! Yet the actors are the very spectators who bave forgotten themselves. What is it all due to? How, why, where and when it began? How, why, where and when will it end? How, why, where and when came the spectators to engage themselves as actors? It is no good putting these questions;

can a dreamer expect to get statisfactory answers to such questions while the dream persists? No; you should similarly wait till you are safely out of it. Even this talk about a getting out of it is illusory. You were never in it; how, then, can there be a getting out of it for you? This is *maya* the *anirvachniya* (indescribable)! Underlying this huge panoramic illusion is one reality or existence, immutable, all-pervading, self-subsisting. This ubiquitous existence is characterised by *sat* (existence), *chit* (consciousness) and *ananda* (bliss), and is termed, after its attributes, Sachchidananda (Sat-chit-ananda). It is also called Brahman. It is the only reality; there is nothing else in existence. Individual souls are of the nature of phantoms in a dream; they have no existence of their own. There is no question of salvation or of being saved. Know yourself to be free and you are free there and then. This sublime truth is to be realised to escape from the illusory misery of an illusory world. Self-knowledge is necessary for the realisation of the idea of the Self, that is the true reality and the only existence. Self-realization is attained in *samadhi* which means the merging of the mind in the Reality or Self with body and thought controlled. *Samadhi* is to be attained by practising certain rules laid down ill worth on yoga.

This is Hindu Monism or rigid Idealism of the non-dual Vedanta. Apart from this, there are two other systems also known as Vedanta. They differ from the monistic school in so for as they admit, though with many limitations and qualifications, the existence of a world and individual souls besides Brahman. Inconsistent as it seems, all these schools of Vedanta subscribe to the doctrine of transmigration which is to be terminated on the realisation of the Self.

Vedanta is essentially an Indian, or, to be more exact, a purely Hindu form of belief, but it seems to have influenced non-Hindu thought outside India in one instance at least. For Muslim Sufe-ism of the Idealistic Shahudians is practically a copy of the Vedanta, with slight variations, which cannot be closely looked into here for want of time.

The **Sankhyan school** of Hindu metaphysics, founded by Kapila, starts by positing two eternal realities, *purusha* and *prakriti*. The *purusha* is merely a spectator and is separate from the spectacle. *Prakriti* is the equivalent of nature, conceived, in an abstract way, as being characterised by intelligence (*sattva*), motion (*rajas*) and rest (*tamas*). All that is changing and shifting, all that is impermanent and transient, all that is produced from reflection, as also all that is concerned in the process of reflection, pertains to and is evolved out of *prakriti*. There is an alternation of involution and evolution, the order of the one being the reverse of that of the other. The following is the order of evolution :

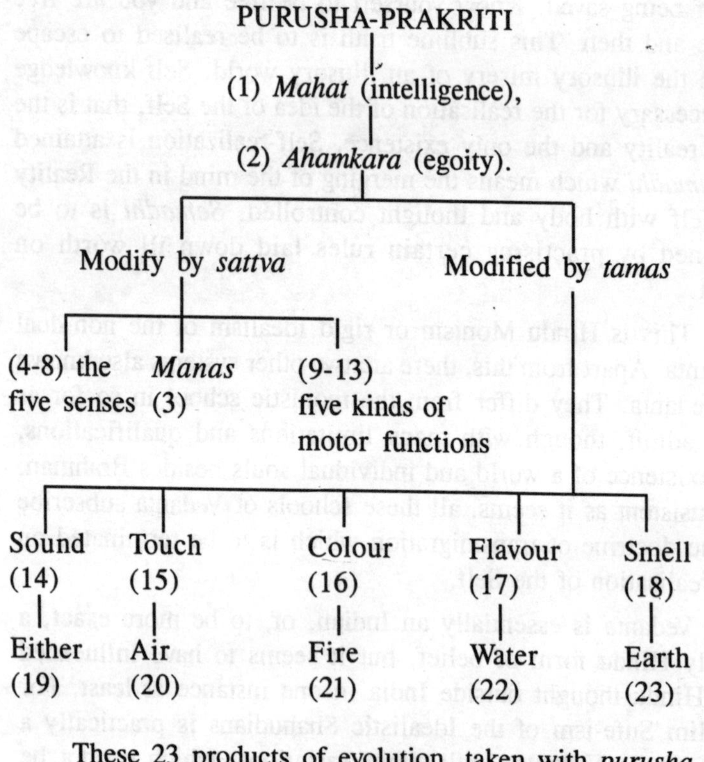

These 23 products of evolution, taken with *purusha* and *prakirti*, constitute the 25 *tattvas* of the Sankhyan school, the knowledge of which is necessary to obtain release from transmigration. Of course, in a system like Kapila's there is no room for the notion of creation, though some of the later writers have endeavoured to drag it within the fold of Ishvaravada (theism). As to every other system of Hindu Thought, *yoga* is also an accessory to Sankhya.

Nyaya (the logical school) lays down no less than sixteen *tattvas* as follows :—

(1) *pramana* (right knowledge or means of knowledge),
(2) *prarneya* (objects of *pramana*),
(3) doubt,
(4) purpose,
(5) illustration,
(6) *siddhanta* (final conclusion or truth),
(7) premises,
(8) confutation,
(9) ascertainment,
(10) discussion,
(11) wrangling,
(12) cavil,
(13) fallacy,
(14) quibble,
(15) futility, and
(16) occasion for rebuke.

The soul, the body, the senses, objects of senses, the intellect, mind, activity, fault, transmigration, fruit, pain and release are the objects of right knowledge. Pain, birth, activity, faults and misapprehension are the things to be destroyed. On their successive annihilation, in the reverse order, follows release. There is no reference to a creator in the Nyaya Sutras of Gautama on which the system is founded, exccpt once incidentally in meeting a Buddhist argument.

The **Vaisesika system** maintains that the supreme good, that is to say the cessation of pain, results from the knowledge of predicables of which there are six, namely substance, attribute, action, genus, species and combination. Substances, are nine in number-Earth, Water, Fire, Air, Ether, Time, Space, Self and Mind. Attributes are colour, taste, smell, touch, number, measure, separateness, conjunction, disjunction, priority, posteriority, understanding, pleasure, pain, desire, aversion and volition. Throwing upwards, throwing downwards, contraction, expansion and motion are actions. Release from transmigration is obtained when action does not originate in the mind that has become steady in the soul. Like the Naiyayikas, the Vaisesikas, did not originally acknowledge a world-making god, though they bowed to the authority of the Vedas as the word of a qualified Teacher.

The **Yoga** school of Hindu philosophy recognises

(1) God, as the ideal for contemplation,

(2) Souls, and

(3) Matter.

Release from transmigration is the aim of the soul. It results in the cessation of pain which is to be attained in *samadhi*. *Samadhi* itself is the culmination or the last of a series of steps, called limbs of yoga. These steps are termed (1) *yama,* (2) *niyama*, (3) *asana*, (4) *pranayama*, (5) *pratyahara*, (6) *dharana*, (7) *dhyana* and (8) *sarmadhi*.

Yama consist in the following five kinds of restraints:—

(i) *ahimsa* (not killing or injuring),

(ii) truthfulness,

(Hi) non-stealing,

(iv) sexual abstinence, and

(v) avoidance of avarice, that is of worldly goods.

Niyama signifies.

(i) restraints on movements,

(ii) control of actions,

(iii) fasting,

(iv) study, and

(v) service.

Asana is posture for meditation, and *pranayama*, the regulation of breath; but *pratyahara* signifies the 'annihilation' of the senses, consequent on the state of catalepsy to be induced by practice. Of the remaining limbs, *dharna* is mental concentration, *dhyana*, meditation or contemplation, and *samadhi*, the culmination of them all in an ecstatic trance.

Buddhism was originally an Indian religion, though it is now almost extinct in India. It was founded some two thousand five hundred years ago by a man who subsequently came to be known as Buddha. Buddha's teaching comprises the sponteneity of the world, that is a denial of its creation as well as of a creator, and non-permanence of things, including the soul. Nirvana is the extinction of the will to be which is the cause of transmigration. Buddha's description of transmigration has the merit of novelty and is altogether unique. There is no continuity of individuality from life to life, according to Buddha, but only of the quintessence of individual character or experience, which, finding a suitable soil of which there is no lack, immediately sprouts forth, and is thus engrafted upon a different stock from the one on which it was nurtured and formed. It is the destruction of this *nucleus* of re-birth which is thrown out by each "bundle" or aggregate of being—and according to Buddhist Metaphysics, everything including life or soul is only an aggregate of impermanent processes—that is to be brought about to escape from transmigration. Great stress is laid in all Indian religions on the painful nature of existence, and Buddhism is no exception to the rule. To exist is to suffer; but the suffering is not due to existence; it is caused by desire. Suppression of desire is effected by observance of the "good law' which means Buddhist principles. Accordingly, the four noble truths of Budhism are:

(1) the existence of pain—

(2) the cause of pain,

(3) the removal of pain, and

(4) the method of the removal of pain.

These noble truths constitute the eternal immutable Law, which had been proclaimed by twenty four infallible Teachers or Buddhas in ancient times. The eight-fold path consists in :—

(1) right views,

(2) right aspirations,

(3) right speech,

(4) right conduct,

(5) right livelihood,

(6) right effort,

(7) right mindfulness, and

(8) right rapture, that is mental tranquillity.

This eight-fold path is intended to stop the wheel of Life, which revolves because of twelve kinds of *nidanas* each of which is caused by the one preceding it, according to the following enumeration :—

(1) ignorance,

(2) mental predisposition or *karma*,

(3) consciousness,

(4) individuality (name and form),

(5) sensibility,

(6) contact (sensory stimuls),

(7) sensations,

(8) craving,

(9) attachment (clinging to life),

(10) becoming (existence),

(11) birth, and

(12) old age, death, grief, lamentation, suffering, depression and despair.

How consciousness gives rise to individuality? is to be worked out in this way: it is the union of aggregates which makes the individual; consciousness arises from aggregates; "every person or thing or god is therefore a putting together, a compound" (Early Buddhism, page 57). The question whether the soul is the same as the body or different from it, was one of the Indeterminates—proscribed questions (ERE. IV. 234).

Christianity which claims to be the fulfilment of Judaism and which is complementary to that religion, is grounded principally upon the following seven points of belief:—

(1) the blissfulness of existence in the Garden of Eden,

(2) the temptation to eat the fruit of the Tree of Knowledge of Good and Evil,

(3) the consequent fall,

(4) redemption by the "Key of Knowledge",

(5) crucifixion,

(6) resurrection, and,

(7) ascension.

Christians profess no definite belief about the soul, and openly range themselves against transmigration. Salvation, too, is not to be 'bought' by merit or works, but is a matter of grace to be obtained through the favour of Christ. According to the Nicene Creed, a Christian is expected to subscribe to the following formula of faith:

"We believe:—

I. (1) in one God

II. (2) And in one Lord Jesus Christ the Son of God, begotten of the Father, only begotten, that is of the substance of the Father, God of God, Light of Light very God of very God, begotten, not made, of one substance with the Father,

(3) who for us men and for our salvation came down

and was made flesh, and lived as man among men,

(4) Suffered,

(5) And rose the third day,

(6) Ascended into heaven,

(7) Is coming to Judge the quick and the dead,

III. (8) And in the Holy Ghost."

There are many parallels to this form of belief among the ancient and extinct faiths, but they shall be dealt with in a subsequent lecture separately.

Islam, the youngest of the most widely spread religions, was founded in Arabia by one Muhummad on the ruins of the neighbouring creeds. It consists in the belief in the existence of one god, termed Allah, in the revelation of the Qur'an and in the messengership of Muhummad. The doctrines of Islam include a belief in resurrection and in the existence of heavens and hell where souls are sent by way of reward or punishment for their deeds on earth. Muslims generally deny transmigration, though several notable philosophers among them, e.g., Al Ghazali, Ahmed Ibni Yunus, Abu Moslem of Khorasan (*vide* Philosophy of Islam, p. 27) openly subscribed to the doctrine. Meritorious deeds in Islam include prayer, fasting, pilgrimage and purification generally.

Brahmanism by which term I mean later Hinduism is two fold; (1) Puranicism, i.e., the worshipping of Puranic gods, and (2) *Yajna-ism*, the sacrificial cult. Puranic deities are a legion numerically, but the most important ones among them are Brahma, Vishnu, Shiva and Krishna. It is believed that all kinds of boons can be obtained from the gods by their worship. The sacrificial cult, or *Yajna-ism*, as I have termed it, is the sacrificing of living beings to propitiate supernal powers in favour of the sacrificer. Human beings, too, it is certain, used to be sacrificed in the past on certain occasions, and the diabolical practice had survived in the form of the immolation of little children to the spirits of rivers etc., which has only been put a stop to in recent times. The most widely-practised sacrifices were those of the ram, the bull and the he-goat, which seem to have been universally selected by all sorts of sacrificial cults. In India *gomedha* and *ashvamedha*, that is, respectively, the cow and the horse sacrifice, were also practised in ancient times, but they have since been abandoned, and the former has now become even one of the chief causes of contention and quarrel between Hindus and Muhammadans.

Mysticism, Shaktism and **Occultism** are all terms which more or less convey the same idea. They all aim at the acquisition of certain vaguely-defined, vaguely-conceived powers by means of secret instruction. **Rosicrucianism** and **Free-Masonry** are two other such systems which claim familiarity with the secret Alchemy of Life. Many kinds of "Mysteries" are known to have been practised in the past in connection with the cults of different gods in different lands. Their teachings were kept secret and only imparted to approved candidates at different stages of initiation. In the Yoga Sutras of Patanjali a great many nervous ganglia in the body are mentioned as points for concentration for the acquisition of psychic powers. The idea underlying all these diverse notions is that psychic powers are developed in the soul by means of certain practices, principally by the concentration of mind on certain nervous centres in the body, and the acquistion of these powers is the principal if not the sole aim and ambition of life. In modern times, **Radha-Swami-ism** (founded in the last century) has attracted some notice on account of a certain part of its teaching which is imparted in secret and which its followers are bound, probably under an oath of secrecy to preserve. The founder is simply worshipped as a god, and even the succeeding *gurus* (preceptors) are held so high in esteem that certain products of their body are swallowed by their followers without demur. The teaching of Radha-Swami-ism resembles in most parts that of the Vaishnavite sect of Hindus, but Hindu incarnations of deity are not recognised. A long list of Muhammadan saints and half-saints, Shams-i-Tabrez, and other, set up as messengers of the new faith, is a special feature of Radha-Swami-ism.

This practically disposes of all important religions. Of the remaining ones, **Shintoism**, the religion of Japan, is a jumble of ancestor-worship, demonology, witchcraft and divination. Immortality of the soul was, however, clearly recognised in Japan, and many divine heroes and illustrious personages were believed to have been translated to the "plain of High Heaven" (ERE. I. 457).

Babism or **Bahaism** which is centred round the mystic teaching about the last Imam of the Muslim church, who is said to be biding his time to appear at the end of the world, is a recent offshoot of Islam, its founder claiming to be the missing Imam in person.

Amongst the Indian creeds, **Kabir Panth**, **Dadu Panth**, **Sikhism** and **Arya-Samaj** are some of the newer faiths, arising in response to some kind of a need felt by their respective founders in their time. For instance, Sikhism was originally intended to reconcile both Hinduism and Islam, though ultimately bitter hostility arose between Muhammadans and Sikhs than that which had originally prevailed between Hindus and Muhammadans. All these faiths are devotional in nature, and they all subscribe to the doctrine of transmigration. Of the remaining Indian religious, **Brahmo-Samaj** is the westernised *Ishvaravada* (one-god cult) founded in the last century in Bengal, one of whose followers and missionaries, a man known by the name of Sheonarain Agnihotri, ultimately set himself up as the founder of an independent faith which he called **Deva-Samaj**. The tenets of Deva-Samaj include belief in a soul that is liable to extinction unless developed to reach a higher life, which can be accomplished by uniting with one who has already reached it in his own person. The founder of Deva-Samaj, it is said, has reached the highest point that can be reached by any soul. He. is, therefore, to be adored by his followers as the most reverend, most worshipful, most exalted divine teacher and blessed lord.

Theosophy, the only other noteworthy creed amongst the newly-founded faiths, was founded by a Russian woman, named H. P. Blavatsky, whose mysterious feats described by her as due to the agency of certain invisible *mahatmas*, or masters, and as pure and simple deception by certain investigators (*vide* Forquhar's Modern Religious Movements in India), attracted much notice about the close of the last century when it was established. There seems to have been at first much talk about these mysterious *mahatmas* who were said to be working miracles from behind the scenes, but in a recent work ("Who Wrote the Mahatma Letters"?) by H. E. and W. Loftus Hare, the authorship of their letters has now been definitely proved to lie in madame Blavatsky herself. Mrs. Anne Besant, who succeeded the Russian woman, as a president of the movement, tried to go down the pages of world's History as Foster mother of a Messiah; but the 'Messiah' himself felt bared with the title, and may be taken to have renounced it for good.

To pass on now to a consideration of the Chinese religions, the oldest faith of that country is **Taoism**, which will be described in a later lecture. Another of the Chinese religions is **Confucianism** which was founded by one Confucius a little over two thousand five hundred years ago. But this is almost wholly a code of moral laws put together by a wise man and so unlike religion in its essential features that I shall not deal with it in these lectures. Confucianism might, no doubt, be possessed of an esoteric side, like certain other religions, but if that be so, it must be left to the better equipped future explorer for its unravelment and elucidation. Buddhism, the third prevailing religion of China, has already been described in today's lecture.

There remain the American cults to be dealt with; but from what is known to me of them they appear to be most unlike religion, and, except for a passing observation or two here and there in their tenets, appear to have consisted almost exclusively in wars and the most blood-curdling of human sacrifices, without anything in the shape of a redeeming feature. If there ever was an esoteric side to these inhuman cults—and it is not impossible for them to have evolved out round an evaporated symbolical *nucleus* imported from Asia or Europe—it was soon lost to view, and its place taken by the most revolting of sanguinary, human sacrifices devoid of every vestige of religion. I shall leave them out of account in these lectures as purely barbarous ritual and savage demonology.

Our survey of the principal religions of the world is now finished, and my only regret is that it is not as complete as I should like to see it. No account is taken here of the ancient religions that are now extinct, the religions of Babylonia, Assyria and Egypt which are expected to throw much light on the situation. The reason for this is that our knowledge of these ancient but extinct religions is so scanty and comes from sources so misleading and unreliable that it is much better to leave their elucidation to the future generation of better qualified researchers than to start on a course of error and misapprehension from the very outset. I shall, however, deal with some of these ancient cults in a subsequent lecture, so for as I can safely go.

Of the minor schisms and cults and other speculative miscellany, *e.g.*, New-Platonism, Pythagorianism, *etc.*, I shall purposely say nothing, since we already possesss sufficient material to form a basis for scientific comparison in our subsequent lectures and since time does not permit our going into minute details. I have said nothing about **Charvakism**, because I propose to deal with it under the head of Materialism later.

Our survey of the principal religions of the world is now complete; it only remains to ascertain their common features of resemblance as well as their striking differences and disharmonies. The following points will be found to be common to all religions-

(1) a hereafter and a future life:—.

(2) the existence of a soul apart from the body, except in Buddhism where a nucleus of *sanskaras* (*karmic*

forces) is posited as the basis of transmigration;

(3) the possibility of a better life in the future;

(4) the freedom of human will to make or mar its future by following the right path or its antithesis, and,

(5) the existence of some kind of divine life, manifesting itself in certain deified Beings, or gods, or in one monotheistic god.

Their differences may also be summed up as falling under the following heads :—

(1) the nature, names and functions of divinity, and the number of Gods;

(2) the nature and origin of the world;

(3) the nature and prospects of the soul, including transmigration and resurrection, and

(4) the means of attaining the *summum bonum* including *ahimsa* and sacrifice of living animals and men.

These points will be generally found to cover all the features of resemblance as well as dissimilarity among the numerous creeds examined by us today, and to furnish a proper basis for the elucidation of the mystery surrounding the origination and differentiation of religion amongst men. As we have now reached a point which exhausts the subject-matter of this evening's lecture we shall stop here for today, beginning with the description and means of speedy acquisition of the power of intellectualism in the next lecture.

CHAPTER - II

THE INTELLECTUAL METHOD

It was stated in the preceding lecture that the method of comparison of different doctrines and beliefs should be exclusively rational. It shall be our task today to define the method of comparison with greater definiteness and to lay down the means for arriving at accurate knowledge of things. The first thing to do is to get rid of the mental bias which in 99 cases out of every 100 is sure to be lurking behind the loudest protestations of impartiality. We are so constituted that there is an overwhelming sub-conscious predisposition in us in favour of the faith in which we are born that unconsciously forces the most critical of us to reject, and that on the flimsiest of grounds, any and every hostile or seemingly hostile theory and fact. And even where extreme tolerance is the guiding characteristic of the enquiring mind, the burden of proof of every point contrary to the cherished notion is sure to be thrown on the opponent, and that only too often in defiance of reason and good sense. It does not require any great familiarity with the canons of logic to predict that no really satisfactory results are to be achieved while this frame of mind predominates over the spirit of enquiry. It is certainly not the proper disposition or attitude for a really enquiring mind,—for a mind that is truly *anxious* to discover the truth for itself. Belief in the religion of birth depends merely on the incident of being born in a certain family and surroundings; but surely that is no criterion of truth. If instead of being born in religion X,I were born in religion Y,I should have had Y as my religion; and Z, if born in Z. But because I thus believe in religion X, and not in Y or Z, is no test of the truth of X, for those born in Y and Z also regard them just as true as I regard X. Private beliefs do not, therefore, establish the truth of the matter of belief. Even Scriptural text, as stated in the first lecture, is no test of truth, for why should one scripture be preferred to another? This does not mean that all Sacred Books are to be rejected by us *en bloc*, but that we should try to find out for ourselves which of them, if any, is the word of a qualified Teacher and worthy of being accepted and followed.

How, then, is the truth to be known? By means of rigid rationalism and scientific method! Broadly put, the sources of knowledge are

(i) observation,

(ii) reflection or meditation, i. e., inference, and

(iii) testimony.

Of those three, the first, namely, observation, is the foundation of science; the second, that is inference, is the basis of philosophy, and the third, i.e., testimony, when it proceeds from the most unimpeachable and fully qualified source, that is to say, the word of an Omniscient Teacher, is scripture. In short, perfection of Observation is Science; perfection of Inference is Metaphysics; and perfection of Testimony, Scripture.

Science is the accurate knowledge of nature, tested by experiment, and capable of yielding immediate and certain results. It divides itself into two parts, physics and metaphysics, of which physics may be taken to be the department of knowledge dealing with concrete things and the other as concerned with their analysis, classification and generalisation, as well as with the systematization of all knowledge or thought itself. True metaphysics must, for this reason, always remain in touch with concrete nature. It has nothing in common with those ambitious flights of fancy which seek to break away from the *terra firma* of fact to enjoy a wild romp in cloudland. It will be noticed that where science and metaphysics do not agree on a point, the disagreement is generally due to the latter having somewhere lost sight of the concrete reality.

The philosopher who would acquire fame as such should harness both "Fancy" and "Fact" to the chariot of his mind, curbing the tendency of the one to rush for the peak, through loose impassable bypaths and cuts, and rousing up the other, whenever necessary, to prevent its lapsing into rumination at the roadside. As for the criterion of truth, it is generally safe to lay down that where science and metaphysics agree truth may be said to be established there; but in the department of Religion there is an additional safeguard imposed upon this agreement which consists in confirmation by Scripture. For Scripture is the word of an Omniscient Teacher and cannot but be in agreement with truth. The notion that the word of God is beyond reason is itself devoid of reason, for omniscience and reason are not contradictory terms. From this point of view, philosophy may be defined as the science in which

(i) facts are taken from nature,

(ii) conclusions are checked by logic, and

(iii) final confirmation is sought in scripture, *i.e.*, the irrefutable word of an all knowing Teacher.

And, certainly, where the three agree, the case is put beyond doubt and dispute.

Observation is the principal instrument of science, which should be supplemented with experiment to get at the exact knowledge of causation of things, that is to say, of the great Law of Cause and Effect. Causes in nature are constituted by the properties and qualities of things, and effects are produced by physical processes and chemical action, *e.g.*, the sweetness of the pudding is due to sugar, so that whenever sugar is not put into the material of the pudding no sweetness is to be found in it. This is pure science, though in its most domesticated form; and it is thoroughly reliable, and the only thing that can be relied upon to produce immediate, certain and unvarying results.

The chief instruments of philosophy or metaphysics are :—

(i) Inference,
(ii) Classification, — Logic
(iii) Analysis,

and

(iv) *Nayavada* (appreciation or system of standpoints).

Of these, inference is the method of accurate deduction; classification, of accurate determination of general attributes; analysis, of accurate knowledge of ingredients and component parts of ideas and things, and *nayavada*, of accurate appreciation of truth with reference to diverse standpoints. We shall deal with each of these subjects here; but I must first point out how logic can be easily mastered in less than three quarters of an hour by a school boy of ordinary intelligence. The first thing to understand is that in order to become an expert logician it is not at all necessary that the mind should be burdened with complex definitions and purplexing formulas to be found in modern text books on logic. Real logic is a very simple thing and requires no technical terminology to be learnt by *rote*. This is evident from the fact that many illiterate men are highly rational and logical; and even little children at times display a remarkable talent for accurate deduction. This should be impossible if logic depended upon the study of a highly complex and complicated system of technicalities, definitions and terminologies. The fact is that logic is simply the science of deduction with the aid of all invariable unalterable rule. If I ask to tell me what day it will be tomorrow, you will immediately say, Tuesday, today being a Monday; but you cannot tell me the number of keys in my bunch, nor the amount of money in my pocket, nor the metal of my watch, whether it be gold or silver or any thing else. The reason is that while there is a fixed unalterable order according to which a Monday is always followed by a Tuesday, there is and can be no fixed invariable rule, neither nature's nor man's, that I would always have so many and only so many keys in my ring, or only so many rupees and neither more nor less in my pocket, or that my watch should be made of one particular metal and never of any other. If there were even one single exception in the case of a Tuesday following a Monday, you could not say with certainty that it would be Tuesday tomorrow, for it might be the turn of the exception, in which case it would not be a Tuesday but some other day that would occur tomorrow. From these cases we can deduce the principle that wherever there is an invariable rule, *without a single exception*, there alone can a logical conclusion be drawn in agreement with that rule; and that no proper inference is possible in the absence, or in defiance of such a fixed unalterable rule. This is the one simple rule of logic which everyone understands more or less clearly, and a text book must be deemed to have failed to fulfil its function if it muddles up such a simple proposition. It is according to this rule that the illiterate rustic, and, for the matter of that, even a moderately small child who sees smoke issuing from a place, immediately infers the presence of fire there. Your cultured "text-book" logician also does this, but in an unnatural, round about way. He will first of all construct a proposition in the form of a formula.

S is P.

Here

S = smoke.

P = fire.

Hence, we have

Smoke is fire.

This is the first of the premises of a modern syllogism. The second is—

This is smoke.

Our logician will now try to ascertain whether his middle (or common) term be distributed or not. But there is so much room here for error and bewilderment through technicalities and forms that he deserves to be congratulated if he can actually settle the point. We now have

(1) All S is P.
(2) This is S.

as our premises, which, put in popular language, should read:

(1) In all cases smoke arises from fire.

(2) This is smoke.

And now we are entitled to draw the conclusion—

(3) This smoke also arises from fire.

All this bewilderment, confusion and entanglement is avoided by natural logic, which simply requires a fixed rule to proceed upon.

The distribution of the middle term, I may point out here, is not in the nature of a special charm or magical formula designed to guarantee the validity of an Aristotelian deduction in some mysterious way. It is simply another way, and a highly involved one for that, of stating the logical principle which is the true foundation of deduction. For a term is said to be distributed when it is used in its entire extent, that is universally; in other words, when reference is made to all "individuals" or cases falling within its definition. Modern logic itself has to recognise that "inference always implies an effort on the part of the mind to see how phenomena are *necessarily connected according to some general principle* and, in carrying out this purpose, the mind *must begin with the knowledge which it already possesses*. When the general law of connection is known, and the object is to discover the nature of some particular fact, the method, of procedure is deductive. But when the in problem by which we are confronted is to read out of the facts of sense-perception the general law of their connection, the method of inference which must be employed is that of induction" (quoted from S. N. Banerjee's Handbook of Deductive Logic, pp. 80 and 81).

It is this necessary, general connection, the true basis of valid deduction, which Western logic endeavours to enunciate in the confusing and confounding "scholarly" terminology of its text-books. No wonder that even college students find their brains in a muddle over it.

It is also to be noted that modern logic does not guarantee the accuracy of the conclusion though natural logic does. I shall again quote from Mr. Banerjee's excellent little text-book where he cites Dr. Ray.

"In deductive or syllogistic reasoning we draw conclusions from given propositions as data. Given the premises, we infer the conclusion that follows necessarily from them. We are not in any way concerned to prove our premises; but our conclusion must be true, if the premises be true. Hence it is evident that the truth we arrive at by deduction or syllogistic reasoning is entirely of a hypothetical character, depending for its trustworthiness entirely on the trustworthiness of the data."

To illustrate the contrast between artificial and natural logic in this respect, it is prefectly correct according to the former to say :

All men are fools.

Socrates is a man.

∴ Socrates is a fool.

But it is simply impossible for natural logic to commit such a blunder, since it only proceeds where there is a fixed rule, and since there is no such fixed rule that declares all men to be fools.

It should be noted that every rule of practice does not give rise to a logical inference, no matter how long so ever it might have been observed and how strictly so ever followed. For instance, if a particular person has been known for the last fifty years to pass my door every morning without a single exception we cannot infer from this fact that he will for a certainty pass by my house tomorrow also, for there are a thousand and one reasons which might prevent his doing so. This shows that the true logical rule, termed *vyapti* in Sanskrit, is something in the nature of a law which has not only held good in the past but which must hold good also in the future. A mere rule of practice will not do here.

There are five kinds of logical relations with reference to which it is possible to have a fixed rule (*vyapti*) giving rise to logical inference. These are :—

(1) Cause and effect,

(2) Antecedence and Consequence,

(3) Concomitance,

(4) Whole and Part, and

(5) Identity.

These relationships give rise to seven kinds of inferences, as follows :—

(1) From cause to effect, *e.g.*

Moist fuel is burning in the kitchen.

∴ There is smoke in the kitchen.

(2) From effect to cause, *e.g.*,

There is smoke in this place.

∴ There is fire in this place.

(3) From antecedent to consequent, *e.g.*,

Monday following a Sunday.

(4) From consequent to antecedent, *e.g.*,

Childhood preceding adolescencc and old age.

(5) From concomitance, *e.g.*,

Age and experience going together.

(6) From the principle that the whole includes the part, *e.g.*,

There is no fruit tree in this village.

∴ There is no mango tree in this village.

(7) Identity, *e.g.*,

There is no pitcher in this room;

because there is nothing answering its identity (description) here.

The last form of logical relationship might appear, at first sight, to be misplaced, as one is apt to regard the conclusion—

There is no pitcher in this room :—

as a fact of perception rather than a logical inference; but in that case we should have to assert that the eye can actually perceive *negations*, which would be ridiculous.

This finishes the entire subject; and I may add that there is no room for error in this method of inference if the *vyapti* is carefully and scientifically tested. The final test of the accuracy of any particular *vyapti* is the Scriptural Text, which, being the word of an Omniscient Teacher, holds good for all times, the past present and future. Hence, where one's own observation is supported by the experience of mankind in general and is also confirmed by the word of an Omniscient Teacher there is no room left for any manner of doubt there. This is the true function of Scripture which, as such, should be highly valuable as a Reference Book of Permanent Values.

We might pause here for a while to compare the merit of the different systems of logic which have been known to prevail among men. These are

(i) the Jaina,

(ii) the *Naiyayika*,

(iii) the Buddhist, and

(iv) the European or Aristotelian.

Our treatment of the subject in this lecture represents the Jaina system. The Naiyayika bases the validity of inference on a homogeneous example (*saha-dharmi drishtanta*). Smoke was seen in the kitchen where there was fire; smoke is also seen on the mountain-top; hence there is fire on the mountain top. There is no question of a scientifically valid *vyapti*; the inference is not drawn by the force of a fixed unalterable rule, but simply from a homogeneous example. Even the sofeguards against error laid down. in the form of fallacies do not place the subject on a scientific basis. The fallacies are five in number, namely:—

(1) The erratic, which implies that the reason is sometimes associated with the *sadhya* (that which is to be established) and sometimes with its opposite.

(2) The contradictory which is the reason that is opposed to the conclusion, *e.g.*,

A pot is a manufactured article;

because it is eternal.

(3) The 'equal-to-the-question' which reproduces itself, *e.g.*,

Sound is non-eternal;

because it is not possessed of the attribute of eternity.

(4) The unproved, which itself stands in need of proof, e.g.,

Shadow is a substance;

because it is endowed with motion.

(5) The mistimed, i.e., that which is adduced when the time in which it might hold good is past, e.g.,

Sound is eternal;

because it arises by union, like colour.

Properly amplified, the argument here comes to this that sound is like colour because the one is manifested by contact between a drum and a drum-stick, the other by the contact of the light of a lamp with a coloured article. Now, since colour is eternal because light is only needed to reveal and cannot be said to create it, so, too, sound must be eternal. It is this kind of reason which is termed mis-timed—the basing of a conclusion on an example which has a different time-value.

This exhausts the list of *Naiyayika* fallacies, but it is evident that no such thing as an invariable logical relationship is established with their aid. The point of difference in the main between the Jaina and *Naiyayika* logic lies in the fact that while the latter draws an inference from a similar example in all cases except where an instance can be pointed out to the contrary,—the fallacy of erratic reason—or has not the same time-value, the former will refuse to draw a conclusion except where the reason on which it is to be based is a true logical *vyapti*. The following illustration, satisfies all the requirement of a *Naiyayika* syllogism, but is nevertheless one on the accuracy of which no true logician will ever stake his reputation.

Illustration.

(1) The unborn child of Z is a boy;

(2) Because he is the child of Z;

(3) Like all the other children of Z who are boys.

Here the reason—the quality of being a child of Z—is a homogeneous instance, and neither erratic, nor otherwise open to objection, but as there is no logical connection between it and any particular sex, there is no guarantee that the next child in Mrs. Z's womb will be a boy, too. The reason in this case has always been invariably attended by the *sadhya* (the fact to be proved) in each and everyone of the homogeneous examples on the strength of which the deduction is made. It is certainly not erratic, because no one can point to the quality of being a child of Z residing in a girl; and it is not mistimed, because it actually resides in the child in the womb all along, including the very moment of deduction.

It is sometimes said in defence of this element of weakness in Gotam's logic that possibly be only intended to throw the burden of disproving his statements and propositions on to his opponents, but even if it be so it is a highly dangerous thing to base a logical conclusion on such slippery foundations, leaving it to someone else, if he be willing and able, to correct our errors.

The Buddhist logic, too, like the Nyaya system, ignores tho scientific *vyapti*, and does not hesitate to draw an inference from a homogenous example, provided that the reason:—

(1) is found in *paksha*,

(2) and is present in *sapaksha*,

(3) but is not to be met with in *vipaksha*.

In the following syllogism;

(a) "There is fire on the yonder mountain top;

(b) because there is smoke on it;

(c) like the kitchen;

(d) and unlike the lake;

(e) so, therefore, there is fire on the yonder mountain top;—

the mountain top yonder is *paksha* (the abode of the *sadhya*, the fact to be proved, here fire), the already observed kitchen is *sapaksha* (*sa*=like + *paksha*, i.e., a similar place known to have been the abode of fire on a previous occasion); and the lake is *vipaksha*, (vi = anti+paksha) which is known to contain neither fire nor smoke. But although these requirements are met in the instance of Z's unborn child, there is no knowing that the little imp will not upset the Buddhist calculations in revenge for having had its sex brought into controyersy so early in its career.

Western logic, too, fails to come up to the mark, for not only is its syllogism artificial and unnatural, as must be fully evident by this time, but also because it is not concerned in arriving at truth. It is more like a method of interpretation than a science of accurate deduction.

No doubt, it is more exact than either the Naiyayika or the Buddhist logic in its application, but its scope is almost wholly limited to determining and here we must be fair to admit, with utmost precision—the contents of a given proposition or propositions, so as to ensure consistency of thought. According to Hamilton and Mansel, logic is merely the science of consistency and has no concern with the real relations of things. Mill and Bain certainly aspire to raise it to the dignity of a true science whose conclusions should conform to matters of fact; i.e., the real relations of things; but they leave it as cumbersome and unwieldy and artificial as ever. The practical value of modern logic as a science, judged from the fact that its inferential processes are never actually resorted to by men—not even by lawyers, philosophers and logicians—in their daily life, is nil. Its innumerable technicalities and definitions entail a heavy burden on the memory, and its forms and formulas confound and confuse where they should illuminate and elucidate. It is the natural logic as described here today which can be taught to every one however stupid; and certainly it can be imparted to little boys and girls in the sixth and the seventh classes with the greatest ease. It is enlightening and assures consistency of thought, and thus sweetens life, while the modern method aspires for pedantry, is elucidative of nothing practical and ends with imparting a wrangling disposition to its devotee. Anyone who has understood the subject, I am sure, will not differ from me when I say that the highest achievement of modern logic is the possession of a set of rigid formulas and diagrams for testing the formal validity of propositions, quite irrespective of the fact whether they embody actual truth or not, while the least gain from natural logic is the acquisition of a logical turn of mind that seeks to discover actual relations among things and the true principles of causation of events in nature. The highest gain from natural logic must, therefore, imply a complete mastery over the empire of nature for the highest conceivable form of good. It will be a great day for mankind when natural logic is freely taught to school boys and girls, and I trust it will even be introduced in some simplified form in primary schools.

This finishes the department of logic, which, I am sure, has not taken us more than three quarters of an hour to assimilate.

I must now say a word about classification which means

the sorting or arranging of things into classes or sets according to their characteristics. A characteristic (*lakshna*) may be an inalienable property of a thing, *e.g.*, heat, which cannot be separated from fire, or a temporary one, *e.g.*, beard, of man. The true characteristic is one that is actually to be found in common in every member of the class, but in nothing else outside it.

The next ally of a metaphysician is analysis which gives us the knowledge of the ingredients, material or parts of which a body or thing may be composed; and the last is *nayavada* that requires, on account of its great importance, to be dealt with at some length. It is safe to say of *nayavada* that all the misunderstandings and trouble that have ever arisen among men with respect to religion and metaphysics are simply due to their ignorance of its fundamental principles. Literally, *naya-vada* means a system of standpoints; in metaphysics, it is the keeping in mind, at the time of raising a subsequent mental superstructure thereon, of the particular side or aspect from which any specific statement is made or a specific conclusion reached. This is necessary to prevent the metaphysical superstructure from becoming top-heavy. For instance, we observe all things of matter changing and shifting and perishing in nature, but this is so only in respect of the forms in which matter appears, not in respect of matter itself, which is eternal. Suppose we generalised upon the impermanence of things and left out of account the underlying continuity of matter as matter, to better emphasize the transiency of its forms, and then set out to build up a system of metaphysics upon this one sided emphasis, we should have something like the doctrine known as *kshanikavada*, which maintains that there is nothing permanent in nature, so that things must constantly arise out of and vanish into pure nothing. Here the confusion has obviously arisen from the ignoring of the fact that the impermanence of things is confined to their forms, and does not extend to their material or substance. This one instance suffices to demonstrate the principle of *nayavada* and to warn us against all such one-sided absolutisms. There are many ways of looking at a thing, and so there are many standpoints. The more important ones of these may be classified as follows :—

STANDPOINT

Real or Scientific (*nischaya), e.g.*, calling a pitcher of clay containing water, a pitcher of clay.

Popular or vulgar (*vyavahara*), e.g., calling the pitcher of water, because of its containg water.

Dravyarthika (having reference to substance and pure natural properties of things).

Paryayarthika (having reference to forms and modifi -cations of things).

This is sufficient to give you an idea of *nayavada*, which is very essential for true metaphysics.

I shall now revert for a moment to the true function of Scripture which has already been touched upon to some extent in today's lecture. This is not the place to plunge into the highly controversial subject of what revelation implies and what is its true source, for we shall have better opportunities for that purpose later on; here it is sufficient to state that the true function of scripture is to instruct mankind in the proper way, so that they may obtain the highest good by conforming to truth. To this extent any scripture is valuable, provided that it proceeds from a properly qualified source. As already stated today, the word of an Omniscient Teacher, who directly perceives the past, the present and the future and who knows all things and their relations, is the true criterion and final test of the validity of a logical relationship (*vyapti*), so that what is not in agreement with the Scripture of Truth must necessarily be the cause of error and undoing and downfall.

I ought to add that some of you may not be willing to accept the proposition ,that there can be Omniscient beings; but for the purposes of this lecture I have merely assumed their existence, and hope to examine the proposition in the next lecture.

This exhausts the subjeot of this evening's discourse and we shall, therefore, stop here too.

CHAPTER - III

SCIENCE

(A)

The subject of this evening's lecture is the Religion of Science. The expression Religion of Science is a somewhat misleading one since what is understood nowadays by the term science is a body of materialistic doctrines that subscribe to no religious belief. What is meant here is Religion as a science rather than a set of doctrines or tenets of any particular body or class of men.

The term science is the opposite of nescience, and implies accurate knowledge of existing substances and their properties together with that of the true principles of causation of things,- a knowledge that is free from error, doubt and ignorance and that may be tested by experiment. Exact knowledge is what is signified by the term, and apart from reliable testimony, exact knowledge is obtained only ofter observation and experiment by the finite man.

The first axiom of science is the constancy of nature. This means that substances and their attributes are eternal and unvarying; they never cease to be and are never produced from nothing. This is proved by the experience of men, both in the present and the past; and the experience that proves it is not that of any particular man or woman, nor of any particular class or body of men, but of the whole of the human race without a single exception. For whatever people may think or hold about the origin of the world and the theory of creation, not one man can be found who claims to know, from direct personal observation, that things can arise from or vanish into nothing.

The law of Constancy of nature means that substance is eternal, so that whatever really and truly exists can never be destroyed. When a thing seems to have disappeared, it has merely changed its form, but has not been altogether wiped out of existence, *e.g.*, a piece, of sugar that has melted in water or milk has merely changed its form, having passed from the solid into a liquid state. Similarly, a shower of rain is simply the moisture of the atmosphere cast down in the form of drops of water; it certainly is not produced from nothing by a god working, from behind the clouds. Water evaporates by boiling, and vapour becomes liquid again by passing through colder temperature. As Haeckel points out, nowhere in nature do we find an example of the production, or 'creation' of new matter; nowhere does a particle of existing matter pass entirely away. "This empirical truth is now the unquestionable foundation of chemistry; it may be directly verified at any moment by means of the balance." (THE RIDDLE OF THE UNIVERSE).

The Law of persistence of substance implies that properties and attributes of substances are also constant though liable to modification in different combinations and groupings, *e.g.*, colour, smell and the like which are the attributes of matter, have always been the attributes of matter and will always remain so. As a matter of fact, substance and attributes are the two sides or aspects of the same thing, for there can be no substance apart from its attributes. This is tantamount to saying that attributes only inhere in substances and substances are but bundles of attributes, *e.g.*, gold is only the sum-total of all its properties, yellowness, heaviness, materiality, etc., etc., and cannot be thought of as anything apart from them.

Substance is characterised by the triple function of origination, destruction and continuance at one and the same time. When a bar of gold is melted in the crucible, there is destruction of bar-ness, origination of the liquid state and continuance of gold as gold throughout. This is the triple function of substance. Nor may we hold that the destruction of barness is not simultaneous with the origination of the molten state, because there is no intermediate state between them, so that the assumption of the liquid state is the very form of the destruction of the bar-ness of gold. If you allowed an interval of time between the two states or conditions of the piece of gold, you would be compelled to hold that the destruction of barness left it without any form whatsoever in the first instance, and that it subsequently became transformed into a liquid state from absolute formlessness. But this is absurd, because things cannot be conceived as existing without some kind of form.

The world is resolvable into two kinds of substances in the main, the living and the non-living. The former of these signifies that which is characterised by life or consciousness and the latter, what is not so characterised, *e.g.*, matter. They are technically termed *jiva* (living) and *ajiva* (a=not+*jiva*, the non-living), respectively. We may also call them spirit and non-spirit. Modern science denies the existence of spirit (*jiva* substance), and attributes consciousness to matter. But scientists are hard put to it to account for the origin of life, and invent fanciful theories to explain its first appearance on Earth, some holding that its germ or seed fell on our globe from some other planet in the first instance, others that it arose spontaneously, and so forth. We shall first of all examine the theory according to which there is a primitive *nucleus* of sensitivity bound up in each atom of matter. This elementary consciousness, it is permised, in the course of evolution developed into the keen, refined and complex intellectualism of a Kant, a Schopenhauer and a Tyndall, and may develop still further. Upon this supposition the higher forms of consciousness would arise by the intensification of the original *nucleus*. But this is pure guess work; and it rests upon two kinds of facts of observation and one kind of misconception of theological origin. The facts are (1) that matter is known to offect the manifestations of consciousness, and (2) that all beings are not endowed with the same kind of mental powers; and the misconception is that there can be no soul unless it remains in one and the same condition under all circumstances. I have nothing to say against the facts; they are well attested and cannot be gainsaid. As a matter of fact we shall see that Religion proper has not failed to give them the fullest consideration they are entitled to. The misconception is evident from the following lucid expression of Haeckel's views in his world famous "Riddle of the Universe":—

> "These and other familiar facts prove that man's consciousness—and that of the nearest mammals—is changeable [Haeckel's own *italics*] and that its activity is *always* open to modification from inner (alimentation, circulation, etc.) and outer causes (lesion of the brain, stimulation, etc.,). The ontogenesis of consciousness makes it perfectly clear that it is not an immaterial entity but a physiological function of the brain, and that it is, consequently, no exception to the general law of substance."

As a matter of fact, Religion proper never regarded the soul to be an 'immaterial entity' in the Haeckelian sense of the expression, nor ever maintained that it could not be offected by matter. What the European scientists had to contend with, however, was not the true view of Religion, but a highly misleading theological fallacy of mystic origin which regarded the soul as *absolutely* immaterial and unchanging. For this reason we do not take the scientist's denial of the soul to be absolute, as he has never had a chance of considering the true view.

According to Religion, spirit and matter are both substances which have a number of properties but not consciousness in common between them. Consciousness is the exclusive property of spirit or soul-substance, which, consequently, is not an 'immaterial entity, in all respects, but only in so for as it is not material, that is to say, not made of matter. Both spirit and matter are capable of affecting each other under certain conditions, *e.g.* the curing of disease. by purely mental suggestion, the augmentation and diminution of the degree of consciousness by certain drugs and medicaments, and the like. The effect of the union or fusion of spirit and matter is the curtailment of the faculties and functions of the former, so that *nirvana* actually implies nothing more or less than the *complete* emancipation of the soul from the pernicious companionship of matter. Under the influence of matter, when it is of the very worst type, the soul's consciousness is reduced almost to what may be termed the zero point, and it is then capable of responding only to the barest sensations of touch.

In the above description of the soul which is taken from the Jaina *Siddhanta*, it is clearly recognised that consciousness is liable to be affected by matter. The issue which now arises between Religion and science, therefore, is not whether there is an unchanging immaterial entity in the human or animal organism, but whether consciousness is a function of atomic matter or of a distinct kind of substance which has an affinity for or with matter, but, which, in its real nature, is not matter?

Now, if sensation be regarded as the fundamental property of an atom of matter, the higher consciousness of man and the manifestation of such supernormal faculties as clairvoyance and the like must be due to an intensification or augmentation of that primitive nucleus. But we have not a case of simple augmentation or intensification before us; the difference between the highest and the lowest forms of consciousness is not merely to be represented in terms of quantity; it is qualitative most strikingly. For the most pronounced materialists have not associated atomic sensitivity with either smell or sight or hearing, and the wildest conjecture fails to guess how these faculties could arise, by mere augmentation or intensification, out of the barest susoeptibility to tactile sensations which is all that this supposed atomic consciousness is capable of. The chasm between pure sensitiveness to touch and such higher functions of life as judgment and will is too great to be bridged over by pure jugglery with deceptive-phrases and terms, and demands a satisfactory explanation from those who would explain these phenomena by a simple exaggeration or magnifying of the primal *nucleus*. There is not an iota of evidence to support the proposition that a bare sensation of touch can be transformed into clairvoyant perception or logical inference, and you certainly cannot expect to have the highly cultured mind of a Kant or a Schopenhauer by multiplying a simple sensation of touch a thousand, a million or even a hundred thousand million times by itself.

Besides this, what is bound up in an atom must be altogether inalienable from it, because an atom is indestructible and therefore devoid of separable parts and qualities. The intensification of an inner psychic state of an entity like our supposed atomic soul is altogether out of the question, since no such soul is possessed of any alienable attributes which it might gift away or lend to a brother or sister in need. Nor can you lend any of your psychic properties to any of your needy brethren, for will, memory, judgment and sight are not transferable like worldly goods.

We thus see that the supposition of an atomic sensitivity as the primal *nucleus*, which becomes, by gradual intensification, the highly versatile soul of a Christ or a Kant is utterly inadequate to explain the fact and phenomena of consciousness and must be rejected. But materialism has yet another thesis to advance to account for conscionsness. We are now told by another set of materialists that consciousness is the product of the brain. In summing up his case agaist the view that, consciousness is the function of the soul Ernst Haeckel of the University of Jena writes:—

> "From the fact that consciousness, like all other psychic functions, is dependent on the normal development of certain organs, and that it gradually unfolds in the child in proportion to the developmont of those organs, we may already conclude that it has arisen in the animal kingdom by a gradual historical development."

But this is a pure conjecture, and not a logical influence grounded on any well-founded *vyapti*, without which, as you already aware, no true deduction can be made. Haeckel is himself instinctively forced to realize the weakness of his position, for he immediately adds:—

> Still, however, certain we are of the fact of the natural evolution or conscionsness, we are, unfortunately, not yet in a position to enter more deeply into the question and construct special hypothesis in elucidation of it."

Strange theorising, indeed; the "fact" has not yet been elucidated by special hypothesis and still we are certain of it! Consciousness is produced by the brain, we are told, but whence did the brain acquire it itself? Did it grow out of a supposed primal *nucleus* embedded in atoms of matter, from a crued primitive atomic soul, which has already been seen to be an indefensible position? Haeckel himself is opposed to the notion of an atomic soul, as he distinctly says in Chap. X of the "Riddle". 'Where else could it come from, then? Yon cannot have blood out of stones; neither can you have sensation, feeling, memory, judgement or will out of dead unconscious atoms. The argument put in the mouth of Bishop Butler in the famous Belfast address, which the late Prof. Tyndall declared to be unanswerable, has in no way been refuted since.

> "Take your dead hydrogen atoms, your dead oxygen atoms your dead carbon atoms, and all the other atoms dead as grains of shot, of which the brain is formed. Imagine them separate and sensationless, observe them running together and forming all imaginable combinations. This, as a purely mechanical process, is seeable by the mind. But can you see or dream or in any way imagine, how out of that mechanical act and from these individually dead atoms, sensation, thought and emotion, are to rise? Are you likely to extract Homer out of the rattling of dice, or Differential Calculus out of the clash of billiard-balls? ....You cannot satisfy the human understanding in its demand for logical continuity between molecular processes and the phenomena of conscionsness."

Tyndall himself tried to evade the difficulty by enlarging

the definition of matter to include Life and Consciousness. He said:—

> "If we look at matter as pictured by Democritus, and as defined for generations of our scientific text books, the notion of conscious life coming out of it cannot be formed by the mind. The argument placed in the mouth of Bishop Butler suffices, in my opinion, to crush all such materialism as this. Those, however, who framed these definitions of matter were but partial students. They were not biologists;........ their science was mechanical science, not the science of life..........Let us reverently, look the question in the face. Divorced from matter, where is life? What ever our **faith** may say, our knowledge shows them to be indissolubly joined. Every meal we eat and every cup we drink illustrates the mysterions control of the mind by matter."

Unfortunately Tyndall only knew of the current contemporary misconceptions about the soul; he did not know that no unredeemed soul was free from the companionship of matter or immune from its influence and that redeemed Souls were altogether outside the reach of modern science, having entered *nirvana* of which it had no motion whatsoever. Therefore, it never occurred to Tyndall or any one else of the scientific fraternity in Europe, before or after him, that the association of the mind and matter was not, in any sense, an argument, much less a conclusive argument, against the existence of the soul. For the dependence of consciousness on the development of the brain might be explained not only on the supposition that it is secreted or otherwise produced by the brain, but in other ways besides. The brain may have not necessarily a productive function with respect to consciousness, but of a different kind, *e.g.*, a transmissive one, as Prof. william James, the famous psychologist, points out. These different possibilities have never been considered by modern science and cannot be said to have been excluded from the list. Thus when certain admirers of modern science think that that science has demonstrated the soul to be an illusion pure and simple, their delude themselves with imaginary conclusions that have never even been in issue in reality. The fact is that modern investigators have never applied themselves to ascertain the attributes of spirit and matter, and are, consequently, unable to distinguish the one from the other. A study of the principal characteristics of consciousness will convince anyone that it cannot possibly be a function of the brain, however closely it may be associated with it.

For, as we shall see presently, consciousness is

(1) Individualistic,

(2) Psychic, and

(3) Immoral,

while the brain is

(a) composite,

(b) non-psychic, and

(c) perishable.

Haeckel and his colleagues seem to treat consciousness as if it only meant the highly illuminated discriminative faculty of man and of certain higher animals but as not including the lower manifestations of sensitive impressionability, *e.g.*, the feeling of pain which is common to all living beings, or of shock to which even plants and trees are subject, as the recent researches of the great Indian *savant*, Prof. Sir Jagdish Chandra Bose, have demonstrated, with the utmost scientific precision. The following emphatic statement from Haeckels' Riddle of the Universe is expressive of the materialistic view on the subject:—

> "As everybody knows, **the new born infant has no consciousness**. Prayer has shown that **it is only developed after** the **child has begun to speak**; for a long time **it speaks of itself in the third person**. In the important moment when it first pronounces the word 'I' when the feeling of self becomes clear: we have the beginning of self-consciousness, and of the antithesis to the non-ego."

The crucial points in this passage are marked in thick print. The statement is simply astounding, especially as it comes from a person accustomed to very exact and sober thinking. If *the new born infant has no consciousness*, who *feels* the pain that finds its expression in the cry that accompanies child-birth? *If consciousness is only developed after the child has begun to speak*, how account for the likes and dislikes of the infant before it has acquired the power of speech? The position becomes perfectly ludicrous when it is sought to strengthen the conclusion by the fact that for a long time the infant speaks of itself in the third person. Does it mean that the child feels its affections also in the third person, as if a pure spectator to someone else's conditions?

Let us not deceive ourselves by such seeming truths and half-truths. Intellectualism, ratiocination, intelligent speech all come from the same source as the capacity to feel one's affections and impressions. Intelligence and sensation or feeling are the two phases or functions of the same entity, of the power that makes one aware of the conditions of one's being, that is to say of the power of self-awareness. Sensation and feeling are as much states of consciousness as intellectual conceptions and verbal ideas that pass by the name of knowledge. There are not two different kinds of sensitiveness or consciousnesses in nature. Intelligence is one, whether it be manifested through instinct or intellect; and sensitiveness is present all along and is never altogether extinct or destroyed though its manifestation be reduced to the barest susceptibility to tactile sensations alone for the time being. There are certain conditions that are necessary for the manifestation of instinct and intelligence, some sort of an instrument of control or self-control is needed to rise above a purely automatic existence. Here you have your brain which is imposed, like a loop, over the sensory and motor systems to enable the ego to attend to the incoming sensory stimulus from without, and to regulate or control the motor movements of the organism in response from within. But it is a fallacy to imagine that sensitiveness originated with the brain.

For automatic response in brainless creatures does not negative the existence of consciousness; it is accompanied by sensation and feeling. Sensation and feeling are not purely physical in their nature; their type is *psychic*, though they may not be presided over by deliberated intelligence. It cannot be urged, I think, that the excitation always suffices, in or by itself, to produce a movement in the motor reflexes. Such a supposition would reduce the whole thing to pure mechanical activity where consciousness would have absolutely no function to serve. It is, moreover, to be doubted if there is any proportion between the excitation of a sensory filament, or nerve, and the ensuing movement of the organism or limb, *e.g.*, a pin-prick may cause a mammoth to move its colossal foot; and a mosquito-bite, a sleeping giant to turn over in his bed![1] What seems actually to happen in such cases is this that the sensory excitement has no more function to perform after it has given rise to a sensation, and that the resulting reaction of the experiencing consciousness is the source of the bodily movement which is performed through automatic reflexes where the deliberative faculty is lacking, and automatically or through selected appropriate channels in the converse case.

May it not, then, be that psychic automatism represents a faculty asleep rather than the crude beginning of a function that is to grow and develop through a long, tortuous and protracted course of evolution? May it not also be that the development of the brain is intended to meet a demand from an ego already advanced in self-control rather than as a distillery or factory for the manufacturing of the ego itself ? It is significant that the highest function of the mind, namely, selection, discrimination or judgement is performed only by such of the living beings as are able to arrest their psychic automatism, that is to say, to arrest the ceaseless flow of action to obtain a pause for deliberation. Hence, the brain is needed only by such beings as happen to possess some degree of control over the motor springs of their actions—desires.

As is well known, there are many highly intellectual men

and women who are simply unable to exercise their discrimination in certain circumstances, especially when faced with some ever-powering temptation. They invariably then do things of which they repent in their calmer moments. It seems to me that there is a clear conflict here between the faculty of judgment and emotion, the latter overruling the former for the time being. It would be difficult to conceive how this could happen if discrimination were a function of the brain and the brain were actually functioning at the time when it was overruled by emotion and continued to forgo the ego thereafter. Everything becomes lucid, on the other hand, by the simple acknowledgment of a pre-existing ego that brings with it all its pre-natal tendencies evolved out elsewhere in earlier surroundings, such tendencies constituting the demand in response to which its future organism is to be made. The brain would, then be an instrument of discrimination made to meet the demand of an individual already sufficientlly advanced in self-control, and its functioning would depend both on its own conditions and on the emotional states of the ego. The inablity of the newly-born infant to *define* his own being clearly to himself or to any one else, in an intellectual way, would thus be due to the difficulties involved in handling a new and extremly delicate tool, while the failure of the intellectual wrong doer to utilise the services of his discriminating faculty simply result from his inablity to control his desires.

But we must now define the ego in more definite terms. The first thing noticeable about our consciousness is that it is individualistic. This is tantamount to saying that every one is aware of himself as himself and as nobody else, however much the definition of what he knows as himself may vary from timeto time, from different causes. Similarly, nobody ever knows himself as more than one or a multitude of personages. There may be a conflict between our emotions and desires on one side and judgement and farsightness on the other; but one never feels oneself as a corporation or board consisting of many individualities, with the decision of matters resting on a preponderance of votes. Reflection shows that our sense of awareness which we term consciousness is an inner, subjective, psychic state that is best described by the term *feeling* of awareness, so that my knowledge of a thing is my feeling of awareness of its existence or presence. As such my consiousness of an object implies the simultaneous awareness of my own being as well as that of the object of my knowledge. This will be clear to anyone who has understood knowledge to consist in a *sense* or *feeling* of awareness, for one can only *feel* one's own being and the states or conditions of that being as modified by the influence of another being or thing. It will be monstrous to suppose that I can *feel* another's being but not my own! As a matter of fact my knowledge of another's being depends on my capacity to *feel* the states of my own being. Hence it is wrong to say that in knowing an object the ego only knows the object but not itself. The fact is that only that which has a concrete existence can be felt by the soul, and as the states of consciousness, that is to say, of the soul-subtance, have no existence apart from the soul-substance itself, they can only be felt simultaneously and along with the soul's own being. This is even so with reference to the feelings of pleasure and pain with which all of us are familiar.' When I say 'I am feeling pain' or 'I feel pleasure: I do not mean that pleasure and pain are concrete things outside me which I have alighted upon in some mysterious way. What I do mean is that I am aware of a state or modification of my own being which is painful in one case and pleasant in the other. Pleasure and. pain are thus only states of my consciousness, that is to say, of that general feeling of awareness which I have of my own being. The newly born infant that cries out on coming into the world, undoubtedly, also *feels* pain as a *state of his own consciousmess*, though he is unable to form a clear picture of his little personality in his mind, for want of intellectual lucidity at the time. Notwithstanding what modern wisdom may urge to the contrary, the fact is that a feeling of pleasure or pain cannot be experienced except in the first person. If one could accomplish the fact of *experiencing* them in the third person, it would be a miracle; for what one witnessed in another could only be a spectacle, never an *affection* or *experience*. Preyer's infant, too, if Preyer ever observed him under the influence of hunger before he learnt to talk, could not but have felt hungry in the first person singular, and in the first I person singular also must have been experienced by I him the satisfaction that followed the nourishment on such occasions. We thus conclude that the first characteristic of consciousness is individuality which is inseparable from it even in its lowest form, the barest susceptibility to sensations of touch. It is, no doubt, possible for us to conceive this low form of consciousness in association with an atom of matter, but a majority of leading materialists themselves are opposed to this view, and it is altogether untenable for the reasons that have been already given as well as for those that will be given later on.

But if, not the property of an atom of matter, consciousness cannot be a function of the brain, also, for the individualistic attribute of conscious life is altogether inconceivable as the product of a human or animal brain, which is itself devoid of indivisibility" hence individuality. For the brain is composed of atomic matter and can have nought but a 'corporational' personality,—a board of consciousnesses presiding over the affairs that might be placed before them. I grant that one's ideas about oneself, may change from time to time from different causes, disease, hypnotic suggestion and the like; but that is not the same thing as making out consciousness to be like a board of councillors,[2] at a country council meeting.

If a composite substance like the brain can produce individuality at any time, it must be the individuality of an atom of its material, for nothing else in the brain has a claim to individuality; but we have already agreed to reject the hypothesis of an atomic soul.

The notion of a 'County-Council' chamber of consciousness is further negatived by the fact of logical inference which becomes possible only where the conclusion is to be drawn by the same unit of consciousness as is in possession of the premises from which it is to be drawn, not otherwise. For if one councillor of our County Council be only aware of one premise and another of the other premise, then neither of them nor anyone else can draw any inference whatsoever from the given premises. Similarly, if one part of the brain be possessed of one premise and another part of the other premise, it will be impossible for a conclusion to be drawn from them. But since the ego is capable of drawing a logical conclusion, it follows that it is not the same thing as the brain, but a different kind of thing, that is to say, not a compound or composite substance or thing, but a simple, indivisible, that is, partless, individuality.

With respect to memory also, we can see that it cannot be a function of a changing perishable thing like the brain; for the brain that experiences a sensation today will not be the same that will recollect it or its experience fifty years hence. Recollection would thus be a miracle, if the brain be the recollect or of events; it would be tantamount to our recollecting the experiences of a being that existed 50 years back, in other words, to recollect having been some one else, which, as Maher S. J., a great Roman Catholic thinker, points out, is an absurdity pure and simple (see Maher's Psychology). It is thus evident that memory cannot be the function of that which is generated afresh every moment, like a stream, which consciousness must be if it is to be regarded as a function or secretion of the brain. In order that the events of a life-time may be remembered by an individual, his recollecting faculty must have subsisted uninterruptedly throughout. One who comes into existence, for the first time, at a particular moment of time, only to be gathered to his forefathers in the very next instant, cannot, by any possibility, know what its predecessors knew, or feel as they did in certain associations. A substratum of individuality which continues in time, *i.e.*, a something which *endures*, is necessary for the purpose; and no amount of "learned talk" can explain the facts of consciousness, that is, feeling, memory and willing if we posit a consciousness that is generated afresh, every movement, from the physical matter of the brain in place of the true individual, namely the *atman* or soul.

The next characteristic of consciousness is its psychic nature as distinguished from the physical nature of matter and material things. There is an inside to conciousness which may become the repository of even infinite knowledge, enthusiasm, goodness, will, etc., etc.; but the atom of matter has no inside to expand. Evolution in reference to matter means the improvement or modification of bodies through continuous readjustment of molecular groupings. Evolution in respect to mind means the enrichment of consciousness by internal lucidity and expansion of thought. Consciousness is a world in itself which can be peopled by an infinity of ideas, impressions and concepts; but matter has no interior to its atom to accommodate even a thought. Intellectual lucidity is obtained not by the intensification or magnifying of a supposed primal tactile nucleus, but by the *removal* of dullness, cloudiness and mental fog. This is so most certainly with respect to what is known as *avadhi jnana* which means *roshan zimiri* روشن ضمیری the clairvoyance of saints, that is acquired by severe asceticism, fasting and self-denial. Clearly here we have a case of recovering a buried Pompeii out of slabs of *lava*, and not of building and *peopling* a new city, by some mathematical jugglery of imagination, out of a single brick! The truth is that every individual, soul, or ego, is endowed with potential omniscience and may recover it by discovering himself. This might appear astounding at first sight but will be readily assented to on mature reflection. For knowledge is not a thing that can be said to have a concrete existence outside the being of a conscious entity or ego, consisting, as it does, in nothing other than *states* of the ego itself, that are usually described as states of consciousness. There are things outside ourselves, not knowledge; and our sense of awareness of things is called their knowledge. With respect to such thing as the notion of time, space, infinity, causality and the like, Kant has shown them to be given a *priori* to the knowing consciousness, that is to say, as not being derived from perception in any way, and there is not one materialist known to me to-day who claims to differ from this great German philosopher in this regard. If our consciousness has evolved out of a primitive form of sensitivity, this a *priori* knowledge must have been there within that primitive *nucleus*. But how can you think of these a *priori* conceptions, in connection with or as coming out of the crude *nucleus* of sensitivity supposed to be residing in an atom of matter ?Why were they not functioning in that primitive form of sensitivity? Did they, too, exist then in some primitive form? But Kant would absolutely decline to listen to, such a thing, because these notions are not the outcome of experience. Causality, certainly, is not such a concept as may be said to have been developed by evolution, nor could a notion like that of infinity be conceived as *growing along with* the development of the brain. The human mind fails to picture a primitive form of these conceptions from which they could have developed or grown by evolution. They are inherent in the mind whence they arise with lucidity of thought, Inalienable assets of consciousness, they must have slumbered in the bosom of understanding when the intellect lay wrapped up in the lowest form of sensitivity. Thus do all ideas-knowledge itself lie dormant in the ego.

We have said that every ego is potentially omniscient by nature. This is easily proved. The soul being not an "immaterial entity," but a kind of substance, the natural properties of the soul-substance must be the same wherever it may be found. This is tantamount to saying that all souls are alike in respect of their attributes, however, much they may differ from one another in respect of their actual manifestation. As the attributes of pure gold are the same whether you come across it in India, or China, or England, so are the natural attributes of the soul. substance the same; and as the differences in the qualities of gold are due to the presence of the alloy in different proportions, so are the differences among souls due to the admixture of a foreign substance-matterin varying proportions. It follows from this that what one soul knows all others can know also,—a sound principle of practical utility which is the very foundation of our educational institutions. For if there were fixed limits of knowledge for different souls, it would be simply waste of time to raise schools and colleges in every city and suburb.

Now, since what is known to one individual is capable of being known by every body else, it follows that everyone has an inherent capacity within him to know all that everyone else knew in the past, all that every one knows in the present, and also all that everyone shall ever lmow in the future. In other words, every soul is potentially omniscient, though the actual knowledge it may possess at any particular time of its career may, owing to. the presence and influence of a knowledge and lucidity-obstructing agent, in the form of a foreign material or alloy, be so poor as will not entitle anyone to boast of.

With reference to the significance of omniscience, it is to be borne in mind that the fullest degree of knowledge is what is implied by the term. According to some writers there are certain limits on human knowledge which are imposed by a being or thing termed, in a spirit of more or less subdued awe, 'the unknown.' But this is merely begging the question. Actually there can he no such thing as the unknown in the empire of nature. For we have right to ask whether in talking of an unknown, you be talking of things which you *know* of or not. Now, if you reply that you *know* that there is an unknown thing existing which will never he known to anyone, then, my dear sir, your own admission—that you know that such a thing exists—falsifies your proposition; but if you say that you do not, then you should take my advice and say no more about it, because then you will be babbling, like babes, of things which you know nothing about and which you have absolutely no reason to suppose exist! You may now seek shelter behind the plea that your unknowable is a paragon of virtues some of which will ever remain impervious to the obtruding gaze of an explorer. But here again you are merely repeating your earlier error. Have you any reason to suppose the existence of those attributes that can never be known by anyone, or are you only talking for talking's sake? In the one case you already know the thing, since you have inferential or reasonable kowledge of it, like that of ether and space, but in the other you have no right to be in the arena of metaphysics and should retire from it at once. The argument that if living beings come to an end before the completion of scientific enquiry, things must ever remain unknown is beside the point; for that would not make them *unknowable*. That term, it will be seen, is not a synonymn for what is termed *unknown*, but possesses the additional attribute of never being known to anyone, although capable enquiring minds exist and become engaged in the exploration of nature and the investigation of truth. Hence, if radium, wireless telegraphy, gramophone and other such discoveries and inventions of the nineteenth century A.D. had remained for ever unknown because of the total destruction of knowing beings at the end of the eighteenth century, it would only have been a case of *knowable* things remaining unknown, but not of any of the unknowable sort. The fact is that without strict proof nothing can be taken to be a fact of existence, so that what can never be known by anyone at any time will never be proved to have an existence. The *unknowable*, whether you spell it with a capital 'u' or a small one, is thus a mere bug-bear invented by a slovenly metaphysics with which to frighten immature untrained novices. On the side of concrete nature, also, it is obvious that things offect one another and are known through their effects on other things even when not perceivable by the senses, *e.g.*, *ether*, which is invisible but is known through its properties. Hence, to say that a thing can never be known is to say that it Beyer enters into relations with anything else in the universe throughout the unimaginably vast infinity of duration that is implied in our conception of time, past, present and future. But this is only possible for things that are outside the universe, that is to say, outside the possible range of existence. Hence, what never entered or enters into relations with anything else is non-existent.

We thus come back to the proposition that all things are knowable and that there are no limits to the knowing-capacity of the soul. Thus, every soul is omniscient potentially.

If you have followed me thus far you will now see more clearly than ever how absurd is the position of the materialistic philosophy which posits a consciousness that is the outcome of a rudimentary sensitiveness in an atom of matter. We know that intellectual lucidity is obtained by the removal of mental cloudiness, opacity, dullness or fog, which are conceivable in connection with a composite personality, arising from the union of more than one substances where each one tends to curtail the functions of the other. But an atomic soul is not encumbered with any such curtailing agent, because an atom is a simple indivisible thing. Hence, the fullest degree of mental lucidity should be the characteristic of the soul, on tho hypothesis of its being synonymous with atomic sensitivity. This is fatal to the hypothesis of atomic consciousness, which proceeds on the assumption of a rudimentary form of sensation in atomic matter. The hypothesis of a brain consciousness, too, fores no better with reference to the powers and faculties of the soul ill respect of knowledge. If any one will pause and reflect over what is implied in the term knowledge-observation, investigation, classification, comparison, inference, interpretation, judgment, etc., etc.,—and recollection, he will not, I am sure, refuse to lend his assent to the following considered dictum from the pen of Prof. Bowne (see Bowne's Metaphysics, pp. 407-410):—

> "By describing the mind as a waxen tablet, and things as impressing themselves upon it, we seem to get a great insight until we think to ask where this extended tablet is, and how things stamp themselves on it, and how the perceptive act could he explained even if they did...... The immediate antecedents of sensation and perception are a series of nervous changes in the brain. Whatever we know of the outer world is revealed only in and through these nervous changes. But these are totally unlike tho objects assumed to exist as their causes. If we might conceive the mind as in the light, and in direct

contact with its objects, the imagination at least would be comforted; but when we conceive the mind as coming in contact with the outer world only iu the dark chamber of the skull, and then not in contact with the objects perceived, but only with a series of nerve changes of which, moreover, it knows nothing, it is plain that the object is a long way off. All talk of pictures, impressions, etc. ceases because of the lack of all the conditions to give such figures any meaning. It is not even clear that we shall ever find our way out of the darkness into the world of light and reality again. We begin with complete trust in physics and the senses, and are forthwith led away from the object into a nervous labyrinth, where the object is totally displaced by a set of nervous changes which are totally unlike anything but themselves. Finally, we land in the dark chamber of the skull. The object has gone completely, and knowledge has not yet appeared. Nervous signs are the raw material of all knowledge of the outer world, according to the most decided realism. But in order to pass beyond these signs into a knowledge of the outer world, *we must posit an interpreter who shall read back these signs into-their objective meaning. But that interpreter, again, must implicity contain the meaning of the universe within itself;* and these signs are really but excitations which cause the soul to un*fold what is within itself.* Inasmuch as by common consent the soul communicates with the outer world only through these signs, and never comes nearer to the object than such signs can bring it, it follows that the principles of interpretation must be in the mind itself, and that the *resulting construction is primarily only an expression of the mind's own nature*. All reaction is of this sort; it expresses the nature of the reacting agent, and knowledge comes under the same head."

I have italicised the important passages in this lucid statement of Prof. Bowne's to emphasize the point. We can see that education, from *e*, out, and *duco*, to lead, is, really, the bringing of knowledge out of the recesses of the mind, as the etymology of the word rightly points out. What comes from the without, in the shape of sensory stimulus, is always matter or motion in some form, *never knowledge*, and it will be a miracle if matter or motion could ever give rise to knowledge of themselves. Hermann Lotze well puts the case when he says:—

> "The second reason which led to the conception of the soul was the entire incomparability of all inner processes, —sensations, ideas, emotions, and desires—with spatial motion, figures, position, and energy; that is with those states which we believe we observe in matter. We may imagine a quantity of movements of material elements and we may attribute to them whatever degree of complexity we choose; but we shall never reach a given moment at which we can say, Now it is obvious that this sum of movements call remain movements no longer but must pass into sweetness, brightness or sound. The only obvious change we could ever anticipate from them would be into a fresh set of movements. We shall never succeed in analytically deducing the feeling from the nature of its physical excitant; we can only connect the two synthetically; and the physical erent does not bccome a condition of the rise of the feeling until the sum of motions which it (the physical event) consists in meets with a subject which in its own nature has the peculiar capacity of producing feeling from itself."—Lotze's Metaphysics (English translation, Oxford 1887) Book III. Chap. I. p. 167.

The final conclusion Lotze arrived at in regard to the soul may be expressed in his own words:—

> "The conclusion we have now reached is usually expressed by saying that the soul is an indivisible and simple substance."—Ibid, p. 178.

Let us now go back to the hypothesis that the brain is the producer of consciousness for a moment, You know that the brain is not a permanent substance; the matter of which it is composed is constantly passing out and is being replaced by other such matter. You also know and can take it as an indisputable fact that this changing perishable brain cannot give rise to aught but momentary products which exist for a moment and pass out almost as rapidly as they are formed. A consciousness that is produced by such a brain must resemble, then, a rapidly rushing stream in which the same volume of water is never at a place for more than a moment. Or you may like it to a continuous series of flashes of light which are not continuous in themselves. Now, you know the amount of education, the years of toil and hard work that are necessary to produce a statesman, a lawer or a physician. I now ask you, who know all this, whether you can think of, or in any way imagine, a method whereby the knowledge, the education and the general mental equipment of a passing flash of consciousness can be instantaneously transferred, whole and entire, to another such flash of illumination that follows on its heels, and is being pushed by yet another member of its tribe eager to take its place? Nay, can you further conceive how complex mental processes can be carried on, without interruption or break through long hours, with, the aid of these self-taught meteor-like infant prodigies of the brain, and in the total absence of an 'enduring reasoner? To me the whole supposition appears to be nothing short of the miraculous, and I reject it as such.

How do I, then, account for the lesions of the brain offecting recollection? Well, the explanation is this: conscious life is like a current composed of diverse kinds of forces of desires, passions, emotions and inclinations which firc constantly being modified as a result of the contact with the outer world, in other words, by experience. These are purely active forces, usually bent on action, so that if their function is not arrested or cancelled by deliberation they will constantly engage themselves in action and sensation, except when unable to do so from one cause or another. Intellectualism, which is the other branch of conscious functioning, however, requires, as already pointed out a little earlier, a more or less complete suspension of this ceaseless action to obtain a pause for deliberation. Intellectualism thus signifies the stoppage of the current of life's tendencies and inclinations, and reflection requires its being *reflected* (in the fullest etymological sense of the word) on itself, to obtain a principle of guidance in the experience of the past. This is accomplished by the merest change of attention, by its not running with the present, but lingering over a moment that is passing, or by turning to the past. Now, memory is not preserved in the shape of ready-made images or photos, for the simple reason that there is no picture gallery or photo album anywhere in the system, not even in the much-lauded brain, but in the form of mental mechanisms for recalling perceptions? for memories are but perceptions recalled. Hence, the character of our perceptions must also determine the nature of our recollections. But perception is the sense of awareness rosulting from the action of the external *stimulus* on the perceiving consciousness. Memory, too, is, then, necessarily, the reproduction of the original stimulus from inner excitation. The part, or parts, of the organism concerned in perception are the nervous system and, the sensory centers of the brain, where the greatest sensitivity is enjoyed by the ego. These sensory centres of the brain have a two-fold function to perform with reference to our mental life, namely, (i) in perception they receive the incoming *stimulus* and pass it on to the ego, and (ii) in recollection they assist in setting up corresponding vibrations, to reinvoke past perceptions. In other words, every perception sets up a characteristic mark or trace in the constitution and disposition of the will, which, when set in motion, from internal causes will recall the original idea that constituted the percept. So for as the ideas are concerned, they arc not crcatcd any more in recollection than they are in perception. For an idea is not the product of the external or internal *stimulus* in any sense. It is a psychic 'fact,' and cannot be deemed to be the product of material *stimuli*, though a material *stimulus* has the power to invoke or provoke it into manifesting itself. Now, a lesion of the brain centers just does this and no more: in perception it interrupts the external *stimulus*, in recollection, the agitation started internally. It does not affect the ego otherwise, nor diminish its individuality or life in any way. If you ask me where memory is preserved, I must tell you to search for it within that mysterious faculty known as attention. The current of activities of life, already alluded to, is loaded with the entire past experience preserved in the form of modifications of its constituents, and its point is the, organ of attention, which is now turned to this and now to that channel of information or communication with the outer world. It is the high tension of attention (from *ad*, to, and *tendo*, to stretch) which keeps the mind engaged in the present and which prevents the *stimuli* of the other senses: than the one to which it is actually directed at any particular moment of time from penetrating to the ego. But when this high tension is slackened, the rhythm of the current of activities is changed, and attention, travelling back along the tracks of similarity and contiguity, busies itself in rousing up buried treasures of recollection in the cemetery of memory. The diseases of re-collection would thus have a two-fold character; they would either arise from the inability of attention to be thrown back sufficiently for, or the lesion of the memory centers in the brain would prevent a mental agitation from rousing up the image of the past. But this does not mean that memory is altogether immaterial. That hypothesis would be as absurd as the one which makes it out to be a pure product of the matter of the brain. All *samskaras* (impressions) are material in nature, no exception being made even in the case of those formed from the data of the senses other than sight. There are constant streams of vibrations impinging on the mind from the -without, so that there is nothing surprising in the fact that some of this fine material should enter into the formation of memory. Indeed, the surprise would be all the other way, should it be urged that a memory impress is devoid of all materiality whatsoever. As said in the Key of Knowledge, memory is a faculty which pertains neither to pure spirit nor to pure matter, but to a soul vitiated by the absorption of matter. For pure spirit is endowed with omniscience, which is inconsistent with limited knowledge like recollection; and matter is unconscious, hence devoid of memory. The latest views of the modern thinkers on the nature of the functions of the brain agree mostly with what I have stated above. Here is an article from the Daily Telegraph of London dated 30/10/34 which may be said to sum up the result of recent investigation on the subject:—

Dr. James Collier's recent address to the Harveian Society has called attention both to the immense strides in knowledge and the very considerable changes in conception that have taken place during what may roughly be called the first sixty years of modern neurology.

During that time the distinction has been emphasised, as never before, between the two structurally different nervous systems by means of which the human body functions.

The enormous importance of the more primitive, sympathetic system, as it is called, has been recognised—the system associated with the basic acts of living. It is this lowlier system that controls such essential, involuntary acts as the beating of the heart, the respiratory movements of the diaphragm, the muscular reactions, or some of them, of the digestive tracts, and is largely responsible for what may be called the general muscular tone.

In its turn the sympathetic system is largely under control of such glands as the thyroid and the suprarenal, and appears to be stimulated, or "braked" by the discharge from these of their internal secretions or hormones. The exact chemical composition of some of these is now known. They can be reproduced in the laboratory, and have already entered the armament of practical medicine.

All these glands are, in their own turn, largely controlled by the pituitary, or master, gland, in the floor of the skull; and this may almost be described as the earliest and most elementary form of brain. It held the reins of reproduction; it responded to such simple emotions as anger and fear. And the chain of communications for which it is still responsible in respect of the more or less animal and instinctive functions of life has loomed into an importance that only lately has been fully appreciated.

What may be termed the higher, and evolutionarily later, nervous system—with its subservice of such special functions as hearing and taste and sight; its intricate network of channels of sensation, touch, temperature, sense of position, and pain—has become the servant of intellect, reason, and their purposive motor reactions. Nerves of reception and nerves of action—motor nerves—complete the orderly service, as it were, by which the will of man finds its way.

It has of course, long been recognised that it is the' brain wherein these inward and outward messages are co-ordinated—wherein the delights or horrors of sight and hearing are appreciated and physical pain is felt. And in the earlier days of modern neurology, as the result of superficial observation and various experimental tests, the brain was regarded as a congregation of "centres," each of which was geographically distinct and responsible for some special function.

This seemed to have received confirmation from the observed effects of certain accidents and diseases. But later and more extensive investigations, largely the result of radiography and the great advances in the surgery of the brain, have tended to modify these views.

Where diseases or accidents have appeared to abolish centres it now seems more probable that they have merely destroyed communications; and conversely it has been found that considerable areas of the brain—hitherto considered the sites of such centres—can be destroyed or removed without any permanent impairment of the functions that they were deemed to control.

In other words, the tendency of modern neurology is more and more to regard the brain as a telephone exchange with a far greater number of alternative connections than was hitherto supposed. What, then, of the mind in its relation to the brain ? There is as yet no answer. But it may perhaps be said that neurology is tending, if only temporarily and tentatively, to regard the brain less as its residence than its instrument.

This somewhat lengthy quotation sufficiently proves my point, and I shall now, accordingly pass on to a consideration of the other important attributes of the soul. It must have already occurred to most of you that our analysis of the substance of consciousness necessarily proves it to be an immortal entity; for it is indivisible or partless in its constitution, and as such absolutely imperishable and deathless. The same reason which proves that an atom of matter is eternal also establishes the eternity of the soul, inasmuch as that which is not composed of parts, that might fall apart, is necessarily immune from destruction and death. The soul is, therefore, immortal by nature.

I think this will suffice on the subject which I will now conclude with a couple of quotations from certain famous scientists to show that the hostility of modern sciences to the existence of the soul is now beginning to vanish. Our first quotation is taken from a learned work on Physiological Psychology by the pen of Prof. William Mac Dougall, who is one of the greatest living authorities on Psychology—Says he:

> "We are compelled to admit....... that the so called psychical elements are......partial affections of a single substance or being; and since.......this is not any part of the brain, is not a material substance but differs from all material substance in that while it is unitary, it is yet present, or can act or be acted upon, at many points in space simultaneously,......we must regard it as an immaterial substance or being. And this being thus necessarily postulated as the ground of tbe unity of individual consciousness, we may call the soul of the individual."—Physiological Psychology (Temple Primer Series) p. 78.

This really is the death-knell of materialism. I recommend Mc. Dougall's "Body and Mind" which deals with the materialistic view in detail and shows it to be an untenable conjecture altogether. But the times are now changing, and the opposition of modern science may be deemed to have been overcome when men like W. D. Halliburton and R. J. S. Mc Dowall of the King's college, London, are led to reject the materialistic view. In "A Handbook of Physiology", which is jointly edited by them, they say on pages 648 and 649:—

"The conscious state is of great general interest and medical importance, but unfortunately we are far from a clear understanding of its nature.

"It is sometimes argued that states of consciousness are the product of the activity of nerve cells, just as bile is a product of the activity of the liver cells, or as contraction results from the activity of the muscle fibre. But this analogy will not bear close investigation. It is, however, true

(1) That the different senses are dependent for their manifestation on the integrity of different definitely localisable areas of the cerebral cortex.

(2) That such drugs as alcohol, coffeine, and chloroform which have a known action on living substance, also affect the course of consoious processes.

(3) That disease or malformation of the brain is acompanied by impairment or absence of intelligence.

"But because nervous substance is essential for the manifestation of conscious states, one cannot legitimately infer that this substance produces those states. Indeed, by a vast number of philosophers a very different position has been upheld........They maintain that, were it not for mental activity there would be no conception, nay not even existence, of those qualities (e. g. sound, colour, force, weight, hardness) of which our non-mental world of matter is composed.

"There is no difficulty in accepting the statetnent that bile is secreted by the liver; in this case the product is physioal, and it is produced by physiological (i. e. presumably, by chemical and physical) conditions. On the other hand, if we state that consciousness is secreted by the brain, we are linking together two sets of phenomena, the psychical and the physiological, between which a connection is inconceivable.

"Consequently, instead of stating that physiological

activity is the cause of mental (or psychical) activity, it is more satisfactory to assume that the two activities run parallel with one another; and to recognise that the nature of their relation is unknown."

(B)

We shall now study the nature of the soul with reference to joy, delight or happiness, which we all are unceasingly engaged in extracting, in one way or another, from our surroundings. Unfortunately there is no such thing as happiness in the world outside ourselves. There are things and events, no. doubt, in nature fram which we all try to slake our insatiable thirst for eternal joy; but it is not in the nature of things and events to be the repositories of happiness. We see one man rejoice in the birth of a son, while another who expected to succeed to that man's enormous wealth laments his own bitter fate, for a direct descendant now stands between him and the much coveted riches. The child is, however, only a fact or an event, and neither pleasure nor ill luck in itself. The same is the case with all other things. The *pan*, for instance, which is so pleasing to the Indian palate is actually distasteful to the European. Further, if there were real happiness in any of the things outside my being it could anly reach me through the gateways of my senses, but I only see matter passing through them but never happiness or joy itself. We thus see that our sensations of pleasure arise from an agreeable modification of the soul-substance, when acted upon by the properties of the things from without or from mental *stimulus*; and that painful sensations are similarly due to a like modificatian, but of a disagreeable type.

Both pleasure and pain are transient, the latter being mostly the lot of living beings in this world of ours, aptly described as the Vale of Tears. For even the little pleasure that is to be had here is obtained after so much worry and trouble and is generally productive of so much suffering, both in its procurement and subsequently, that it is no exaggeration to say that it is born in pain and ends in tears.

Fortunately, however, there is another kind of joy, available to us, but of this we are almost wholly ignorant. This joy consists in the natural 'pulsation' of pure delight (from *de*, a prefix of intensity and *light* as distinguished from heavy, hence, intense *lightness*) of the soul, which being its very attribute becomes an inalienable asset in its hands the moment we destroy the causes that obstruct its realisation. We are all more or less familiar with the feeling of mixed light-heartedness and satisfaction which arises on the successful performance of some task imposed on our will, *e.g.*, on the passing of a University examination. The question is whence does this feeling of joy arise?

Obviously, it is not an affection of the soul like pleasure, for pleasure arises on the real or imaginary contact between an external object and a sense-organ. But in the instance under consideration there is no such contact between the ego and any object real or imaginary, though the eye is undoubtedly deemed to have fallen on a scrap of pink paper containing the telegraphic message relating to success.

Observation shows that neither the scrap of paper, nor its peculiar colour, nor even the writing on it has anything to do with the state of joy which arises on a perusal of its contents. If you do not agree with me on this point, then you may put down the words of the message on the same or on a similar piece of paper and read it as often as you please. This will suffice to convince you that there is nothing in the communication or the paper on which it is written to cause an effervescence of joy. Analysis makes it clear, on the contrary, that the feeling of *de*-light arises, like the effervescence of sparkling vintage, from within the soul itself, the message being the occasion, but not the cause, of its display. What seems to happen in such eases is this that the communication, if believed to be true, removes something of the load of worries and anxieties that lay heavy on the soul, thus enabling the natural state of its being to manifest itself to a certain extent. It is, thus, not the imbibing or absorbing of anything from without but the removal of an obstruction, the pulling or drawing out of a kind of mental stopper" which enables the natural effervescence of the soul to be enjoyed at the time. The idea of pleasure cannot here keep pace with that of joy, in any sense; for while true joy is the sense, or rather the sensation, of freedom from the burden of worry and anguish imposed by some liability or limitation, pleasure depends on contact, whether real or imaginary, with an external object, and conveys no idea of freedom in its unqualified import.

The feeling of joy which is rooted in the idea of freedom, it will be further noticed, is not a momentary sensation like pleasure, but lingers in the soul till the imposition of some fresh obstruction or obligation or infliction of pain or worry in some other form, again obstruct its manifestation.

We also observe that success in more than one enterprise at the same time augments our sense of delight and intensifies its quality. It is, therefore, safe to say that the greater the sense of freedom, the greater the pulsation of *de*-light, so that absolute freedom from all kinds of undertakings, limitations and obligations must actually be the signal for the coming into manifestation of the intensest kind of blissful ecstasy, the undying, unabating, and unchanging emotion of joy. We thus conclude that the soul is itself the real source of all bliss and blessedness. Nor can its springs of happiness ever run dry, for the joy that arises from within one's being can only be an attribute of one's own self, since there can be no other meaning to the term 'inside' with reference to an indivisible, partless substance like the soul. Now, since a substance and its natural attributes are eternal, it is impossible that the happiness which pertains to the soul should ever become exhausted when once the obstacles to its realisation are completely removed.

We can now perceive why everyone feels happy when the desires and passions that robbed him of mental serenity and peace have subsided. As for grid and pain, they arise from causes external to the soul, and are, for that reason, but temporary conditions of our life. If it were otherwise, that is to say, if pain and misery were the attributes of our being, then they should have arisen in the soul from the quiescence or subsidence of desires and passions, because whatever is a natural attribute of a thing always arise without a cause, as soon as the obstacles which bar its way are removed from its path. Now, both grief and misery arise from extraneous causes which may be summed up under two general heads for the sake of brevity, namely:—

(1) the association, real or imaginary, with that which is undesirable, and

(2) the dissociation from what is desirable and desired.

They do not, certainly, arise when we are left to ourselves, that is without the one or the other or both of the causes just enumerated. Indeed, so for as physical pain is concerned, it is the resulant of physical processes or of chemical action between different substances and elements going on in the body, and not a spontaneous manifestation from within the soul.

From the above analysis or happiness we are entitled to conclude that the soul is itself the repository of purest joy, which it vainly seeks to extract from its surroundings.

How is it, then, that this natural happiness is not always enjoyed by the soul? The answer to this all important question is furnished by the fact that our infatuations and ignorance have defiled the natural attributes of our being, whose properties have become vitiated in consequence. To the extent to which these infatuations and ignorance are destroyed in us, do the natural attributes of our souls become ours to be enjoyed by us. Verily shall the soul experience full perfect happiness and enjoy all embracing infinite knowledge when the forces that stand in the way of their realisation are destroyed. Immortality shall also be the reward of the conqueror of these enemies of the soul.

The decreasing of omniscience, Bliss and Immortality in favour of the soul is tantamount to declaring it to be its own God, inasmuch as these. are the principal attributes associated with our most exalted conception of Divinity. And this is the literal verification of the old Biblical text: "the stone which the builders refused is become the head of the corner" (Ps. CXVIII. 22; Matt. XXI. 42). Verily, the soul which the materialist builders (=philosophers) rejected has turned out to be the "head of the corner," endowed with all divine attributes and perfections. These divine attributes are not enjoyed by the soul now, because they are vitiated and neutralised by certain forces operating on the soul-substance, so that they cannot come into manifestation till they are set free from the dominion of these defiling, neutralising agents.

As said the Jaina Theory of Karma (See Indian Philos. Rev. Vol. III. p. 153), the soul is a reincarnating ego which passes from life to life in an unbroken succession, till *nirvana* be attained. This is evident from the fact that the soul is immortal by nature, so that it *must* have had a past, however much it might be ignorant of it in its present incarnation. The nature of memory, of the causes that obstruct it, and of the process of its recovery have been explained in the Key of Knowledge to which you are referred for further enlightenment on the point. But when even the events of a few moments back are forgotten and cannot be recalled by us, what is there surprising in our inability to recollect anything of a past which has since been followed by wholesale cataclysmic changes in our being? Immortal by nature, the soul must have been in existence throughout the whole of the past eternity of time, as surely as it will continue to exist in the future.

But the soul could not have existed as a pure spirit in the past, for in that case it would be impossible for it to be born in the world. This is because in its natural purity the soul is the en joyer of full prefect knowledge, infinite perception, unbounded happiness and all other divine attributes, which, in the absence of a restraining force or body of some kind, must be deemed to be manifested in the fullest degree in its nature. The idea of such a perfect being descending to inhabit a body of flesh and thereby crippling its natural unlimited perfections in a number of ways is too absurd to be entertained for a moment. It follows from this that the soul did not exist in a condition of perfection prior to its present incarnation, and that the existence of some force capable of dragging *jivas* (souls) into different wombs is a condition precedent to their birth in the different grades of life. But how shall we conceive force operating on a soul and dragging it into an organism, if not as the action of some kind of matter? It is, therefore, clear that the soul has always been in union with matter in the past.

It is the influence of matter, then, which is responsible' for all those conditions of the soul which are not natural to a pure spirit; for the fusion of different substances always results in the limitation or suspension of their pure natural functions, *e.g.*, hydrogen and oxygen which are deprived of their gaseous nature so long as they remain locked up in each other's embrace, as water. But it is not a case of actual annihilation of an attribute, because the separation of substances is marked by the immediate restoration of their natural properties in full (Indian Philos. Rev. p. 155). Observation shows that the soul involved in impurity is unable to enjoy its natural perfection in respect of knowledge, perception and happiness, which, therefore, must be held in abeyance by some kind of forces operating on it. We thus get three different kinds of forces namely:—

(i) those which obstruct knowledge (*jnanavarniya*),

(ii) those that interfere with perception (*darshanavarniya*), and

(iii) those that stand in the way of happiness, leaving the soul to experience pleasure and pain through the senses (*vedaniya*).

Besides these, observation also proves the existence of another kind of force, which does not permit the adoption of the right faith (Scientific Truth). The energies falling under this head are divisible into two classes: those which interfere with the very acquisition of faith, and those that offer opposition to its being put into practice. To the former class belong such forces as prejudice, bigotry, false beliefs and all those other kinds of mental energy—passions and emotions of the worst *(anantanubandhi)* type—whose uncontrolled and uncontrollable impetuosity deprives one of the full and proper exercise of the faculty of reflection, the most essential requisite for the discernment of truth; and under the latter type fall all those deep-rooted mental traits—anger, pride, deceit and greed of different degrees of intensity. Other than the *anantanubandhi*, already referred to—that rob the mind of determination and serenity and prevent the adoption of what is known to be useful and good, also certain minor faults, *e.g.*, joking, attachment and the like, as well as certain bodily habits and propensities (*e.g.*, sexual lust) which are; prejudicial to an attitude of self-control. All these are termed *mohaniya* (infatuation), which is of two kinds, *darshana-mohaniya* (infatuations opposed to the acquisition of right faith) and *charitra-mohaniya* (infatuations opposed to living up to right faith). There is also another kind of force which interferes with the doing of what is desirable and desired and prevents effectiveness in general with reference to mental resolves. This is known as *antaraya*. These are, broadly speaking, the forces which debar us from the enjoyment of our natural prefections and divine attributes, omniscience and the like. It follows, therefore, that the destruction of these inimical forces must immediately lead to the acquisition of all its suspended divino powers and prerogatives on the part of the soul, since they are its own natural attributes and have not to be acquired from outside its own being. Religion claims to be the method which enables the soul to attain to divine perfection. This it accomplishes by studying the nature of the properties and attributes of the soul as well as of the causes that interfere with the functioning of those properties and of the means to be employed for the destruction of the forces of obstruction. I need not tell you that all this study must be made with the utmost scientific rigour, for nothing but science or scientific thought can be relied up on to produce immediate, certain and unvarying results.

Religion, thus, may be defined as the Science of Bliss which knows nothing of dogma or unreasoning faith. It proceeds on the principle of cause and effect, and furnishes a complete explanation of the whole misery and suffering of being, prescribing, at the same time, ascertain unfailing remedy for all concievable forms of woe.

The field of enquiry is comprised in seven *tattvas* (heads or ultimates of knowledge) which must be clearly understood. These *tattvas* are the outcome of a logical treatment of the subject, and can be understood with ease. The deliverance of the soul from the power and forces of darkness and evil being the end in view, the first thing to know is the nature of that which if' to be freed—whether it is or is not capable of being liberated? The very first point or subject for study, therefore, is the nature of the soul. Hence, soul (*jiva*) is our first *tattva*. The next thing to know is the nature of the material of which the forces that are inimical to the well-being of the *jiva* that is, the soul; are composed. This gives us our second *tattva*, namely, *ajiva* (non-living substance). How does the *ajiva* approach the *jiva*?, how is it converted into obstructive forces?, how can its further inflow be stopped?, how to destroy the existing forces? are further points for investigation. Accordingly, the third *tattva* is termed *asrava* (inflow of matter into the soul), the fourth, *bandha* (the generation of forces from the inflowing matter), the fifth, *samvara* (the stoppage of the inflow), and the sixth, *nirjara* (the destruction of the existing forces). The last *tattva* is termed *moksha* (liberation). Tersely put, the result of the scientific investigation may be expressed in the following sentence, with the small numerals pointing to the *tattvas*: the *jiva*[1] (spirit) is defiled by *ajiva*[2] (non-spirit, here matter) which flows[3] (*asrava*) into it and is transformed by combining with it into powerful forces[4] (*bandha*), destructive of its natural attributes; the stoppage[5] (*samvara*) of this influx and the destruction (*nirjara*) of the existing forces lead to liberation[7] (moksha), *i.e.*, salvation, which signifies the wholeness of perfection.

Ethics, *i.e.* the entire range of duty, and the fruition of virtue and vice are really covered by the third and fourth *tattvas*; but they may be dealt with separately, in which case they constitute, along with the *tattvas*, the nine (7+2=9) *padarathas* (principles or categories of the Science of Bliss).

To have a full grasp over the entire subject of emancipation, in the religious sense of the term, it is necessary that you should clearly understand the nature of *asrva* and *bandha*, the third and fourth *tattvas*, respectively. The coming together of spirit and matter is what is signified by *asrava*, and tho law which governs it may be described in the following words: *all actions of embodied living beings, whether mental, or physical, or vocal, are accompanied by an influx of matter towards the soul*. There is a constant stream of material vibrations eternally knocking and pressing against the senses, which they are constantly engaged in transmitting to the soul. Whether I see, hear, smell, eat or touch anything I only extract and draw to myself a quantity of different kinds of sensory *stimuli* or material. Even when I do not attend to this ceaseless traffic from the without and shut my self up in the closet of the mind, sensations, implying actual intercourse between the ego and the sensory centres of the brain, continue. If I speak, I am conscious of hearing my own voice and of percieving the muscular sensations of the organs involved in the articulation of words. Here also the inflow of the raw material of sensations is continued undiminished. There is no rest; no interruption; no holiday with these intruders on the senses. The eye, no doubt, may obtain a sort of respite if it be shut, and the tongue is also capable of being protected in a similar manner to a great extent. But the condition of the skin, the, nose and the ear is altogether pitiable; they are meant to serve as the open door of a courtesan's house and must give admission to whosoever may care to pass in.

Such briefly is the nature and description of *asrava* which is, our third *tattva*. The law that governs *bandha* is to be deduced by observing the consequences that follow the *asrava* of matter.

Now, observation shows that sensation does not always follow the external influx which we have just seen is constantly impinging upon the senses. If the mind is engaged elsewhere no, relish is experienced of the food that may be actually on the tongue; the ear is then deaf to music, the sense of smell, dead to odour, and tactile sensitivity, to contact. The rule of impressionability would appear from these facts to be this that the mind has an inhibiting action on all the senses except the particular one, to which it may be attending for the time being. On the other hand, faint impressions received in a mechanical way are magnified by our attending to them. The explanation of the taste of the morsel of food on the tongue not being felt when the mind is busy elsewhere lies in the fact that no new state of consciousness has resulted from it. The physiology of taste seems to indicate that while the bulk of food passes through the gullet into the stomach, some fine particles of its relish reach the soul through the glands of taste, and by 'knocking at its door' call forth a corresponding idea. If the particles of matter are admitted still further, and allowed to affect the feeling-tone of the individual; pleasurable or painful kind of, feeling would ensue, and the soul would know whether it liked the relish of the food or not. But these relish particles must be, there all the same whether the soul attend to them or not. It would follow that they do not combine with the soul except when they find the door open and attention ready to take them into the presence of her mistress. But attention always implies interest, whether it indicates the merest wish to know or the most passionate longing to embrace. We may, then, say that the fusion of spirit and matter cannot take place unless the soul be first thrown into an attitude of desire, signifing its willingness to mate with the stangers from without. This gives us our second law of interaction between spirit and matter, which may be enunciated thus; *the fusion of spirit and matter does not take place except where the soul is thrown into a condition of expectancy, i.e., weakness*. When existing in a vitiated condition the soul is generally unable to exercise any discrimination and has little or no will of its own. In the worst cases it is even ignorant of the inimical nature of the "cavaliers" from the outside world, who, like the Russian Vampyre Dracula, only need the first invitation to get in, after which they do not leave their victim in a condition to resist any further onslaught on their part.

We can now understand why the harmful forces engendered by the fusion of spirit and matter are termed karma-*prakritis* in the Jaina *Siddhanta*. Because they originate in a desire on the part of the soul, which is its own action; they signify *karma* (action in English), and being in the nature of powerful forces are termed *prakritis* (energies or forces).

The compound resulting from the fusion of spirit and matter is termed *karmana sharira* (the body of *karmas*) This subtle, invisible inner body is the root of the soul's troubles, and along with another similar body, made of highly magnetic matter, is only destroyed at the time of liberation. This second subtle body, known as *taijasa sharira*, is a necessary link between the extremely subtle *karmana sharira* and the outer body of gross matter. There is a continual readjustment of the form of the *karmana sharira* from "life to life" in the course of transmigration, and the varying conditions of the different phases of life in the highly chequered career of the eternal pilgrim are due to the organising forces and agencies residing in that body itself. In consequence of the magnetic affinities residing in its *taijasa sharira*, the soul is drawn into a new "womb" immediately after its "death" in a given incarnation, when the forces dwelling in the *karmana sharira* become operative to organise a new outer body for it, The body, its longevity, the bodily limbs, as well as the status in life which is really dependent on the family of one's birth, are thus conditions which directly spring from one's own *karmas* in a previous life, and it is madness to throw the blame for one's own shortcomings, defects and deformities on another, whether God or man.

The *karmana sharira*, then, is the seed of re-birth. Its

absence will make it impossible for the soul to incarnate in flesh and blood; for he who is free from the crippling companionship of matter must be pure Divinity in actual manifestation, and there is no power in nature which can drag a perfect God into bondage and transmigration. This is the true sense in which a Perfect Soul is said to be all powerful; for outside the holy land of *Nirvana karma* is all powerful every where else, so that the greatest of *Indras* (Ruler of heavenly worlds), *devas* (celestial beings), *asuras* (demons) and men are helpless before it. There is no power in nature that can interfere with the Perfect Souls in *Nirvana*; Their happiness is unexcelled in all the three worlds; Their perfection simply immeasurable. And who can describe the power of that Great One whose merest "glance" can acquire knowledge of all that is, of all that has been, and of all that shall ever be, unlimited by time and space? How, again, shall we guage the measure of the glory of that most High Conqueror of the forces of darkness and evil whose supreme bliss nothing can mar, and whom none can disturb even for the millionth part of a second. The Perfect Soul is never affected by sleep, stupor, or laziness; death, disease and senility cannot approach His presence, and Time attends upon Him only to place the choicest blossoms of Eternal Youth and Immortality at His holy worshipful feet! If omnipotence only mean all this, then such a Perfect Being alone is Omnipotent; none else.

To revert to transmigration, I must tell you that it rests on the solid foundation of the eternity and indestructibility of souls, so that being eternal, and, therefore, also, uncreated, they must have existed in some form or other in the past. Furthermore, miracles being inadmissible in science, the present incarnations of the souls now existing in the world cannot all have been determined by anything in the nature of a lawless occurence, but must be due to a law or laws which are concerned in the shaping of our destinies. Take now into consideration the infinite variety of circumstances surrounding all the different grades of life in the scale of being, and see what explanation nature offers of the pain and misery that are only too evident all round. The fact is that all that a living being undergoes, all that he feels, and all that he experiences is in consequence of his own actions in the past!

That the unredeemed soul must have existed in an embodied condition in the past is evident from the fact that it is involved in matter now. For, as we have already seen, a pure spirit is incapable of being effectedly matter. It must, then, have existed in a condition of impurity, which is tantamount to saying that it was involved in matter. But matter is incapable of effecting it by mere juxtaposition or contact, howsoever close, as is clear from the instance of the food on the tongue, when its taste is not appreciated and enjoyed, till there be a chemical fusion between the substance of consciousness and the subtle particles of relish, as already explained, through the intervention of attention. The soul must then have existed in an embodied condition so that the present incarnation cannot but owe its being to the termination of the form of embodied life immediately preceding it.

We need not discuss the laws and forces of reincarnation any further; they have been sufficiently described today.

It only remains to consider the Weapons and means for over-coming the forces of ignorance and evil, which stand in the way of the soul. The question is an easy one, and can be answered in a few words. Your trouble is wholly due to your desires; therefore, you should destroy your desires. Whatever your circumstances, do all you can to curb your appetites and longings. Whenever you have time, wherever you may happen to be, decline to yield to your internal cravings. You must engage yourself in a deadly struggle with this foe of yours—desire—never letting go, but always tightening your grip on it. No good postponing it either; You may have no opportunity for it later on. Whether it be penance or fast or any, other method of self-denial, you must impress each and everyone of them into service to vanquish the foe. It is no use your expecting to reach *nirvana* by lolling in your arm-chair; you cannot destroy the forces of *karma* that way. Begin to prepare yourself from now for a life and death struggle with the enemy in all seriousness of purpose, or be ready to face the inevitable consequences—birth as a dog, a cat or a caterpillar, long-continued intolerable suffering in hell and the like—that flow from a life abandoned to passion and desire.

Thus while there is no royal road to perfection, there is a narrow scientific path out of this Vale of Tears; it is one for all, from which you can only deviate to fall into the ravines below, to be broken against the hard boulders of falsehood and infatuation. It is not a question of individual taste either; there is and can be no choice of means in a scientific pursuit of the ideal. We cannot allow the soldier to determine for himself whether he will go through the prescribed drill. He has got to do so if he wishes to join the army.

This narrow rigidly scientific 'path' ,consists in the acquisition and adoption of Right Faith, Right Knowledge and Right Conduct. Of these, Right Faith has its eye constantly fixed on the great ideal of Perfection and Bliss, and never loses sight of it for a moment. Its function is to determine the direction of individual activity in the right way, preventing it from becoming self-destructive. Faith is like the man at the helm, always directing and guiding the barge of life, in storm and in calm, to the looked for Haven of Freedom and Rest. He whose heart is not chastened by Right Faith is like the rudderless ship that is soon dashed to pieces against rooks, for want of proper guidance and control. The necessity for Right Faith is fully obvious from the fact that people only live up to their beliefs, never in opposition to them.

Right Knowledge is the detailed knowledge of the process of self-realisation. It is like the chart which is intended to furnish an accurate description of the path to be traversed, of the obstacles to be encountered on the way, and of the means to be adopted to steer clear of them. As no one who has not provided himself with such a chart is ever expected to take his boat successfully across an ocean, so is not the soul that is not provided with Right Knowledge ever likely to land in safety in *nirvana*.

Right Conduct is the third essential for success, since without the doing of the right thing at the right moment no desired results can ever be achieved by anyone.

If Right Faith is the properly directed rudder and Right Knowledge the chart of navigation in the ocean of life (transmigration), Right Conduct is the force which actually propels the Barge of Being Havenwards. Taken singly, Right Faith only opens the outlook of life to embrace the highest good, Right Knowledge is merely the diagram of the action to be performed, while Right Conduct is simply inconceivable in the absence of faith and knowledge of the right sort.

As already stated, this straight, rigid, narrow 'path' consists in the total eradication of desire, so that the harmful forces that are engendered by and through it may be completely destroyed, leaving the soul in its natural state as pure Effulgence of Intelligence, all-knowing, ever-blissful and altogether divine, in every way.

Any one who will reflect on the nature of the gulf that separates this supreme ideal of divine perfection from the low wretched type of sinful humanity that is to attain it, will readily agree with me that nothing but the severest form of asceticism can ever succeed in cutting down the huge embankments of desire to fill up the chasm. To become a God, an all-knowing ever blissful God, is not a joke. A renunciation so complete as to exclude in its last stages everything of personal requirement, even that very last vestige of raiment—the *langoti*—must be practised, if spiritual *wholeness* is to be attained. But the commencement is not so forbidding. There is a ladder of graduated progressive steps which enables the top to be reached by degrees, and with ease and ever-increasing enthusiasm.

The first step to be taken is the acquisition of Right Faith which means unshakable belief in the *tattvas* and veneration for those Great ones who have already attained to Godhood by living it in their own lives. As the man who wishes to attain to eminence in law, as a profession, must sit at the feet of some great lawyer, shaping his own life after that of his model, so must the man who desires to reach the summit of Perfection of Life, follow in the footsteps of those Worshipful Souls that have already attained to the supreme status of Divinity.

The following psychological changes occur in the mind which result in the acquisition of Right faith :—

(i) a general loosening or weakening of the forces of *karma*;

(ii) clarity of intellect, i.e., open mindedness; that is a scientific turn of mind that will listen to and retain the teaching of truth,

(iii) the seeking out of a teacher and hearing the doctrine of truth from him or finding out a suitable book on the subject

(iv) a further general subsiding or quiescence of powerful emotions; and

(v) meditation or reflection on the true nature of the soul.

I have enumerated these steps simply to impress on your minds the inestimable value of a scientific turn of mind, which comes from a proper study of natural logic, especially from an investigation of the true principles of causation of things.

Right Faith being acquired, the knowledge of the believer in Truth is at once transformed into Right Knowledge, since Right Faith only means an unwavering belief, i.e., an undoubting conviction, in the subject matter of the *tattvas*;

The start in Right conduct is to be made by the renunciation of the very worst habits and thoughts as soon as Right Faith is acquired. Wanton cruelty, animal flesh, intoxicating drinks and cruel sport are the very first things to be abandoned. It is no use our endeavouring to make a headway on the 'path' without renouncing these worst forms of *himsa*.[3]

How shall he whose foot has never touched the first rung

of the ladder reach the top? The Gods in whose company we fain would sit are the wellwishers of all; they neither devour nor destroy any living being. How, then, can he who causes pain to living beings to afford momentary pleasure to his palate or tongue ever aspire to become a God?

The aspirant ofter immortality and joy must, therefore, give up these evil habits at the time of the adoption of Right Faith. For similar reasons, he should also give up gambling, profligacy, thieving and falsehood. These most sinful habits broken up, the believer in, truth gradually begins to train himself for the assiduous life of asceticism. He lives in the world, as other men do, and marrying a suitable spouse settles down in' life, striving always to constantly advance in piety, virtue and *vairagya* (renunciation). There are eleven stages of the householder's life, through which the aspirant must pass to reach *sannyasa* (asceticism).

These are:—

(1) the giving up of cruel sport, theft, animal flesh, etc.,

(2) the observance of vows against

  (i) himsa (the inflicting of injury or harm on others),

  (ii) falsehood,

  (iii) stealing,

  (iv) incontinence, and

  (v) an abundance of worldly goods.

(3) practising holy meditation, three times a day

(4) fasting, at least four times a month,

(5) avoidance of fresh vegetables, *etc.*,

(6) refraining from eating after sunset[4] and before sunrise,

(7) total sexual abstinence,

(8) withdrawing from occupations and undertakings,

(9) dispossessing onself of all kinds of property,

(10) refraining from even participation in consultation on worldly matters, and

(11) placing further restrictions on food that is henceforth to be taken only once a day, at the morning meal, at a pious householder's, and on personal apparel, which is reduced to a *langoti* (loin-strip).

The eleventh *pratima* perfected, the aspirant takes to *sannyasa*, and becomes a homeless ascetic. These steps take one roughly to the commencement of old age, between the 45th and the 55th years of life. The householder has hitherto given his best to the world in the form of love, service, advice, charity, and the like; but he now withdraws himself from it to study his own future. As an ascetic, he has no more concern with anything else but the destruction of his real enemies, the forces of passion and desire. The vows he practises are the same as he did in the householder's stage, but they are now characterised with utmost severity. In addition, he observes carefulness in walking, speech, eating, handling things and evacuating bodily excrements. He also avoids the engagement of his mind, speech and body in, worldly traffic, and practises the ten most excellent rules of *Dharma* (Religion), namely, (1) forgiveness, (2) humility, (3) honesty, (4) truth-fulness, (5) dispassion, (6) mercy, (7) self-denial, (8) non-attachment, (9) contentment, and (10) chastity, all qualified by the word *uttama* (commendable, praiseworthy or noble). Both forms of *tapas* (asceticism), internal and external, are practised by him, with ever increasing severity. Meditiation on the nature of the soul and on the transitoriness of the world, its temptations and vanities, constantly occupies his mind.

All this is tough uphill work, but, as I said before, you cannot achieve success anywhere in life unless the means employed are commensurate with the end to be achieved. In reality, Right Conduct only consists in Self-realisation, i.e., the contemplation of one's own greatness and glory, which seems easy enough to do; but just sit down to see if you can do it at present even for the brief space of a second. All your cravings, desires, appetites, tendencies, habits of thought, bodily longings and mental propensities will rise in revolt against you the moment you think of settling down to attend to your inner Self. Each and everyone of these insurgents is a powerful foe, and has to be destroyed before you can hope to be left to yourself. Mercy is not meant for these foes of Life; they are unrelenting themselves and will fight to their last gasp.

Does the prospect of so much hard, uphill work frighten you? There is nothing that man cannot accomplish, if he once gird up his loins for it. And even if one is not suuccessful all at once there is no fear of the fruit of one's labour being destroyed by death. The merit acquired by Faith and conduct is carried from one incarnation to another in the shape of auspicious modifications of the *karmana sharira*, and becomes an important factor in determining the conditions of existence in the next incarnation. Seriousness of purpose and a cheerful disposition are, then, all the essentials to success on the acquisition of Right Faith. If a lawyer, when a babe in arm, were told, and allowed to brood over, the number of books that he would be required to read and of those he would have to consult, there is little doubt that he would have died of fright; but we have among us many eminent lawyers who not only excel in law but in other branches of literature besides! And it is not that there are only troubles and trials in store for him who sets his foot on the 'path.' It is true that you never find a rose without a thorn in nature, but it is equally true that there is also no real thorn that does not lead to a rose, if you only know how to search and persevere. Now, if you only attempt to reach the rose by ignoring the thorn, you will have all the smarting of its sting for your labour, but if you first deal with the thorn, you may take the rose away wherever you please. I have no time to plunge into a detailed analysis of the different stages of the path, but I may say while I am still on the subject that after a while the ascetic begins to experience such happiness as is even beyond the imagination of millionaires and kings. The house-holder, too, at times has his reward in the joyous pulsating of his life, though such moments are rare in his case, and depend on the degree of dispassion and the sense of detachment evolved out by him. The ascetic finally also attains to omniscience prior to *nirvana*, though, owing to bad times, there are no such ascetics just now in our part of the universe. For we men of today are but puny mannikins compared with our ancestors of the past, and not having inherited their adamantine frames fail to approach them in respect of pure contemplation. But though denied this purest form of self-realisation, we are not debarred from the benefits appertaining to the other forms of holy meditation, and would be well-advised to adopt them, according to our capacity and circumstances. It should, however, be never forgotten that the primary root of spiritual knowledge and conduct, the very seed of the ever-green life-giving Tree of Life, is nothing other than Right Faith, concerning which the following occurs in anancient work of authority (the Ratnakaranda Shravakachara):—

> "In the three words and the three periods of time there is nothing more auspicious than Right Faith, nor anything more inauspicious than a false conviction. Those whose hearts have been purified by Right Faith become the lords of splendour, energy, wisdom, prowess, fame, victory, and greatness; they are born in high families and possess the ability to realise the highest ideals [*dharma* (religion), *artha* (wealth), *karma* (pleasure) and *moksha* (salvation)] of life; they are the best of men. Those who have the Right Faith are born in the heaven-worlds where they become the devotees of the Lord Jinendra, and, endowed with eight kinds of miraculous powers and great splendour, enjoy themselves for long millenniums in the company of *devas* and *devangnas* [residents of heavens of both sexes]. Those who are endowed with Right Faith are attended upon by great emperors and kings; they acquire all the most wonderful things in the world; the entire earth comes under their sway, and they are competent to command all men.
>
> "They who take refuge in Right Faith finally attain to the Supreme Seat, which is free from old age, disease,

destruction decrease, grief, fear and doubt, and implies unqualified prefection in respect of Wisdom and Bliss and freedom from all kinds of impurities of *karma*. The *bhavya*[5] who follows the creed of the Holy *Tirthamkaras*[6] acquires the immeasurable glory of *deva*-life and the discuss of a *chakravarti*[7] before whom kings and rulers of men postrate themselves, and, attaining to the supremely worshipful status of God-hood, finally also reaches *nirvana*."

It only remains to say that the conclusions drawn in this evening's lecture are all those that are embodied in the Jaina Siddhanta, which is seen to be in full agreement with scientific thought. We shall also find most of these conclusions in the other creeds as we get on with our studies in comparative religion.

FOOTNOTES

1. *Cf*. "A reaction, as the term is here used, means more than the mere transmission of energy from one object to another as when a moving billiard ball, striking another, throws the latter into action. The amount of energy released or transformed may be very much greater than the amount transmitted to the organism by the stimulus. A tiny prick ocacasioned by a very small amount of force may cause a reaction in which a relatively huge amount of energy is consumed, or more accurately, transformed. The organism contains at all times, stored in various reacting mechanisms large amounts of energy, which when released by appropriate stimulation occasion the body's activity."—"elementry Psychology" by Gates, pp. 33-34.
2. The individuality of the soul is not affected by the fact that there are to be found more living beings than one in certain organisms. As Jainism points out, there are two kinds of organisms, namely, firstly, those that are inhabited by one soul each and, secondly, those that resemble a colony of souls. The characteristic of the latter is that they generally have a common mouth or share certain other organs of their bodies in common: but are otherwise separate and distinct from each other. They certainly do not combine to form one soul by intensification or any other process or method;

and the destruction of one or more of them does not necessarily mean the destruction of them all. They are like the Hungarian twins one of whom tiled without in any way offecting the individuality of the other: although the latter must have suffered grievously, in mind and body both, from the demice of one so closely affiliated to her as to share her lower limbs.

3. It is interesting to note that the ancient Jewish creed prohibited the eating or flesh from a living animal (ERE. Vol. vi. 245). The Parsis, too, say (The Teaching of Zoroaster, p. 43):—

"Of all kinds of sins which I have committed with reference to Heaven against the Ameshaspend Bahman with reference to the world against the cattle and the various kinds of cattle, if I have beaten it, tortured it, slain it wrongfully, if I have not given it fodder and water at the right time, if I have castrated it, not protected it from the robber, the wolf and the waylayer, if I have not protected it from extreme heat and cold, if I have killed cattle of useful strength, working cattle, war horses, rams, goats, cocks, and hens, so that alike these good things and their protector Bahman have been injured by me and not contented with me, I repent."

In Shayast La-Shayast (chap. x. 8-9) it is said:— "The rule is this, that reverential should be the abstinence from unlawfully slaughtering of any species of animals; for in the Studgar *Nashk* it is said, concerning those who have unlawfully slaughtered animals, the punishment is such that each hair of those auimals becomes like a sharp dagger, ano he who is unlawfully a slaughterer is slain. Of animals, the slaughteriug of the lamb, the goat, the plonghing ox, the war-horse, the.....hare the cock.........is most to bo abstained from" (SBE. v. p. 319).

With reference to Christianity, too, there is good reason to believe that the use of meat was regarded as highly objectionable by its zealous adherent.

"There are", says Mr. Hatch, in the 'Influence of Greek Ideas and Usages on the Christian Church' (p. 165), "there are proofs of the existence in the very earliest Ohristian communities of those who endeavoured to live on II higher plane than their fellows. Abstinence from marriage and from animal foods were urged and practised as 'counsels of perfection.' In some communities there was ap attempt to make such counsels of perfection obligatory."

4. I am happy to note the following correspondence cf this rule in the Books of Zoroastrianism:

"This, too, is declared; 'When in the dark it is not allowable to eat food; for the demons and fiends seize upon one-third of the wisdom and glory of him who eats food in the dark," (SBE. Vol. V. 310).

The Mahabharata also has it: "Offerings, bathing, the performance of *shraddha*, worshipping, making of gifts and, in particular, eating should not be done at night."

It is also interesting to note that वस्त्रपूतंजलंपिवेत (water should be taken after straining it through cloth) is the common injunction of both the Jaina *Siddhanta* and the Mahabharta, as Prof. Virupaksha Beriyar points out (see the Jaina Path Pradarsbaka, Vol. iii. part 3. p. 114.)

5. The soul that is destined to reach *nirvana*.
6. An Omniscient Teacher.
7. The title of twelve great kings who possessed the divine weapon called chakra (=discus).

CHAPTER - IV

METAPHYSICS

This evening's lecture is concerned with what is termed metaphysics. There is some doubt as to what is precisely meant by the term, but it was orginally applied to a certain group of the philosophical dissertations of Aristotle which were placed in a collection of his manuscripts after his treatise on physics. But whatever be the significance the term was intended to express, I think we may sofely take it to refer to that department of knowledge which transcends physics. Thus while physics deals with what may be termed concrete facts, metaphysics assorts them into concepts and relations, and, finally, reduces them into consistent systematised knowledge. As we have had occasion to observe ere this, philosophy and science are wedded together, so that the divorcing of the one from the other is fatal to both. For science must tend towards the comprehensive consistency of systematic thought to rise above the petty trivialities of life, and philosophy must adhere rigidly to rationalism of nature to secure the generally neglected harmony between imagination and actuality, on fact Metaphysics may thus be defined as the process or expression of reflection on *the facts of experience*, culminating in an all-comprehensive consistent system of thought that is explanatory of the nature of our surroundings, and, therefore, capable of being harnessed into service for the obtainment of the highest good. This definition is all the more important for our purpose as we are not concerned here with every form and type of mental speculation, but with that alone which has a bearing on religion. We are also not interested in, nor can offord to be interested in compiling a history of human thought or in collecting what speculators of different countries and times have thought with reference to religion. Such treatment of the subject will not only be quite irrelevant and unnecessary for our purpose, but will also involve an amount of time and labour altogether beyond the scope of the present lecture and the capacity of the lecturer before you.

We shall, therefore, confine our investigation to the region of the practical, that is to say, to those schools of metaphysics which are associated with the prevailing religions; and with respect to these even we shall not attempt anything like a thorough criticism except where this is absolutely necessary to understand, the fundamental tenets of any particular system.

I shall begin my investigation with the monistic Vedanta which teaches that there is only one reality behind this phenomenal show that is termed the material universe. This one reality is termed Brahman, and as *it* is the only existent being or thing, everything else necessarily has only a seeming being. The universe is, therefore, nothing but a bundle of names and forms; in plain terms, an illusion. What, then, is the individual soul? Brahman itself, and as such omnipresent, omniscient and omnipotent, but neither the doer of works, nor the gatherer of their harvest (Deussen's System of the Vedanta, p. 468). The *summum bonum*, therefore, does not consist in becoming Brahman; for the soul is always Brahman, even when it does not know itself. Liberation implies the knowledge, on the part of the individual soul, of its being the *sat-chita-ananda* (=Exisience-Consciousness-Bliss), which is descriptive of the essence of Brahman, though the usual method of defining Brahman is by the words *neti*, *neti* (not this, not this). I should have taken this purely negative description as being in the nature of an emphasis on the point that Brahman is devoid of sensible qualities, but for the fact that the Vedantists take it literally. After the Brahmanhood of the soul is recognised, liberation follows at once ("that thou art" is the pharse, not "that thou wilt be"); simultaneously with the attainment of knowledge of the identity with Brahman the soul becomes the soul of the Universe (Deussen).

The salient features of Vedanta may now be put down as follows:—

(a) the unreality of the world,

(b) the being of only one reality, or soul, and

(c) the attainment of 'liberation' by knowledge.

As to the first of these points it is interesting to note that Logic takes for granted certain self-evident truths; and it is no use our trying to found anything like a system of metaphysics without acknowledging them in the first instance. These truths are tersely summed up in a small work on logic (A Handbook of Deductive Logic) by S. N. Banerji, already referred to ere this, and may be enumerated as follows:—

(1) that there exists a material world apart from our mind;

(2) that our mind can frame things, so that things are as we actually percieve them.

(3) that amidst the ceaseless minor changes of the universe there is order and uniformity, so that the world remains essentially the same in all ages (past, present and future) for all observers; and

(4) that there are or must be universal tests to distinguish truth from falsehood—rules to guide all reasoners in their way to truth, avoiding the snares of fallacy.

These are self-evident truths which you have to adopt, and it is no use our denying them. They are the very foundation of a logical *vyapti*, which cannot be established in their absence. Now, the first proposition of Advaitism is that the universe is an illusion, which contradicts the first and the third axioms of Logic, as laid down above,—that there exists a material world apart from our mind, and that it remains essentially the same in all ages (past, present and future). Order and regularity are found to prevail in the world, and these certainly are not the distinguishing features of illusion. Vedanta, which persists in calling this orderly world an illusion, is, therefore, not entitled to be admitted in the council of Rationalism.

As regards the second characteristic feature of Vedanta, that there is only one reality or soul in existence, we shall let the propounders of the Sankhyan School refute that view. "If there were but one *Purusha*, as the Vendantins hold, then if one were happy, all would be happy; if one were unhappy, all would be unhappy, and so on ill the case of people affected by trouble, confusion of race, purity of race, health, birth and death. Hence, there is not one *Purusha*, but many, on account of the manifoldness indicated by form, birth, abode, fortune, society or loneliness."-(SSP. p. 256)

I think it is not possible to deny the force of the Sankhyan objection in this instance.

With respect to the third distinguishing feature of Vedanta, namely that liberation consists in the knowledge of Brahman, it seems to me that there is a great deal of confusion even here with respect to the ideas of bondage and liberation. There is only one soul we are told, and that an immutable unchanging existence. Who then is there to be liberated? For whose benefit is all this teaching and preaching intended? And what about those that have been liberated in the past, if any? Are they still in existence or have they totally disappeared from all existence? The confusion is further confounded by the doctrine of transmigration which Vedanta subscribes to. It is a vain endeavour to construct an infinity of transmigrating souls out of one solitary *individual*, or, what is the same thing in other words, from one partless individuality. If the Liberated Souls are all parts or phases or aspects of one and the same reality, are we not forced to the conclusion that certain *parts* of a *partless* entity are liberated while certain others are still undergoing the pain and misery of repeated births and deaths? There can also be no significance of liberation if the liberated soul is to remain what it already is (not "thou *wilt* be that," but "thou *art* that").

These observations also apply to certain forms of Sufi metaphysics which mark the nearest approach of Muslim speculation to Vedanta. The Shahudians, for instance, maintain that the *alam* (world) is a reflection of God.

> "A man enters a glass-house and sees himself reflected in a hundred directions. These reflections virtually depend on the man and have,no existence of their own. The attributes and the ego of man are thus the reflection of the attributes and essence of God. The *alam* (the world) is the rupee of the juggler, which in reality is a piece of pottery (a nothing); but by the skill of the juggler shows itself like the silver of the *rupee*, Thus everything is 'with him'," (The Philosophy of Islam, pp. 5 and 6.)

We have already seen in our last lecture that the souls are eternal, being simple, that is to say indestructible, by nature. They cannot, therefore, be the reflection of anyone. Unfortunately it never occurred to the author of the view just quoted that there was absolutely not one particle of proof or evidence in support of the proposition that mere reflections could be endowed with consciousness, feelling, willing, memory and judgment. The analogy of the sun and its reflection through a magnifying lens is not to the point, because, firstly, that is not a case of true reflection inasmuch as the sun's reflection is in reality the concentration of the Sun's rays at a point by means of the magnifying glass; secondly, because the sun itself is not comparable to a partless immutable spirit that does not radiate any kind of rays, and, thirdly, because feelings, judgment, willing and the other functions of consciousness are not alienable in any sense, as was proved in the last lecture. The notion is not supported by any kind of logical *vyapti* (see lecture II) and has to be rejected.

We shall now turn to *Sankhya* which is unlike any other system, oriental or accidental. Much has been written both in friendly and hostile comment on this famous school of Hindu Metaphysics; but curiously enough not one writer ever succeeded in getting anywhere near the founder's original line of thought. You remember the enumeration of *tattvas* as given by Kapila, the originator of this school. For facility of reference I reproduce them again here.

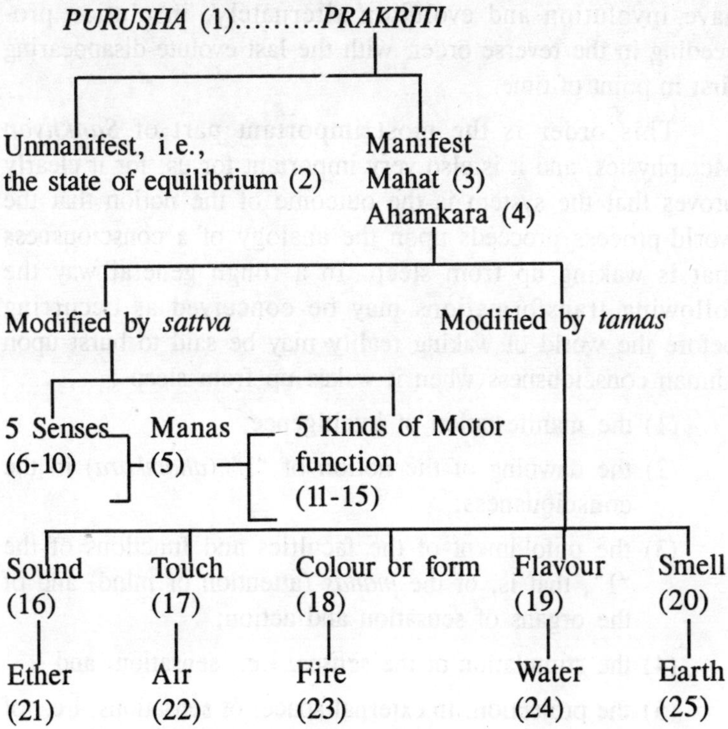

You have in this table the principles as well as the order of their appearance, beginning with *mahat* No. (3), as the first two are eternal. According to Kapila, the *purusha* principle is merely a spectator, neither an actor nor an enjoyer (*bhogta*) of the fruits of action. All changes, therefore, appertain to the spectacle, which is, consequently, conceived to be chara acterised by intelligence (*sattva*), in addition to movement (*rajas*) and rest (*tamas*). The equilibrium of these essential attributes, *sattva*, *rajas*, and *tamas*, is taken to mean the cessation of the spectacle, so that there is nothing which a *purusha* can then perceive. When this equilibrium is again disturbed after some time, in obedience to some unknown heartbeat of nature, the curtain is rung up again, and the process of evolution begins through the steps, as described. We thus have involution and evolution alternately; involution proceeding in the reverse order, with the last evolute disappearing first in point of time.

This order is the most important part of *Sankhyan* Metaphysics, and it is also very important for us; for it clearly proves that the system is the outcome of the notion that the world-process proceeds upon the analogy of a consciousness that is waking up from sleep. In a rough general way the following transformations may be conceived as occurring before the world of waking reality may be said to burst upon human consciousness when it wakes up from sleep :—

(1) the manifestation of intelligence;

(2) the dawning of the notion of "I" (*ahamkara*) in the consciousness;

(3) the unfoldment of the faculties and functions of the "I", that is, of the *manas* (attention or mind) and of the organs of sensation and action;

(4) the stimulation of the senses, i.e., sensation, and

(5) the projection, in external space, of sensations, i.e., of the data or bundle of sensible qualities of which objects are composed.

If you will only bear in mind the notion entertained by certain idealists that the sensible world is only neld in the mind of its percipient and the objects are but our sensations spatially projected, you will have no difficulty in comprehending the position of Kapila. We shall compare the Sankhyan order of evolution side by side with the manner in which Kapila appears to have understood an awakening mind to perceive the world.

The Awakening Mind.	*World-process or Evolution.*
(1) Alternation of waking and sleeping.	(1) Alternation of evolution and involution.
(2) In deep-sleep the ego is not destroyed, but there is nothing to percieve.	(2) In involution (*pralaya*) *purusha* is not destroyed but the world performence has stopped, so that there is nothing to preceive.
(3) In awakening, intelligence is roused first of all.	(3) In evolution, Intelligence (*mahat*) is produced first of all.
(4) From Intelligence arises "I-ness" (*ahamkara*).	(4) *Mahat* is then transformed into the *ahamkara*.
(5) From the sense of "I -ness" flow the functions of "I", manas (attention or mind), the senses and motor faculties.	(5) From *ahamkara* the *manas*, the five senses, and the five kinds of organs of action, hands, feet and the like, are formed.
(6) Sensations are then felts.	(6) The ahamkara is then transformed into sensations, i.e., sound, touch, colour, flavour and smell.
(7) Finally, the data of sensations are projected and constitute the perceptible world.	(7) The data of sensations, *i.e.*, the subtle elements of smell, etc., are, finally, transformed into the five gross elements, ether, air, fire, water and earth, of which the phenomenal world is composed.

It is thus clear that the metaphysical inspiration of Kapila was derived from the simple analogy of an awakening consciousness.. It must be now evident that Kapila knows nothing of an outside world apart from the projections of his own mind, *i.e.*, the transformations of his own sensations, touch, smell and the like. Unfortunately for this view, it never seems to have occurred to Kapila that a sensation did not wholly originate in the mind, and that there was such a thing as external stimulus which played an important part in our sensations. Had he noticed this distinguishing feature of sensation, he would not have described the gross elements, fire, water, etc., as transformations of the subtle *tanmatras* of sensations.

Time does not permit my going into the further inaccuracies of the system of Sankhya about the correspondence of elements and sensations, the relations of elements amongst themselves, and the like. You will find some of them dealt with in my, '*Key of Knowledge*' to which I am content to refer you for further information.

But though not valid as Metaphysical explanations of the world, both Vedanta and Sankhya are highly valuable to us in so far as they throw interesting side light on the tenets of the ancient Vedic faith of our Hindu brethren, since they both acknowledge the authority of the Vedas and, like the other systems of Hindu Metaphysics, only profess to furnish philosophical explanation of the revealed word. The Hindu mind, it is obvious, would have sooner or later plucked off these new offshoots if they did not furnish, or at least, did not profess to furnish, Metaphysical props for the accepted doctrines of the faith. It is certain that they would never have been acknowledged as belonging to the family. And what is true of these diverse schools of Hindu Philosophy in relation to the tenets of Hinduism also holds good with respect to the relationship between the Shahudian Metaphysics and Islam. The most important thing for us to know, then, is that all these three systems regard the human soul to be fully divine in nature and essence.

I must now pass on to a consideration of the *Nyaya* or the "logical" school. We have had occassion to find fault with its quaint conception, of *vyapti* which is described as a homogeneous example; but it is refreshing to note how Gotam proceeds to tackle the argument of the eternal *purvapakshin* (opponent) who denies the existance of an external world. Gotam objects to this doctrine, "first of all because if it were impossible to prove the existence of any external things it would be equally impossible to prove their non-existence. And if an appeal were made to dreams, or visions produced by a mirage, or by jugglery, it would be remembered that dreams also, like remembrance, presuppose previous perception of things; and that even in mistaking we mistake something, so that false knowledge can always be removed by true knowledge" (SSP. p. 427).

Gotam maintains that knowledge belongs not to the senses and mind but to the soul; he believes in transmigration, and considers attachment, aversion, and stupidity to be the chief faults of which stupidity is the worst. The separation of the soul from the body is obtained by the cessation of deserts. The notion of a god occupies a very secondary position in. Gotam's philosophy, his existence being simply necessary to decree fruits of action to the infinity of em bodied souls.

The categories of Nyaya do not include the true essentials of knowledge, as laid down in our discourse on the scientific side of Religion, and there is no description even of the state of *Moksha*, the end in view.

The Vaisheshika school, founded by Kanada, is practically a sister to Nyaya Philosophy. There is not much in it that is peculiar to it. Kanada's chief merit lies in the further development of the atom theory which is also to be found in a crude form in the Nyaya school. His categories, however, are:—

(1) substance,

(2) attribute,

(3) action,

(4) genus, or general qualities,

(5) species, or special attributes,

(6) combination, and

(7) non-existence.

Amongst the substances is mentioned *atman* or soul; but attributes are said to be "colour, taste smell, touch, number, measure, separateness, conjunction and disjunction, priority and posterity, understanding, pleasure and pain, desire and aversion, and volition" (SBH. Kanada Sutras).

There is no mention of bliss amongst these unless it be included in the term pleasure, which according to Naiyayikas is only a form of pain (The Nyaya Sutras by S. Vidyabhushan, pp. 122-123). No positive contents of knowledge are mentioned even with reference to *moksha* which is simply described as consisting in "the non-existence of conjunction with the body, when there is at the same time, no potential body existing, and consequently no rebirth can take place". No true explanation is given of bondage or transmigration and there is no mention or consideration of the real *tattvas*. The arguments employed are chiefly concerned with fanciful abstractions, while scientific treatment is almost invariably wanting.

The difficulties of the Vaisheshikta school are also to be found in the Yoga philosophy. According to some writers the word *Yoga* is derived from a root which means to join. This is certainly the sense in which the mind, speech and body are regarded as the three *yogas* (channels) of *asrava* in Jainism.

Mr. Ram Prasad, M.A., the learned translator of the Yoga Sutras in the series known as the Sacred Books of the Hindus, takes it to mean "to go to trance, to meditate." According to Max Muller, the word more probably signifies harnessing oneself for some work, to prepare oneself for hard work, for restraining the activities or distractions of our thoughts. There is no question of joining oneself to anyone else, not even to an *Ishvara* or Lord, for the idea of absorption in the supreme godhead forms no part of yoga. "Patanjali, like Kapila, rests satisfied with the isolation of the soul, and does not pry into the how and where the soul abides ofter separation" (Rajendra Lal Mitra quoted in the Six Systems of Hindu Philosophy, p. 310).

Certainly, there can be no absorption of one individual into another. The soul is an individual and will continue to exist as an individual. The idea of Ishvara in Patanjali's mind is not that of a maker or creator or ruler of worlds, but simply that of a Pure Spirit that is not offected by *karmas*, ignorance and pain, and whose perfection in respect of omniscience is full and unexcelled by anyone else. He is not the giver of *moksha* or joy or anything else, but only an object of meditation, or contemplation. This view is almost identical with that of the Jaina *Siddhanta*, which prescribes contemplation of the glory of a Perfect Soul and the study of His life-story, as a transmigrating ego, as the surest means of leading the devotee to become steady in the contemplation of the glory appertaining to his own soul.

Patanjali also is right when he says that the *jivas* (souls) are involved in matter, and the aim of Yoga is to free them from the meshes of matter (Int. to SBH., Yoga Sutras of Patanjali). But Patanjali has no idea of the true *tattvas*, and is unable to give any explanation of the why and wherefore of the means to be employed for getting rid of matter.

We should, however, remember that he does not claim to be the founder of the system, but only a compiler. This is evident from the very first verse which reads :

अथ योगा नुशा सनम्

which means "now a revised text of yoga." We have no right, therefore, to blame Patanjali for the shortcomings of what he only set out to collect and revise. Apparently there has been a great deal of borrowing in the course of this compilation, for we find the five kinds of restraints to be not only identically the same as are known as the five kinds of vows in the Jaina

Siddhanta, but they are also mentioned in the same order in which they are given by the Jaina writers.

Of these restraints, *ahimsa*, which is the first in the order of enumeration, is again the one which is a special characteristic of Jainism, its very motto being *ahimsa paramo dharmah* (non-injuring is the highest dharma).

The greatest stress is laid in the Yoga system on the attainment of *samadhi*, which is, no doubt, the culmination of the process of self-contemplation, but its description is vague and meagre, and the steps which are said to lead to it impracticable and abstract. For pure self-contemplation is not possible for a house-holder; it arises as the culmination of a long course of training both as a pious layman and an ardent ascetic. *Pranayama*, on which so much stress is laid by the Hindus in modern times, is in reality a very secondary affair. Patanjali himself only just alludes to it. It is merely a device to prevent mental distraction. It is not even touched upon in some of the other systems, and in Jainism also much importance is not attached to it (see the *Jnanarnava*). The real *samadhi* is internal and arises from a subjugation of one's desires and lusts. The forms of meditation which lead to pure self contemplation are also not described by Patanjali. I refer those of you who are interested in the subject to chapter XIII of my "Key of Knowledge" where the whole subject has been discussed and described. The space at my disposal does not admit of my going into so intricate a subject here.

I now come to the most fascinating part of Yoga which is concerned with the acquisition of miraculous powers. I presume some of you must be very eager to know what the final verdict of research is going to be on this point. Well, gentlemen, I am a lawyer, and the instincts of the learned profession to which I belong are, as you know, opposed to the admission of 'hearsay'. There is, however, a very large body of tradition of different creeds and faiths which undoubtedly supports the view that miraculous powers can be acquired by leading the life of purity, virtue and asceticism. I think this tradition is admissible, though a certain amount of caution is indispensable in letting it in. On the other hand there is the fact, and a very significant fact, too, that India boasted of many more *yogis* and *mahatmas* about the time of the invasion of Mahmud of Ghazni and the subsequent influx of Musalmans into India. I take it that the early Muslim invaders were heartily hated by the Hindus, and would have been wiped out if *yoga* knew of any method of encompassing their ruin. But *yoga* proved of no avail. A few centuries later when the beaf and pork-eating Christan came to India, we again witnessed a failure of Hindu occultism, and this time not alone, but in company with Muhammadan thaumaturgy. Personally I have seen very little of occultism, but from what I have seen and read about it I have come to the conclusion that there is no reason why a fairly large bulk of *ancient* tradition should be regarded as *outside the bounds of possibility*; but I should not like to substitute any other words for those I have used. It seems to me that occultism is not a reliable science by itself, that is, when taken apart from religion, and that truly miraculous powers spring only from regular asceticism, though fanatical fervour is also not unlikely to produce some minor mysterious effects, owing to the abnormal development of the inner psychic forces of life. The latter are, however, most likely to deceive one in the hour of need, and also lead to unhappy conditions and results. For Religion has nothing in common with the ambition for world-power or show. Dispassion and *vairagya* (desirelessness or renunciation) are the essential conditions for progress on the path, so that he who aspires for power, whether temporal or spiritual, can hardly be said to have put his foot on it. Hence, even if these psychic powers can be acquired in the way they are described in the Yoga Sutras, they can only be acquired by those saintly ascetics who do not long for them and who will certainly not use them to harm even an enemy. For others it is useless even to think of them.

I must now say a few words about the sixth school of Hindu thought before summing up the results of our investigation in respect of these world-famous *darshanas*. This sixth *darshana* was founded by Jaimini, who, again, seems to be only a compiler and not the original author. It is known as *Purva* (prior) *Mimansa* while Vedanta is termed *Uttara Mimansa* (a subsequent dissertation). But there is nothing, in this literal significance to furnish a ground for inferring a real chronological priority in time in favour of Jaimini's system (SSP. 197). On the other hand, it is quite likely that the notion of priority of his compilation is associated with a preconceived priority of "works" (*dharma*) which are supposed to precede *jnana* (knowledge).

As for the subject-matter of this *darshana*, its opening line—*athato dharma jijnasa* (now, therefore, for an enquiry into the philosophy of "works")—sufficiently indicates its scope. This is very significant in comparison with *athato Brahman Jijnasa* (now therefore, for an enquiry into Brahman), which is the opening line of the *Uttara Mimansa*, better known as Vedanta.

The idea of "works" in Hinduism is centered round the principle of "Sacrifice" which is practised for the obtainment of Heaven and other kinds of divine blessings and good. Jaimini's work deals with the doctrine of sacrifice, and its purport is evident from the list of its contents which I give here.

(1) Authoritativeness of injunctions, explanations etc., etc.

(2) The mysterious effect hymns and sacrificial formulas (the *Apura*).

(3) Revelation, context, etc., and the duties of a sacrificer.

(4) The influence of the principal and subordinate rites on other rites.

(5) The order of performance of a sacrifice.

(6) Qualifications of a sacrificer, substitutes for sacrifices, etc., etc.

(7) The transference of the ceremonies of one sacrifice to another.

(8) Further treatment of the subject of transference.

(9) The adaptation of hymns, etc.

(10) The non-performance of rites, etc.

(11) Repetition and combination of acts.

(12) The chief and subsidiary purposes of sacrificing, etc.

This abridged list of the contents of the *Purva Mimansa* should suffice to give you an idea of the subject-matter dealt with. I shall not comment on this subject here, but shall only say that Jaimini does not believe in a god as creator or governor of the universe, holding even that no judging divinity is necessary to determine the effect and to adjudge the degree of punishment and reward of our actions, which bear their fruit themselves.

> "In order to explain this, Jaimini assumes that there was a result, *viz.* an invisible something, a kind of after state of a deed or an invisible antecedent state of the result, something, *Apurva* or miraculous, which represented the reward inherent in good works. And he adds, that if, we suppose that the Lord himself caused rewards and punishments for the acts of men, we should often have to accuse him of cruelty and partiality; and that it is better therefore to allow that all works, good or bad, produce their own results, or, in other words, that for the moral government of the world no Lord is wanted" (SSP. 211).

Max Muller, commenting upon this theory of *karmas* bearing their own fruits, says :—

> ".....Jaimini would not make the Lord responsible for the injustice that seems to prevail in the world, and hence reduced everything to cause and effect and saw in the inequalities of the world the natural result of the continued action of good or evil acts. This surely was not atheism, rather was it an attempt to clear the Lord of those charges of cruelty or undue partiality which have

so often been brought against him. It was but another attempt at justifying the wisdom of God, an ancient Theodicee, that whatever we may think of it, certainly did not deserve the name of atheism," (Ibid. pp. 211-212).

So much for Jaimini's view as to the efficacy of " works". As for the cult of sacrifice, it will suffice for the present to quote what the Mahabharata declares on the subject:—

अहिंसा सर्व भूतानातेतत् कृन्यतमं मतम्॥
एतत्पदमनुद्विग्नं वरिष्ठं धर्म लक्ष्णम्॥
हिंसा पराश्चये केचिद्वेच नास्तिक वृत्तयः।
लोभ मोह समायुक्तास्ते वै निरयागमिनः॥

[Tr. "The real characteristic of the best Dharma, is *harmlessness*. Atheism, inclinations to injure, avarice etc., lead to hell."—Ashva-Medh Parva (PHB. Part II. pp. 636, 637 and 639.)

Our survey of the different systems of Hindu Philosophy is now complete. We find them in several instances contradicting one another as well as the sound principles of good reason. They are ignorant of the true *tattvas*. The *summum bonum* they try to encompass is obscure and indefinite, though they all agree upon showing respect to the Vedas. As Prof. Max Muller, whose treatment of Hindu Metaphysics is marked with great sympathy and good-will, remarks;-

"......while we can understand that each of the six systems ....may succeed in removing pain, it is very difficult to see in what that actual happiness was supposed to consist which remained ofter that removal. The Vedanta speaks of Ananda, of bliss, that resides in the highest Brahman; but the happiness to be enjoyed by the souls near the throne of Brahman, and in a kind of paradise, is not considered as final, but is assigned to lower class only. That paradise has no attraction, and would give no real satisfaction to those who have reached the knowledge of the highest Brahman. Their blissful knowledge is described as oneness with Brahman, but

> *no details are added*. The bliss held out by the Sankhyas is also very vague and indefinite. It can arise only from the Purusha himself, if left entirely to himself, for from all the illusions and disturbances arising from objective nature, or the works of Prakriti.

"Lastly, the Apavarga [bliss] of the Nyaya and Vaiseshika systems seems entirely negative, and produced simply by the removal of false knowledge. Even the different names given by each system of philosophy tell us very little. Mukti and Moksha mean deliverance, Kaivalya, isolation or detachment....Amrita, immortality, Apavarga, delivery........I doubt even whether the Upanishads could have given us a description of what they conceived their highest Mukti or perfect freedom to be. In fact they confess themselves (Taitt. UP. II. 4, 1) that 'all speech turns away from the bliss of Brahman, unable to reach it', and when language fails, thought is not likely to fare better." (SSP. pp. 372-373).

The *italics* are mine.

It is not that only European writers have been unfavourably impressed with these attempts at philosophising the teaching of the Vedas; Hindu savants, too, have had to write very much in the same strain. It is frankly acknowledged in the preface to the ninth volume of the Sacred Books of the Hindus, edited by a highly qualified editorial staff of learned Hindus themselves:—

> ".....none of the six Darshanas......was, as we have hinted more than once, a complete system of philosophy in the Western sense, but merely a catechism explaining, and giving a reasoned account of some of the truths revealed in the Vedas and the Upanishads, to a particular class of students,....without attempting to solve to them the transcendental riddles of the universe, which in their particular stage of mental and spiritual development, it would have been impossible for them to grasp."

This attempted justification, no doubt, does great credit to the faith of the writer, but there is nothing in the entire range of Hindu *philosophy* to support it. As said earlier, these systems are valuable as furnishing important evidence of Hindu ideals and beliefs which they vainly sought to place on an intellectual basis.

As our interest lies in getting at the real Hindu tenets of faith, I shall now endeavour to give you the points which the *darshanas* hold in common with one another.

(1) That the soul is a reality which is immortal, either as Brahman or an individual.

(2) That it is in bondage and undergoes transmigration.

(3) That the condition of transmigration is full of pain and misery.

(4) That there is a way out of this mundane suffering and pain.

According to certain European thinkers, there is one additional striking feature of all these schools, which Prof. Max Muller describes in the following words:—

> "Though there is a strong religious vein running through the six so-called orthodox systems, they belong to a phase of thought in which not only has the belief in the many Vedic gods long been superseded by a belief in a supreme deity,...... but this phase also has been left behind to make room for a faith in a supreme power or in the Godhead which has no name but Brahman, or Sat, 'I am what I am' (SSP. pp 449-450).

We also learn from Max Muller (Ibid. p. 450):—

> "Atheism with Indian philosophers means something very different from what it means with us. It means a denial of an active, busy, personal, or humanised god only who is called Ishvara, the Lord. But behind him and above him Hindu philosophers recognised a higher power, whether they called it Brahman, or Paramatman, or Purusha. It was the denial of that reality which constituted a Nastik, a real heretic."

Before concluding the subject of Hindu Metaphysics I must

not omit to quote a very healthy piece of advice from the Mahabharata:—

> "Manifold philosophical doctrines have been propounded by various teachers; but cling to that only which has been settled by arguments, by the Veda and by the practice of good people" (SSP. p. 455).

I shall now briefly deal with the Buddhistic Metaphysics during the remaining time at my disposal today, and in the next lecture we shall apply ourselves to unravel the mystery of the Vedas and the Holy Bible along with some other mythological conceptions.

It would seem that metaphysical knowledge was at first no essential part of the Buddhist discipline. The true Law was a practical training and nothing more. Deliverance from pain was to be obtained by saintliness; saintliness, by deliverance from desire; and deliverance from desire, by asceticism and meditations that fired the mind with *vairaygya* an overwhelming sense of disgust for the world and the objects of pleasure. Buddha's own attitude was uncertain at times; he spoke sometimes as a believer in permanence (*shasvata*), sometimes in favour of annihilation (*uchchheda*). But on the whole the Buddhistic Metaphysics lays all the stress it can on the impermanence of the soul. According to the *Hinayana* or *Abhidharma* School of Buddhism:—

> "There is no self (*atman*), person (*pudgala*), living being (*sattva*), or principle of life (*jiva*)—a flat negative not only of an unchangeable Self as recognised by the Brahmanic philosophies, but also of the substantial principle that the popular philosophy considers as a transmigrating entity a soul different from the body. Man is a complex composed of five *skandhas*—the material element *rupa*, or body, and four intellectual elements, *samjna*, (feeling), *vedana* (sense-perception) *samskaras* (impressions) *vijnana* (consciousness). The ego, or 'man' is described in terms of its constitutive elements, and is compared to a chariot which lacks personality beoause it is composed" (ERE. Vol. IX. p. 847).

The other sect, the *Mahayana* School, goes considerably further and denies the very existence of things. It is the doctrine of voidness (*shunyata*), a sort of Idealism pushed to the extreme. There are not only no external things, but there is even no self, an individual generator of thoughts. Even thoughts are void, not substantial. Voidness characterises all.

With notions such as these it was, of course, impossible to think of a *nirvana* that did not imply annihilation out and out, or of a doctrine of transmigration that did not mean the punishment of someone other than the doer of evil.

Mrs. Rhys Davids in her Buddhist Psychology points out (p. 26) that the Buddhists are unenlightened as to the nature and medium of the rebirth-force, though its logic is irrefutable for them. The Buddhists certainly have no scientific ideas about the four most important points with reference to transmigration—*asrava*, *bandha*, *samvara* and *nirjara*—though they employ the terms *asrava* and *samvara* in their books. As the latest authority confirms (ERE. Vol. VII. p. 472):—

> "The Jains understand these terms in their literal meaning, and use them in explaining the way of salvation (the *samvara* of the *asravas* and the *nirjara* lead to *moksha*), Now these terms are as old Jainism. For the Buddhists have borrowed from it the most significant term *asrava* ; they use it in very much the same sense as the Jains, but not in its literal meaning, since they do not regard the *karma* as subtle matter, and deny the existence of a soul into which the *karma* could have an influx. Instead of *samvara* they say *asavakkhaya* (*asravakshaya*), 'destruction of the *asravas*', and identify it with *mugga* (marga, 'path'). It is obvious that with them *asrava* has lost its literal meaning, and that, therefore, they must have borrowed this term from a sect where it had retained its original significance, or, in other words, from the Jains. The Buddhists also use the term *samvara*, e.g., *shilasamvara* 'restraint under the moral law', and the participle *samvuta*, 'controlled,' words which are not used in this sense by Brahmanical

> writers, and, therefore, are most probably adopted from Jainism, where in their literal sense they adequately express the idea that they denote. Thus the Same argument serves to prove at the same time that the karma theory of the Jains is an original and integral part of their system, and that Jainism is considerably older than the origin of Buddhism,"

Personally I am inclined to think that Buddhism was intended as a protest against the caste system of the Hindus and the severe asceticism of the Jainas, not as a new metaphysical system, at least, not in its inception. Buddha had spent a number of years in the company of monks of different religions and was familiar with their doctrines though probably not with their explanation.

On one occasion he said;-

> "There are, brethren, certain recluses (Achelkas, Ajivikas, Niganthas, etc.) who thus preach and believe: Whatsoever an individual experiences, whether it be happy, or painful, or neutral feeling, all has been caused by previous actions. And thus from the cancelling of old actious by *tapas*, and by abstaining from doing new actions, there is no influx: into future life; by this non-influx *karma* is destroyed and so ill is destroyed and so feeling is destroyed, and so all pain will become worn away. This, brethren, is what the Niganthas (Jains) say ......Is it true, I asked them, that you believe and declare this ?......They replied........Our leader, Nataputta; is all-wise out of the depth of his knowledge he tells us: You have done evil in the past. This you do wear away by this hard and painful course of action. And the discipline that here and now, by thought, word, and deed, is wrought, is a minus quantity of bad *karma* in future life.....thus all *karma* will eventually be worn away, and all pain. To this we assent (*Majjhima*, ii. 214ff.; *cf.*1. 238)"—ERE Vol. II. p. 70.

Notwithstanding this knowledge, when faced with the severity of *parisha-jaya*, which signifies cheerfully enduring all kinds of hardships incidental to asceticism, and finding them only leading to enfeeblement and emaciation, but not to the enlightenment that he sought, Buddha declared:—

"Not by this bitter course of painful hardship shalll arrive at that separate and supreme vision of all-sufficing, noble [Aryan] knowledge passing human ken. Might there be not another path to enlightenment?"—ERE. Vol. II. p. 70.

He thenceforth began to look after the welfare of the body once more. At last the middle course that he was looking for occurred to him under the famous, Bodhi tree. It was a compromise between rigid asceticism on the one hand and the life of unrestrained licentiousness under the guise of karma-yoga (the, doing of all worldly actions, but without attachment, to their fruits) on the other. Whether the middle course thus arrived at was scientifically valid or not, was not the point; what mattered was the avoidance of pain in any form. If asceticism itself led to pain, how could it lead to its destruction? "*Dukkha* is evil", said the Enlightened one, "and must be removed. Excess is *Dukkha*. *Tapas* is a form of excess , and multiplies *Dukkha*. It does not even lead through suffering to any gain; it is unprofitable" (ERE. Vol. II. p. 70). What Buddha would have thought or said on the subject if he had known that he was trying to perfect himself, in *sannyasa* without ever having passed through the prescribed stages of a householder's preparatory course, we do not know. Probably it never occurred to him that a ladder was necessary to reach the top, and that asecticism never led to anything but distress and pain unless accompanied by faith and knowledge of the right sort.

Thus did Buddha live to a ripe old age, preaching the 'noble' middle path, and exhorting the people to seek release from pain in the extinction of being in *nirvana*. He died after eating from a dish of boar's flesh in the 80th year of his life.

Buddha's teaching has appealed to a vast majority of mankind chiefly because it did not entail a severe discipline and went a long way to tone down the rigours of Hatha Yoga, truly a useless system of physical distortions which must be clearly distinguished from the true form of *tapas* as given in the Jaina *siddhanta*. But whatever we may say or think of the Buddhistic metaphysics, of its theory of metempsychosis,that would make another being than the doer of deeds the recipient of rewards and punishments flowing from them, and of the teaching about the impermanence of souls, there can be no withholding of praise for Buddha's very clearest perception of the misery of unemancipated life and for the most faithful picture that he drew of it in words. Such language has seldom been surpassed.

> "Woe upon youth, threatened by old age ! Woe upon health, which so many maladies destroy! Woe upon human life which lasts but a little space! Woe on the temptations of the flesh, which lure the heart of the wise! Would that there were neither old age, nor illness nor death and the pains of death" (The Lalita Vistara, quoted trom Metchnikoff's Nature of Man).

In the same strain,[1] again, it is said:—

> 'Miserable in truth in this world, in which there is beginning, birth, growing old, death, disappearance and renewal! Alas......to all who are there comes old age, and illness, and death and their like'—(Ibid).

Truly, is this world, which appears so beautiful and full of pleasure and fun to the thoughtless, like the Giant's Island in the Arabian Nights Entertainment, the unfortunate captives of which are fattened only to be devoured a while later! Here also we have nothing but old age, misery and death in store for us as the end of life in everyone of its recurring phases. Those of us who have understood the nature of being and the terms of existence, and are sorrowful in heart, are the wise who withdraw themselves as completely as they can from the lusts and temptations of the flesh to ultimately escape from this huge cannibal's cave, but the rest, who abandon themselves to the pleasures of love and song and dance, or who only cultivate refined Epicurean tastes, are seized upon and crushed and mangled in the powerful jaws of the monster (Death), over and over again, in the course of their perennial (eternal) rovings!

FOOTNOTE

1. Cf. "For we know that the whole creation groaneth and travaileth in pain together until now. And not only they, but ourselves also, which have the first fruits of the script, even we ourselves groan within ourselves, waiting fot the adoption, to wit, the redemption of our body."—Romans viii, 22-23.

CHAPTER -V

MYTHOLOGY

(A)

This evening's lecture deals with a subject which is of the utmost importance to the proper study of Religion and, therefore, also to humanity at large. We are going, to explore today the region of mythology which has defied the best attempts of the moderns at unravelment. The greatest confusion has hitherto prevailed amongst the propounders of the sacred text, and scholarship, both autochthonous and foreign has been only knocking its head against a dead wall. For some have perceived in the gods of the different countries and pantheons real actual beings, and in their strange doings and impossible relationships, ir-refutable evidence of their superhuman nature, while others, who have either had no superstitions to warp their judgment or who have shaken themselves free from them, by education, or otherwise, have taken these innumerable gods and goddesses to be personifications of such natural phenomena as light, rain, fire and the like, or of different kinds of sciences and arts, the art of governing people, the culinary art, etc. etc. But to each and everyone of these learned scholars have the Vedas, the Holy Bible, the Qur'an and the Zend Avesta remained a sealed book.

The Orientalist thinks that he has a complete solution of the mystery as soon as he has identified the Vedic Surya, Indra and Agni with the sun, clouds and fire, and read the Old Testament and the New Testament compilations historically; and the learned of our day have banded themselves together into a sort of mutual admiration society, whose members are ever ready to ascertain to whom the credit of their diverse discoveries belongs and to proclaim it in a spirit of commendable self-less impartiality.

If I have to criticise even a tenth parth of what these learned explorers of the Bibles of the world have written or said on the subject, it will require at least a volume of about a thousand pages. It is not that they are insincere, or uneducated; some of them are really men who have not their equal in respect of learning in this age. But unfortunately they are all, each and everyone of them without a single exception, suffering from mental myopia of which they are altogether ignorant. This mental short-sightedness is further aggravated by their lavish praises of each other's insight and breadth of view, already hinted at.

If the learned professor who identified *Agni* with fire, and the eloquent Arya-Samajist who took it to represent the culinary art had taken the trouble to note its strange characteristics, they would have surely found much that would have jarred, in the most unwholesome manner, upon their self-complacent nerves. They would have found that the ancient *rishis* described this strangest of gods as

(1) having three legs, seven hands and seven tongues,

(2) the priest of gods,

(3) at whose invocation they appeared,

(4) by feeding whom they were fed and strengthened, and

(5) a devourer of clean and unclean both.

There are several other characteristics of *Agni*, but these are by themselves quite sufficient to arrest any one's attention. I ask you now to show me these distinguishing marks of Agni in fire or the culinary art.

I ask you also to see if you can discover in the elucidations of the learned and the eloquent an explanation of how rain or clouds committed adultery with a Brahmana preceptor's wife, and the where abouts of the marks of disease that were ultimately turned into eyes by Brahma. But you may search as long as you please; modern explanations have nothing to tell you on these points!

Besides this, it is permissible to ask what may be the relevancy of fire to religion, and what the connection between the art of cooking and the salvation of the soul? But there is no reply to these questions! reproduce here a portion of a hymn translated by the Arya Samajists to show the flimsy nature of their interpretation.

> "(1) We shall describe the power generating virtues of the energetic horses endowed with brilliant properties, or the virtues of the vigorous force of heat which learned or scientific men can evoke to work for purposes of appliances (not sacrifice).
>
> "(2) They who preach that only wealth earned by righteous means should be appropriated and spent, and those born in wisdom, who are well-versed in questioning others elegently in the science of forms and in correcting the unwise, these and such alone drink the potion of strength and of power to govern.
>
> "(3) The goat posessed of useful properties yields milk, a strengthening food for horses. The best cereal is useful when made into pleasant food well prepared by an apt cook according to the modes dictated by specific knowledge of the properties of foods."

Here you can see at a glance that the distinguishing features of this composition are that

(1) it has no bearing on religion, and

(2) it is like a school-boy essay in style, and not a scientific exposition of any art or craft. Needless to say that it is also not the recognised reading of the Vedic hymn of which it purports to be a translation. If this is not dragging down the Vedic text from its high place of sanctity, where the spirit of Hinduism places it, we do

> not know what it can be. It is certainly not complimentary to the Hindu intelligence that composed the Vedas.

Neither have the Sanatan-dharmists (orthodox Hindus) fared any better in this respect. They have blindly repeated, the errors of their predecessors, never stopping even to consider whether the attributes mentioned with reference to the diverse gods and goddesses were or were not the true components or constituents of divinity. Indra committed adultery with a Brahmana's spouse; Brihaspati, the *deva guru* (preceptor of gods), seduced his elder brother's wife during her pregnancy; and Soma, also known as Moon, begat a son on the better halt of the *deva guru* himself! But the Sanatan-dharmist has no eyes for these and other similar escapades of the gods.

The strangest thing about these strange deities is that they are no longer making history. Their deeds were all finished. and accomplished, so to speak; prior to the composition of the scriptures. How is this possible with living beings, especially with actors such as those who cannot live peacefully for a moment without thinking of running away with their neighbours' wives? This one peculiarity of the gods should have sufficed by itself to open the eyes of any seeker ofter the truth; but, unfortunately, the majority are content to follow blindly in the wake of usage!

What, then, is the true explanation of Vedicism, and what the secret of the divers gods mentioned in the hymns I But before I undertake to answer these questions I should tell you something about the reason why all these three kinds of Vedic scholars, the superstitious Sanatanist, the Darwinised European, and the half-Darwinised Indian, have failed in getting at the truth. This reason lay in the fact that the Vedas are not written in Sanskrit, just as the Holy Bible is not written in Hebrew and Greek, or the Qur'an in Arabic! Does this astonish you? It is nevertheless a fact; these sacred scriptures that I have named are all written in two languages, not in one. The word symbolism used in their composition, no doubt, is the spoken tongue of a particular people, but there is a sense symbolism behind the words which is the real language of the text. It is this language which I have termed Picto-krit (the language of Pictures) in the Foreword. The scholars knew nothing of this sense-symbolism and exhausted themselves on the outer husk. They missed the kernel of truth altogether. This is why the Vedas, the Zend Avesta, the Bible and the Qur'an have appeared to contain only such childish stuff as nature myths, and the personifications of lakes and rivers and brooks. Generally these scriptures themselves caution us against a literal interpretation. Louis Jacolliot, citing the authority of the Agrouchade Parikchai, says of the Hindu Scriptures (see the Occult Science in India, p. 102)—

> "The sacred scriptures, ought not to be taken in their apparent meaning, as in the case of ordinary books. Of what use would it be to forbid their revelation to the profane if their secret meaning were contained in the literal sense of the language usually employed.....The Vedas do not explain themselves, and they can only be understood when the *guru* has removed the garment with which they are clothed, and scattered the clouds that veil their celestial light."

Unfortunately Jacolliot himself acquired no true insight in Hinduism though he understood the true principles of reading these Books. His mind was too much obsessed with current materialistic notions to enable him to get at the underlying spiritual significance. "The Sacred text," writes Mr. K. N. Iyre in his highly valuable work, 'The Permanent History of Bharatavarsha', "the sacred Text never tells tales of past history, but contains valuable instructions in the best interest of humanity. The proper scientific method or procedure for religious development is described in the garb of histories and geographies, law and politics."

The Vedas require the aid of the Vedangas to be understood, and the most important Vedanga is Niruktum (the method of interpretation) without a knowledge of which no one is allowed to explain the Vedic Text. In Greece, too, grammar had come to include all that in later times has been designated *belle lettres*. It included the study of the explanations of tb,e names of the gods and heroes, the legends and histories (see Hatch's Influence of Greek Ideas and Usages upon the Christian Church p. 129).

In the preface to his highly interesting Mahabharata or Karma Yoga, Mr. K. N. Iyre again points out:—

> "For the purpose of enlightening the ordinary people in the manner above described, the ancient authors have explained valuable scientific truths in the guise of stories for conveying religious instructions. Suitable teachnical terms were coined and defined which in themselves would suggest their intended meanings by the very roots of their formation, known as Niruktam, one of the six Angas of the Vedas......The technical terms so coined were also carefully defined in the texts to prevent possibilities of error from the very beginning.

We may or may not agree with Mr. Iyre as to the origin or justification for this method of instruction, but there can be no doubt but that the text was not intended to be read in the literal sense of the words. Not only has a derivative significance been employed to alter the current purport of words, but free use has also been made of allegory and other forms of subtle symbolism to depict human thought in a garb so alluring and enchanting as to elude the gaze of the prying intellect at every turn. In Judaism a method of what may be termed numerical equation of words was also resorted to to conceal the real sense of the writers. The Kabbalah is the Esoteric side of Judaism.

The Kabbalah is divided into three parts; Gematria, Notariqon and Temuru. Of these Gematria is based on the numerical values of words and phrases, those of an identical value being taken as synonymous. The other two are complex methods of forming sentences by taking the letters of a word to stand for a complete word each, and the like, with which we have no concern here. Great stress was laid in Jewish Esotericism on the science of numbers as this method of equation of words may be called. For every letter in the Hebrew language has a definite numerical value. Thus aliph=1; beth=2; gimel=3; daleth=4; and so forth. This is the foundation of the doctrine that every word is a number and every number a word. We have the Identical system of numerical values of letters in Urdu and Persian, commonly known as the *abjad* method. The Jews seem to have made the greatest use of this system in composing their scriptures. The scriptures thus represent a real body of secret doctrines that can only be known by the elucidation of the symbolism and the numerical equations in which they are couched. "According to the Kabbalah, all these esoteric doctrines are contained in the Hebrew Scriptures. The uninitiated cannot perceive them; but they are plainly revealed to the spiritually minded, who discern the profound import of this theosophy beneath the surface of the letters and words of the Holy writ" (Ency. Brit. Eleventh Edi. Vol. xv. p. 621, art. Kabbalah).

> "This secret mysticism," we learn from ERE (vol. vii. p. 622 art. Kabbalah), "was no late growth. Difficult though it is to prove the date and origin of this system or philosophy and the influences and causes which produced it, we can be rairly ccrtain that its roots stretch back very far, and that the medieval and Geonic Kabbalah was the culmination and not the inception of Jewish esoteric mysticism."

The secret mysticism was extended even to the animals that were regarded as lawful for food. As pointed out in the Encyclo. Religion and Ethics (Vol. xii. p. 143): "In the Letter of Aristeas[1] (which can scarcely be later than the 2nd century B. C. and which may well belong to a century earlier) the enactments as to the animals lawful for food are explained symbolically."

The same view of the commandment is taken in the Epistle which is traditionally ascribed to St. Barnabas, and the purpose of which is to warn the readers against accepting the Old Testament, in a literal sense. Leading lights among early Christian writers, too, accepted this view. (See Ante-nicene Christian Library Vol. xii pp. 251-252 and 488; also Origen's Philocalia p. 131). According to Tertulian, "literal prohibitions about clean and unclean kinds of foods would be quite contemptible" (see Farrar's Rist. of Interpretation, p. 178).

It is not a new case that I am making out before you. As early as the third century A.D. Origen, a famous Christian, who was, on the authority of the Encyclo. Britannica, the most distinguished and most influential of all the theologians of the ancient Christian church, had applied the allegorical method with reference to the interpretation of the Holy Bible. Origen fully believed that there was not either in the Old or the New Testament a single syllable that was void of divine meaning and import.

> "But how" he asks, "can we conciliate with this tenet of their entire inspiration the existence in tbe Bible of such tales as that of Lot and his daughters, of Abraham prostituting first one Wife and then another, of a succession of at least three days and nights before the sun was created? Who will be found idiot enough to believe that God planted trees ill Paradise like any husbandman; that he set up in it visible palpable tree-trunks, labelled the one 'Tree of Life,' and the other 'Tree of knowledge of Good and Evil,' both bearing real fruit that night be masticated with corporeal teeth; that he went and walked about the garden; that Adam hid under a tree; that Cain fled from the face of God? The wise reader may well ask what the face of God is, and how anyone could get away from it ? Nor is the old Testament only full of such incidents as no one regardful of good sense and reason can suppose to have really taken place or to be sober history. In the Gospels equally such narratives abound. How can it be literally true, how a historical fact, that from a single mountain-top with fleshly eyes all the realms of Persia, of Scythia, and of India, could be seen. adjacent and at once? The careful reader will find in the

> Gospels any number of cases similar to the above" (quoted, from the History of The New Testament Criticism, by F. C. Conybeare. pp. 9 and 10).

Read historically the Bible, like the Vedas, can only yield a harvest of contradictions and absurdities. Even the genuineness of the Bible as an historical record is seriously open to question. Impartial Biblical scholars, professing Christianity, have found themselves forced to regard certain portions of the Old and the New Testaments as simple forgeries (Encyclo. Britannica, art. Bible). I have no time to point out to you the contradictions in the Holy Bible, but here is an abridged extract from a learned article, which summarises a few of them (see The Theosophist, Vol. xxxv. p. 396):—

> "The gospels constantly contradict each other and *S. John's* is so different from the other three that a division has been made by all scholars between it and what are called the three synoptic Gospels.....Apart from the fact that *S. John's* way of speaking of the Christ is very different from that we find in the synoptics, he does not mention the Lord's supper, he gives a different day for the Lord's death, speaks of three feasts of the Passover whereas the others speak of but one, and relates almost all the incidents of the life of Christ as taking place at Jerusalem, whereas, according to the synoptics, only the end of his life was spent there. In *S. John's* version the character of ,John the Baptist loses almost all its importance, the miracles are quite different, becoming more astonishiug and, at the same time, more symbolical; the whole character of Jesus is much more divine and more like an aspect of the LOGOS than in the synoptics; but at the same time he speaks of Jesus as the son of Joseph, and does not mention the birth from a virgin...... Neither do the so-called synoptics agree together. To begin with the date of the birth of Jesus is fixed by Matthew as occurring four years before our era at the very latest (under Herod). Luke makes it ten years later (during the enrolment), or in the year 6 A.D., yet states, further on, that in the fifteenth year of

Tiberius—our 29 A.D.—Christ was about thirty years old. The Miraculous birth is not related by S. Mark; S. Matthew and S. Luke give two quite different genealogies for Christ's descent, *through Joseph*, from King David, but these are in contradiction with the story of His birth from a Virgin. Had Mary and Joseph known of the miraculous birth, would they have been astonished when Christ spoke in the Temple of His Father's business (Luke, ii. 58)? The miracles related by the synoptics, are much alike but the circumstances under which they are stated to have occurred are very different.... The greatest miracle—the raising of Lazarus—is related only by S. John. The other miracles are......often allegories (the multiplication of loaves, the changing of water into wine, etc.) The names of the persons at the foot of the cross are not given in two places alike. On the subject of resurrection the synoptics differ considerably. What Mark says in XVI. 9-20 is an appendix added afterwards.....[Luke's] historical indications are false. Herod has never King, but a governor. Cyrenius, whom he brings into his history of Jesus, governed from the year 7 to 11 A.D., and had consequently nothing to do with the story. He also mentions the name of Lysanius, although he had died thirty-four years before Jesus was born......The Gospel writers cannot have been familiar with the customs of the Jews in Palestine, whell they speak of baptising in a river, and especially in the Jordan, where even bathing was prohibited. In *Luke* we find two high priests, Caiaphas and Annas, existing at the same time which is impossible. We find Jesus teaching in tbe Temple where only sacrifices took place, the synagogue serving for preaching.....If we compare the Jewish Legal Code with the Gospel stories we come across very strange contradictions. It was strictly prohibited to hold judicial proceedings on days of religious feasts, so Jesus can never have been judged on the day of the Passover. It was also forbidden to carry arms on such days, so that the chief priests would never have sent the Temple Guard to arrest Christ, and Peter would certainly not have worn a sword."

The above is a summary of but a few of the Biblical contradictions. But European Scholarship has not been content with pointing out mere discrepancies in the Biblical text; it has also busied itself in tracing the sources of the various doctrines of the Gospels themselves. It has now been shown, as the result of this scholarly investigation, that

> "a number of data in the Christian gospels, both miraculous and non-miraculous, held by Christians to be historical, or at least, accretions round the life and doctrine of a remarkable religious teacher and creedfounder, are really mere adaptations from myths of much greater antiquity and that accordingly the alleged or inferred personality of the Founder is under suspicion of being as mythical as that of the demigods of the elder lore. Broadly, the contention is that when every salient item in the legend of the gospel Jesus turns out to be more or less clearly mythical, the matter of doctrine, equally so with the matter of action, there is simply nothing left which can entitle anyone to a belief in any tangible personality behind the name. Such a view, as scholars are aware, is not new in the history of criticism, though the grounds for it may be so. In the second eenlury, if not in the first, the 'Docetoe' had come to conceive of the Founder as a kind of supernatural phantom, which only 'seemed' to suffer on the cross; and many Gnostics had all along regarded him as an abstraction. One or the other view recurs in medieval heresy from time to time. A 'Docetic' view of Jesus was professed by the secret society of clerics and others which was broken up at Orleans about 1022; and in England, as elsewhere, in the sixteenth century, sectaries are found taking highly mystical views of the Founder's personality. In the fifteenth century, again, Voltsire tells of disciples of Bolingbroke who on ground of historical criticism denied the historicity of Jesus; and in the period of the French Revolution we have not only the works of Volney and Dupuis, reducing the gospel biography to a set of astronomical myths, but the anonymous German work mentioned by Strauss as reducing it to an ideal which

had a prior existence in the Jewish mind, though admitting divergences."—("Christianity and Mythology" by J. M. Robertson, p. 276).

Another writer of note, and one who was for a number of years associated most intimately with the Christian Church from which he ultimately withdrew himself, is Joseph McCabe, who writes in his "Bankruptcy of Religion," pp. 162 *et seq* as follows:—

"The science of comparative religion.....enquires how the mythical Jesus of the Gospels was evolved and the task is not difficult. We do not know where the gospels were written, but we know that at the time they were written Christianity was spread over the eastern end of the Mediterranean at least from Alexandria to Corinth, and the final Gospels were most probably written in that region. Now in these cities the myths and creeds and priesthoods of all religions were richly represented. Priests of Egypt, Syria, Persia, Greece, Rome and of the less known provinces of the Empire, set up their temples and vigorously proselytised everywhere. Myths, legends and rites passed easily from one religion to another. Many of the myths were found to resemble each other closely in religions which came from quite distant countries. There never was such a melting-pot in the history of the world as that eastern shore of the Mediterranean in the first century of our era when Rome fused the nations into one empire.

"Careful research into the movements of the old empires, the sacred books of the old religions, the writings of the Christian fathers and certain of the pagans have now established that all the chief mythical elements of the life of Jesus already existed in that cosmopolitan World. The healing and other miracles do not, of course, require any special study. Such things are not only ascribed to holy men, in the Old Testament, but they were claimed in every nation and religion of that uncritical age.....The works of the Right Hon'ble J. M. Robertson... contain an exhaustive and learned study of this important branch of comparative religion. Mr. Robertson has,

> in fact, traced mythical parallels to the Gospel stories in such minute details that he is convinced that no such person as Jesus ever existed; that the whole story is a mythical compilation founded on a sacred drama or mystery-play......The evidence accumulated by Mr. Robertson, and in part repeated and expanded by Sir J. G. Frazer in his Golden Bough, must convince any impartial person that the stories of the birth, resurrection, and the atoning mission of Jesus are but the application to Jesus of myths that were widely current in religions of the time......The death and resurrection of Christ are probably to the average believer the central and unique truth of the Christian religion. Now every well-informed theologian has known for ages that in the Roman World in which Christianity arose the annual commemomtion of the death and resurrection of a god was the most common religious feature. The Egyptian cult of Osiris, the Babylonian cult of Tammuz (or Adonis), and the Phrygian cult of Attis had celebrated this annual solemnity for unknown ages, and had, in the fusion of nations in the Roman Empire, spread it over the whole eastern world. The Greeks adopted the festival centuries before Christ was born; the Persian cult of Mithra also adopted it. It is safe to say that there was not a city of that old world, before the time of Christ, which had not one or more temples of different religions, attracting full public attention to the annual celebration of the death and resurrection of a god."

The resemblance in the Mithraic temples actually went so for that the rasurracted god was hailed as "the Lamb of God that taketh away the sins of the world."

All this is certainly fatal to the historicity of Jesus himself who is the central figure in the New Testament. It is certainly most astonishing that Jehovah should not have revealed the existence of his son to any of the earlier or later prophets, especially of such a son as Jesus who was to redeem the world. On the contrary we were distinctly told (Isaiah, xiii. 11):-

"I, even I, am the Lord; and beside me there is no saviour."

This is not contradicted, but confirmed by Ecclesiastes (iv. 8):

> "There is one alone, and there is not a second, yea he hath neither child nor brother."

Is it the same god that is supposed to be the Father of Jesus who is speaking here? If so, why does he deny his having a child? And is it the same Supreme Divinity that the Hindus worship as Ishwara, the Muhammadans as Allah and the Parsis as Ahura Muzda? If so, why did he not tell them, too, that he had a son?

The fact is that the Gospels themselves make no secret of being written in a secret script, the meaning of which is requried to be elucidated. The sayings of Jesus were imparted in parables that had to be explained to the disciples over and over again, and yet they understood not at times even then (see Mark ix. 31-32; Luke xviii. 32-34; Mark ix. 10). Jesus is even said to have opened the understaning of his disciples after his resurrection (Luke, xxiv. 45), *so that they might understand the scriptures*.

> "I have also spoken by the prophets, and I have multiplied visions, and used similitudes; by the ministry of the prophets" (Hosea, xii. 10)

The injunction against enlightening the profane is recorded in these memorable words in Matthew vii. 6:—

> "Give not that which is holy unto the dogs, neither cast ye your pearls before swine, lest they trample them under their feet and turn again and rend you,"[2]

Israel had already been told by Isaiah (vi. 9): "Hear ye indeed but understand not; and see ye indeed, but perceive not." Jesus conforms to and fully confirms this when he says:—

> "Therefore speak I to them in parables; because they seeing see not, and hearing they hear not, neither do they understand.......For this people's heart is waxed gross, and their ears are dull of hearing, and their eyes they have closed" (Matt. XIII 13 and 15).

"Who hath ears to hear, let him hear"—was the oft-repeated word of warning with Jesus (Matt. xiii. 9). There was something, then, in the teaching of the New Testament which required *seeing, hearing and understanding*!

It was not a case of plain-speaking; the divine teacher was not preaching history, even though he became a very great factor in its subsequent making. The Gospel-writers did not take even the earlier records of Judaism in their literal sense. Jesus is once reported to have said: Ye shall know the truth, and the truth shall make you free" (John, viii. 32). To the Doctors of Law who set themselves up as the teachers of truth he said:—

> "Woe unto you lawyers! for ye have taken away the key of knowledge; ye entered not in yourselves, and them that were entering in ye hindered" (Luke, xi. 52).[3]

The learned cleric has absolutely no idea of what this passage means. He certainly knows nothing of a key, much less of a *key of knowledge*, and has never—heard of any Hall or Place from which the unfortunate & lawyers' debarred themselves and their followers by 'taking it away'! To him all is history,. and nothing but history,—the history of a mad love for the unbelieving idol-worshipping Israel on the part of Jehovah, or of the doings of a newly-announced son of God, become flesh to redeem the sinners! In vain do the Gospel-writers cry themselves hoarse in shouting "whoso readeth, let him understand" (Matt. xxiv. 15); so sure are we of our "history" that we cannot offord to be moved by the injunction! In the book of Revelation also we have it:—

> "He that hath an ear let him hear what the spirit saith unto the churches. To him that over-cometh will I give to eat of the tree-of life, which is in the midst of the Paradise of God" (chap. ii. 7).

It is useless to multiply further authorities; but I must tell you what one of the apostles of Jesus, a person no less than St. Paul, himself says as to the interpretation of one of the most supposedly historical portions of the Holy Bible, namely, the doings of the patriarch Abraham and his wives and sons. He writes in his Epistle to the Galatians (see chap. iv.21-26):—

"Tell me, ye that desire to be under the law, do, ye not hear the law?

"For it is written, that Abraham had two sons, the one by a bondmaid and the other by a free woman.

"But he who was of the bond-woman was born after the flesh, but he of the free woman was by promise.

"Which things are an allegory; for these are the two covenants; the one from the mount Sinai that gendereth to bondage, which is Agar.

"For this Agar is mount Sinai in Arabia, and answereth to Jerusalem which now is, and is in bondage with her children.

"But Jerusalem which is above is free, which is, the mother of us all."[4]

I think it is useless to multiply further instances. it is a clear case of non-historical documents being treated as narratives of fact. The impossible relationship of a father and a son both of whom are said to be co-eval and eternal is a sufficient reason in itself to falsify the historical sense. As I stated in the Key of Knowledge, we are not dealing here with a case where an historical *nucleus* is needed to account for Subsequent deification; the documents before us are purely mythological in nature, and cannot be construed as history. The only real person at the back of this huge tangle of mythical lore is the composer of the original work which seems to have furnished the source and substratum of the mutually contradictory accounts of the gospels; but unfortunately he has not deemed it fit to reveal himself to the world. That he' was a man of considerable wisdom and enlightenment and familiar with the Doctrine of Salvation, as a science, is evident from his work, though, for obvious reasons, we are precluded from regarding the gospel narratives as his auto-biography.

The nature of the contradictions which exist in connection with the life of Jesus, when we try to study it from the standpoint of the historian, is so deliberate and determined that no single fact can be seized as an actual event in the world of men. There is piling up of allegory upon allegory and metaphor upon metaphor, on the one hand, and a delightful determination to violate the order of events, invent personalities, defy facts, disregard chronology, and, in every possible way, to act as if history were only meant to be topsy-turvy, on the other. The inference is plain: the narrators were anxious to guard against being understood in the historical sense, and took every precaution to set it at nought. The gospels, thus, constitute the records of the spiritual progress of "Jesus", the soul, rather than so many editions of the "Life arid Teachings of Jesus, the Man", written by so many writers.

Our theory, then, is that the Biblical contradictions, like those of the Hindu Scriptures, are either due to a deliberate effort on the part of the gospelwriters to discredit the historical sense,[5] or arise as a natural consequence of mythological symbology. We shall presently see that this theory will not only prove to be the true explanation but will also at once bring the teaching of the Bible in a line with the earlier scriptures, reconciling it with the true scientific view of things at the same time. Let me repeat that I am not the first in the field of interpretation; other thinkers, too, have arrived at the same conclusions.

"The spirit intended," says the author of the Influence of Greek Ideas and Usages on the Christian Church (p. 78), "the spirit intended in all such narratives on the one hand to reveal mysteries to the wise, on the other hand to conceal them from the multitude. The whole series of narratives is constructed with a purpose, and subordinated to the exposition of mysteries. Difficulties and impossibilities were introduced in order to prevent men from being drawn into adherence to the literal meaning. Sometimes the truth was told by means of a true narrative which yielded a mystical sense; sometimes, when no such narrative of a true history existed, one-was invented for the purpose."

"But I will draw your attention," writes Mr. Hatch, "to the fact that the basis of this use of the old Testament was not so much the idea of prediction as the prevalent practice of reading ancient literature as symbolical or allegorical. The method came to be applied to the books which were being formed into a new volume of sacred writings, side by side with the old. It was so applied in the first instance not by the Apologists but by Gnostics. It was detached from the idea of prediction. It was linked with the idea of knowledge as a secret" (Ibid. pp. 74-75).

Thus,

"Odyssey is the. picture of a man who is tossed upon the sea of life, drifted this way and that by adverse winds of fortune and of passion; the companions who were lost among the Lotophagi are pictures of men who are caught by the baits of pleasure and do not return to reason as their guide: the syrens are the pleasures that tempt and allure all men who pass over the sea of life, and against which the only counter charm is to fill one's senses and powers of mind full of divine words and actions, as Odysseus filled his ears with wax, that no part of them being left empty, pleasure may knock at their door in vain" (*Ibid*. page 64).

Aristobulus (about B. C. 170-150) is the earliest Jewish writer of the school of allegorists whose views have descended to us. According to him, "Moses using the figures of visible things tells us the arrangements of nature and the constitutions of important matters." Then comes Philo whose works are a veritable monument of exegetical enterprise. "They are based throughout on the supposition of a hidden meaning. But they carry us into a new world. The hidden meaning is not physical, but metaphysical and spiritual. The seen is the veil of the unseen, a robe thrown over it which marks its contour, and half conceals and half reveals the form within" (*Ibid*. pages 66.67).

It is to be noted that allegory is nota thing of recent invention or growth, even in Europe. The oldest known allegorist in that continent is Theagenes of Rheguim who wrote an 'Apology' for the Homeric poetry. As a matter of fact, the Cynical school had, with conscious purpose, reduced the allegorical interpretation of Homer to a system. Lecky in his History of European Morals (chap. iii) mentions Eusabius as his authority for the statement that the ancient Romans had divided religion into three parts—the mythology or legends that had descended from the poets; the interpretations or theories by which the philosophers endeavoured to rationalise filter or explain away these legends; and the ritual or official religious observances. We learn from the Encyclopaedia of Religion and Ethics (Vol. 1, page 328) that the Stoics undertook the completion of the system, and that under Crates of Mallus this method of interpretation extended itself to the exposition of Homer as a whole.

These views made their way into Judaism. Philo is the chief representative of this line of thought and it is certain that even before him there had been other interpreters who made use of the same method of explanation. According to Philo, Abel is pure piety without intellectual culture, Cain the Egoist, Seth, the virtue which is imbued with wisdom. Enoch is hope, Sarah virtue and wisdom, in the law; the one beloved wife is pleasure, the other who is hated is virtue. St. Paul confirms this view in his Epistle to the Galatians (chapter iv. 21-31) already referred to. With reference to another part of the O. T. Maimonides points out how the poetical narration of the account in Proverbs vii. 626 is a charming allegory, depicting the influence of the physical body as a handsome and seductive young whore. This compares very remarkably with the story of Puranjan and Puranjini in the Bhagvata Purana of the Hindus, which is a similar allegory. In the hand of Origen allegorical interpretation acquired a scientific aspect. Unfortunately much of the ancient literature is now lost, though we learn from ERE (vol. I. 331) that among the Jewish interpreters of the Bible at the present day the allegorical method is the method of interpretation which finds most favour.

Here are a few other correspondences from alleg-orical thought to show you the nature, the extent and the variety of the symbols adopted. The tree of life is a symbol of the life-giving power of the Law (ERE. xii. 144; Proberbs iii. 13 and 18); the tree of the field is man's life (Deuteronomy xx. 19); Jerusalem is a widow (Ante Nicene Christian Library ix. 33); Egypt represents the world (A. N. Ch. Lib. ix. 91); Chaldea is sensual understanding, Haran ('holes'), the five senses which are nothing without the soul, and Jordon, baseness (Forrar's Hist. of Interpretation pp. 140-141). Again, Rachel stands for contemplative virtue, and Leah, for practical virtue (*Ibid.* 23); but water is repentance (Jewish Encycl. i. 406); idolatry, love of the things made with hands (A. N. C. Lib. ix. 91); and staff[6], discipline (Hist. of Interpretation p. 141). Similarly, the seven-branched candle-stick is symbolical of the soul (ERE. xii. 144; Proverbs xx. 27), while golden vials full of odours signify prayers of saints (Revelation v. 8), and nations of the world, groups of qualities of the soul (Origen; A. N. Ch. Library vol. x. p. 234).

Again side (rib) represents the spirit of truth[7]; harps are bodies[8]; willows[9] , chastity (*e.g.*, in the text, we have hanged the harps on the willows); Zion signifies' the commandment of the watch-tower[10]; Babylon is pleasure,[11] and the rivers of Babylon stand for the streams of voluptuousness[12]. In the same way, oil stands for wisdom and Righteousness[13]; but morning signifies the coming of Christ[14]. The first born represent the sons of Satan (i.e., evil inclinations and lusts).[15] And the significance of marking the door-posts of the houses with blood is the sealing and marking of the soul with the blood of Christ that preserves it.[16] Further, whale stands for time[17]; the fig tree is the command given to man in paradise[18]; Olive is the law given to Moses in the desert[19]; and uramble represents the law given to the apostles for the salvation of the world.[20] Vine generally refers to Christ[21] ; and the fig-tree to the Holy Spirit[22], as the Lord maketh glad the hearts of men, and the Spirit healeth them. Birds are an emblem of the purification of speech (Yonge's Philo Judaeus ii. 287).

I shall now take up Islam, which, as you know, was founded a little over thirteen hundred years ago, by an Arab called Muhammad, who became ultimately intimately associated with history. The sacred book of Islam, too, is couched in mythological garh. It mostly follows the teaching of the portion known as the Old Testament of the Holy Bible-, and has a body of tradition of its own besides. There is a tablet of destiny on which Allah wrote, at the commencement of the world, with the Pen of Fate, of which however, the Jews and the Christians were both kept ignorant.

The story of Dhul Qarnein, the history of the brothers Yajuj and Majuj, and the disobedience of Satan are some of the other items of interest in Al Qur'an. That these are pure mythologies, like the fall of Adam, is hardly open to doubt in our day. As a matter of fact there was a sect of Muslims themselves who maintained that the allegorical method was the only true method of interpretation of the Quranic text. As shown in ERE (vol. ix. p. 881):

> "One of the main problems of Muslim philosophy was naturally tile definition of its relation to religion, as presented in the Qur'an and the Tradition. Many theologians more or less conscious of this problem, were already working towards its solution by spiritualising the letter of the law, having taken over from Hellenism the allegorical method ot interpreting sacred writings. Those who applied this method in thorough going fashion were called Batinites (adherents of the inner sense, [batin, 'interior', inside]). Extreme mystics, rationalists, and free-thinkers all came in this way to the same results. Another theory common to them all was that the inner sense of the word—the truth—was revealed to only a few, whether by divine enlightenment (mystics) or by one's own reflection (rationalists and free-thinkers)."

We are further informed that Muslim Aristotelians agreed with this view in the main, Averroes, for instance, holding that there was no ground for conflict between reason and faith, since tbe doctrines of religion were simply symbolical expressions of philosophic truth (Ibid).

As a matter of fact the early admiration for philosophy on the part of the leaders of Islam is clear evidence of the belief in an underlying harmony between the scriptural text and science, however, much Muslim Vandalisln may be responsihle for the destruction of knowledge in later times. The Prophet himself had, according to the Tradition, highly extolled the faculty of intellect, saying; "He dieth not who giveth (his) life to learning" (see "The Sayings of Muhammad") Ali is also reported to have said: "Philosophy is the lost sheep of the faithful; take it up again, even if from the infidel" (ERE. vol. ix. p. 878).

Muslim Aristotelians, too, we learn from the same source, held that their philosophy was the highest form of truth attainable by man. Amongst later thinkers, S'adi of Shiraz lays the greatest emphasis on knowledge when he says :

که بے علم نتواں خدا را شناخت

(he who is without knowledge cannot know God).

As for the Sufis who may be called the Gnostics of Islam, they clearly held that

> "the Koran without the interpretation was only an assembly of words void of sense." [The Dervishes, by John P. Brown p. 306].

The Sufi alone understood the purport of the book, for it was distinctly said :—

> "Paradise and Hell and all the dogmas of positive religion are only so many allegories, the spirit of which was only known to the Soofee" [*Ibid*. p. 11].

The allegorical interpretation was known as the *ma'anae batin* (hidden significance) concerning which Sufis taught:—

> "......most parts of the Koran have a hidden, inner or spiritual significance, called the.....ma'anae batin" [*Ibid*. P 106].

The Sufi also recognised that the essentials of religion were the same for all times, which, indeed, is true of all sciences. Accordingly, it was maintained:—

> "The historical and biographical portions of these books (scriptures) may even comprise errors, omissions, and

> exaggerations, and even may have been more or less changed from time to time by copyists; whilst that which is purely spiritual and essential to the soul of man commenced with his creation, has always existed unchanged and will so continue to the end of time."—*Ibid*. p 106.

The reason for the existence of allegory was not, always clear to the Sufi's mind, hut he knew that it must have been a proper one. Accordingly, one of the order declares:—

> "Why parts of it (scriptural wisdom) were veiled in allegories we scarcely dare to ask, and may only suppose that the knowledge was withheld for a good and wise cause." *Ibid* p. 21.

The secret teaching was not to be divulged to the unworthy, the penalty for violation of the rule being some form of physical violenee or chastisement. How rigorous the rule was will appear from Mr. Brown's highly interesting work ("The Dervishes," p. 183):--

> "They (the dervishes) must not divulge the secrets to their family (wives and children) nor to anyone who is not the seeker of the truth (Talib Sadik) and asks for assistance in attaiuing t() the path of God (Hakk). In that case violence must not be used towards him who does divulge them to another in the view of engaging him to join the order........"

It is thus clear that the scriptural text of Al Qur'an too, is not to be taken in the literal sense of the words, and the inclusion of such myths as the Tablet of Destiny, the eating of the forbidden fruit, and the like at once stamps the Bible of Islam as a work of the same type as the Vedas and the Books of the Old and the New Testaments. That the above conclusions are true is fully borne out by ancient Muslim tradition? and belief. The author[23] of the interesting work, entitled "Studies in Tasawwuf," who is himself a learned Muhammadan, has brought together a good deal of evidence on the subject and has thrown much interesting light on the true tenets and doctrines of the elders of the Islamic church. As to why resort was had to the hidden script by these elders, the book last named explains:—

It was not thought advisable......to deal with the subject in a plain matter of fact way, and lay bare the truth before ordinary people, whose minds were not prepared to receive them, and who mismanipulated the same........Secondly, propaganda work was best done in those days by means of poetical effusions. Poetry could not put a philosophical subject in a precise and mathematical style..............." (Intro. p. viii).

Again it is said in the same book ;—

> "......our great thinkers line made themselves purposely obscure" (Intro-. p. ix).

And still further:—

> "Direct exposition of a spiritual theme is avoided in the holy scriptures of most religions Direct facts are misleading and confusing to the ordinary man; esoteric writers and speakers have all along clothed realities in many-hued garbs, so that those who have eyes to see may see" (*Ibid* p. 1).

As a matter of fact, the Qur'an itself makes no secret of the kernel being concealed within the rind. It is said in Suratul Baqara; "God has fixed his seal in their hearts, and on their ears; and before their eyes there is a great curtain, and for them is great calamity "(Studies in Tasawwuf" p. 115). In another place the matter has been put even more clearly still: "Verily we have cast veils over their hearts, lest they should understand the Qur'an, and unto their ears caused thickness of hearing" (quoted in the "Studies in Tasawwuf," p. 2).

As in Hinduism and other religions, technical terms were coined with a double purport, the outer and the inner, *i.e.*, the plain and the hidden. The outer, *i.e.*, the plain significance was intended as a mask, the inner and the hidden was what really mattered. Thus animal signifies lust; man, the mind; jin, suspicions of the mind; bones, mountains; arteries and veins rivers and streams; and the stomach, ocean; hairs represent trees; teeth the carnivora; birds spirituality. The face stands for populated areas; the back, for the barren land; infancy means spring; youth, summer; old age, winter; and dotage, autumn.

Angels are good affections; Gabriel signifies the tongue; Israfael, the nose; Michael the body, and Israel, the ears.

I think it is advisable to stop here for the day. We shall do more systematic explorations in mythology tomorrow, and shall take up the different systems one by one.

(B)

We shall today undertake to solve same of Hindu mythologies ourselves. To begin with the god Ganesha, who insists an being invited before other gods, he is described as

(i) riding an a rat;:

(ii) having a body composed of a human trunk and an elephant's head;

(iii) the youngest of gods;

(iv) yet the most mischievous, if neglected at the commencement of an undertaking;

(v) engaged in eating a *laddu* (an Indian sweet-meat ball); and

(vi) called, *ek danta*, because of his having only one tusk instead of two in his trunk.

This child-god has hitherto defied unravelment, because the scholars have only searched in the outside world for the object which he represents. The true secret was given in the Key of Knowledge for the first time in this age. Ganesha represents Intellect or Wisdom, as is evident from the following correspondences:—

(i) the rat, which is chiefly known an account of cutting up things, is a symbol for analysis;

(ii) Ganesha himself with an elephant's trunk joined to a human body is the very form of synthesis (piecing up or putting together);

(iii) Wisdom is the youngest of gods (divine qualities), because the soul that has wandered in transmigration for the whole of the past eternity of time acquires it only when about to obtain salvation:

(iv) though the youngest of gods Wisdom or Intellect insists on being the first to be consulted at the commencement of an undertaking, disaster being but a natural result of its being neglected;

(v) the *laddu* represents the fruit of Wisdom, since the wise naturally enjoy happiness (sweets);

(vi) *Ek-danta* stands for the true monistic view that the real God for every individual is, only one, namely, his own soul, to associate another with whom is the deadliest of sins. This is the final conclusion Wisdom ultimative establishes.

Such is the charming personality of Ganesha. It is interesting as well as instructive. The original composer of this elegant impersonation was, as we learn from the visiting card, hidden in the missing tusk, a learned thinker whose knowledge of the Science of Life turns out to be as exact as it is astonishing. Ganesha to whom we have just had the pleasure of being introduced is, thus, not the outcome of a primitive savage mind bent on presonifying wind, clouds or rain, but an idolising, in poetical garb, of the mast essential element for salvation as is clear from such texts as rite *jnanan na mukti* (no salvation without knowledge).

Having offered our obeisance to the divinity of Wisdom, we shall now proceed to study the scheme of the Vedic gods. As Savana, the most distinguished of the Vedic commentators, says, there are three principal gods that are really reducible to one in the Vedas. These are Surya, Indra and Agni, who have been grossly misunderstood by one and all in modern times.

Now, in order to understand their nature fully, it is necessary to bear in mind the scientific truths established by us in an earlier lecture. I shall summarise them for facility of reference once more.

(i) The soul is a substance which is endowed with potential Omniscience, that is to say, which will be omniscient but for the clogging impurities adhering to it.

(ii) The impure soul is constantly engaged in traffic with the outside world through the doorways of the senses, and undergoing metempsychosis.

(iii) The means to the attainment of divinity and perfection is *tapas* (severe self-denial, *i.e.*, asceticism).

In other words, every soul is a *paramatman* (God) in potency; it is, however, a *jivatman* (unredeemed or impure ego) so long as it is involved in matter; and escape from matter is possible through *tapas*.

The three subjects which everyone desirous of obtaining salvation must study are, therefore,

(i) the nature of the soul-substance,

(ii) the characteristics of an impure *jiva*, and

(iii) the method of its purificatlon.

These three, I must now tell you, are also the subjects which are represented by the three principal gods—Surya, Indra and Agni—in the scheme of the Vedic Pantheon.

(i) Surya is a symbol for Omniscience for, as the sun reveals all objects when it rises in the sky, so does Omniscience reveal all objects of knowledge when it arises in the soul;

(ii) Indra stands for an impure ego, trafficking with the world through *indriyas* (the senses); and

(iii) Agni is *tapas* personified, which is the cause of salvation.

In a detailed way, Indra

(i) committed adultery with a Brahmana Preceptor's wife,

(ii) in consequence of which he was afflicted with ugly disease spots all over his body;

(iii) these were later turned into eyes at the intervention of Brahma.

(iv) Indra is also the father of his own father.

The correspondence of these peculiarities is as follows:—

(i) (a) The adultery is the penetration of spirit into matter, a forbidden act, since emancipation only signifies release from the embrace of matter.

(b) Life and Intellect are the two faculties of the soul of which Life is *continuous* or enduring but Intellect subject to vicissitudes, *e.g.*, its suspension in sleep.

(c) The source of education to Life is Intellect, external books and teachers being only instrumental but not the real causes.

(d) Intellect is as a rule inclined towards matter, and but rarely turns to the study of Life, e.g., European Intellectualism which has hitherto been confined to 'soulless' materialism[24] The conception of the penetration or entry of pure spirit into matter is that of a forbidden act (adultery) with what is most in-timately related to (hence the wife of) Intellect, that is the true teacher of life (hence its *guru*).

(ii) The disease-marks are the ignorant *jivas*, the product of the interaction between spirit and matter; they are 'blind' at first on account of ignorance.

(iii) But when they become self-conscious in consequence of Brahman *Jnana* (prayer to Brahma) their eyes are, as it were, opened. Hence, Brahma is said to have converted the ugly spots on the body of Indra into eyes.

(iv) Indra is the father of his own father, because,

(a) the term father is a symbol for what is termed the material cause of a thing, and

(b) because the material cause of it purified spirit is an impure ego; while the latter is itself the product of the union of pure spirit and matter. Hence, is the one conceived as the source (father) of the other.

Such briefly is the nature of Indra and snch the description of his highly reprehensible adultery with a Brahmanȧ preceptor's wife. We have no time to go into further details here, but it may be stated that the enemy of this god is the demon of darkness which stands for ignorance, and the rain that is associated with his name is the peaceful shower of *shanti* (tranquillity) which descends when the heat of passions and *mithyatva* (error) has subsided.

Agni, the third member of this most important trio, is the symbolisation of *tapas* already stated. We saw how irrelevant and absurd it was to treat this deity as a personification of fire or the culinary art; but the relevancy of *tapas* needs no demonstration. Even the word *Agni* (fire) is the most appropriate one for *tapas*; because asceticism is really the purification of the mind by the fire of *vairagya*, or the *baptism* of *fire*, as it is termed in the sacred books of Christianity.

As for the special characteristics of Agni, the god

(i) has three feet,

(ii) seven hands, and

(iii) seven tongues:

(iv) he is the priest of gods who appear at his invocation;

(v) he is the devourer of the clean and the unclean both, and

(vi) the giver of strength to gods, so that the more he is fed by sacrificial oblations, the greater is the strength imparted to gods.

The Explanation of these highly artistic conceptions is as follows:

(i) *Tapas* rests on three kinds of controls, namely,

(a) the control of the mind,

(b) the control of the body, and

(c) the control of speech.

There can be no *tapas* if only two of these controls are exercised, and there is no fourth thing to coptrol. Because *tapas* rests on these three kinds of controls, it is said to have three legs or feet.

(ii) The seven hands probably represent the seven kinds of occult powers that are acquired by ascetics. As power is exercised by hands generally, these seven kinds of occult powers are described as the seven hands of Agni.

(iii) The seven tongues are the five senses, *manas* or mind, and *buddhi* (intellect), which are to be offered up asa sacrifice to Agni.

(iv) As the divine attributes of the soul become manifest by the practising of *tapas*, Agni is said to be the priest of gods (= divine attributes) who appear at his invocation.

(v) Virtue and vice are both causes of bondage, the former leading to pleasant and the latter to unpleasant kinds of rebirths. Both of them have to be given up ultimately for pure self-contemplation. Hence *Agni* is the devourer of the clean (virtue) and the unclean (vice) both.

(vi) The food of Agni is self-sacrifice, i.e., the sacrificing of desires, because asceticism consists in curbing one's desires. The divine qualities and attributes of the soul are developed and strengthened by the destruction of desires. These divine qualities and attributes are termed gods in the language of symbolism. Hence, the gods are strengthened by the offering of sacrifices to Agni.

Such is the character of Agni, which as you are aware, is not only venerated by the Hindus but also by the followers of the Zend Avesta. The entire scheme of the Vedic mythology is thus clearly reducible to the following important points;

(1) the individual soul is its own Gods—the *jivatman* and the *paramatman* are one;

(2) the pure soul is fully divine, being endowed with Omniscience which is a mark of divinity;

(3) this natural divinity of the soul is marred by its union with matter; and

(4) asceticism is the path which leads to Perfection and Godhood.

We thus see that the Vedic Mythology is nothing but an expression in symbolical language of some of the most important scientific truths about Life. The subject is highly interesting, but I cannot offord to (dwell any longer on it. You will find it discussed in my "Key of Knowledge" which deals with different mythologies in a cosmopolitan spirit of enquiry. Another book to which I would like to refer you in this connection is the Permanent History of Bharatavarsha that has already been quoted in yesterday's lecture. It is a compilation containing an explanation of hundreds of mythological symbols for which the authar qnotes chapter and verse, though no attempt is made at an original study, by determining the correspondences of the allegorical attributes of the diverse gods and goddesses.

It would seem that the Hindu mind at one time evolved out a mania for personification, and devoted itself whole-heartedly to adorning the progeny of its exuberant thought in all sorts of ways. Not one ward of its sacrad literature is therefore valid historically not even the narratives of the Ramayana and the Mahabharata, though they are in the nature of historical allegories. Its indicatians of time and place are as unreal scientifically as thc persanages associated with them.

Vasishta *rishi* is not a human being but a symbol, expressing *sruti* (revelation), while Vishvamitra is meditatian (*manana*),[25] their quarrels signify the canflict between revelation and reason which his fairly common with mystic creeds. *Sruti*, however, always triumphs in the end, and so we have *Vasishta* overcoming his rival The fourteen *lokas* (regions) are 'the fourteen *shānas* or positions assigned to man in his religious development.' The creation of the world has reference to the 'peopling' of the mind with spiritual thoughts; preservation signifies the development of spiritual life; and destruction is of the evil tendencies and traits. Brahma, the creator, is thus, the spiritual *buddhi* (intellect) that reduces the mental chaos into orderly thought, peopling the mind with holy conceptions and ideas. Vishnu, the Preserver, is *dharma* which is the cause of increased merit; he preserves what Brahma has created and nothing else. Lastly, Shiva or Mahesha is *vairagya* (desirelessness or renunciation) that is the destroyer of the forces of *karma* and evil. From another point of view, Rishabha is *dharma*, Bharata, the son of Rishabha, devotion, and *bull* the symbol of *dharma*. *Jambudvipa* is the devotional sphere for the mortal man, and Bharatavarsha, the processes and scope of devotional *karmas*. Kurukshetra is the psychic *chakra* (plexus) at the junction of the nose and eyes in tin human body; Prayag, in the heart, Mathura, the thousand-petalled lotus, in the head, and Gobardhana is the mind. Haridwar stands for dispassion, the Ganges, the Jamna and the Saraswati, for the three nerve-currents known respectively as the *Ida*, the *Pingala*, and the *Sushumna*; and *yugas* are divisions of *tapas*, with the human body reckoned as a year. The *avataras* (incarnations of deity) are the gradual steps on the path of *dharma*, leading to the goal of perfection.

Amongst the 'revolting' myths, we have the *lingum* and the *yoni* rapresenting joy. Since sexual union is conceived to be the highest form of earthly joy, it naturally becomes the symbol of the spiritual joy which the worshippers of Shiva (*vairagya*) obtain on Emancipation. The same import is to be understood in connection with the grotesquely vulgar and obscene statues that have been placed on the dome of the temple of Jagan Nath at Puri.

I must now turn to the great Hindu Epic, the Mahabharata, which is one of the most ingenious of its kind. The central figure in this wonderful story is, of course; Krishna; but the other personifications are also very instructive and striking. Karana, for instance, is born wearing a coat of mail and golden ear-rings in his ears. He represents Duty, being born ready for action; and being decorated with the distinction of Nobility, namely, the ear-rings, he belongs to the class of virtues. Another interesting personification is that of Shikhandi who was born a girl, but who longed to be a boy and was made one by the gods, on his supplication The great Warrior Chief, Bhishama, refused to raise his hand against him, although attacked by him, saying it was not proper for a soldier to wage war against at woman. Now, Shikhandi simply stands for a Boaster, who is timid (a girl) at heart, but wishes to pass himself off as a hero.

Krishna is the Lord of *Gopis*, and the Protector of the Kine. He is the Hindu Messiah, the Saviour God and the Guide of the souls. But I can here only just harely touch upon the basic principles of this personification in the briefest way, considering that the events of his life have filled whole *puranas*. The need for the elucidation of this impersonation is also not very pressing now that we have an authoritative Hindu *exposition* (The Permanent History of Bharatvarsha) of the whole of the mythical teaching of the Mahabharata, including the part assigned to Krishna. In a general way, when the fruition of good *karmas* leads an individual to turn to his inner self, the conception of the divinity of the soul is formed by the intellect, and the quickening of his spirit takes place in consequence of the acquisition of Right Faith. St. Paul aptly describes this in the following terms:

> "And so it is written, The first man Adam was made a living soul; the last Adam was made a quickening spirit" (1 Cor. xv. 45).

This quickening of spirit is the birth of Krishna, the true Saviour of man; for when fully quickened, the soul is itself transformed into a full, perfect God. For this reason, Krishna is the abode of all Godly attributes. He is the Lora Gopis and Gopas (sacred hymns, rites etc., etc.).

At an early period in life he subdues the Serpent-King, Kaliya, which has already been explained, as representing *manas* (desires). When lndra (the impure ego) endeavours to interfere with the cows, Krishna raises the Gobardhana hill (the desiring manas) on the tip of his little finger and thus protects the kine. The luring of *gopis* from the beds of their husbands in the darkness of night, the giddy moon-light dances on the banks of the Jamuna, the stolen kisses and embraces, all of which would be highly condemnable from a moral point of view, if ascribed to an actual being, are fully appropriate for Messiah, or Christos. For Krishna is the divine ideal for the soul (*gopi*), to pour forth all her affection upon. She must wander out in the solitude of night (when the mind is not occupied with worldly things) on the banks of the placid Jamuna (mind stuff, hence the mind), disregarding both her love for the husband (worldly attachments) and the fear of society. When she stands before the Redeemer, stripped of her clothes (worldly possessions), when she gives up even the last vestige of feminine modesty, and, standing upright joins her hands above her head, disregardful of her nudity and the rules of worldly decorum, then is the notion of duality between the Lover and the Object of Love dispelled from the mind, and the fruit of Love enjoyed.

The hopes and fears of the love-lorn *gopis*, their neglect of their household duties, their abandonment of their children and husbands, their passionate yearnings to be enfolded in the arms of the Beloved—all these are pure allegories, describing the degree of devotion or zeal necessary for the realisation of the great ideal of perfection, personified as Christos or Krishna, the Redeemer (The Key of Knowledge).

The birth[26] of Krishna is a symbol for the commencement of the greatest battle (the Mahabharata) that the soul has ever fought. The *quickening* spirit cannot remain idle; there is work to be done; the business of the Father (in Christian thought) must be attended to. It is said in St. Luke's Gospel:-

"Every valley shall be filled, and every mountaill and hill shall be brought low; and the crooked shall be made straight, and the rough ways shall be made smooth (Luke. iii. 5).

But this work is not to be done unopposed; there are the Giants of Darkness to be reckoned with, and they are prepared for fight. Then is there a gathering of clans; heroes are born, warriors trained, armies assembled. Under the guidance of Krishna,[27] the frail, doubting soul (Arjuna) engages the enemy hosts in mortal combat. At last, Evil is overpowered, victory attained, and the bondage overthrown. Then there is *nirvana* and joy and bliss, with no more battles to fight, no enemies to be dreaded or conquered!

Such briefly is the purport of the Mahabharata. Some times this mortal combat is described as a war between *devas* (divine beings) and *asuras* (demons of darkness and fury). The leader of the *devas* is Indra, and they fight well when he is in their midst. This is because the *devas* are only so many attributes of the soul and have no existence apart from it. The enemies of the gods are the forces of darkness (ignorance) and fury (passion). The *devas* are immortal, though liable to suffer defeat at times; but the *asuras* are mortal. The explanation is that the divine qualities of, the soul are really the attributes of the soul-substance, which may be curtailed, limited, or suspended from time to time but can never be completely destroyed, while ignorance and passions are the products of a soul vitiated by the union of matter, and must disappear completely on their separation from one another. Most of the world's mythologies contain stories of such wars between the *devas* of Light and the powers of Darkness and Evil. The Celtic, the Teutonic and the Greek systems of mythologies seem to have been conceived on a gigantic scale, though nowhere near approaching the grandeur of the Hindu Epics; but owing to spoliation on the part of their pious and "enlightened" translators, these "pagan" myths rarely yield their secret through the medium of modern European works. The Greeks, however, openly applied the allegorical method of interpretation to their sacred literature, and a solution of some of the classical legends has also been given by me in the 'Key of Knowledge.' But I must not linger any longer over this fascinating subject

This much I think will suffice for our understanding of the mysteries of the great Mahabharata.

Turning now to the Ramayana, I need only refer you the work known as the Adhyatama Ramayana, which seeks to explain the allegory of Rama's story, though the language is involved and often puzzling. There is a smaller book also on the subject which is rather excellent, and which I have translated into English. This is known as the Atma Ramayana, the Ramayana, of the Soul. The author of the original work is a Hindu *sannyasin* (ascetic), and he has taken pains to elucidate the whole story. I shall give you a brief account of the allegory, to enable you to perceive its beauty for yourself.

Dasaratha, the king of Ajudhya, prays for the birth of the great Vishnu as his son. This wish of his is granted, and he begets 4 sons from his three queens. Rama Chandra, or simply Rama, is the eldest and the incarnation of the deity. The seer Vasishta one day called to take a way Rama and his full brother Lakshamana, while they were still in their teens to fight certain demons, who were interfering with his sacrifice. The boys successfully accomplished the undertaking. Rama is thence taken to Janakapur where he marries the lovely princess Sita, after proving his skill, at a great gathering of veteran fighters and chiefs, by breaking a terrible Bow, which no one could bend. Afterwards he is appointed the heir apparent by his father which causes uneasiness to Kekai the mother of Bharata. She ultimately succeeds in her designs, and makes the king to exile Rama for a period of 14 years from his kingdom. Lakshamana and Sita accompany Rama into the forests where they are to spend the term of the exile. Here Sita is abducted by a powerful demon king, the redoubtable Ravana, and carried off to the distant Lanka; but Ravana does not succeed in winning her favour.

Rama comes across the Monkey host in the course of his wanderings in search of his wife, and with their aid invades Lanka. A terrible battle is fought at the gates of Lanka; Ravana is killed; and Sita released. Rama thence returnes to his kingdom, and takes over the reins of the government from Bharata, who had succeeded on his father's death in the interval to the throne, but who had remained loyal to the rightful successor.

The significance of the story is as follows: Dasaratha is the mind that has acquired control over its activity, and is desirous of obtaining the boon of Wisdom Divine. Such a mind naturally speedily obtains knowledge of the Truth, so we witness the birth of Rama (representing Divine Knowledge) to him. But Wisdom Divine does not dwell anywhere alone; it has Discrimination (Lakshamana); Meditation (Shatrughna) and Renunciation (Bharata) as its inseparable companions; and these are accordingly born to Dasaratha also.

The ascetic Vishwamitra is Faith which is disturbed in its devotional practices (sacrifice) by Desire (the interfering demon), whom Rama soon puts to flight by telling the saint that the element of disturbance realy only resided in his own heart. This only means that Desire is soon curbed and subdued by a study of its nature and consequences. In other words, Knowledge Divine is the destroyer of Desire and the longings of the Heart.

Janakapur is also called Videha, which means bodilessness, and is a good symbol for *nirvana* in which state the soul exists without the material body. Sita is the daughter of Janaka, the king of Janakapur, and means Divine Tranquillity or Bliss. The Bow that Rama destroys is the sense of egoity or self-love.

Kekai is Action which is naturally opposed to the Inaction of Wisdom; she cannot abide with Wisdom, and plans to have it sent away. Rama is thus turned out from his home. But Discrimination (Lakshmana) and Divine Bliss do not stay behind, and accompany Rama in exile.

Rama now assumes the role of the aspiring soul who is seeking Spiritual Perfection. He has to part with Tranquillity for this reason. She is carried off by IGNORANCE (Ravana), who is the King of demons. In the course of his wanderings Rama comes across the Monkey King, Sugriva (Contentment), and his generalissimo Hanuman (Good Company). With the aid of the Monkey Host (Holy Practices) Ignorance is destroyed and Sita released. The party now return home, and are welcomed by Bharata (Renunciation) who has no more work left to do.

Here is a further list of the remaining important personifications in this interesting poem. Agasta (the doctrine of non-dual Unity); Ahilya (Forgiveness); Ahiravana (Hatred); Ayodhya (5 Envelopes of the Soul); Akriya (Arrow); Angada (Angerlessness); Anusuya (Patience); Atri (non-Action); Bali (Greed); Asoka Batika (Freedom from Grief); Boat (a form of Contemplation); Bridge (sport); Chitrakuta (Divine Status); Churamani (Faith); Deer (Illusion) ; Dhanusha (Egoism); Drona-giri hill (Scripture) ; Gotama (Asceticisim) ; Jala (Water, Desired Object); Jatayu (Religion); Kaushalya (Actionlessness); Khardushana (Infatuation); Kumbhakarana (Anger); Kushaketu (Salvation); Lanka (Error); Maricha (self-love); Mandavi (Understanding); Meghanada (Attachment); Narada (Detached Action); Pampa Lake (Deep Meditation); Panchabati (Control of the 5 Senses); Parasurama (Love) ; Ring (the Divine Message); sailor (the Seeker after Truth); Sajivana Herb (Basic Truth); Shakti (Seducement) ; Sampati, the Eagle (Intelligence) ; Shavri (Unreasoning Devotion, or Love) ; Sphatika Slab (Pure Heart); Sulochana (Indulgence) ; Sumitra (Devotion); Surpanakha (Thirst for Pleasure); Sushena (Passion, Affection); Sutikshana (Dispassions); Taraka (Doubt); Urmila (Meekness); Forest (Fearlessness) ; Valmika (Restraint); Vibhishana (Right Action); and Yajna (Sacrifice, i.e., Self-Contemplation).

I think this much will suffice for an insight into Hindu Mythology and the Allegorist's work. We shall carry on our investigation in other directions tomorrow.

(C)

I shall now proceed to unravel the doctrine of the 'fall' which is the basis of Judaism and Christianity.

To begin with, you must banish from your minds the notion that there ever was a spot on the earth or in heaven, known as

Eden, where a Supreme Being planted a grove of beautiful trees once upon a time. We have seen in the quotation from Origen, how absurd such a supposition really is. If you try to picture to yourself further the two famous trees, that of Life and that of Knowledge of Good and Evil, you will see the absurdity of the supposition becoming still more ridiculous. Then, why should knowledge of Good and Evil be forbidden to man? Why, again, should he be punished so cruelly for just one piece of the fruit as to be cursed and turned out of the Garden, to become subject to death, and to have his children and grand-children, and their remotest descendants, down to the very last man, inflicted with wretchedness and misery?

And if the punishment was what was intended from the very first—and an omniscient god must be deemed to have known from the very outset that Adam will prove disobedient—why do we find Jehovah repeatedly sending down prophets for the guidance of the fallen humanity? Could he not redeem them with a word, just as he had cursed them with a word?

If you ponder over these and other similar questions that arise on the literal interpretation of this legend, you will agree with Origen that it is not to be taken as a narrative of facts. Its purport is hidden like the purport of the Vedic deities.

I shall now place before you the esoteric interpretation of this fable.

(1) The Garden of Eden is a representation of the attributes of the soul.

(2) The Tree of Life and the Tree of Knowledge of Good and Evil are two such attributes that are the most important of all; hence, they grow in the centre.

(3) Adam is the individual ego that has reached the stage of evolution known as "human birth."

(4) Eve is Sensual Pleasure that is made from Adam's rib taken out in sleep—an apt simile since the Pleasure

impulse is only a hidden longing with which the ego is equipped and associated in the state of waking.

(5) Man alone is qualified for salvation and therefore entitled to be taught *dharma* (religion). Animals are debarred from salvation because of their general deficiencies in respect of intellect and other bodily and mental functions. Even the residents of heavens and hells are not entitled to salvation, because they are not fitted to perform *tapas*. Hence, 'man is the principal recipient of *dharmic* injunctions.

(6) The Tree of Life represents Life itself, and the Tree of Knowledge of Good and Evil, the determination of the value of external things.

(7) The fruit (consequence) of knowledge of good and evil represents what are termed *raga* (attachment) and *dvesha* (aversion), because we long to possess what we regard as good and to destroy what is bad. If you will now pause for a moment to ponder over the nature of good and evil you will find that they are not concrete things, nor even constants in nature, but mere terms of comparison. In the already noticed instance the birth of an heir is hailed with joy by the childless millionaire, but it is the actual source of despair and gloom to the expectant reversioner. The child is himself but an event; it is auspicious, lucky and therefore good to its parents; but the source of lifelong despair and misery to those whom its presence debars from stepping into the jewelled shoes of the millionaire. In the breast of the former it excites love and affection (attachment), in that of the latter hatred and anger (aversion). Thus, attachment and aversion are the fruits of the 'tree of knowledge of good and evil.

(8) Attachment and aversion (*raga* and *dvesha*) are the two general forms of desire, which is the cause of

bondage, as demonstrated in an earlier lecture. Hence, the injunction against the fruit of the Tree of Knowledge of Good and Evil.

(9) The soul is immortal by nature being a simple substance, but birth and death are imposed on it on account of its embodied condition. Hence, the statement: "In the day that thou eatest thereof thou shalt surely die" (Genesis, ii. 17). It is noticeable that Adam did not die on the day that he ate of the forbidden fruit, but lived for a very considerable period of time thereafter, dying at the age of 930 (Genesis, v. 5). The true interpretation of the text of Genesis, ii. 17, then, can only be this that the liability to death is incurred as the result of the eating of the forbidden fruit.

(10) The force of desire which drags the soul away from the path of *dharma* to what is forbidden is the serpent through which came the temptation.

(11) The ego entangled in the discrimination of good and evil of the objects of the senses has no knowledge of the true nature of the Soul—that it is the true God—and hides himself from external deities through superstition.

(12) Adam throws the blame for the evil deed on his pleasure-seeking nature (Eve), while Eve asserts that she was misled and overpowered by desire (the serpent). This is fully in keeping with the psychological functions of the will, or ego and desire. For the will is addicted to pleasure, and pleasure is itself rooted in desire.

(13) The punishments of the transgressors are all descriptive of the nature of the diverse functions and attributes of the will, the intellect and the *manas* (desires collectively).

(a) The serpent is cursed above all cattle, and above every

beast of the field. It is to go upon its belly and to eat dust all the days of its life. The element of sensuality (the serpent) may degrade one even below the level of the lowest beasts and brutes; hence is sensuality rated below the lowest grades of "cattledom". The *manas* (sensuality) is constantly engaged in trafficking with matter (that is in extracting and imbibing the raw material of sensations from the objects outside). This raw material of sensations, constantly pouring in through the door-ways of the senses is the "dust" which the serpent (*manas*) is to eat all the days of its life. Desires are finally subdued by asceticism, as the result of true Wisdom. This is beautifully described in the Hindu Books as the subduing of the Serpent-king, Kaliya, by the Child Krishna, the latter being, not an *avatara* of an extra cosmic divinity, but only the allegorical representation of the divine Ideal of Perfection, as we have already seen.

The serpent-sacrifice instituted by Jenamejaya is another beautiful allegory of the sacrificing of desires (see The Mahabharata or Karma Yoga, by K. N. Iyre, B.A., pp.191 *et seq*). According to the Book of Genesis (iii. 14) the serpent is also doomed to go on its belly. This is because sensuality can never aspire to soar to spiritual heights, never having a moment's respite from the enjoyment of *vishaya-bhogas* (objects of sensual pleasure) to pause for self-contemplation.

(b) The curse on Eve is also fully descriptive of the nature of Pleasure. Her sorrow and conception are greatly multiplied. "In sorrow shalt thou bring forth children, and thy desires shall be to thy husband, and he shall rule over thee" (Genesis. iii. 16). Pleasure is governed by the Will, her husband in allegorical speech; her children are the niceties and refinements and novelties which are ever sought by pleasure-seekers to escape from the boredom of *ennui* and dull in sipidity, which are the source of perennial worry (sorrow) to her.

(c) The curse on Adam is also typical of the nature of the impure ego:

(i) "Cursed in the ground for thy sake;

(ii) "in sorrow shalt thou eat of it all the days of thy life;

(iii) "thorns also and thistles shall it bring forth to thee; and thou shalt eat the herb of the field;

(iv) "in the sweat of thy face shalt thou eat bread, till thou return into the ground for out of it wast thou taken: for dust thou art and unto dust shalt thou return"—(Genesis, in 17-19).

The significance of these terms is that the distress, privations, wars and suffering that appear on the earth are the result of the lusts, vices, villainy and hypocrisy of man; that not withstanding all his efforts to rule over the world or the empire of nature, only thistles and thorns shall be the lot of the greedy lustful man; and that it is not in the province of a soul-less materialism to impart the true strength that only comes from Religion. The term ground means the soul-substance, that is afflicted (cursed) in various ways by the ego's misbehaviours and lustful actions. As for the earthly nature of the ego, there are three kinds of personalities:—

(i) the *bahiratman* (the lower ego).

(ii) the *antaratman* (the soul), and

(iii) the *paramatman* (God).

The foolish man only looks upon himself as the bodily self that is a pure compound of matter, perishable and mortal. The enlightened man knows himself as a soul that is immortal and to be perfected, when he shall become a *paramatman* (God). It is the first kind of conception of the self, the *bahiratman*, of the fallen ego, that is described in the Biblical curse.

(14) After the fall Abel and Cain are born to Adam, of whom Abel is the keeper of sheep and Cain, the tiller of soil. They both take the offerings of their respective occupations before God, but Abel's offering is approved and not Cain's. Cain thereupon murders Abel, for which he is cursed by God. Seth (the appointed) was the next son of Adam, and Seth's son was Enos: "then began men to call themselves by the name of the Lord" (see Marginal Notes to Genesis, iv. 26).

(15) Now, Abel is faith which is turned towards life, while Cain is reason wedded to matter. Hence, is Abel a keeper of sheep (the symbol of Life) and Cain, the tiller of soil (=Matter). The offerings of the brothers signify the fruit of their respective occupations, Abel's consisting in the best products in the department of Life—gentility of the 'lamb' (*uttama-arjava*=excellent meekness), and the like—and Cain's, in the highest achievements—electric light, aero-planes., etc. etc.,—of a purely material science. Abel's work is naturally acceptable to God, the Ideal of divine perfection and joy, because virtues like *uttama arjava* are really the first steps on the "path." But reason and Faith are incompatible by nature, for the one is critical and the other dogmatic. For this reason is Abel murdered by Cain.

(16) The curse pronounced on Cain is also in keeping with the nature of Reason and has been fully explained in the fourth chapter of the Key of Knowledge. Here we have no time to go into the subject. But Seth which means the appointed is the divine Wisdom which is to take the place of the murdered Abel (unreasoning faith). It is Enos, the child of divine Wisdom, who calls himself by the name of the Lord, that is to say, who regards himself as a God.[28]

Such is the true purport of the legend of the fall in the

Jewish Scripture It is not a narrative of the anger of an omniscient god at the petty transgressions of a couple of puny mortals, nor a nursery tale composed by a primitive savage humanity, soon ofter its emergence from the monkey race; but a description of some of the most valuable principles of a spiritual science, the psychological analysis of which is more exact and rational than anything known to what is termed science in our day.

I shall now tell you the purport of the Abraham story, as explained by St. Paul (see Galatians iv. 21-31). The text has already been quoted in full by me in a previous lecture. The bond woman is the condition of the bondage of the soul, while Jerusalem represents the state or condition of the spiritual nature. Hence, Hagar (the bondwoman) is symbolical of Jerusalem which now is, that is to say of the present condition of (the spiritual nature of) the unredeemed soul. But Jerusalem that is above is Spirit in its natural purity, free) from all kinds of bondaga and bonds. The son of the bond-woman is the apparent or outer ego, the lower self; and the son of the free woman is the Real or Higher Self that is to be saved. But the lower self is the fleshly lustful ego of desires, and the persecuter of the Real Self. Hence, is he to be cast out, so that the true Self may enter into life that is glorious and blissful and eternal. The barren woman is the spiritual nature that is at present destitute of divine attributes. She is the one that is bidden to rejoice, for she shall soon bring forth the glorious divinity and the infinity of divine attributes, on the acquisition of Right Faith. Thus, Isaac and Ishmael stand for two different types of Men, the former representing those who are promised the Crown of Glory by Life, on perfection in respect of Faith and Knowledge and Conduct, and the latter, the ordinary humanity that are characterized by ignorance and (unrighteous) living after the flesh. These types are also referred to in the ninth chapter of the Epistle to Romans from which I shall quote only the relevant portion:—

6. "…….for they are not all Israel, which are of Israel.

7. "Neither, because they are the seed of Abraham, are they all children: but, in Isaac shall thy seed be called.
8. "That is, they which are the children of the flesh, these are not the children of God; but the children of the promise are counted for the seed."

Read literally, that is in the historical sense, it will be absurd to say that an the children of Israel are not Israel, or those of Abraham, not the seed of Abraham! But from the spiritual standpoint, the allegorical reading is fully in harmony with the Teaching of Truth with which alone is Religion concerned. We also read in Galatians (chap. iii. 29):—

"And if ye be Christ's, then are ye Abraham's seed, and heirs according to promise."

It is needless to say that the Jewish allegorists, both before St. Paul's time and afterwards, held exactly the view which he takes of the life story of the "Patriarch".

According to Philo Judaeus, too, Abraham stands for a man who is really wise. Noah is righteousness, and his three sons Shem, Ham and Japheth, respectively represent what is good, what is bad, and what is indifferent. Noah's ark is the symbol of the body; but Miriam is the purified outward sense (Yonge's Philo Judaeus, vol. i. p. 394). Lot is the emblem of an unsteady mind; Esau is vice, or savage nature; Ephraim, memory; Manasses, recollection; Isaac, happiness. The wives of the patriarchs also represent psychological and psychical functions and aspects of Life: Eve is the pleasure-seeking outward sense; Sarah, who is described as "princess and guide" is virtue; Rebecca represents perseverance in what is good; Leah is virtue, fainting and weary at the long continuance of exertion; Zipporah, winged and sublime righteousness (virtue); and Agar is encyclical, that is to say, secular instruction.

Angels stand for virtues:

"For as many angles of God as there are, so many nations and species of virtue are there,"—Yonge's Philo Judaeus vol. i p. 306.

They are also regarded as *logoi* (doctrinal truths ,or knowledge) by Philo (Ibid. vol. ii. p. 307). Jacob's vision indicates the rise and fall in spirituality.

'Brother' is the body (Ibid. i. 466), since it is most nearly related to the soul. The four principal passions and the five senses taken together are termed (the nine) kings; but the term eunuch represents what is barren of wisdom. The senses are collectively the neighbour, while the near one is speech (see Exodus xxxii. 27 and Yonge's Philo Judaeus, vol. i). Amongst the animals, camel is the emblem of memory; the ass stands for labour; and sheep is improvement. Beasts and birds generally are passions. The significance of the names of the rivers is thus given by Philo: in the general sense, a river is descriptive of generic goodness; Phesion (Pison) is prudence; Gihon, courage; Tigris, temperance; Euphrates, justice; and Jordan is descent.

As regards the limbs of the human body, hand is action; bone, strength; rib, a hidden faculty or function or power. Sleep of the mind is the awakening of the outward sense, the pleasure-seeking will or impulse. Staff is discipline and asceticism.

The horseman is the mind riding on the passions which are kept under control; but he who is not able to control his passions is only a rider.

Amongst other allegories we have the description 'pleasant to the sight' as meaning what is good in theory, and 'good for food' signifying what is good in practice. The face of the earth represents sensations; the fountain of the earth is the mind; grass is the food for the senses (cattle); the green herb of the field is "that portion of the mind which is perceptible only by intellect" (Yonge's Philo Judaeus, 1. 57); heaven is mind, earth, sensation. Again, serpent is pleasure, but the brazen serpent is temperance. Fatness is mental fatness, produced by a life of pleasure.

The significance of the text which shows that Adam named all things is thus given in Philo's work:

> "The mind which is in each of us is able to comprehend all other things, but has not the capability to understand itself."—Ibid. vol. i. p. 76.

This is the reason, according to Philo, why Adam did not name himself.

Unmixed wine is excessive greed, trifling, and playing the fool (Ibid. i. 453).

In Judaism allegory is piled upon allegory in the most bewildering manner. It is said with reference to the Jewish law-giver himself that two Moseses were seen, "one alive in the spirit, the other dead in the body." The explanation of the mystery is furnished by the Lost Apocrypha of the Old Testament (see the Fragments: 'Seth'): "Wherein of course this is indicated that if thou look at the bare letter of the law, empty of all the things that we have mentioned, that is Moses dead in the body; but if thou canst take away the veil of the law, and understand that the law is spiritual, that is Moses who liveth in the spirit."

A very charming allegory in Judaism is the Vision of Ezekiel. Its meaning may be surmised from the following correspondences, which suggest themselves to the mind. The Wheel is the symbol for the cycle of transmigration. The rings that are full of eyes may stand for the innumerable incarnations, or re-births, the soul goes through in the course of transmigration. "Their appearance and their work was as it were a wheel within a wheel,"—this is so because works (*karma*) modify a soul's disposition, which is the maker of the outward appearance, that is, the physical personality and the body from within (see the Key of Knowledge). Wings are used for soaring, and represent aspiration, those covering the body entirely signifying embodiment—the embodiment, hence personification, of aspiration or ideal. The lion, the calf, which is also the young of the sea mammals (see the Imperial Dictionary), the eagle and the face of man suggest, as in the vision of St. John, the four elements of Matter, hence, the souls that are embodied in Matter (see the eleventh lecture *post*).

The 'quadruple' being, with straight legs, represents the fourfold ideal which souls have in view. It comprises Virtue and Piety (*dharma*), wealth (*artha*), pleasure (*kama*) and salvation (*moksha*). It is in the nature of an Ideal not to turn or deviate from its purpose; and because an ideal is an ideal and not a shuffling, shifting thing, the fourfold being in the vision has straight legs and goes straight forward, without turning to right or left. The calf's sole which is divided in the middle is suggestive of discrimination. The form of the Glory, in the likeness of the appearance of a man, on the appearance of a sapphire throne, that has the appearance of the colour of amber, with the appearance of fire within it, and round about it and from the loins upwards as well as downwards, that is to say, all over, is the personification of Divinity, which is KNOWLEDGE permeated with RENUNCIATION (Fire within the translucent Amber). Because the Perfect SOUL, that is a GOD, has no material body, all the reference to HIM is made in the strange way, as the likeness of the appearance of a man, on the appearance of a sapphire throne, and so on. On account of its deep rich colour the sapphire is a good representation of Right Faith. The gist of the entire symbolism may now be shortly expressed as follows: Souls involved in the corruption of Matter have the four kinds of ideals before them, of which the highest is that which leads to the attainment of the Divine Status! The departure of the Glory of God from Israel would only mean the departure from the soul of the Great Ideal; in other words, the forgetting of it on the part of the soul; and the return thereof, the re instatement of the Ideal again in the human heart.

The relation between spirit and matter has been beautifully allegorized in the following fable :

> "A certain king had all the men in his kingdom enrolled in the army and had no '*pagan*' ('civilian' we should say) but two only, one lame and one blind, and each abode separately and dwelt apart. And the king made marriage-feast for his own son and invited all that were in his kingdom, but neglected the two *pagani*, the

lame man and the blind. And they were angry in themselves and set about contriving a design against the king. Now the king had a garden, and the blind man called out from a distance to the lame man and said. 'How much would the breaking of our bread have been (what would have been the extra cost of entertaining us) with the multitudes that are invited to the merry-making? Come, then, and as he hath done to us, let us requite him.' The other asked—'In what way?' and he said, 'Let us go into his garden and destroy the things there.' But he said, 'How can I, who am lame and cannot walk?' And the blind man said, 'What can I myself do, who cannot see whither I am going? but let us devise means,' (Then the lame man) plucked the grass that was near him and plaited a rope and threw it to the blind man and said, 'Catch hold of it and come along the rope hither to me.' And when he had done what he was told and was come to the place, the lame man said, 'Come, be feet to me and carry me, and I will be eyes to thee from above and guide thee to the right and to the left' And so they did, and went down to the garden. Thee, for the rest, whether they spoiled it or not, at all events their tracks were to be seen in the garden. And when the feasters dispersed from the marriage, they went into the garden and were enraged at finding the tracks there, and reported it to the king, saying.—'We are soldiers in thy kingdom, and there is no *paganus*. Whence, then, are the tracks of the *pagani* in the garden? But the story says that the king sent for the lame and the blind men, and asked the blind man: 'Didst thou go down into the garden?' And he said, 'Alas Lord! thou seest our infirmity; thou knowest that I cannot see when I walk.' Then he came to the lame man and asked him, 'Didst thou go down into my garden?' And he answered and said, 'O Lord, wouldst thou afflict my soul in respect of my infirmity?' And then the judgment was at a standstill. What, then, does the just judge do? Having discerned in what manner the two men yoked together, he sets the lame man on the blind man's back, and examines both of them with scourges, and they cannot deny the fact. Each convicts the other, the lame man saying to the blind,

> 'Didst thou not bear me and carry me off?' And the blind to the lame, 'Didst not thou thyself become eyes to me?

The above is given *verbatim* from the Apocryphal Book of Ezekiel (see the Lost Apocrypha of the Old Testament, by M. Rhodes James, pp. 64-67). Its explanation is obvious to the thoughtful allegorist, but for the benefit of others it may be given in the words of Epiphanius who was writing against the Origenists (see the work quoted):—"God cannot separate the soul from the body for the final judgment. For immediately the judgment will be found at a standstill. For if the soul be found all by itself, it would reply when judged. 'The cause of sin is not of me, but of that contemptible and earthly body, in fornication, adultery, lascviousness. For since it left me I have done none of these things,' and it will have a good defence and will paralyse the judgment of God.......The body cannot be judged apart from the soul: for it also could reply, saying, 'It was not I that sinned, it was the soul; have I, since it departed from me, committed adultery, fornication or worshipped idols?' and the body will be withstanding the judgment of God, and with reason. On this account therefore......God.......brings our dead bodies and our souls to a second birth......."

We are not concerned here with the quarrels of Origenists and Epiphanius; but the story gives us a true insight into the nature of both spirit and matter. For pure Spirit is absolutely sinless, and matter is dead and unconscious: separately from each other, they are incapable of sinning. On page 67 of "The Lost Apocrypha of the Old Testament" the subject is again referred to in the following striking terms:—

> "The soul will say, 'I have not sinned; it is the body. Since I came out from it I have been like a pure bird that flies in the air.' The body says, 'I have not sinned; it is the soul. Since it went forth from me I have been like a stone that is thrown on the ground'."

Freedom from the clutches of tantamount to sinlessness, divinity, eternal life and glory for the soul.

Matter it is that is described as the Devil in the ancient Hebrew literature. We read in the "Lost Apocrypha," already referred to (see p. 46): "For the devil resisted, trying to deceive, saying, 'The body is mine, for I am the lord of Matter.'" He was snubbed (see the work quoted, p. 46) with, "The Lord rebuke thee, that is the Lord who is Master of all spirits." The contrast is true to nature, and constitutes one of the basic principles of Religion. Accordingly, it has been said (*loc. ci.* 54):

"But the saint of the Lord shall inherit the Glory of God
and matter is thus eternal life and His power,"

This means nothing if not the soul's becoming God which is the end in view. It was for this reason that Seth, whose name signified resurrection, was also called God (Ibid. p. 9). This is, indeed, the old Indian teaching, which maintains that the *ātman* (soul) itself becomes the *Paramātman* (the Supreme Soul, hence God) on deification, that is by ridding himself of the companionship of matter. In the Hebrew apocryphal thought, the promise to the devotee is significant:

"......I.....will raise you out of your coffins."—Ibid. 88.

This surely did not signify the raising of the dead on a specified judgment day, at the end of the world-cycle. Its true (allegorical) interpretation only is the conquest of death by attaining to immortality, so that the soul who is really divine in its real nature may on the cessation of the evil influence of matter—coffin signifying the body of flesh—attain to its inherent natural godhood. Accordingly the apocryphal doctorine puts it:

"Behold, I make the latter things as the first."—Ibid. 88,

We may compare this with the Hindu teaching, as embodied in the hymn to Yama:

"All imperfections leave behind:

Assume thy ancient frame once more—

> Each limb and sense thou hadst before,
>
> From every earthly taint refined!"

The attainment of the inherent Divinity is possible by means of *tapashcharana*; that is to say, asceticism. The story of Job is an allegorising of the severity of *tapashcharana*. For the love of God, which m.eans devotion to the Ideal of Divinity, Job had to endure all kinds of suffering. The tormentor is the Evil One (Desire in the suppressing of 'which torments have to be borne). Everything is taken away; yet Job, the personification of asceticism, remains cheerful and calm. The result is that he gets in the end much more (real Bliss) than what he loses. In Apocryphal language *tapascharana* becomes the Intelligent Fire.

> ".......a fire which distinguishes between the good and the bad......destroying the worse and preserving the better, for which reason this fire is called in the Prophets intelligent."—Ibid. 90.

The "Pistis Sophia" speaks of 'a very great, very vehement wise fire which will burn up sins' (Ibid. 90). It is to be distinguished from the ordinary fire which can only burn up the flesh.

> We say that the fire sanctifies not the flesh but the sinful soul; we do not mean the all-devouring ordinary fire, but the intelligent, that penetrates the soul that passes through the fire,"—Ibid. 90.

The baptism of fire of the Christian creed, in reality, only bears reference to this Intelligent Fire. The Holy Ghost, again, is just another form of this elegant personification.

The evil to be destroyed is described as evil spirits or giants; they arise from the association of spirit and the lustful actions of embodied beings:

> "And now, the giants, who are produced from the spirit and flesh, shall be called evil spirits upon the earth, and on the earth shall be their living,"
>
> "And the spirits of the giants afflict, oppress, destroy,

attack, do battle, and cause destruction on the earth, and cause trouble: they take no food but nevertheless hunger and thirst, and cause offences. And these spirits shall rise up against the children of men and against the women, because they have proceeded from them."—The Book of Enoch, p. 43.

It is these forces of evil, termed *karmaprakritis* in the Jaina Siddhanta, which resist the onward march of the aspiring soul. They will be destroyed completely, by individual effort, prior to the obtainment of *nirvana*. The divine powers of the soul which lie dormant now shall be revivified into activity again, or, to use the poetical language of Hebrew Mysticism,

"And in those days shall the earth also give back that which has been entrusted to it. And Sheol also shall give back that which it has received. And hell shall give back that which it owes. For in those days the Elect One shall arise,"—Ibid. p. 69.

On page 38 of the work quoted is given a somewhat graphic account of the final processes:

"And then shall the whole earth be tilled in righteousness, and shall be planted with trees and be full of blessing. And all desirable trees shall be planted on it, and they shall plant vines on it: and the vines which they plant thereon shall yield wine in abuudance and as for all the seed that is sown thereon each measure (of it) shall bear a thousand, and each measure of olive shall yield ten presses of oil. And cleanse thou the earth from all oppression, and from all unrighteousness, and from all sin, and from all godlessness: and all the uncleanness that is wrought upon the earth destroy from off the earth. And all the children of men shall become righteous, and all nations shall offer adoration and shall praise Me, and all shall worship Me. And the earth shall be cleansed from all defilement, and from all sin, and from all punishment, and from all torment, and I will never again send (them) upon it from generation to generation and for ever"

The term earth signifies the soul-substance, which prior

to its entry into *nirvana* must be purified and dressed up, like a bride, in all the most elegant and charming of 'raiments,' for it is said:

> "And in those days I will open......the store chamber of blessings which are in the heaven, so as to send them down upon the earth over the work and labour of the children of men. And truth and peace—shall be associated together throughout all the days of the world and throughout are the generations of men."—Ibid. p, 38.

The Saved Ones, we learn from the Book of Enoch (p. 34) "shall all live and never again sin." They shall spend in "eternal gladness and peace all the days of their life......And they shall not again transgress. Nor shall they sin all the days of their life. Nor shall they die of.......anger or wrath,"—Ibid. p. 34.

> "And from henceforth there will be nothing corruptible: for the Son of Man has appeared; and has seated himself on the throne of his glory. And all evil shall pass away before his face. And the world of that Son of Man shall go forth, and be strong before the Lord of spirits;"—The Third Parable of Enoch, see the work quoted, p. 92.

We learn from "The Ascension of Isaiah" (see p. 32) that

> "[those] who believed in the ascention into heaven, withdrew and settled on the mountain. They were all clothed with garments of hair, and they were all prophets. And they had nothing with them, but were naked."

This is but only the description of the Digambara (Jaina) saint who has only his skin (the garment of hairs) for his covering, who possesses nothing and who is absolutely naked! Only when a world-flight of such a type is attained does the 'flesh' leave the soul unmolested and depart from it for ever! Then only can the soul attain to full continuity of consciousness and to knowledge that remains unbenumbed and unclouded by the stupor of somnolence and sleep. Those who have already attained to the Supreme Status have, accordingly, been described in "The Book of Enoch" as those who sleep not.

> "And here my eyes saw all those who sleep not....."(p. 59)

A very large number of men have attained to the Supreme Status already. In mystic language (*vide*, as for instance, the description of a similar spectacle in the 4th and the 5th chapters of the Book of Revelation in the New Testament of the Holy Bible). They are described as standing or seated round the Throne of LIFE and engaged unremittingly, in (appreciating, that is to say, enjoying, and, therefore) praising its Divinity.

> "Those who sleep not bless thee: they stand before Thy glory and bless, praise and extol, saying, 'Holy, Holy, Holy is the Lord of Spirits.'"—The Book of Enoch, p. 59.
>
> "And here my eyes saw those who sleep not: they stand before him and bless and say: 'Blessed be Thou and blessed be the name of the Lord for ever and for ever.'"—Ibid. p. 59.
>
> "And the Great Glory sat there on the Throne.
>
> "And the Most Holy Ones who were nigh to Him did not leave by night nor depart from Him."—Ibid. p. 42.

The Divinity of Life is revealed, but with great caution, in the mystic work known as "The Ascension of Isaiah", p. 47.

> "Worship neither throne nor angel which belongeth to the six heavens —for this cause was I sent to conduct thee—until I tell thee [in the seventh heaven] For above all the heavens and their angels hath thy throne been placed, and thy garments and thy crown which thou shalt see."—The Ascension of Isaiah, p. 47.

Isaiah is, no doubt, speaking of his own self here in his vision; but all souls are alike and there is no difference among them as regards their nature, that is to say, as regards their natural qualities and traits. We cannot even attribute the language exclusively to any particular individual, e.g., a Saviour or a Christ.

> "I have therefore been empowered and sent to raise thee here and thou mayest see this glory And that thou mayest

see the Lord of all those heavens and those thrones undergoing (successive) transformation until be resembleth your form and likeness."

This is surely not applicable to any external Saviour or Christ, by any stretch of imagination: the lord undergoing transformations to resemble the spectator or devotee's form and likeness! The seer is, however, promised in clear language:—

"Then thou wilt become equal to the angels of the seventh heaven.",...—Ibid, p. 50.

In the sixth heaven Isaiah saw no thrones; but was able to 'praise' on terms of equality with those who were there.

"And there were no angels on the left, nor throne in the midst, but all bad one appearance and their (power of) praise was equal. And (power) was given to me also. And I also praised along with them and that angel also and our praise was like theirs and then they all flamed the primal Father and His beloved, and Christ and the Holy Spirit, all with one voice."—Ibid. p. 50.

Isaiah is also informed:

"......and he who permitted thee is thy Lord God, the Lord Christ who will be called Jesus, but this name thou canst not hear till thou hast ascended out of thy body."—Ibid. p. 52.

The reference here is clearly not to a Christ, or a Jesus, who is openly named, but to the aspirant himself who cannot attain to Christhood so long as he remains cnsouled in the body of flesh, that is to say, till he separates himself *completely* from the harmful association with matter, inasmuch as salvation only signifies attainment to the purity of spiritual nature, by the elimination of every particle of the foreign substance—matter—from it.

This is made clear in the imagery of the highest heaven, the seventh:

"And he raised me lip unto the seventh heaven, and I

> saw there a wonderful light and angels innumerable."
> —Ibid. p. 62

All the Saved Ones dwell in the seventh heaven :

> "And there I saw Enoch and all who were with him stript of the garments of the upper I saw them in their garments of the upper world, and they were like angels, standing there in great glory"—Ibid p. 52.

We are also told about these Holy Ones:

> "There is nothing hidden from the thrones and from those who dwell in the heavens and from the angels"—Ibid. p. 48.

The heavenly Guide does not claim any superiority for himself above his companion. The latter's style of address as "my Lord" immediately elicits the gentle but clear disclaimer of superiority: "I am not thy lord, but thy fellow-servant." The idea is simply that of a 'co-worker,' of one who has by his own work attained to a position which qualifies him to guide others, who have still to work out their destiny.

This is to be consummated in the last generations along with the end of the world for we are told:

> "Both the ends of this world and all this vision will be consummated in the last generations."—Ibid. p. 61.

In vain shall we search for an external Christ to appear into the world towards its end and to fulfil the vision; what is meant by the end of the world is the end of the wandering of the soul in transmigration, while the last generations imply nothing more or less than the last few incarnations prior to one's entering *nirvana*. The inner Divinity has alreay appeared as Christ in the life of innumerable souls, towards the end or their *samsara* (transmigration) in the last two or three generations (lives or incarnations); and they became Gods. They are Those who sleep know all things, and who have the best reasons for praising the blessed and blissful nature of Life. They enjoy sleepless bliss, and are above the trouble and turmoil of the world! These Holy Ones are termed Siddhas in Jainism; but four and twenty out of Them who attain to the utmost glory as

Divine Teachers are termed Tirthamkaras, who will be described more adequately in the eleventh lecture. With reference to transmigration of souls, we have it from Philo :

> "Now of these souls some descènd upon the earth with a view to being bound up in mortal bodies, those namely which are most nearly connected with the earth, and which are lovers of the body. But some soar upwards.....Of these those which are influenced by a desire for mortal life, and which have been familiarised to it, again return to it.....—Yonge's Philo Judaeus ii. 321.

According to Philo escape from transmigration is attained by the practice of virtue, which implies the suffering of hardships (asceticism):

> "To these men (devoted to labour and virtue) the soft earth is their most costly such, their bed is rushes, and grass and herbage, and a thick byer of leaves; and the pillows for their heads are a few stones, or any little mounds which happen to rise a little above the surface of the plain, Such a life as this is, by luxurious men, denominated a life of hardship, but by those who live for virtue, it is called most delightful; for it is well adapted, not for those who are called men, but for those who really are such,"—Yonge's Philo Judaeus ii. 319.

"According to Philo, the mind when it has been initiated into divine things—and" it is not lawful to speak of the sacred mysteries to the uninitiated" (Yonge's Philo Judaeus iv. 245)—and is inspired, resembles unity, and he who "cleaves to the nature of unity is said to approach God with the intimacy as it were of a kinsman." The reason is thus given by the great revealer of the Judaic mysteries:

> "For abandoning all mortal types, he is transferred to the Divine type so that he becomes akin to God and truly divine"—Philo's Contribution to Religion, by H. A. A. Kennedy, 233.

Further light is thrown by Philo on the point which is more elucidating still:

> "......the good man does not die, but departs, that it

> might declare the inextinguishable and immortal nature of the fully purified soul, which soal, experience a departure from this world to hea ven, not that dissolution and destruction which death appears to bring."—Ibid. 138.

This only means the attainment of *nirvana* by the soul which is rid of the companionship of the body, and is, therefore, left as a simple substance. Philo, too, says:

> "*God is not a compound being.*"—Yonge's Philo Judaeus, vol. i. p. 81.

All this amply proves the existence of a scientific basis for Jewish allegories. Unfortunately the understanding of these allegories has been lost to-day, and misunderstandings have arisen in its place. Perhaps these will depart too, and we shall have the Wisdom Divine once more shedding its lights on the hearts of men. We shall stop now for the day.

(D)

We may now proceed to an elucidation of the doctrines of the New Testament, which is said to be the fulfilment of the Older Testament. The most noticeable feature of the Gospels which are the foundations of the New Testament doctrine is their parabolic teaching. The "Key of Knowledge" for the loss of which Jesus found fault with the Lawyers of Israel is also needed to open the hidden sense of the Messianic speech. Here and there we, no doubt, come across real gems of great value lying on the surface, but just because they are loose and unset they are liable to be twisted and forced into any kind of a setting. On the whole, the cardinal doctrine of the Messiah in the New Testament may be taken to be as follows.

(1) *Perfection and Divinity of the soul-substance.*

(i) "I said, ye are Gods" (John, x.34).

(ii) "Ye are the light of the world. A city that is set on a hill cannot be hid" (Matt. v. 14).

(iii) "Ye are the salt of the earth" (Matt. v. 13).

(iv) "Beloved, now we are the sons of God, and it doth not yet appear what we shall be, but we know that, when he shall appear, we shall be like him; for we shall see him as he is " (John's First Epistle General, iii. 2).

(v) "Behold, the kingdom of God is within you" (Luke, xvii. 21).

(vi) "And no man hath ascended up to heaven, but he that came down from heaven; even the son of man which is in heaven" (John, iii. 13).

(2) *The fallen condition of the soul.*

(i) "For all have sinned and come short of the glory of God" (Romans, iii. 23).

(ii) "For God hath concluded them all in unbelief" (Romans, xi. 32).

(3) *Redemption by the Key_of Knowledge.*

(i) "Woe unto you lawyers! for ye have taken away the Key of Knowledge; Ye entered not in yourselves, and them that were entering in ye hindered" (Luke, xi. 52).

(ii) "Ye shall know the truth, and the truth shall make you free" (John, viii. 32).

(iii) "Be ye therefore perfect, even as your Father which is in heaven is perfect" (Matt. v. 48).

(4) *The bondage is the bondage of sin, that is to say, of wrong-doing (karmas=actions, that bind the soul.)*

(i) "Neither do men light a candle, and put it under a bushel" (Matt. v. 15).

The allusion here clearly is to the *jnanavarniya* (knowledge-obstructing) *karmas* that act as a covering over the faculty of infinite knowledge of the ego.

(ii) "Whosoever committeth sin is the servant of sin" (John, viii. 34).

It is this servitude or bondage of sin which is to be terminated by the knowledge of truth (John, viii. 32).

(5) *This bondage is destroyed by the practising asceticism and other forms of purification that are destructive of desire.*

(i) "For if ye live after the flesh, ye shall die; but if ye through the spirit do mortify the deeds of the body, ye shall live" (Romans, viii. 13).

(ii) "He that soweth to his flesh shall of the flesh reap corruption; but he that soweth to the spirit shall of the spirit reap life everlasting" (Galatians, vi. 8).

(iii) "Mortify therefore your members which are upon the earth" (Colossians, iii. 5).

(iv) "For to be carnally minded is death; but to be spiritually minded is life and peace."—(Romans, viii. 6).

(v) "Enter ye in at the strait gate; for wide is the gate, and broad is the way, that leadth to destruction, and many there be that go in thereat: because strait is the gate, and narrow is way, which leadeth unto life, and few there be that find it" (Matt. vii. 13-14).

(vi) "Woe unto you that are full! for ye shall hunger..... Blessed are ye that hunger now: for ye shall be filled" (Luke, vi. 25 and 21).

(vii) "If any man will come after me, let him deny himself, and take up his cross, and follow me" (Matt. xvi. 24).

(viii) "He that taketh not his cross, and followeth after me, is not worthy of me" (Matt. x. 38).

(ix) "If any man come to me and hate not his father,

and mother, and wife and children, and brethren and sisters, yea and his own life also, he cannot be my disciple" (Luke xiv. 26).

(x) "Whosoever shall seek to save his life shall lose it; and whosoever shall lose his life shall preserve it" (Luke, xvii. 33).

(xi) "The foxes have holes, and the birds of the air have nests; but the son of man hath not where to lay his head" (Matt. viii. 20).

(xii) "In weariness and painfulness, in watchings often, in hunger and thirst, in fastings, often, in cold and nakedness" (2 Corinthians, xi. 27).

(xiii) "......there be eunuchs which have made themselves eunuchs for the kingdom of heaven's sake" (Matt. xix. 12).

(xiv) "But I keep under my body, and bring it into subjection" (1 Cor. lx. 27).

(xv) "And they that are Christ's have crucified the flesh with the affections and lusts" (Galatians, v. 24).

(xvi) "I beseech you therefore, brethren, by the mercies of God, that ye present your bodies a living sacrifice, holy, acceptable unto God, which is your reasonable service" (Romans, xii. 1).

Such is the nature of the light that is thrown by these stray gems and jewels of real philosophical worth. Christian Gnostics, too, "regarded perfection as the prerogative of the 'spiritual'—those redeemed from the bondage of matter and the flesh- for it was assumed that sin was an inseparable assooiation of matter." Perfection, according to these Gnostics, was only attained by knowledge acquired through initiation; "it was an esoterio state entered through theosophic insight and had no living connection with Christ" (ERE. vol. ix. p. 733.)

On the Esoterio side of Christianity we find the doctrines

of crucifixion, resurrection and ascension as utterly misunderstood by Christians as Agni, Indra and Surya by the Hindus. The whole life of Jesus is a series of ingenious symbolisms, depicting the glory of a self-conscious Soul.

When the conception of the divinity of Life is formed by the mind, Christos or Krishna is said to be born. Being intimately connected with Life, He is associated, from his very birth, with kine (go in Sanskrit, signifying the senses, whose control is intended by ,*go-rekshya*, *vide* PHB. Vol. II. p. 520.) Jesus, too, is associated with shepherds. Mary, the virgin mother, is the intellect which conceives in consequence of spirit's brooding over it. The father is a carpenter, which term is another ingenious symbolism for the faculty represented by the Hindu deity Ganesha, since he outs up (analysis) and joins together (synthesis) things. The conception is immaculate, because it is intellectual, not sexual. The child develops in secret, till its enemies are destroyed, which means that the manifestation of Christhood is delayed after the acquisition of Right Faith so long as the evil tendencies and habits and beliefs are not sufficiently eradicated from the heart, by the quickening of the germ of Spirit from within. Then there is a course of asceticism in consequence of which certain psychic powers are acquired by the soul. Now comes the important moment in the life of a novitiate when he stands at the cross-roads of destiny, so to speak, with the forces of life and death in his power; for he has only to suffer himself to be worshipped by the World to mar his true progress. This is the temptation, the Evil One showing the worldly empires to be acquired by obeisance to him. But the ascetic cannot turn away from his determination to crucify his lower self. He thus carries his cross, and is crucified at the place of Golgotha which means the place of the skull. The special significance of the skull is that it is the seat of an important psychic plexus in the brain which is intimately associated with the progress of *dhyana* (meditation).

The following passages from the Bible may be cited here as confirmatory of this view:

(i) "Jesus was not yet glorified" (John, vii. 39).

(ii) "Who for the joy that was set before him endured the cross, despising the shame" (Hebrews, xii. 2).

The effect of the crucifixion of the *bahiratman* (bodily self), to come into the real life which is at once abundant and glorious, is manifested in

(i) the rending of rocks,

(ii) the darkening of the sun,

(iii) the rending of the veil of the temple from top to bottom, and

(iv) the opening out of the graves and the appearing of the dead.

These are all mystic allegories which have a hidden meaning that are being revealed to you for the first time in modern times.

(i) The rending of the rocks means the rending of the adamantine knots of *karmic* forces in the inner constitution of the soul. You must have read in the Hindu and Jaina Puranas that the throne of Indra in the heavens is shaken by the asceticism of saints and that the attainment of omniscience on the part of *Jinas* (Conquerors of the *Samsara*) is accompanied by the spontaneous ringing of bells in the regions of devas. Well, the explanation of these phenomena is probably to be found in the fact that the powerful vibrations set up by the rending of karmic knots, in consequence of the one-pointed *dhyana* (self-contemplation), are carried by the 'wireless' medium of a subtle electricity, and impinging upon the ethereal matter of Indra's thrones and bells in the regions of the *devas*, set them shaking and resounding and reverberating.

(ii) The darkening of the Sun signifies the loss of the lower mental equipment, *i.e.*, of sense-perception and intellectual function. These disappear with the dawn of omniscience,[29] and are no longer needed. Much as we prize our senses and intellect, they are really the obstructors of the full blaze of the inherent, all-embracing knowledge of the soul. Their loss is a blessing when it arises in the course of asceticism, since it is then immediately followed by the acquisition of infinite simultaneous knowledge of all that has happened in the past, all that is happening in the present and all that is to happen in the future, though at all other times it is a calamity pure and simple.

(iii) The rending of the veil of the temple is also an allegorical description. The veil that is rent is not of a man-made temple of brick and mortar, but of the temple of the soul. It is the 'busher' over the inner light that is removed, revealing the true divinity within! There is no question of the destruction of a temple or of a part of a temple of masonry or stone. Inner illumination (روشن ضميري = *roshan zamiri*) is the immediate result of the destruction of this internal veil.

(iv) But the most beautiful metaphor of all employed in this connection is the opening out of the graves. What is meant is, of course, not the graveyard in a cemetery, where dead bodies lie buried, nor the appearance in public of the rotting carcases of the dead, thrown out by some sort of a volcanic force; but the cemetery of human memory where lie stored up the events, sensations and impressions of the past, as if buried underground. The allegory is indicative of the recovery of the memories of the past lives of the soul, obtained as the fruit of advanced asceticism.

As regards metempsychosis, in vain shall we be told that transmigration is not a fundamental tenet of Christianity and that the teaching of Jesus is on the whole opposed to any such doctrine; the truth is that those who say so have not read their Bible in the light of the injunction : "whoso readeth let him understand," which we had occasions to refer to ere this. There are, as you are no aware, in the Bible secret tenets and concealed doctrines, hidden behind apparently meaningless words. But for this we should not have been told:—

> "I will open my mouth in parables; I will utter things which have been kept secret from the foundation of the world" (Matt. xiii 35).

The text of John, viii. 32 becomes very important here. It was the bondage of *karmas* which Jesus referred to when he said:—

> "And ye shall know the truth, and the truth shall make you free"—John viii. 32.

The fictitious discourse recorded in the verses that follow this dynamic truth was only designed to furnish a hint to the thoughtful as to the nature of the bondage referred to. The important verses bearing on the the point are reproduced below:—

> 33. "They answered him, We be Abraham's seed and were never in bondage to any man: how sayest thou, Ye shall be made free?
>
> 34. "Jesus answered them, Verily, verily, I say unto you, whosoever committeth sin is the servant of sin.
>
> 35. "And the servant abideth not in the house for ever; but the son abideth ever.
>
> 36. "If the son therefore shall make you free, ye shall be free indeed."

If we are to construe these verses correctly, we must first endeavour to find out the truth each of them lays down. Careful reflection will show that the 34th is intended to settle the question raised in the 33rd—whether the bondage meant national or political subjection? The answer is plain: it is the servitude of sin that is meant, not national captivity!

In the 35th verse a distinction is made between the conditions of servitude and sonship, the former of which is pronounced to be terminable, but the latter, eternal. The 36th, finally, lays down that the true freedom from all kinds of bonds—note the force of, 'indeed' after 'free'—can only be conferred by the Son who is to abide for ever.

Now, the word 'son' in the mouth of Jesus signifies the soul that has inherited the status and glory of God. According to St. Paul, "as many as are led by the spirit of God, they are the sons of God......The spirit itself beareth witness with our spirit, that we are the children of God. And if children, then heirs; heirs of God, and joint heirs with Christ, if so be that we suffer with him, that we may also be glorified together" (Romans viii. 14, 16 and 17). Thus if we put down our conclusions categorically we get,

(1) that the word bondage in religion means the servitude or thraldom of sin;

(2) that this thraldom is not ever-lasting, but the condition of Sonship is eternal; and

(3) that the soul obtains true freedom only when it acquires the status of the Son.

These propositions are fully in harmony with the teaching of Jainism, and only reproduce three of the most fundamental truths of religion. They are not exhaustive of the why and the *wherefore* of the doctrine of transmigration, but only intended as a hint to the wise. Let the reader ask himself as to what is meant by sin, and he will soon perceive that there can be no being or substance corresponding to the term. It is a mere word, and were we to search for it from now till the Judgment Day, it is certain that it would always remain what it is to-day—a pure wordy abstraction. The truth is that sin only conveys the idea of wrong doing, there being no concrete being or thing to corre-spond to it in nature. The bondage of sin, thus, is clearly the thraldom of actions, i.e., *karmas* (actions or deeds), which is to be shaken off to bring the state of "son-ship" into manifestation.

Now, if the reader will further pursue the theme, and enquire how the soul can be bound by its acts, he will not be long in coming to the conclusions which have been already established regarding the nature of *asrava* and *bandha*. For there can be no binding of real subsisting beings or things with mere imaginary notions, or by pure ideas and words. A force is need-ed for the purpose, and no force is conceivable apart from a substance of some kind or other.

It is here that the exact teaching of Jainism is found to be of inestimable service; for while some creeds have pure words, illusion, *maya* and the like to bind the soul with, others vaguely talk of desire, and others again of such generalities as *karma*, action, sin and *taqdir* (destiny or fate). The importance of scientific knowledge has been pointed out ere this, and it is clear that vague generalities are wholly responsible for the amount of confusion which has prevailed in theological circles hitherto.

It is not likely that a man would now be found to msist on interpreting the word son to mean Jesus of Nazareth in the 36th verse of the 8th chapter of St. John's Gospel; but should one venture to entertain that supposition, it would be well to remember that no one can help another in the spiritual region, except to the extent of pointing out the way for obtaining release from the turmoils of *samsara*. And the case is nowise altered by our individual beliefs; for the laws of nature are not dependent on the whims of men and other higher or lower beings, but work independently of them. Hence, when people say that it is more comforting to believe that some one else will, out of grace, do the needful for them, they lull themselves into false security and allow themselves to fall asleep on the verge of an innocent looking volcano whose apparent quietness is soon to be changed into a sudden outburst of destructiveness. It is a corollary to be deduced from the spiritual laws already described that the bondage of the soul cannot possibly be terminated by any agency outside its own self. The reason "for this is to be found in the fact that *no one can possibly control the desires of another, which, being the causes of the fusion of spirit and matter, must continue to produce their effects so long as they exist.*

The teaching of Jesus with reference to resurrection, which is the last stronghold of Christian hostility to the theory of transmigration itself leads to no other conclusion when studied philosophically. Here is the text, in full, which was propounded in answer to a question put by certain Sadducees as to whose wife a certain woman would be in resurrection, she having married, here on this earth, seven brothers in succession, that is one after another, as they died:

> "The children of this world marry and are given in marriage;
>
> "But they which shall be accounted worthy to obtain that world and the resurrection from the dead, neither marry, nor are given in marriage:
>
> "Neither can they die any more: for they are equal unto the angels; and are the children of God, being the children of the resurrection."—Luke, xx. 34-36.

Here we are distinctly told

(i) that resurrection is not open to everybody but only to those who *are accounted worthy to obtain that world and the resurrection from the dead*;

(ii) that there is no such thing as marriage in 'that world'; and

(iii) that those who obtain resurrection acquire immortality, and are known as the children of God, by virtue of being the children of resurrection.

But the very first of these statements is fatal to the popular sense of resurrection according to which everyone shall be made to rise up irrespective of worth. Jesus distinctly says that it is open only to those who *are accounted worthy to obtain it*.

The second particular is still more fatal to the popular belief according to which men and women shall be made to rise up in their physical bodies, with the prospect of a re-union of families. Now, if there is to be a distinction of the male and the female amongst the risen dead, their condition would resemble that of Hindu widows, whose cause Christians are ever ready to champion, on the ground of its being inhuman and unjust to enforce a life-long widowhood on them. What, we ask, must be the plight of those residents of the post resurrection world who are formed male and female and who are never to know the happiness of married life? Will not the gift of the organ without its function be the source of the greatest conceivable misery in their case? It is too much even to expect from everyone of the undisciplined souls, that shall enter the 'kingdom,' not through the strait gateway and narrow path of 'works,' but through the favour of a saviour, to betake himself or herself to practising eternal celibacy, after the manner of a Jaina or a Hindu widow ! Well, this is the kind, of muddle in which unscientific thought finds itself when bent on theorising against facts.

The third particular, the obtainment or acquisition of immortality by each and every risen individual, is equally astonishing. An embodied soul is a compound of spirit and matter, and it is not in the nature of compounds to be eternal. Nor is immortality a thing that can be purchased in two-penny packets at a chemist's. The fact is that the doctrine of resurrection is really the doctrine of transmigration of souls, though couched in mystic symbology. It was not unknown to the Jews, and the Pharisees actually subscribed to it. Before them it was well known to the Egyptians who had probably borrowed it from Persian sources. But the original of the Lord of the Judgment Day is to be found in the god Yamaraja of Hindu mythology, who weighs the merit and demerit of creatures on their death and disposes of them accordingly.

Now, Yamaraja is a personification of the Law of *Karma*, which being the effect of the operation of the forces bound up in different substances, is absolutely unerring. The idea of a general rising of the dead on a certain day at the end of the world-cycle was, however, never associated with this doctrine in any religion, though some of the passages of the scriptural text are liable to be twisted in that direction. What was meant was that as each individual died his future was determined automatically by the operation of the Law of *Karma*, personified as the Lord of Death, and he was drawn into the most suitable 'womb' for his next incarnation. The process continued till *nirvana* was attained, which meant the conquest of death, hence resurrection from the dead. The dead[30] are all those souls that are not spiritually alive, as in the text:

"Let the dead bury their dead" (Matt. viii. 22).

This is also the sense of the passage in Revelation (i. 18) where the Redeemed Soul is made to say:

> "I am he that liveth, and was dead j and behold, 1 am alive for ever more, Amen j aud have the keys of hell and of death."

Resurrection from the dead, then, meant the con-quest of death, the removal of the liability imposed upon the soul as a consequence of the 'fall'. This liability is due to the entertainment of *raga* and *dvesha* (euphemistically, the eating of the tree of knowledge of good and evil) and is put an end to by the conquest of death by 'works,' when he who is accounted worthy to obtain that world and the resurrection from the dead *cannot die any more* (Luke xx. 36). We thus have the region of death confined to the sphere within which *raga* and *dvesha*, i.e., private loves and hatreds, prevail. As explained in the lecture dealing with the scientific aspect of Religion, *raga* and *dvesha* are the real causes of the bondage of *karma* and transmigration; they lead to the union of spirit and matter, thereby crippling and maiming the soul. This is precisely what Christian Gnostics themselves held.

The Jewish Esotericism, which is the true side of Judaism, as must be quite clear by this time—for 'literalism' is only the kernel-less husk—also professed belief in metempsychosis (ERE. vol. vii. p. 626).

As a matter of fact the doctrine is implied in the very fundamentals of Judaism from the very earliest times. But to continue with our subject, death is the consequence of the fusion of spirit and matter; for independently of each other they are death-less, pure spirits as well as atoms of matter being both simple indestructible substances. He who would attain immortality must, therefore, seek it within himself, by separating from his soul every particle of the foreign material that may be adhering to it. This is possible only in one way—by *tapas*. When the individual is rid of *raga* and *dvesha* in every form, he is said to conquer death, though he lingers in the world of men so long as his body (or rather bodies) are not completely 'dissolved'. He is then called a *jivanmukta* (Liberated One). Finally, when he is completely freed from all kinds of connection with matter, He immediately ascends to the top-most part of the Universe, as pure Effulgence of Spirit, and is termed the Most High.

Why there is no marrying or being married in 'that world' is because there is no distinction of sex there. Sex appertains to the body, but not to the spirit,[31] hence the same soul becomrs now a male, now a female in the course of transmigration. But when 'the other shore' is reached both the longings of sex-passion and the physical bodies that are necessary to support sex-organs are burnt up with the fire of asceticism and *jnana* (knowledge), and there is consequently neither marrying nor giving in marriage in nirvana.

The Sons of God, thus, are those pure and perfect Souls who have attained their high Ideal, and become Gods. They have destroyed the bondage of *karmas* and the consequen'l; liability to repeated births and deaths, and are now living at the top of the Universe as the Conquerors of the Dragon of Ignorance and its chief ally-Death. They are called the Sons of God, because they are heirs to the heritage of divinity, so to speak, having attained the perfection of Godhood, which is the goal of spirit's evolution. They stand for manifested godhood, which is the successor (or heir) to the divini-ty unmanifest of the soul. Pure, perfect happiness, *i.e.*, eternal, unabating bliss, the power to defy Death, *i.e.*, immortality, infinite power, infinite knowledge and infinite perception, called the *ananta chatushraya* in Jaina Scriptures, are the attributes of Their divine Souls. They are the true Teachers of mankind and the fountain-head of perfect Wisdom, hence Religion. Their chief characteristics, as given in the Bible (Luke xx. 34-36), are;

(1) the possession of spiritual merit which entitles them to obtain 'that world' i.e., nirvana,

(2) freedom from sex, that is, the absence of all material bodies,

(3) non-liability to death, and

(4) the enjoyment of Godly status.

It is not possible to lay too much stress on the words 'any more' in the Messianic. observation recorded by Luke (xx. 36). The statement will lose all its merit, if souls are born and die only once in their career. The fact that it was made only with reference to those Great Ones who obtain 'that world' and the resurrection from the dead, is sufficient to show that it is not applicable to all souls indiscriminately. Thus, while all those who have not perfected themselves remain liable to repeated births and deaths in the course of transmigration, those who attain the fullest degree of spiritual unfoldment are necessarily exempt from dying *any more* (The Key of Knowledge).

We can now understand what is meant by the saying:—

> "Blessed are the meek, for they shall inherit the earth" (Mdtt v 5).

This clearly means that they shall be born as kings and rulers of men on earth in their next incarnation. The orthodox interpretation of the resurrection text will make this saying a dead letter; for what shall the meek inherit if the earth is to pass away before the resurrection day?

Similarly, it is said:

> "And everyone that hath forsaken houses. or brethren. or sisters, or father, or mother, or wife, or children or lands, for my name's sake, shall receive an hundred fold, and shall inherit everlasting life" (Matt. xix. 22).

This is precisely what the Jainas say, as will be evident from the following from the *Ratna Karanda Shravkachara*, a work of great authority, dealing with the rules of conduct applicable to a house-holder:—

> "Those whose hearts have been purified by Right Faith become the Lords of splendour, energy, wisdom, prowess, fame, wealth, victory and greatness; they are born in high families and posses the ability to realise the highest ideals.....of life; they are the best of men.
>
> "He who has quaffed the nectar of *dharma* becomes freed from all kinds of pain, and drinks from the endless, unsurpassed and exalted fount of blissfulness of liberation.
>
> "Those who follow the rigid path of renunciation and dharma dwell unexcelled for all eternity, in the joy of final beatitude, endowed with infinite wisdom, faith, energy, dispassion, bliss, satisfaction and purity. And if there be a cosmic disturbance violent enough to destroy the three worlds still no change is observable in the condition of the Perfect Souls even after the lapse of hundreds of *kalas* (cycles of time)."

If further proof is required to show that transmigration was a part of the Christian Doctrine, it will be found in the writings of the Ante-Nicene Fathers (see my "Jainism Christinity and Science.)

We shall now work out the connection between Jesus and John the Baptist whose personality is one of the most puzzling in the whole Bible. John is the cousin of the Messiah, to being with, and jumps up with delight, while yet an unborn babe, on hearing the voice of his cousin's mother (Luke i. 41). John, it is said, met Jesus at the Jordon, and, when asked to baptize him, meekly entreated, saying;

> "I have need to be haptized of thee, and comest thou to me?" (Matt. iii. 14).

It was only when he was assured by Jesus that it behoved Christ to be baptized by him in the first instance that he performed the ceremony.

"Suffer it to be so now for it becometh us to fulfil all righteousness" (Matt. iii. 15)

John saw the heavens opened and the spirit of God alighting on Jesus in the form of a dove. This is what he says about it himself:—

"And I saw, and bear record that this is the Son of God" (John i. 34)

The next day John pointed out Jesus to two of his disciples, saying:

"Behold the Lamb of God" (John i. 36)

Asked to explain his mission, he declared:—

I am not the Christ, but I am sent before him. He that hath the bride is lhe bridegroom: but the friend of the bridegroom, which standeth and heareth him, rejoiceth greatly because of the bridegroom's voice: this my joy therefore is fulfilled. He must increase but I must decrease. He that cometh from above is above all: he that is of the earth is earthy and speaketh of the earth; he that cometh from heaven is above all," (John iii 28-31).

He also said:—

I indeed baptize you with Watter: but one mightier than I cometh the latchet of whose shoes I am not worthy to unloose: he shall baptize you with the Holy Ghost and with fire" (Luke iii, 16).

John said all this, yet a few months later when he was thrown into prison by Herod, he actually sent his disciples to ascertain whether Jesus was "he who should come," or should they look for another (Matt. xi. 2 and 3).

I need not comment upon this grotesque change of front on the part of John in my own words; I shall simply let Mr. Evanson (a curate of the church from which he ultimately withdrew on account of his critical views) tell you what he thought on the subject:—

"Now it seems simply impossible that John, after being from his earliest infancy personally acquained with Je-

> sus and not only in possession of all the information respecting him, which he must have learnt from the two families, but so miraculously impressed with affection and reverence for him as to exult with joy, though but an embryo in the womb, at the mere sound of his mother's voice, could at any time have entertained the least doubt of Jesus being the Messiah" (see the History of the New Testament Criticism p. 91).

The author of the work quoted, Mr. F. C.Conybeare, gives us the verdict of modern criticism on Luke's version in the following significant words (Ibid. p. 91):—

> "The true view, of course, is that Luke, in spite of his .pretensions to accuracy, was a careless and credulous writer."

Evanson himself regarded the first two ohapters of the Gospel acoording to St. Luke as "the daring fiction of some of the easy-working interpolators of the beginning of the second century from among the pagan converts, who, to do honour as they deemed it to the author of their newly-embraced religion were willing that his birth should, at least, equal that of the pagan heroes and demigods, and who thereby laid the foundation of the succeeding orthodox deification of the man Jesus, which, in degree of blasphemous absurdity, exceeds even the gross fables of pagan superstition" (Ibid. p. 92).

Unfortunately, it never occurred either to Evanson or to any of the modern critics or even to the clerics themselves that the New Testament was not writiien in the language of the script and was not to be read as a narrative of facts. What might have been their conclusion had they known this, I cannot say, but let me proceed to unravel the secret teaching to enable you to determine its value for yourselves.

Jesus and John are two different aspects of the soul which arise when the individual consoiousness is awakened to spiritual Life. Jesus represents Life Triumphant while John stands for Intellect Repentant. Being but different 'faculties' or aspects of the soul substance, they are described as related to each other.

Hence is John the cousin of Jesus. John's mission is described as the voice of one crying in the wilderness, and the purport of his cry, to exhort humanity to repent and to straighten the path for the coming of the Lord (Mark i, 3 and 4), This is characteristic of the mind that has begun, in seriousness, to reflect on its destiny. When the lower self is tired of the pursuit of worldly pleasures and has reached the end of its tether, it begins to reflect on its destiny, and realises that neither friends, nor riches, nor position, nor physical prowess, nor anything else can come to its rescue or relieve it of the impending gloom of death and extinction which stare it in the face. It then Cries out in the anguish of its loneliness in the midst of the world, and, becoming disgusted with the pleasures and joys of the mortals which had hitherto diverted its attention from its real nature, gradually learns that the source of all bliss, blessedness and immortality is none other than its own true self. This is the stage which is likened to the voice of one crying in the wilderness, saying, 'Repent for the kingdom of heaven is at hand.' Now, because, the activity of the intellect is exhausted with the purification of beliefs, which can be accomplished by means of the water of wisdom (Right Faith), and since the willi rather than the intellect, is the real cause of the subsequent progress, the baptism of John is necessarily that of water. The intellectual self is of the earth, earthy; but the soul is from heaven, and, therefore, heavenly. Hence, the Intellect is made to say that it is unworthy to loosen the latchet of the shoes of the Messiah. Again, because it is only through the Intellect that one can become convinced of the existence of the higher self, it (the Intellect) is the solitary witness to the coming Messiah, at whose birth it leaps with joy. But in so for as wisdom is a necessary attribute of the Christos, he cannot do witllout the baptism of the Intellect, in the first instance. Hence the remarkable words of Jesus: "Suffer it to be so now, for it becometh us to fulfil all righteousness" (Matt. iii. 15). The Intellect, again, is not the enjoyer of bliss, hence, not the bridegroom, but it is natural for it to feel joy at the bridegr8om's voice, for he is to turn the wilderness into a veritable paradise. Lastly, because the freedom of the soul means the attainment of omniscienc which arises on the destruction of the lower mental equipment—judgment, memory, and the like—the Intellect is described as saying, 'he must increase, but I must decrease.' The sending of his disciples by John to ascertain whether Jesus (soul) is the Messiah, i.e., the Redeemer, in spite of the fact that he had exulted with delight at his mother's voice, is in keeping with the nature of the Intellect, which always doubts and hesitates, and is seldom satisfied with its own conclusions. It is, thus, clear that the personality of John, the Baptist, is typical of the intellectual self of the man who has become conscious of the fuller Life of the higher Ego. The Holy Ghost is the spirit that makes one holy; it is the giver or source of saintliness, in plain language it is *Vairagya* (an overpowering sense of detachment from the world). Fire is *tapas* (fasting and other forms of asceticism). *Vairagya* and *tapas* are the two purifiers of the spirit. Hence does the Messiah baptize with the Holy Ghost and with fire. The Holy Ghost is also termed the comforter, because though asceticism appears to be austere and forbidding in its outer aspect, it is really accompanied, in its advanced stages, by such joys as cannot even be described in words. The power of asceticism to lead to full knowledge is also implied clearly in the following statements of Jesus ;-

> "But the comforter which is the Holy Ghost, whom the Father will send my namé, he shall teach you all things, and bring all things to your remembrances whatsoever I have said unto you" (John xiv 26).

> "I have yet many things to say unto you, but ye cilnnot bear them now. Howbeit when he, the spirit of truth, is come. he will guide you unto all truth" (John xvi. 13-14).

As to whence this knowledge is to arise, we already know that *education* is a drawing out from within, in a strictly etymological sense—from e, out, and *duco*, to lead. In the Gospel according to St. Matthew also we are told:

> "Ye are the light of the world. A city that is set on a hill cannot be hide. Neither do men light a candle, and put it under a bushel, but on a candle stick: and it giveth light unto all that are in the house" (Matt. v. 14-15).

The relation between devotion and asceticism is indicated in the following from the fourth Gospel (Joh xvi. 7):—

> "Nevertheless I tell you the truth; it is expedient for Jon that I go away: for if I go not away, the comforter will not come unto you; but if I depart I will send him unto you."

This plainly meant that the disciples' devotion stood in the way of their practising asceticism which is the source of joy (comfort).

Joy itself is conceived as a bride, the giver of happiness to the bridegroom whence the speech of John, the Baptist:

> "He that hath the bride is the bridegroom."

John's dissertation about him that is earthly and speaketh of the earth, and of him that cometh from heaven is also highly instructive. The intellectual ego is not a pure spirit, but a compound of spirit and matter, the *bahiratman* that is made out of the dust of the ground with ,the vital breath infused in him. It is this outer self, the ego that discriminates between good and evil, and the function of which is exhausted as soon as it has intellectually conceived the divinity of the soul—it is this half material half spiritual self, personified as John, the Baptist, that is to decrease and disappear, while his cousin, the dematerialising ego of Life Triumphant is to wax and increase. In other words, while the process of unwinding in dematerialisation leads to the perfection and divinity of Life, it signifies the disruption of all those faculties and functions which are useless and burdensome to a pure spirit, however serviceable they might be to a fallen ego. Hence, the highly significant speech of John :—

> "He shall increase, but I shall decrease."

(E)

To proceed to Islam, there can be no denying the fact that the Al Qur'an is also a document of the same description as the Bible and the Vedas. As a matter of fact, Islam is a descendant of Judaism and Zoroastrianism as the Revd. W. St. Clair Tisdaill has so well, shown in his very admirable work "The Sources of the Qur'an." A good deal has been said by non-Muslim writers by way of attack upon Muhammad for his shortcomings. But we cannot listen to all that, for the very simple reason that Muhammad really did not set himself up as an ideal to be imitated and followed by men. Mahavira, Buddha and other Teachers had invited men to follow their example; but not Muhammad. He never said to anyone: 'Go sell off all thou possessest; give it away in charity, and come and follow me.' If Muhammad, therefore, had married twenty times or more, if he framed special rules for his own convenience, if he did not perfect himself in respect of renunciation and *charitra* (conduct), these are his private concerns, though they must be fully taken into account in determining the degree of self-realisation attained by him.

There can be no doubt but that Islam was at first only intended as a sort of reform over the unrestricted libertinism and mammon-worship that were rampant among the Arabs in Muhammad's day; but the sword the Prophet was forced to draw to defend himself did not admit of the idea being fully carried out. I am here not concerned with the political aspect of the faith, but it is evident that the teaching of the earlier creeds as to the excellence of the extreme degree of forgiveness and dispassion for the *sadhu* could not and did not find any place in the Bible of Islam. The product of necessity, the Qur'an could not, and as a matter of fact did not, teach the offering of the other cheek if smitten on one. Jehad became the outward symbol, though the crescent moon still remains the inward mark, of Islam. It is to be doubted whether any living Muhammadan knows whence the crescent Moon was taken. Probably a great many of them connect it in their minds with the miracle of the splitting of the moon; but the esoteric significance of that is very different. Probably that miracle only signified the acquisition of the power to visualise thought—a kind of second sight, what the mystics might call the opening out of the individual's conciousness on the 'Astral plane'. It is supposed that the first of the series of veils that obstruct clairvoyance is made of a kind of subtle material, the 'astral matter,' which is supposed to have a marked affinity for the moon, and it was the penetration of this, the first veil of matter, which was possibly intended by the miracle. As for the proper significance of the crescent moon, I had better refer you to the ancient symbol of Jainism which consists of the crescent moon placed above a *swastika*, with one cipher on the top and three such ciphers below the crescent, thus:

The explanation of the symbol is this: the four limbs of the *swastika*[32] indicate the four types of life, through which souls wander in the course of transmigration, namely,

(i) *deva* (as a resident of heavens),

(ii) *manushya* (as a human being),

(iii) *naraka* (as a resident of hells), and

(iv) all others, collectively termed *tiryancha* (birds, beasts, insects, plants, etc.).

The three ciphers symbolise Right Faith, Right Knowledge and Right Conduct, and the crescent moon is the mark of the *quickening* Spirit who is bound to grow and wax strong till He become Full and Perfect. (like the full Moon). The cipher at the top is, of course, an emblem of Godhood, full and perfect.

As for the arch-angel, Gabriel, Sir Syed Ahmad declined to believe in his existence, holding that when the Prophet said that an angel had appeared unto him, he meant nothing mere or less than the simple fact that an unknown person had met him (The Philosophy of Islam by Khaja Khan, p. 54).

According to the Sufis Gabriel signifies Reason. It is said in the "Studies in Tasawwuf" (p. 102):—

> "Salat (namaz) was instituted in Miraj........Gabriel who had accompained him (the Prophet) stopped short att he great Fig Tree.......i.e., Reason could not soar beyond the tree of life. The Prophet himself had to progress into that non-spatial region. When he reached there he had the injunction. 'Sit down, my beloved and utter my praises!' The Prophet replied, Why do I sit down?' The answer was: 'God is saying His own Namaz !'

It is said in the Shiva Samhita, a notable work on Yoga:—

> "When the yogi thinks of the great Soul, after rolling back his eyes, and concentrates his mind to the forehead then he can perceive the lustre from tge great Soul. The elever yogi who always meditates in the abovementioned way, evinces the great soul within himself and can even hold communion with Him."

It is this lustre from the "great Soul" which seems to have been personified as the arch-angel Gabriel. According to Muslim mysticism, he represents the tongue (probably meaning speech). Of the other angels, there are two that are deputed to take an account of a man's behaviour, "one sitting on the right hand, and the other on the left: he uttereth not a word, but there is with him a watcher ready to note it" Al Qur'an, chap. 50). These are probably the forces of good and evil (like or dislike) which are the modifiers of disposition, hence, recorders of one's behaviour.

To come now to the real doctrines of Islam, there is no doubt but that the same fundamental principles are to be found in the Qur'an as in other religions, though for obvious reasons the admixture of the useful and the useless is the most bewildering in that scripture. Times out of number is God defined in the Qur'an as he who seeth and heareth. We know that seeing and hearing appertain to consciousness or life, not to one particular being or soul. In Suratul Hadid it is said:—

> "God is with you wherever you are,"

In Suratul Rahman He is said to be the first and the last, the apparent and the real, all knowing. Sura Fatah points out:

"The people who strike palm with thee, do not strike it with thee, but with God,"

Elsewhere it is said that God is nearer to man than his camel's neck. Sura Wakiya records:

"We are nearer to man than you, but you do not observe."

In Sura Zariyat it is recorded:

"I am nearer to man than his jugular vein,"

Finally it is openly said in this Sura:

"I am in your individuality, but you do not see."

These expressions need no comment now from me. The reason why these highest truths of philosophy were imparted to men in this ambiguous laconic way is to be found in the attitude of the people and the state of human society at the time of the different prophets. Mạnsur was impaled for saying "analhaq" (I am God), as you know, and there were others who had been put to death for similar "faults" by fanatical mobs, championing the cause of exoteric gods,—whence the practice of speaking in 'proverbs' (cf. John xvi. 25 and Matt. vii. 6).

The hidden sense of these parables is clear enough once you are familiarised with the Scientific Truth and the mystic way of expressing it, but otherwise might easily pass for poetical licence or elegant diction without exciting comment.

How did Muslim esoterics understand these sayings is evident from Ali's injunction to acquire philosophical wisdom even from an infidel if necessary. The Prophet himself said; "Man, know thyself." Amongst mystics we may mention Al Hallaj, commonly known as Mansur, whom we have already referred to. There is Shamsh of Tabrez also who says:—

عجب من شمش تبریزم که گشتم شیفته بر خود
چون خودرا خود نظر کردم ندیدم جز خدا در خود

[How wonderful I am Shamsh of Tabrez; When I came to look into myself, I found none but God in the self!]

Maulana Rum writes;

"Oh my soul, I searched from end to end, I saw in thee nought save the Beloved. Call me not infidel, O my soul, if I say that thou thyself art He.

"Ye who in search of God, of God, pursue.

Ye need not search for God is you, is you!"

The Sufi thought approached perfection with Forid-ul-din Attar who said:—

تا تو هستي خداے درخواب است
تو نه ماني چو اوشود بيدار

Rendered into Urdu it would read ;

تيري هستی هے باعث ایک خدا کے خواب غفلت کی
رهے جب تو نه عالم میں تو وه بیدار هو جاوے

[Tr. So long as *thou* art in evidence a God is asleep; when thou shalt cease to be, He shall wake up.]

Is this any thing other than a repetition of the old Indian teaching that the soul is its own God, or different from the Messiah's word:

"He that findeth his life shall lose it: and he that loseth his life for my sake shall find?" (Matt. x. 39).

Here are a few of the more precious gems from the Sufi Treasury of Thought:

(۱) مقام روح برمن حیرت آمد
نشان از وے بگفتن غیرت امد
(۲) توئی عاشق بظاهر در طریقت
توئي معشوق باطن در حقیقت
(۳) گر بکنه خود ترا باشد رهے
از خدا و خلق بیشک آگا هے
(۴) هم ازیں گفته است در بحر صفا
نیست اندر جبه ام غیر خدا

(٥) عین آبے آب مے جوئي عجب
نقد خودرا نسیه میکوئي عجب
(٦) بادشاهي ار چه میمانی گدا
گنجها داري چرائی بے نوا
(٧) یار پنها نست در زیر نقاب
همچو دریا کو نهاں شد در حباب
(٨) پردہ بردارو جمال یار بیں
دیدہ واکن چهرہ اسرار بین
(٩) کشف در معني بود رفع حجاب
بود تو آمد بروے تو نقاب

These may be translated into English as follows :—

(1) The ‘place’ of the soul was full of wonders for me; I feel ashamed of my failure to describe it in words.

(2) Thou thyself art the outward lover, conformably to usage; thou thyself art in reality the Beloved!

(3) Couldst thou but find a way to thine own mystery, without doubt, thou wouldst know God and the world.

(4) For this reason, it is said in the Behr-i-sofa: there is none but God inside my cloak.

(5) Purest water thou art, and seekest thou water: it is strange! Thine Treasures thou hast forgotten, and now askest for them; it is strange!

(6) Thyself a king why remainest thou a beggar? Owner of all treasures, why art thou penniless?

(7) The beloved is hidden under the veil, like water that lieth concealed beneath a bubble.

(8) Lift up the veil and behold the glory of the Beloved; open thine eyes and perceive the face of the mystery!

(9) Separateness is destroyed by the sense becoming illuminated; thine own being hath come over thy face as a veil.

As you might be knowing, Bayazid of Bestam, the founder of the order of the Bestamee dervishes, too, openly proclaimed himself to be God in the presence of his disciples, and said:—

> "Glory to me, I am above all things......." The Dervishes p. 339.

Another mystic free-thinker, quoted in the work cited (see The Dervishes, p. 9) thus delivers himself in charming style:—

> "The seeds of Sufeeism were sown in the time of Adam; germed in that of Noah, budded in that of Abraham, and the fruit commenced to be developed in that of Moses They reached their maturity in that of Christ and in that of Mohammad produced pure wine. Those of the sectarians who loved this wine have so drunk of it as to lose all knowledge of themselves and to exclaim, praise be to me! Is there any greater than me? ...I am the Truth (that is to say, God)! There is no other God than me ....

No less emphatic is the statement of mysticism when it says:—

> "The Ehl el Hakk consider that every one may, by superior piety and love of God......even become God" (The Dervishes p. 294).

So is the one which holds:—

> "......a religious (man, intoxicated with the cup of Divine Communion, exclaims, 'I am God!' In fact fact man's attributes are of a divine character......what do I say?......His substance is even that of God."—The Dervishes, p. 10.

All these are beautiful commentaries on the simple statement of truth by the Prophet;

> "He who knoweth himself, knoweth God" (Saying of Muhammad).

Such is the nature of the soul according to Islam; and it is source of real pleasure to me to find animal life placed on the same level as the human in the Qur'an.

> "There is no kind of beast on earth, nor fow!" which flieth with its wings, but the same is a people like unto you: we have not omitted anything in the book of our decrees: then unto their Lord shall they return" (chap. vi.).

It is also very refreshing to find in the Qur'an such passages as acknowledge prior revelation of truth amongst other nations and countries. As a matter of fact, it is a part of the teaching of Islam that men were professors of one religion only at first; afterwards they dissented (Al Koran by Sale, p. 151).

As for reincarnation, the Muslim idea of predestination, which has brought upon Islam the stigma of fatalism itself suffices to prove the doctrine ,of transmigration, if investigated philosophically.

> "Taqdir, or the absolute decree of good and evil," says T. P. Hughes in 'A Dictionary of Islam,' " is the sixt.h article of the Mahemedan creed, and the orthodox believe that whatever has, or shall come to pass in this world. whether it be good or bad, proceeds entirely from the Divine will, and has been irrevocably fixed and recorded on a preserved tablet by the pen of fate."

This preserved tablet is the Perspicuous Book, the Book of God's decrees, called *lauh-i-mahfuz* in Arabic, and is said to contain all that has happened in the past and all that is to happen in the future.

> "Nor is anything added unto the age of him whose life is pro-longed, neither is anything diminished from his age, but *the same is written in the book of God's decrees"* (Sura, xxxv.).

It is pointed out in the Sura Y. S.:—

> "Verify, it is we who will quicken the dead and write down the works which they have sent on before them, and the traces which they shall have left behind them: and everything have we set down in the clear book of our decrees."

The actions of men are determined according to what is

written in the Book of Decrees; and the same holds true with respect to every other creature, for

> "all things have been created after fixed decrees" (Sura, liv. 49.)

To the same effect are the following:

> "No one can die except by God's permission according to the book that fixeth the term of life" (Sura, iii. 139).

> "The Lord hath created and balanced all things and hath fixed their destinies and guideth them." (Sura, xxxvii. 2).

> "By no means can aught befall us but what God has destined for us" (Sura, ix. 51).

Such is the nature of the Perspicuous Book. But the question which remains to be answered is; how are the decrees contained in the book of fate to be enforced in the world of men? Where may be a book, or even a whole library, in the cosmic archives, but unless there is a force which connects every individual soul with the action it is destined to perform, it is inconceivable how the decrees of fate can be worth anything more than the cash-value of the tablet on which they are inscribed. If our Muslim friends will take the trouble to work out the problem of the connection between the decrees of fate and the actions of men and other beings in the three worlds, they will not fail to perceive that the force which compels obedience to the decrees of fate is none other than the force of brmrl, and the (*lauh-i-mahfuz*), the Perspicuous Book, whose decrees can never be challenged, is the self-registering Ledger of karma, in which are recorded all things that have happened in the past and also those that are to happen in the future, or, in the language of the Qur'an, all actions of men, including '*the works which, they have sent on before them,* and the *traces which they shall leave behind them.*' The reader has only to turn to the doctrine of *karma*,[33] as propounded in the Jaina Siddhanta, to understand the nature of the Perspicuous Book and of the process which automatically records and registers the actions of men and their future, hence predetermined, fruits.

The whole doctrine, thus is a highly abridged and condensed version of the theory of *karma*.

I must now turn to Muslim philosophy. According to Avicenna (Ibn Seena), "the rational soul, being a simple substance, is out of space and time, and independent of the body" (see the "History of Psychology" by J. M. Baldwin, page 91). Kindi describes it as an "uncompounded, imperishable substance, descended from the world of reason [intelligence] into that of the senses" (see de Boer's History of Philosophy in Islam, p. 101). Abu Ali Ibn Maskawiah, too, held the soul to be a simple substance. Said he :

> "The soul of man is a simple incorporeal substance, conscious of its own existence, knowledge and working...... Length is not long in the soul, nor does it become longer in memory. Accordingly, the knowledge and endeavour of the soul extend for beyond its body......Moreover it possesses an inborn rational knowledge, which cannot have been bestowed by the senses, for it is by means of this knowledge that it determines the true and the false......Finally, it is in Self-consiousness, or knowing of its own "knowing, that the spiritual unity of the soul is more clearly shown—a unity in which thinking, that which thinks and which is thought—all coincide" (Ibid.)

From Ibn Baddja we learn: "Thus it is by rational knowledge, and by religious and mystical dreaming, with the sensuous invariably clinging thereto, that the human spirit arrives at perfection" (Ibid.). Ibn Khaldoon fully supports the view that the soul is omniscient by nature, and says that "as the soul is spiritual, the forms of events exist in it actually......It becomes spiritual through being stripped of all material substance and of the channels of bodily apprehension" (see my Gems of Islam, Eng. Trans.).

The above views are quite in accord with the conclusions established in the course of these lectures; but I must not omit to mention Al Ghazzali who is the greatest Muslim philosopher.

He was a great thinker and a voluminous writer, and understood the tenets of the Science of Salvation in the clearest way (see my Gems of Islam, part 2). With reference to the soul, he says:—

> "Although the Heart is a simple thing, nevertheless all departments of knowledge may be contained in it. Indeed, the whole World appears in it like a speck of dust in a desert........The knowledge that ordinary humanity acquire by learning, the man who has attained to this [supreme] status knows without the effort of learning. So long as the Heart is not emptied of the wisdom of the world the inner Illumination of Knowledge will not be obtained."

Al Ghazzali actually believed in transmigration and the bondage of karma, which he says can be worked off by very much the same kind of life as we have described in the third lecture.

Jalal-ul-Din Rumi, the author of the great Masnavi, is another great philosopher in Islam, though he conceals his attainment in the guise of a poet. So was Farid-ul-Din Attar. Many other saints and mystics and poets, *e.g.*, Hofiz, Nyaz, Muaiyen-ul-Din Chishti, also understood the scientific side of the Doctrine, hut did not care to show their knowledge or claim to be ranked among thinkers. They all believed in the Divinity of the soul and the effect of karma, and also in the power of the prescribed means to be rid of the bondage (see my Gems of Islam, parts I and II). They knew that the Qur'an was misleading if read literally, and said so openly. This was also the view of Ibn Tofail who said that the utterances of Muhammad should be interpreted allegorically (see T. J. de Boer's History of the Philosophy of Islam, p. 185).

Of course, transmigration was not openly taught in Islam, but it was accepted as a truth by all the really enlightened men. Here is a passage from Mr. Brown's valuable work, The Dervishes, which shows that the doctrine was openly preached by the order of Baktashee Dervishes :—

> "The soul is a divine emanation incorporated in a human form. It exists in five conditions, *viz*: it is awake, it dreams, it is plunged in slumber, it fills a state of half-death, and finally, *even perfectly sepamted from the body*........After death it must pass through several new existences. Virtuous souls occupy spheres superior to that of this soul and enjoy the fruits of their good works, whilst the guilty ones are condemned to fill conditions inferior to that of humanity. Wicked people who have degraded humanity in this life will live again in the shape of animal existence.......Baktashees believe that the soul ofter its separation from the human frame may enter into the body of an animal....."—The Dervishes, pp. 46-47.

The Dervishes, who held the soul to be altogether divine, maintained that God was a simple substance (see the Dervishes p. 61). They also maintained that "the soul existed before the body and is confined within. the letter as in a cage. Death, therefore, should be the object of thc wishes of the Soofee" (The Dervishes p. 12). Of Religion (*deen*) it was said that it was "the.........right path leading to eternal happiness" (The Dervishes, p. 65). This is precisely the view of Religion Proper, as described in the third lecture.

How is eternal happiness to be attained? The reply is:

> "The man must die, so to say, before the saint can be born" (The Dervishes, p. 300).

The next step is to become God.

> The Ehl el Hakk consider that everyone may, by superior piety and love of God......even become God" (The Dervishes p. 294).

Renunciation, termed *terk*, was prescribed for the attainment of "death". 'The Dervishes' again tells us:—

> "The Terk, or abandonment required by the Tareeket, is .thus explained:—To abandon the world, its comforts and dress,—all things now and to come,—conformably with the Hadees of the Prophet, *i.e.*, 'The world is forbidden to those of the life to come; the life to ,come is forbidden to those of this world; *and both are forbid-*

> *den to the true servants of God*,' which is thus explained:—The true Dervish in heart not only willingly abandons all the joys and pleasures of the world I but he is willing also to *give up all hope of the pleasure of Paradise*, and to be satisfied with the enjoyment derived from a submissive and devout contemplation of the beauty of God, and the hope of attaining to that primte Paradise, occupied only by the pious, the holy and the prophets."

Finally, we are told:—

> "The.....Hadees says, 'The Faithful do not die'; perhaps they become translated from the perishable world to the world of eternal existence."

But this is the true Indian or rather the Scientific doctrine once more, and in no sense different from it.

Turning to the allegorical vogue, Muhammadans are not found to be behind any other community that employed or patronized the pictorial soript. Some of their compositions are really possessed of superfine merit. A good many of the Muslim allegories have been explained in the useful little book of Mr. Khaja Khan which has already been referred to in one of the earlier lectures. The legend of the cow sacrifice will be explained by me in one of the succeeding lectures when I come to deal with the sacrificial cult.

In the Suratul Kahf a strange story is related of the vanity of Moses. It is said that Moses once declared that there was no one wiser than himself, whereupon he was directed in a vision to see Khizr at the junction of two streams. Moses accordingly proceeded to the appointed place where he met Khizr. Moses requested Khizr to be allowed to follow him, but the latter said, " Verily thou couldst not bear with me." Moses replied, "Thou shalt find me patient, if God please." Thence they proceeded together on the. seashore and finally got on board a, ship. Later on Khizr made a hole in the ship, when Moses accused him of the intention to drown all on board. Khizr replied, "Did

I not tell thee that thou couldst not bear with me ?" Upon this Moses apologised for his breach of faith, and they left the ship and plocceded on land. Here they met a youth whom Khizr slew at once. Moses now aceused Khizr of killing an innocent person and thereby committing an unjust act. Khizr gave the same curt reply as before and reminded Moses of their solemn pact. Thus rebuked, Moses said: "If I ask thee concerning anything hereofter, suffer me not to accompany thee!" From here they proceeded to a certain city where the inhabitants proved to be the most inhospitable, so much so that no food could be obtained there. Here Khizr found a wall that was in a dangerous condition and about to fall down, and he promptly put it right. This time Moses could not contain himself and remonstrated: "Thou mightest doubtless have received a reward for it.' Upon this Khizr declined to have anything further to do with Moses; but he condescended to enlighten him as to the significancy of his actions.

He said:—

> "The vessel belonged to certain poor men, who did their business in the sea; and I was minded to render it un serviceable, because there was a king behind them, who took away every sound ship by force. As to the youth, his parents were true believers and we feared lest he being an unbeliever should oblige them to suffer his preverseness and ingratitude, wherefore we desired that their Lord might give them a more righteous child in exchange, and one more affectionate towards them. And the wall belonged to two orphan youths in the city; and under it was a treasure hidden, which belonged to them and their father was a righteous man; and thy Lord was pleased that they should attain their full age and take forth their treasure through the mercy of thy Lord; and I did not what thou hast seen, of mine own will, but by God's direction. This is tho interpretation of that which thou couldst not bear with patience."

Khizr's explanation is only a partial lifting of the veil.

Further explanation is furnished by Mr. Khaja Khan in his Studies in Tasawwuf. He explains that the two rivers at whose junction Moses met Khizr signify love and humanity.

> "When one is on this cataract one requires a boat and a boat-man to tide over it. Moses met the boat-man in the person of Khizr and the boat was the boat of spiritual training When the boat reaches the other side of the river, there lives a King who confiscates sound boats. To save his ship Khizr, the spiritual guide, springs a leak in it. This is the hole of Love in the bottom of Humanity. Satan is unable to confiscate it; a leaky boat is of no good to him. In such a boat Humanity passes over to spiritnality."

The explanation of the rest of the story given by Mr. Khaja Khan,is that the youth, whom Khizr slew, represents Nofs (desires). "In the second stage of tile journey one has to kill his desire-body; unless desires are killed there can be no progress, this demon in the shape of a youth will be shadowing our steps." The wall that was toppling over stands for *Shariat* (law), under which lie two precious treasures, 'Pro-phet-ship' and 'Saintship' which are the two orphans referred to. In the country of plunderers the wall of *Shariat* (law) is protecting these two treasures. If the wall were allowed to collapse these treasures would have fallen into unworthy hands (Studies in Tasawwuf, pages 2 to 5).

I shall avail myself of the present opportunity to show that the Muslim conception of resurrection, too, is intended to yield the same significancy as that of *nirvana*, when properly understood. Its esoteric interpretation is to be found in the invaluable work of Mr. Khaja Kaan, entitled "Studies in Tasawwuf" from which I shall take the following passage:—

"Qiyamat.—The state of stability—a static state as opposed to dynamic. When the soul Eevers its connection with the body, the faculty of Wahm [imagination] accompanies it, according to Ghazzali, to the other side of the grave, and renews, in kaleidoscopic form and with a hundredfold vigour, the changes wrought and nurtured in it during the man's life-time on the earth, and he takes the form of the predominating characteristic of his life, still retaining the identity of his earthly ego, which links him on to resurrection in the next life. These changes, whether pleasant or unpleasant, go on recurring till........ qiyamat, when he feels his proximity to God and is lost in Transcendental Wonder The time of Qiyamat is not known to any creature. In the Hadith of Gabriel, the stranger also asked the prophet to I enlighten him regarding the day of judgment. The answer was: 'The questioned one is himself no more enlightened than the questioner.' 'Then,' said he, 'enlighten me regarding the signs that shall precede it.' The prophet said: It shall be when the maid-servant shall bring forbh her master, and you see the naked and the bare-footed and the grazer of sheep enjoying themselves in palaces.' According to Abdul Karim-i-Jili, 'Man is compared to Maid-Servant and the Occult Truth to her master.' This, therefore, means that Qiyamat will be when Divinity will manifest itself in Man..........The Wujud-i-Batini (the interior or real existence) of Man is God. The nature of this existence will become more apparent, and the reality of abd will become more clear in that 'state, and the naked (the interior; will enjoy in palaces' (illuminations). When the ariff (the knower) will become aware of asma (names=namarupa, of Indian origin, *i.e.*, objects of the senses) and ignores them in the light of Dhat (the Reality) and when also he will ignore sifat (qualities) and envisage Dhat, he will be like a shepherd, who is enjoying himself in a palace, i.e.,—the humane man will enjoy tile light of epiphanies. These are the minor signs; the major signs are that Yajuj and Majuj will appear on the earth. These are the seditious thoughts and evil intentions overpowering the nofs [soul] of man. They will be finally killed; and in their places Rahmani Khatras [Divine-affections] will appear. The second major sign is the appearance of the Dabbatul-ard, a talking beast, who will warn people against evil impulses. Jili considers that this refers to Ruh-ul-Quds (the Holy Ghost). The third is Dujjal, who will wander over the earth, but will avoid the direction of Mecca and Medina; he will stop short at Ramilah, a village built of mud near Jerusalem. Here Christ will descend and kill him with a lance. The Dujjal will have hell on his left-hand side, and heaven on his right-hand side. Jili considers that Dujjal is the Nofs-i-Ammara [the desiring nature] which is the repository of evil thoughts. On its left is the hell of ascetic life; and on its right, the heaven of licentiousness. Whoever is put into his hell will at once find a place in God's heaven, and *vice versa*. The Christ referred to is the soul that will scorch the nofs. The two cities that Dujjal will be unable to enter are the cities of Sukr [a state of ecstasy] and Sahw [a lesser state of ecstasy], and the village Ramilah that will obstruct his path is the state of the causal body. The fourth is the appearance of Mehdi. The fifth is the rising of the sun in the West and his setting in the East. This means man will have illuminations from a quarter least anticipated. All these signs mean that the ghayb [invisible] world will become the apparent world. This is the expected Millennium, wherein evil will disappear from the world before the coming of the Judgment Day."—Studies in Tasawwuf, pp. 192-194.

The square brackets are mine. Yajuj and Majujn stand for Good and Evil which are the causes of the influx of matter into the soul (see my Vision of St. John). The rising of the sun in the West and its setting in the East signify the dawning of the sun of Omniscience and the destruction of the organ of finite knowledge, which is described as the darkening of the sun in the Bible. The invisible world is the world of Reality, *i.e.*, of the attributes and virtues of the soul that are unmanifest to-day. Mehdi is probably the state of self-consciousness in the advanced soul that becomes his own guide and ceases to depend on external leaders. As for Dujjal's heaven and hell, the worldly man regards asceticism as a painful and undesirable process, and regards the ascetics as needlessly tormenting themselves. Hence is hell likened to asceticism, *i.e.*, torment, and being less easily acceptable is placed at the left hand. The heaven of the worldly-minded, on the other hand, consists in the enjoyment of the pleasures of life which comes easy naturally.

The paths to the real heaven and hell are, however, the reverse of this; asceticism leading to heaven and licentiousness to hell. It is said in a *hadis* (quoted in Extracts from the Holy Qur'an by Abdullah Allahdin p.76): "Hell is veiled in delights, and heaven in hardships and ,miseries." Hence he who enters into Dujjal's hell will find himself in the real heaven, and *vice versa*.

The interpretation of the term grazer of sheep will become clear with reference to the significance of Abel in the legend of the 'fall,' but nudity was the mark of saint-ship, as is evident from the following significant passage in the Holy Bible:—

> "And he stripped off his clothes also, and prophesied before Samuel in like manner, and lay down naked all that day and all that night. Wherefore they said, Is Saul also among the prophets ?" (Samuel, xix. 24.).

In Isaiah (xx. 2) also it is said:—

> "At the same time spake the Lord by Isaiah the son of Amoz, saying, Go and loose the sack cloth from off thy loins, and put off thy shoe from thy foot. And he did so, walking naked and barefoot."

Nudity was also a sign of world-renunciation amongst the Arabs about whom Washington Irving says in his "Life of Mahomet" (Appendix):—

> "The Towaf, or procession, round the Caaba was an ancient ceremony observed before the time of Mahomet, and performed by both sexes entirdy naked. Mahomet prohibited this exposure ami prescribed the Ihram, or pilgrim dress."

In India the Jain *nirgrantha* saints discard all clothes, and there are *nanga* (naked) *sadhus* also amongst the Hindus. Buddha's contemporary Mankhali Goshal, and the Achelakas, both went naked (*vide* Mr. Barna's Ajivikas). The seamless coat of Ohrist (st. ,John, xix. 23) is suggestive of the bare-skill esoterically.

Thus it is clear that the real significance of the passage "when you see the naked and bare-footed and the grazer of sheep enjoying themselves in palaces" is that redemption is nigh when those who go naked and bare-footed (*i.e.*, saints) and the grazers of sheep (*i.e.*, devotees of Life) enjoy themselves in palaces (*i.e.*, enjoy the joys inherent in the 'palace', that is to say the Kingdom of tho Soul).

We shall now briefly dwell upon the means prescribed by Islam for the obtainment of salvation. They comprise:

(1) sacrifice,

(2) prayer,

(3) fasting,

(4) pilgrimage and

(5) the general rules of piety.

We shall consider the first two of these in a subsequent lecture, but pilgrimage is common to all religions, as it is a powerful means of intensifying faith, and fasting[34] and general piety call for no special mention here. They all were intended to uproot the poisonous tree of desire which is the root of all trouble; and there have been many notable Muslim saints who understood these injunctions in this sense. Here are a few striking Terses from the writings of Shamsh of Tabrez and Forid-ul-din Attar in support of this view:—

(۱) ز دنیا ترک گیر از بهر دین تو
توکل بر خدا کن بالیقین تو

(۲) قلم اندر بصورت خویش در زن
حصار نفس را از بیخ برکن

(۳) حواس خمسه را چون دزد بربند
چو بستن دزد ایمن باش میخند

(۴) چو بائد رفتنت زین دار دنیا
چرا بندي تو دل درکار دنیا

(۵) بغفلتهاے دنیا خلق مغرور
بکردہ یاد مرگ از دل همه دور

(۶) علایقهاے دنیا قطع گردان
حزین دل باش دروے چون غریبان

(۷) زهے غفلت که مارا کور کرداست
که یاد مرگ از دل دور کرداست

(۸) تا نه گردن نفس تابع روح را
کے دوا یابی دل مجروح را

(۹) مقام فقر بس عالیمقام است
مني و مادر انجا بس حرام است

(۱۰) درآن منزل بود کشف و کرامات
ولے بائد گزشتن زان مقامات

(۱۱) اگر دنیا و عقبیٰ پیش آئد
نظر کردن درآن هرگز نشاید

(۱۲) اگر کردي تو در توحید فانی
بحق یابی بقائیے زندگاني

The English rendering of these couplets would be something like the following :—

(1) For the sake of din (religion or salvation) retire thou from the world; assuredly thou shouldst trust in God.

(2) Thrust the pen through the image of self ("I" and "mine"); pull down the Fortress of Desire from its foundation!

(3) Close the five senses, as thou wouldst lock up a thief; having secured the robber thou mayest rest in peace and laugh.

(4) When thou hast to leave the world, why dost thou tie thineself to its concerns?

(5) Inflated with pride are men with the vanities of the world; [alas!] they have altogether put aside the thought of death!

(6) Out off the chains that tie thee to the world; like a stranger thou shouldst live, sad of heart!

(7) strange is the infatuation that has blinded us-that has banished from the mind the thought of death!

(8) So long as the desiring nature is not brought under subjection to the soul, how shalt thou obtain a salve for the aching heart?

(9) Saintliness (asceticism) is the true exalted seat; 'me' and 'mine' are forbidden in that state.

(10) Illumination and miracles occur in that state [of self-contemplation]; but one should not) linger there.

(11) If both this and the future worlds lie before the saint, he should not look at them.

(12) If thou losest thyself in the unity of being, thou shalt find eternal life in the Truth!

The insistence on knowledge as a means of true progress is clear from the following passages in the Qur'an, the reference being to the pages of Sale's Translation:

(i) "Use indulgence, and command that which is just, and withdraw for from the ignorant" (p. 125).

(ii) "That they may diligently instruct themselves in religion" (p. 119).

(iii) "How few revolve (*these things*) in their mind" [po 353]!

(iv) "It is not *fit* for a man, that God should give him a book *of reveiations*, and wisdom and prophecy; and then he should say unto men, Be ye worshippers of me, besides God; but he ought to say, Be ye perfect in knowledge, and in works, since you know the scriptures and exercise yourselves therein" (p. 41)

The last quotation is also a direct authority for the view that "works" are necessary for salvation. In the Suratul Ankbut in the Qur'an (see xxix. 67) it is further said; "Those who labour in God's ways, we guide them to the right path." It was upon this text that Suhayl Ibn Abdullah Tasturi founded his sehoul of 'works,' which ultimately came to be known as the Suhayliyah school, after its founder.

All these facts and the inferences they give rise to definitely go to show that the real teaching of Islam is based on the same scientific principles which have enabled innumerable men to attain to Salvation in Jainism. I have no time to quote from other Muslim writers' works or to take you through further allegories of Islam; but I may ask you to read my Gems of Islam and other books where I have given further explanations. I can also recommend Mr. Khaja Khan's Studies in Tasawwuf for an explanation of Muslim mythology.

I propose to stop now for the day and to continue the investigation of mythology in another direction in the next lecture.

FOOTNOTES

1. Here are a few extracts from un English Translation (see pp. 53-54, 56 and 57) by H. St. J. Thuckeray, M. A:—
"........all these ordinances have been solemnly made for righteousness' sake, to promote holy meditation and the perfecting of character. For all the winged creatures, of which we partake, are tame and distinguished by cleanly habits, reeding on wheat and pulse.......But as touching the forbidden winged creatures, thou wilt find that they are wild and rarnivorous, and use the strength whioh they possess to oppress the remainder of their kind and get their food by cruelly preying upon the aforesaid creatures; and not on these only, but they also oarry off lambs and kids, and do violenoe to dead men and living. By these creatures which he oalled unclean, the law-giver gave a sign that those for whom the laws were ordained must praetise righteousness in their hearts and oppress no one trusting in their strength nor rob one of anything, but must direct their lives by righteous motives......He has, then, set forth all these rules as to what is permitted us in the case of these and the other creatures by way of allegory. For the parting of the hoofs and the dividing of the claws symbolize discrimination in our every action with a view to what is right......Mice mar and

injure everything not only for their own food, but in such a way that anything which they have begnn to injure becomes utterly useless for man. And the weasel tribe is peculiar, for beside the aforenamed habit it has a characteristic which defiles it; it conceives through its ears and gives birth through its mouth. And therefore the like habit of man is unclean; that it to say, whenever they have embodied in speeoh the things which they have received through the ear and involved others in ills, they are guilty of gross uncleanness and are themselves utterly tainted with the pollution of their impiety.....So, then, all that is said concerning meats and......animals relates to righteousness and righteous dealing between man and man."

2. The Jews also enjoined secrecy in respect of their secret doctrines and esoteric faith, including the mystery of Creation. As for the Hindus, they are notorious for forbidding the perusal of the Vedas to Shudras.
3. Cf. "Open ve the gates, that the righteous nation which keepeth the truth may enter in"—Isaiah xxvi. 2.
4. The concluding portion of the allegory is thus given in the Epistle of St. Paul (see Galatians, iv. 21-31):—

   "For it is written, Rejoice thou barren that bearest not; break forth and cry. thou that travailest not: for the desolate hath many more children than she which hath an husband.

   "Now, we brethren, as Isaac was, are the children of promise.

   "But as then he that was born after the flesh persecuted him that *was born after* the spirit, even so it is now.

   "Nevertheless what saith the scripture? Cast out the bond-woman and her son: for the son of the bond-woman shall not be heir with the son of the free woman.

   "So then brethren, we are not the children of the bond-woman, but of the free,"

   The sense of this allegory will be explained after the explanation of the mystery of the 'Fall'.
5. Cf. The nabi (prophet) wrote not in plain words, but in pictures. The meaning of the pictures was often purposely obscured. The Greek word 'prophet' sometimes properly belonged not to the nabi himself, but to those who, in his own time or in after time explained the riddle of the message." (The Influence of Greek Ideas and Usages upon the Christian Church by Hatch, pp. 72-73).

6. "Because the stoff is the symbol of discipiline (i.e., self-control), therefore, its reversal must be indicative of sense-indulgence, which is represented by a serpent. Hence, when Moses threw down his staff, it became a serpent. The superiority of Moses renunciation is to be sought in the fact that his serpent devoured all other similar serpents, which meant that his stoff stood for a renunciation much greater than that of any of his rivals!
7. See the Writings of Methodius p. 28.
8. Ibid. 39.
9. Ibid. 40.
20. Ibid. 103.
21. Ibid 107.
22. Ibid. 107.
23. In the Foreword to Mr. Khaja Khan's book, Nawab A. Hydari Hydar Nawazjung Bahadur, B.A., Finance Minister to H. E. H. the Nizam, thus delivers himself on the subject:—
"While the esoteric side of the other great religions is made more and more accessible to English readers, it is a matter of great misfortune that similar service is not being rendered to Islam, with the result that the majority of non-Muslims and even many Muslims, who have been brought up entirely under a European cultural environment, remain ignorant of that particular side in Islam which is its core and centre, which really gives life and vitality to its outward forms and activities, and which can most appeal to followers of other faiths owing to the universal character of its contents,"
24. *Cf.* "The mind that is concentrated most on the properties of matter is predisposed to derive all ideas from the senses..." (The History of European Morals chap. i)
25. See Atma Ramayana; also PHB. Vol. i. Chapter iii.
26. Krishna is conceived in the womb of Rohini and is then transferred into that or her co-wife Devaki, according to the Vishnu Purana of the Hindus. The significance of the allegory is this that the conception of divinity is first formed in the intellect, and is thence transferred to the soul-substance, which assuming its form itself becomes a manifested God.
27. The allegory of God, as the Ideal, becoming the charioteer of the soul, is one of the most fascinating ones. the individual has got to fight his battels himself, the Ideal cannot do so for for him; but it

is the ideal's function. to guide and direct all of his movements. Hence, Krishna does not undertake to fight in the great war for Arjuna, but willingly becomes his charioteer, in which capacity he leads him on to the battle field in the middle of the two armies and exhorts him to destroy the fees! These are the forces of delusion and evil-ties and attachments and emotions and all else that men are apt to regard as constituting the joys of life. Arjuna is bewildered at the prospect. What will be left if all that constitutes the joy of life. is destroyed? Life without earthly emotions, existence without love and, destitute of all that appeals to the senses and the mind! No, no, it is not to be thought of! It will be a void, the blankness of which is appalling to the imagination. Thus dismayed, Arjuna would fain turn back from such a battle! He turns. to his sweetly smiling charioteer for a word of comfort which now flows from the Divine (Ideal's) lips in the form of the Song Divine! The world represents but one side of tire shield, the other is represented by the Ideal itself. On its true side, life is so full and abundant and joyous that the very conception, of it is beyond the worldly-minded. One's choice lies between a life characterized by the endowments of such wondrous faculties as Omniscience, Immortality, Blissfulness and the like, on the one hand, and a wretched, impecunious miserable existence which, at its best, is perpetually haun ted by the ever-gnawing fear of death, and decay and calamity and distress and, disease, in one form or another, on the other! There isno rest even in death! The immortal 'pilgrim' may have to pass into the form of a moth, a. caterpillar, an onion, a bird, or a worm that wallows in filth and refuse! But Arjuna is not yet satisfied. Could Omniscience be possible? How was he to realize it? Could the glorious lustre be seen with the eyes of flesh? No, no; it cannot be seen that way; the gift, of the divine eye is needed. The Ideal now opens his internal vision; Arjuna's intuition is stimulated, the sub-conscious is roused into action, to display its hidden treasures! Thus is perceived the Light Divine expanding out to fill the entirety of the Realms of Time and Space! It holds, surrounds, overflows all, on all sides; outside it exists nought alone! It was truly a strange spectacle that lay unfolded before the mental eye of the gazer, staggering in its immensity, bewildering, terrifying, and flouting, by all manners, every well-formed human conception concerning Time, Space, Causality, Energy and Force, derived from the observation of visible nature! No wonder that poor Arjuna is overawed with the sight. At last the awesome vision is withdrawn; Arjuna is convinced now; but the combat still appears fearful to him. How can he be sure that he will succeed against such powerful foes ashe is oalled upon to faoe ? How to hope for a viotory in such an unequal contest? Now is uttered one of the greatest of psychologioal truths:

"Fight, thou shalt kill thy foes:

By Me they are already slain, be thou the outward cause!" The mere fact of the presence of the Ideal in the heart is an indication that the foroes of delusion and evil have been already uprooted. The very inoeption of Right Faith is fatal to their existence. Hence forth they exist like burnt up cordage, which resembles a rope outwardly, but crumbles to dust at the merest touch! Thus induced, Arjuna at last engages the enemy hosts in a mortal combat, and eventually overpowers the foe.

28. According to the Lost Apocrypha of the Old Testament (see Fragments p. 9), "Seth signifies resurrection. He was also called God."

29. Cf. "As long as our reason encompasses us with brightness.......filling our whole soul as it were, with noonday light, we remain in ourselves and do not experience possession. But when the light of reason Sets.......ecstasy and divine possession.......fall upon us. For where the Divine light blazes forth, the human sets, and when that sets, this rises" (Philo's Contribution to Religion, by H. A. A. Kennedy, pp. 229-230). The outward-turned sense is, allegorically, the second sun (Yonge's Philo Judaeus ii. 309).

30. Cf. "The man that wandereth out of the way of understanding shall remain in the congregation of the dead" (Proverbs xxi. 16).

Cf. also....."Awake thou that sleepest and arise from the dead, and Christ shall give thee light" (Ephesians v. 14).

31. Cf. "The soul. leaving the body,' was regularly represented as a little human figure, naked and sexless emerging from the mouth" (ERE Vol. xii p. 137, Art. Christian Symbolism),

32. The following interesting note occurs in connection with the figure of a fylfot (swastika) in Hulme's Symbolism in Christian Art, pages 218-220:—

"The form known as the fylfot is frequently introduced on the vestments of the Greek Church, and is found also somewhat more sparingly in the west, both in ecclesiastical and heraldic work. It was most commonly employed amongst the Western peoples in the thirteenth and fourteenth centuries, and many examples of it may be seen on monuments, brassese, and so forth.......In the use of the fylfot the early Christians merely adopted and diverted to their own purpose a symbol centuries older than the Christian era, a symbol of early Aryan origin, iound abundantly in Indian and Chinese art, and spreading westward, long before the dawn of Christianity, to Greece and Asia. The subject is beset with difficulties, and many theories have been propounded in attempted elucidation, one being that it represents a revolving wheel, and symbolizes the great Sun God; while another is that it stands for the lightning wielded by the omnipotent Deity, whether this Deity be Manu,

Buddha, or Brahma of the East, or Thor or Zeus of the West. The fylfot is abundantly found on the terra-colta objects dug up by Dr. Schliemann at Troy, and conjectured to date from 1000 to 1500 B. C.; and the Greek fret or key pattern is frequently seen in combination with the fylfot, or is itself a fuller and more decorative development of the form."

33. Cf.."Verily, God changes not what a people has unless they change what is in themselves." (The Quran by Abul Fazal, vo), II p 386) Sale's translation of this verse, which is as follows, is also very significant. "Verily, God will not change his grace which is in men, until they change the disposition in their souls by sin" (Al Koran, p, 182), The italicised words in Sale's translation are only intended to develop the sense, which is, however, quite clear even without them. The idea here, clearly, is that of a modification of what is in men by their own evil deeds, in other words of a modification of disposition by action. This is certainly in agreemcnt with truth, as demonstrated ere this.

34. Cf. "In fasting man shows the qualities of angels, who neither eat nor drink, neither marry nor are given in marriage.........In fasting the *abd* (devotee) attains the attributes of God who neither cats nor drinks......Abul Hasan-Nuri defines it as the renunciation of all pleasures of nab, thus emphasizing asceticisrn." ("Studies in Tasawwuf," pages 103 and 122).

CHAPTER -VI

SOME ANCIENT AND EXTINCT FAITHS

I propose this evening to look into certain ancient faiths. As is now well-known, the ancient Babylonians celebrated a sort of mystic rite that was centred round the god Tammuz who was dead and rose again from the dead, through the labours of Innini, his weeping mother, and, finally, also his bride. The Semitic legend of the descent of Istar who descended into Hades to rescue the young god Tammuz, is another myth of the same type. So is the Egyptian cult of Osiris, in connection with which certain forms of ritual were gone, through annually in secret and were known as "mysteries". The following account of this ancient cult is given in the ERE. (vol. iv, p. 243) :

> "The details of his myth do not concern us; but, briefly, the doctrine of the Egyptian religion taught that Osiris, a beneficent god and king, after being S. Jain by the treachery of Set, his malevolent antithesis, was restored to life again, justified before the gods against the accusations of Set, and made God and Judre in the underworld. Already by the time of the 5th dynasty the idea had been conceived that the story of Osiris was repeated in the case of each Pharaoh, and the conception gradually filtered down until it was heltr that every man who was possessed of the necessary knowledge might after death become an Osiris, be restored to life, be justified before the gods, and enter into ever-lasting blessedness. Practically the Egyptians believed, from the earliest historical period that becanse Osiris died and rose again, and after being

> justified entered into ever-lasting life, therefore those who believed in him would share the same destiny ....This belief is held, with no essential variations, throughout the whole historic period."

In the Book of The Dead (chapter cliv) it is said:—

> "Homage to thee O my divine father, Osiris! thou...... didst not decay.........thou didst not become corruption ....I shall not decay......I shall not see corruption.......I shall have my being, I shall live, I shall germinate, I shall wake up in peace,"

The following is the explanation given by Herodotus of these mysteries (ERE. vol. ix. p. 74):—

> "At Sais is the burial place of one whom I scruple to name (Osiris)......On the lake (of the temple), the Egyptians represent by night the sufferings undergone by Him and this representation they call Mysteries. All the proceedings in these Mysteries are well-known to me; but my lips shall piously refrain from mentioning them" (Herod ii. 170 f.).

And Plutarch adds (ERE. vol. ix. p. 74):—

> "Isis would not that her own woes and grievous journeyings, that the deeds of his wisdom and heroism should fall into oblivion and silence. She therefore instituted holy sacred mysteries which would afford an image, a representation in mimic scenes, of the sufferings he endured that they might serve as a pious teaching and a consolatory hope to the men and women who passed through the same hardships" (Plutarch de Is. et Oris. xxvii).

Osiris was murdered, according to an Egyptian legend, by his brother Seth, which means typhoon. The coffin containing his body was then launched into the Nile. It drifted away thence to a place where it was discovered by Isis, and was taken thence by her to Egypt. Here Seth found the corpse and cut it into pieces, which he cast into the Nile. Isis resumed her search for it, and she raised a tomb over every fragment of the body wherever she found it. Then Horus, the son of Osiris,

Thoth and Anubis, his friends, came to Isis' help to avenge Osiris; they justified him before the court of gods, and restored his mummified body to life and immortality. Thus could Osiris hand over his realm to his son, Horus, who became the patron and ancestor of the Pharaohs (ERE. vol. ix. p. 74).

The scheme of the Osirian Mysteries that has now been partially reconstructed with the aid of an old account, dating from the year 1875 B.C., runs as follows:—

(1) Isis and Nephthys have searched and found the body of Osiris upon the river of Nedit; and there is prolonged lament.

(2) On hearing the cries, the gods come in haste; Horus, Anubis and Thoth carry magical implements and vases filled with fresh water; Osiris is cleansed of all stains by four libations and fumigations.

(3) Divine magic effects a series of miracles : (a) the dismemberment of the body of Osiri is restored; (b) by unction with oils and paint and by the agency of the adze of Anubis mouth, eyes and ears in the body of Osiris are 'opened'; (c) the members are put into motion, and each organ recalled to life; (d) other methods are employed to revive 'Osiris' body: it is buried in the earth; (e) Osiris is also revived by simulating an animal rebirth; the priest who plays Anubis lies in a recumbent position—which is that of the foetus in the mother's womb—under the skin of some sacrificial animal. He symbolises Osiris being conceived anew, being reborn in the hide, and issuing, as if from the matrix, after assimilating to himself the life of his sacrificed adversary, Seth. As the result of all these rites Osiris is brought back to life. Offerings are then offered to him, and he is adorned and crowned. He also recovers the privilege of 'creative voice' whereby he is able to baffle all dangers, and to create instantly whatever in any emergency necessity demands (ERE. vol. ix. p. 75).

In addition to these rites, there is reason to believe, there were other rites complementary to these which related to the purification of Osiris, and which were probably only known to the initiates. These ceremonies were performed that they might serve as a pious hint and consolation for the men and women who should suffer the same trials. In the words of the writer of the Article on the Egyptian Mysteries in the ERE., "the Egyptian Mysteries, like the Eleusinian and Isiac Mysteries, claim to.......reveal the way to enter upon a new blissful life. Every notion that we have of them is connected with the cult of Osiris, who is, in the Egyptian Pantheon, pre-eminently the dead and resuscitated god."

We come now to the Greek Mysteries of which there were several sorts, and which were believed to deliver men from the torments of the other world, while the neglect of them was punished by an awful doom. It was clearly stated that happiness in the next world was confined to those who had been initiated in these mysteries. The initiate was enjoined in the following remarkable words:

> "Above all remember and retain in your heart that the remaining space of your life on earth is dedicated to me, to whom you owe all your being" [ERE. vol ix. p 82)

Dramatic art was impressed in these Mysteries into service to illustrate the triumph of Life over Death in captivating symbolism:

> "At night there were the mystic plays: the scenic representation the drama in symbol and for sight. Their torches were extinguished: they stood outside the temple in silence and the darkness. The doors opened—there was a blaze of light—and before them was acted the Drama of Demeter and Kore—the loss of the daughter, the wandering of the mother, the birth of the child.......It was the poetry of nature........It was a drama also of human life It was the poetry of the hope of a worm to come. Death gave place to life. It was a *purgatio anima*, by which the soul might be fit for the presence of God.

> Those who had been baptized and initiated were lifted into a new life. Death had no terrors for them The blaze of light after darkness, the symbolic scenery of the life of the gods, were a foreshadowing of the life to come" (The Hibbert Lectures for 1888, pp. 288-289).

As for the cult of these mysteries, the same theme of the death and resurrection of a god is common to them all. An interesting account of one of these mystery-cults is thus given in the ERE:—

> "The special form of Dionysiac worship.......is connected with the name Zagreus which was applied to Dionysus. The legends which told the story of the birth, death and resurrection of Zagreus are of a particularly revolting kind.......Zagreus was the child of an amour of Zeus and Persephone. While still an infant he was entrapped by the Titans, who attracted him with toys and then tore him to pieces and devoured him. Only the heart survived, which was rescued by Athene and carried to Zeus, who slew the murderers with his thunder. bolts, and produced from the heart another Zagreus."

The legend was thus explained by Orphic teachers:—

> "In all of us there is a divine element not wholly overwhelmed with wickedness of which the Titans are the emblem. By innate impurity men are condemned to a cycle of births and deaths, from which they can escape and be made fit for communion with Gods only by purification and initiation in the Mysteries" (ERE vol. ix. p. 80).

I do not think I am called upon to add another word of explanation to this, as it must be quite plain to you by this time that the resurrection cult in all these 'mysteries' bears reference to the soul's own divinity which is to be rescued from the clutches of the Titans (forces of *karma* and transmigration) and immortalised, with all the lost limbs and members (attributes and powers) restored. This is in full agreement with the following from the Hindu *Puranas* already quoted in our first lecture.—

"All imperfections leave behind.
Assume thine ancient frame once more—
Each limb and sense thou hadst before,
From every earthly taint refined."

I shall now briefly describe the teaching of that ancient religion of China which passes by the name of Taoism.

Taoism was reformed or put together afresh about, the sixth century B.C., by a certain Chinese mystic who was known as Lao-tze. The theories of Lao-tze, in many instances, bear close resemblance to Indian thought and are, in the main, an abridged version of the teaching of Jainism.

The term *Tao* which has proved very troublesome to the translator (see the introduction to SBE. vol. xxxix. pp. 12-15) means Life, and on account of the different aspects in which Life manifests itself, has caused endless confusion in the minds of men. Some think that it means a path or road, others that it was intended for nature, others, again, that it stands for reason. But the true reading is Life, in all its diverse aspects, especially as "the way, the truth and the Iife" (cf. St. John xiv. 6). Accordingly, Lao-tze defines his Tao as the ultimate reality, anterior to and higher than heaven, existing before time began and precedent to the manifested God. Of course, Life is eternal, and its essence is prior to its manifesting itself in its full divinity as manifested God. Taken in the abstract, it is devoid of personality and is without any or those attributes, including Reason which are associated with humanity. Its action is represented as necessary and automatic, and it is devoid of sensible qualities. The ultimate source of all being it pervades, influences, and harmonises all the phenomena of nature, and its quiet but all-effective operation is the example upon which all human activities should be modelled, in contradistinction to the bustling officiousness and blustering self-assertiveness that are characteristic of mankind in general. Tao, of course, is the natural heritage of man, but, in the majority of cases, that heritage has been set aside by other interests. The quest of Tao must be undertaken if men are to regain that tranquillity, that complete contentment, which can never be acquired by the worldly-minded. For Tao is also the goal towards which all beings tend. The means by which the goal is to be reached are generally available to all, demanding only the condition of absolute self-abnegation. To abandon the vaunted 'wisdom' of the schools, to lay aside all self-interest, to throw open every avenue of thought and feeling to the entrance of Tao are the necessary steps to that final consummation, viz. return to Tao. Ambition, luxury, wealth and pleasure have no place in the life-programme of the Taoist. He must strive for the attainment of quietness, for nothing else, not even for the promotion of virtue, or the preaching of his doctrine. The Taoist holds that virtue which is artificially developed is valueless as compared with that which is the unconscious expression of the Tao within. Tao must be attained, therefore, by every means in one's power. It is only when the root is present that flowers will bloom! Amongst the steps the first is purgation. Only he who is eternally free from earthly passions will reach Tao. The second is illumination when dispassion becomes a habit. The third is the attainment of unity, when "without going out of doors one may know the whole world." The process, however, is long and involves many hardships. The novice must first acquire esoteric knowledge of the Truth at the feet of an Adept. He should then establish himself in the principle of 'Quietism,' devoting his whole spare time to self-introspection; he must also develop complete contempt for material things and worldly relations. Then alone will he be qualified to enter into Tao, that is Life Eternal.

The above account which is taken from the article on Chinese Mysticism in the ERE. is really an abridgement of the teaching of Religion Proper, and shows at a glance how widely prevalent its doctrines were in the ancient days. According to a French work, the 'Histoire des Religions' (vol. iii),quoted in Metchnikoff's 'Nature of Man.'

"One of the chief claims of Taoism was the possession of

> a specific against death. And some of the masters of Taoism, such, for instance, as Chang-Tao-Ling, ascended to heaven without dying, by climbing a lofty peak and vanishing into the skies.......To arrive at this, Lao-tseu simply expanded and applied to mankind generally an idea that was already familiar to him, the conception of the transmigration of one soul through several successive bodies. By means of......expiatory transformations, a man who had not reached it directly through the holiness of his life, could attain the immortality of the *genii* and the blessed.

I suppose this only means that if a man failed to attain to immortality in one life, by reason of death intervening before the destruction of the causes of transmigration, the fruit of his labours was not lost and would be his in the next rebirth, so that by means of steady work *nirvana* could be easily attained in the course of a few 'lives.'

Philo Judaeus also says:—

> "The end of virtuous and hold men is not death but a translation, and migration and an approach to some other place of abode". (The Message of Philo by K. S. Guthrie, p. 74).

That this simple doctrine should have puzzled modern investigators is not surprising, because what they have read hitherto is not the scientific explanation of Religion Proper, but only the disconnected mystic or, at best, speculative tenets of mytholgical creeds passing current as Religion.

The vanishing into the skies of Chang Tao-Ling is thus described in the Introduction to the 39th volume of the SBE. (p. 42) :

> "Among Liang's descendants in our first century was a *Kang* Tao-Ling, who, eschewing a career in the service of the state devoted himself to the pursuits of alchemy, and at last succeeded in compounding the grand elixir or pill, and at the age of 123 was released from the trammels of the mortal body, and entered on the enjoyment of immortality......."

I think this is more like a secret teaching than a literal statement of a fact; and a strong hint of the emblematic nature of the teaching is conveyed in the part that refers to release from the trammels of the body, which is certainly an indication of *nirvana*, and opposed to the notion of a perpetuating of bodily existence by means of chemical or alchemical potions and pills.

The Tao Teh Ching, the mysterious Book of Taoism, has it:

> "The further that one goes out (from himself), the less he knows" (SBE. vol. xxxix. p. 89).

And the following from the same work—

> "He who has in himself abundantly the attributes (of tile Tao) is like an infant. Poisonous insects will not sting him; fierce beasts will not seize him, birds of prey will not strike him" (Ibid. p. 99)—

is in the same strain as the prophecy in the Gospel of, St. Mark towards the end of the 16th chapter, or the teaching of Hinduism (the Yoga Vashishta by Narain S. Ayer).

Self-knowledge is pointed out as essential to the knowledge of God.

"By exerting his mental powers to the full, man comes to understand his nature. When he understands his own nature, he understands God" (The religions of Ancient China, by H. A. Giles, LL.D., p. 43).

Shao Yung (1011-1077 A.D.) defines the residence of God thus:

> "The heavens are still: no sound.
> Where then shall God be found?
> Search not in distant skies;
> In man's own heart He lies" (Ibid. p. 58)!

The ultimate end, too, is God (Ibid p. 50). Everyone who attaches importance to the external, becomes internally without. resource (THE MUSINGS OF A CHINESE MYSTIC, by L. Giles, p. 100). Perfection is not constituted by

> "......charity and duty to one's neighbour. It is found in the cultivation of Tao. Perfection of hearing is not hearing others, but oneself.......Perfection of vision is not seeing others, but oneself. For a man who sees not himself, but others, takes not possession of himself, but of others, thus taking what others should take and not what he himself should take. Instead of being himself, he in fact becomes someone else" (Ibid. p. 97).

By mental perfection good and evil cease to exist. A Chinese mystic puts it:

> "The question is, how to bring the mind into a state of calm, in which there is no thinking or mental activity; how to keep the lips silent, with only natural inhalation and exhalation going on. If you give yourself up to mental perfection, right and wrong will cease to exist; if the lips follow their natural law they know not profit or loss" (Taoist Teachings, p. 41).

We also have it from the same source:

> "The only way to etherealise the body being to purge the mind of its passions" (Ibid. p. 42).[1]

The mind is the seat of felicitous influences:

"Look at that aperture: the empty apartment is filled with light through it. Felicitous influences rest (in the mind thus emblemed), as in their proper resting place" (SBE. vol. xxxix. p. 210).

The true man, a Master of the Tao, or the spirit-like Man, is defined as a "recluse of the mountain, whose bodily form has been changed, and who ascends to heaven" (*Ibid*. 237 footnote). The sagely man is "the Great Conqueror" (*Ibid*. p. 385). "Men of the highest spirit-like qualities mount up on the light, and (the limitations of) the body vanish" (*Ibid*. p. 324). the human spirit, it is said (*Ibid*. 367), transforms and nourishes all things, and cannot be represented by any form; its name is "the Divinity (in man)". The Chinese term here used is *Ti*, which, according to a footnote of the translator (on p. 367), is regarded as " a very remarkable use of *Ti* for the human spirit in the sense of God." He to whom profit and injury are not the same is not a superior man (*Ibid*. p. 239).

As to what is the significance of the attainment of the aim:—

> "Complete enjoyment is which is meant by the attainment or the aim. Now-a-days what is called the 'Attainment of the aim' means the getting of carriages and coronets. But carriages and coronets belong to the body; they do not affect the nature as it is constituted. When such things happen to come, it is but for a time; being but for a time their coming cannot be obstructed and their going cannot be stopped……The one of these conditions and the other may equally conduce to our enjoyment, which is simply to be free from anxiety. If now the departure of what is transient takes away one's enjoyment, this view shows that what enjoyment it had given was worthless. Hence it is said, 'They who lose themselves in their pursuit of things, and lose their nature in their study of what is vulgar, must be pronounced people who turn things upside down'" (Ibid. pp. 372-373).

All this is in full harmony with the teaching of the Scientific Religion as we know it now.

Let us pause here for a moment to ascertain the precise significance of the Biblical text "I am *the way, the truth and the life*" (John xiv. 6).—

It is in reality nothing but a·paraphrase, or rendering in other words, that is to say, a literal translation, virtually, of the *Ratna Trai*. (triple-jewel) of Right Faith, Right Knowledge and Right Conduct, which, taken together, constitute the Path of Salvation, according to Jainism.

The way=the true, proper or Right Faith.[2]

The truth=the true, proper or Right Knowledge.

The life = the true, proper or Right mode of living, hence Right Conduct.

The very first *sutra* of the Jaina Bible, otherwise known as the *Tattvartha Sutra*, teaches:—

सम्यग दर्शन ज्ञानाचारित्रारिग मोक्ष मार्गः॥

This means: Right Faith, Right Knowledge and Right Conduct (together) constitute the path to liberation. And it is said in the 27th *sloka* of the *Dravya Sangraha* (see SBJ. vol. I. p. 110):—

> "Because by the rule a sage gets both the causes of liberation by meditation, therefore practise meditation with carefnl mind."

The two causes of liberation referred to are known as *vyavahara* and *nischaya*. Their difference is due to the standpoint from which we may approach the subject. The *vyavahara* is the practical point of view, while the other is the real or natural point of view. From the former point of view (the *vyavahara*),the belief in the doctrine of the *Tirthamkaras* Right Faith, the knowledge of the *tattavas*, as taught in the Jaina Scripture, Right Knowledge, and the observance of the rules of conduct prescribed for the layman and the monk, Right Conduct. But, in reality, the soul being a conscious being, is itself an embodiment of Right Faith, Right Knowledge Right Conduct.

Mr. S. C. Ghoshal writes in his commentary on the *Dravya Sangraha* just referred to:—

> "Perfect faith, perfect knowledge, and perfect conduct are the cause of liberation from tbe ordinary point of view, while really the soul itself possessed of these three is the cause of liberation" (SBJ. vol. i. p. 110).

Plainly put, the difference between *nischaya* and *vyavahara* points of view is simply the difference between the subjective and the objective aspects of Faith and Knowledge and Conduct. Objectively, Faith, Knowledge and Renunciation or *Vairagya*, that is to say, Proper Conduct, are constituted by the rules and descriptions given in the Scripture of Truth; but subjectively, they are only states of the soul itself. Certainly, the scriptures do not contain Faith, Knowledge. and Conduct, but only their description in words, so that they can only be really found in the hearts of men. This is the reason why a selfconscious soul may justly maintain of itself,

"I am *the way, the truth and the life.*"

The order in which these attributes are mentioned is also full of significance; for they are always mentioned in this very order in the Jaina Books. This significance appears sufficiently clearly from Mr. J. L. Jaini's translation of the *Tattvartha Sutra*, which constitutes the 2nd volume of the series known as the Sacred Books of the Jainas.

> "Of these three, right belief is the basis upon which the other two rest. It is an essential preliminary to right knowledge. It is the cause and right knowledge is the effect. Right knowledge always implies it. Similarly, right conduct is preceded and caused by right knowledge, and implies both right knowledge and right belief. For this reason, in the aphorism we find right belief mentioned first, then right knowledge and lastly right conduct" (SBJ. vol. ii. p. 2).

I shall now explain the purport and nature of certain mysteries which adopted the symbols of the builder's art to conceal their religious doctrines from the profane. The society of Dionysian Builders was one of those societies that flourished in ancient days, and their influence has continued through Druids and others, down to our own times in one form or another. The Builder[3] was not a common labourer or mason, in the ordinary acceptance of the term, but the builder of the edifice of his own soul. He built no pagodas or fanes of brick or stone, but employed himself to raise a temple of Divinity and freedom for his Soul to dwell in, for all Eternity to come. A. E. Waite writes (see "The New Encyclo of Free Masonry, vol. 1. p. 335):—

> "On his entrance into Free Masonry the newly received Brother has come into a world of emblems or symbolism and whatever takes place therein has a meaning behind it, being one which is not always indicated on the surface. Import is sometimes manifold, depending

> on those various points of view from which it can be approached.....It is......as if the, candidate on his initiation had been born anew into the universe or that a door had opened to admit him into another analogical cosmos. Indeed at that pregnant moment when he is restored to light, he discovers himself in the symbolical representation of a new world; and when he is told subsequently that he is the corner stone of a new foundation from which he must build up himself, he should realize—if his be the gift of insight—that from such point of view the just, perfect and regular Lodge is also his own symbol, a representation of that state which he is called to attain."

As everywhere else, the initiates "were obliged by solemn engagements to commence a new life of strictest purity and virtue into which they were entered by a severe course of penance proper, to purge the mind of its natural defilements" (The Mysteries of Freemasonry by John Fellows, page 107). The object of this, Mr. Fellows points out, was "to restore the soul to its original purity—to that state from whence it fell, as from its native seat or perfection" (Ibid. page 106). Amongst the moral precepts inculcated in the ancient mysteries were included the honouring of the parents, the offering up of fruits to gods, and the forbearance from cruelty to animals (Ibid. 107). The Pythagorians, too, abstained from animal food and sacrifices (Ibid. 198), and their predecessors of Egypt were not allowed even to wear shoes other than those made from the plant papyrus (Ibid. 218). The Pythagorians also abstained from the use of beans which has puzzled European writers much.[4] But the fact is that the Pythagorians had learnt their wisdom from the Eastern nations including the Gymnosophists (the .Jainas), and the Jainas do not use beans in combination with milk and curd, on the ground that in conjunction with the human saliva such a combination of beans (all kinds of pulses are included under this head) becomes the breeding soil of an infinity of microscopical germs which are destroyed in the process of digestion. To avoid the destruction of so many innocent lives it: was that the Jainas recommended abstaining from the use of beans in combination with milk and curd, and the Pythagorians had probably taken the doctrine from the Jainas.

The initiate was termed *Epoptes*; by which was meant one who sees *things as they are*, and without disguise, whereas before he was called *Mystes*, which has a contrary significance (Ibid. 111). According to Clemens: "the doctrines delivered in the greater mysteries are concerning the universe. Here all instruction ends. *Things are seen as they are*; and nature and the things of nature are given to be comprehended" (Ibid. 114). This may be compared with the Jaina Proclamation of Victory:

जैन धर्म जैवंत नित जाको मर्म सौ पाए।
बास्तु यथारथरूप लखि पहुँचे शिवपुर धाए॥

[Trans.—May eternally victorious be the Jaina Dharma; who so acquires an insight into it becomes familiar with the real nature of things and speedily reaches *Nirvana*.]

In an old Scripture dating probably from the second century A.D., Right Knowledge is defined thus:

> "That which reveals the nature of things neither insufficiently, nor with exaggeration, nor falsely, but exactly as it is, and with certainty, that the Knowers of Scripture call Right Knowledge"— The Householders's Dharma, page 23.

The myth most intimately associated with most of these building mysteries was the death of the Grand Master Architect, Hiram Abif, which is also to be found in the Old Testament in the Holy Bible with slight modification. King Solomon, desirous of building a Temple to the God of Israel, enlisted the co-operation of Hiram, King of Tyre, and with the aid of the Grand Master Builder, Hiram Abif, proceeded to build up a Temple of God which was to be absolutely unparalleled on the Earth. The three Grand Masters, that is, King Solomon, King Hiram and the Master Builder Hiram Abif, who was a widow's son, entered at the commencement of the work, into a solemn agreement that the Master's degree was not to be conferred until the Temple should be complete, that all the three must be present when it should be conferred, and that if any of them were taken away by death prior to the finishing of the Temple, the Master's degree should be lost. Now, Hiram Abif was killed by three assassins, and so the Master's degree could not be conferred without his revivification. The "mysteries" celebrated, in one way or another, the restoration to life of the Grand Master, for though dead he was destined to rise again.

The interpretation of this myth lies in the resurrection of Hiram, issuing gloriously from the tomb, 'reborn to active life.' The three assassins are the world, the flesh and the devil (Waite's Encyclopaedia. Vol. i. 424), that is falsehood or delusion. The three Grand Masters of whom two are kings and the third a builder, and who entered into a pact not to confer the Master's degree except conjointly, are Right Faith, Right Knowledge and Right Conduct, or what comes to the same thing in Christian terminology, the way, *the truth and the life*, as already explained. For while salvation is not possible except the three are present conjointly and simultaneously, the real builder of the Soul's Divinity is the last-named, that is to say Right Conduct, Faith and Knowledge not being directly concerned in the actual building up of the Spiritual Edifice. For this reason Faith and Knowledge are described as Kings, and Conduct as the Master Builder. The significance of the description "the widow's son" will be explained in connection with the elucidation of the cow sacrifice in the twelfth lecture.

The Temple to be built is the individual's own self.[5]

"It was wise of Israel's king
To make such treaty with the King of Tyre;
When he to build the Temple did aspire;
Even now we seem to hear the axes ring
In Lebanon's huge forest. How they fell
Those pines and cedars! and Sidonian skill
Soon carves them into shape: the craftsman's will

Bringing rude matter into forms which all
Admire for strength and beauty. So must we
Carve thoughts and feelings with true Masonry."
—G. Markham Tweddil.

As Mr. Waite points out *ars latomorum*, understood in its true emblematic sense, is the Art of Life; and in the degree of Entered Apprentice there is imposed upon the candidate such, an edification[6] of his own temple as shall in fine produce a structure perfect in its parts and honourable, to the builder. In the last resource the croftsman is always one's own self. The Master-Builder of the third degree does actually rise as Christ. The culmination is reached in the higher degree of the Royal Arch where the soul itself becomes the corner stone, resting on the two pillars, Boaz and Jachin, which again signify Faith and Knowledge. This is the very stone which was rejected by the misguided 'builders,' but which is really divine. As the Biblical text has it,

> "The stone which the builders refused has become the head of the corner."

The pillars are imagined as standing at the two equinoxes, east and west, to support the world.

> "Hence it may be remarked that the pillar representing Boaz, or the Sun, is probably said to denote strength, whereas in the apprentice's degree it is made to denote *wisdom* Jachin, signifying Isis the Moon, was a necessary appendage to the creation and perhaps may be applied metaphorically to 'establish' (The Mysteries of Freemasonry, p. 273).

With respect to the idea of creation "the maintainers of the Egyptian Philosophy held that the: *Supreme Being*, the infinitely perfect and happy, was not the creator of the world, nor the alone independent being" (Ibid. 271). The true divinity is revealed only when the initiate arrives at the Holy Royal Arch where the discovery is made known to him and he is told of the true first person. The lost word is logos, the creative intelligence that removes the prevailing confusion from the mind, establishing a holy Spiritual Cosmos in its place.

The explanation of the more important building symbols is as follows:—

Ashlar.—Literally a kind of stone; hence the Living Stone, the Essence or Substance of Life. The rough ashlar represents the ordinary man, ignorant of himself and deluded by the tinsel show of the outside world. The *perfect ashlar* is the Master who has removed his imperfections and acquired the smoothness, polish and finish of perfection.

The Compasses.—Restraint or Control, hence the placing of limitations on one's desires to acquire Self-Control. In the Lodge Catechism the initiate is asked: 'have you seen your master to-day'? He replies: 'yes.' 'How was he clothed'? 'In a yellow jacket and a pair of blue breeches!' The allusion is to the Compasses with the body of brass (yellow jacket) and steel points (blue breeches). This clearly refers to the daily imposition of restraint on one's desires and activities to subjugate the lower nature.

The Pentalpha.—Bears reference to the five chief sins, *himsa* (causing injury to living beings), falsehood, theft, adultery and *parigraha* (abundance of worldly goods). Probably, the figure of the pentagram in Jewish Mysticism signified A^3 UM (ओ३म) formed by combining the first letters of the following five words expressive of *Parameshthi* (Divinity):

a=*Arhant* (the Tirthamkara),

a=*Ashrira* (the Deified Emancipated Soul),

a=*Acharya* (the Pontiff, i.e., the head of Saints),

u=*Upadhyaya* (the Preceptor of Saints), and

m=*Muni* (a Saint).

This gives us:

3 'a'$s+u+m=A^3$ UM (ओ३म)

The word *Aum*, or *Om*, is associated in Jainism with the holiest of mantras, called the *pancha namokara mantra* (the five-fold obeisance *mantram*) which is as folows:—

Namo Arahantanam (I bow to the *Arhant*),

Namo Siddhanam (I bow to the *Siddha*),

Namo Aieryanam (I bow to the *Pontiff*),

Namo Uvajjhayanam (I bow to the *Upadhyaya*),

Namo loe savvasahunam (I bow to the Saints)

Om is the grammaticl abridgment of this holy *mantram*, and is respected by all kinds of celestials, demons and ghosts. It is pointed out in, the " Masonic Legends and Traditions" (by Dudley Wright) that" according to Masonic Tradition, Enoch was an eminent mason, and preserved the true name of God, which it is said the Jews subsequently lost. This name was known only to the initiated. The descendants of Abraham wrote it *Jao*; in the mysteries it was Om or *Aum*, and most frequently expressed in the latter trilateral form." *The Pentalpha* (5 alphas or 'a's) is so called because it presents the letter A in five different positions (see "The Perfect Ashlar"). Cornelius Agrippa says of it (ibid. p. 98):—

> "By virtue of the number five it has great command over evil spirits because of its five double triangles and its five acute angles within its five obtuse angles without, so that this interior pentangle contains in it many great mysteries."

The *Square*—Rectitude, that is to say, what is characterised by rectangularity in human conduct and opposed to obliquity of motive and purpose.

"I will strive to live with love upon the level by the square."

Plumb Rule.—Uprightness.

The *Level.*—Impartiality of disposition from which all disturbing forces are absent, and which regards the ups and downs of life as but small accidents inseparable from existence, but in no way producing corrosion nor disturbing faith (The Perfect Ashlar by Revd. J. T. Lawrence).

"By square conduct, level steps, and upright actions we hope to ascend to those ethereal mansions whence all goodness emanates" (The Perfect Ashlar).

Apron.—The white apron is the mark of purity. The spotless purity of the heart and the soul is intended, of course.

The *Point in a Circle.*—The point is the worker's own soul in the universe represented by the circle. The master proceeds, to build himself from this point, because in working from the centre no master mason can go astray.

The *Gavel.*—The voice of the conscience which should keep down all vain and unbecoming thoughts (The Perfect Ashlar).

Refreshment.—The renewal (*i.e.*, joy) which follows labour.

Masonic Pavement.—The light and shadows of life that go to make up what is termed chequered existence.

Tracing Board.—Thc *tabula rasa* of a pure and virgin heart upon which are drawn lines and designs for the raising of the Spiritual Edifice.

Blazing Star.—The emblem of Pure Spirit and Divinity.

Geometry.—The science of all sciences which "sees God behind the Circle and Triangle. Those who can penetrate its intellectual mysteries will understand the geometrical point as representing a given disposition in the state of inaction. A symbolic right line is duty persisted in, uninterrupted pleasure, happiness and so forth. As regards the symbolic right angle, the perfect sincerity of one right line to another is as the line of that angle, the line of duty being radius. An acute angle is injustice. A perfect junction between

> sincerity and duty forms justice, and is equal to an angle of ninety degrees. A symbolic perpendicular signifies fortitude, prudence, temperance, while a symbolic solid 'is the whole system of Divine Laws as existing in practice'" (The New Encyclo. of Freemasonry, Vol. i. pp. 453-454). A triangle, of course, is the emblem of Trinity or of the Triple Jewels of Right Faith, Right Knowledge and Right Conduct.[7]

I think I must now turn to that branch of the secret doctrine which hides itself under the garb of alchemy. Here also we find the adaptation of the expression to a special terminology appertaining to a human science concerned with turning baser metals into silver and gold. The interchangeability of terms is pivoted on the common aspiration to turn worthless stuff into the one that is the most precious. As the alchemy of the worldly-minded seeks to transmute the brass in the crucible into the royal gold, so does the Alchemy of Life aspire to transform the base-born sinner into a pure Divinity, and as gold is free from liability to corrosion and deterioration, so is Divinity eternally above misadventure, misfortune and mishap. In the rite of the Black Eagle these considerations have been elaborated into a catechism, and it is explained that gold is not a metal, physically speaking, seeing that it is all spirit, and is an emblem of Divinity because it is incapable or corruption (The New Encyclo. of Freemasonry, Vol. ii. page 350). The "universal dissolvent" which alchemists sought everywherd is the Divine Love, the unwavering impassioned attachment to the great Ideal of Perfection and Bliss which every soul itself becomes on regeneration by Faith. A. F. Waite has the following interesting note on the subject:—

> "The old Alchemists used to seek what they termed" paradoxically the Universal Dissolvent. By some who understood them literally they have been held up to ridicule (for supposing that such a substance could be contained in a vial. There is, however, a gift in man which in its way is a universal dissolvent, by the opera-

tion of which all the externals are transmuted and—to prolong the alchemical illustration—the matter of his work is found everywhere in the condition that he requires for the attainment of his mystical end. It is the gift of Divine love. He who is possessed of this faculty can and does act as his own initiator until God becomes the hierophant, and he finds within the compass. of his own being a hidden sanctuary, in which the great and lactsecrets are imparted" (The New Encyclo. of Freemasonry Vol ii page 204).

We come now to Mithraism which at one time flourished all over the western tract of Asia, extending from India to Rome, in spirit at least, if not in name. The Vedic Mitra is now generally acknowledged to be the original of the Mithra cult, though the picture has been enlarged and considerably tinted afresh. According to the inscriptions found by H. Winckler at Boghazkeui in 1907, especially the one chronicling the treaty between Subbiluliuma, the Hittite king, and Mattiuaza, the son of Tushratta, the king of Mitanni, Mitra, Varuna, Indra and the twin Aswins were worshipped in the district of Mitanni as for back as the fourteenth century B. C.

This is strong evidence of the fact that the Indian Aryans had extended their conquest upto Asia Minor in those ancient days. I am inclined to agree with Moulton, who says that the fact probably means no more than that the chieftains were Aryan, the people whom they conquered being indigenous. This might also indicate a pre-historic migration of Indian Aryans westwards as some have surmised. The Iranian Parsis would certainly seem to be a colony of Indian Aryans who settled down in Iran in remote times, and carried Indian ideas and customs with them, as is made sufficiently clear in the Fountain Head of Religion by B. Ganga Prasad, whose opinion seems to be in agreement with the best of European thinkers on the point. A tablet, from the library of Assurbanipal, the king of Assyria (668-626 B.C.), establishes the identity of Shamsh with Mithra, while Assara Mazash is simply the Ahura (Sanskrit, *asura*) Mazda in his Assyrian form (ERE. vol. viii.

p. 754). Plutarch tells us that the, cult of Mithra was taken to Rome by Cicilian Pirates, taken captive in 67 B.C. (*Ibid*. p. 755).

As to what Mitra represents, there can be no doubt but that he was regarded as a god of light which meant that he represented some aspect of knowledge or *dharma*. Mitra is the god of day and to be distinguished from Varuna who is the god of night, the day and night probably being intended to distinguish the two phases of spirit, namely, purity of essence and the condition of impurity. Mitra (literally a friend) would thus represent Divine Wisdom or Revelation or even the faculty of Intellect which is the best friend of man, and Varuna some specific function of Life, governing conditions of being in the state of bondage. Varuna is, accordingly, the arbiter of our destiny which is automatically adjusted in obsdience to the operation of the Laws of nature. Varuna is thus described in Hindu Mythology :

> "He is said to have good eye-sight, for he knows what goes on in the hearts of men. He is the king of gods and men; is mighty and terrible; none can resist his authority. He is the sovereign ruler of the Universe. It is he who makes the sun to shine in heaven; the winds that blow are but his breath; he has hollowed out the channels of the rivers which flow, at his command, and he has made the depth of the sea. His ordinances are fixed and unassailable; through their operation the moon walks in brightness, and stars, which appear in the nightly sky, vanish in day light. The birds flying in the air, the rivers in their sleepless flow, cannot attain a knowledge of his power and wrath. But he knows the flight of the bird in the sky, the course of tile far-travelling wind, the paths of ships on the ocean, and beholds all the secret things that bave been or shall be done. He witnesses men's truth and falsehood.
>
> "His spies descending from the skies,
> glide all this world around;

Their thousand eyes, all scanning,
sweep to earth's remotest bound.
Whate'er exist in heaven and earth,
whate'er beyond the skies,
Before the eye of Varuna, the king, unfolded lies.
The secret winkings all he counts of every mortal's eyes;
He wields this universal frame as gamester throws his dice.
Those knotted nooses which thou flingst,
O god! the bad to snare,
All liars let them overtake, but all the truthful spare"
(quoted from Wilkin's Hindu mythology).

The omniscience of Varuna is, of course, the poetic omniscience of nature which cannot be evaded, deceived, disobeyed or cheated by any possibility, while the unerring accuracy of results in the domain of a Law that is automatically put in operation by and through the properties of diverse substances and things is a conception of impartiality which human judges in vain emulate. Mitra's omnisoience, however, is the omniscience, of pure spirit, and a very different thing from the poetic omniscience of Varuna.

Among the Persians Mithra occupied a position of equality with Ahura Mazda, who says:—

"When I created Mithra, lord of wide pastures, then, O Spitama, I created him as worthy of sacrifice, as worthy of prayer as myself, Ahura Mazda." (Yt. x. 1).

Mithra is also described as Mithra the Mediator, which would mean that he was regarded as the Messiah. Mithra is generally depicted as slaying a bull, which, in connection with sacrifice, is the emblem of 'cattledom' that is to say, sensuality, For further identity of thought between the Hindu and the Parsi mind, I may refer you to the following striking passage from the ERE. (vol. ix, p. 568):—

"As Ahura Mazda is surrounded by a court of moral hypostases, so the wise Asura of Tndia is the first in a

> group of personified religious abstractions—the Adityas. In India, amongst those abstractions, we find Bhaga, 'good lot,' Amsa, 'the share,' Daksha, 'ability,' etc. If they happen not to be the same as the Amesha Spentas, it is probably a mere chance; because, the equivalents of the various religious hypostases of Iran are to be found also in the Vedic mystic. Not only does, *rta* correspond to *asha*, *arta*, but *aramiti*, 'piety,' 'prayer,' is the equivalent of armaiti, 'piety,' 'wisdom,' *Ksatra* is the kingdom of Varun a as Xshathra Vairya is the realm of Mazdah, *saurvatati*, 'integrity' is Haurvatat, while the conception of good mind (Vohu Manah), though not found in the Vedas, seems to have belonged to the moral vocabulary of the ancient Indians, since one of these Vedic priests is called vasumanas he who possesses good mind."

As the overseer of the world of strife, Varuna may be likened to the Moon who is the lord of the night. In the Assyro-Babylonian Pantheon the Moon-god, we are told (ERE. vol. ix. 569), enjoyed a considerably high position. In Zoroastrianism, too, the Moon is said to be the abode of the Amesha Spentas (archangels): "it is repeatedly called the *ratu*, 'master,' 'patron,' of Asha, "justice" (ERE. vol. ix. 568, quoting Yt. vii. 3).

With reference to the idea of creation also, the esoteric ism of the Zoroastrian thought is apparent at every stage. According to L. H. Mills in the SBE. (vol. xxxi. p. 26).

> "It is undeniably 'abstract.' very, and just in proportion as it lacks colour and myth are its depths visible."

The fact, however, is that it is both mythical and abstract, no part of it, not even the calculations about milenniums, ages, dynasties and years, being intended to be read historically. It may be that we are not able to-day to unravel the mystery of each and every character that has a part to play in this sacred drama of Life, hut neither is our knowledge so meagre as not to warrant our tracing the general outline of the plot with confidence and certainty.

Ahura Mazda is Life in its aspect of *Dharma*, *i.e.*, the Law or 'Path.' The term *ahura* is equivalent to the Sanskrit *asura*, which means deity or lord; and *mazda* corresponds to *medhas* which signifies science. Hence Ahura Mazda is the embodiment of the Divine *Dharma-jnana*, that is the Science of Life Eternal Ormazd, the Parsi form of the Pahlavi Auhar Mazd, popularly known as Ahura Mazda, dwells in 'eternal and endless light,' inasmuch as *Dharma* can only exist in the being of pure Spirit which is Endless Light Eternal.

The enemy is Evil, that is darkness, so thick that you can grasp it by the hand (ERE. ix. 567). This is fully characteristic of matter in which evil has its abode.

The being of a corrupter of souls is proved by the author of the Shikand-Gumanik Vijar in the following manner (SBE. vol. xxiv. 167):—

> "......from the necessity of preserving the soul are manifested the defilement and delusion of the soul, and from the defilement and delusion of the soul is manifested a defiler and deluder of the thoughts, words and deeds of mankind. On the whole a corrupter of the souls is manifest."

The writer might as well have added that the corrupter must be a substantive agent to be able to corrupt a substantive being. The result of this defilemt is thus described in the *Dina-i* Mainog-i Khird (SBE. vol. xxiv. p. 32).—

> "And Aharman, the wicked, miscreated the demons and fiends, and also the remaining corrupted ones, by his own unnatural intercourse."

These demons are lust, greed, anger and other evil traits and propensities of the soul that arise from the adulteration of spirit and matter. But this is purely the Jaina doctrine of *asrava* and *bandha* which was explained in connection with the scientific basis of religion. This is further evident from the teaching of the Zad-Sparam (chap. ii. 9).—

> "......on the whole earth were the snake, the scorpion,

> the lizard, and noxious creatures of many kinds; and so the other kinds of quadrupeds stood among the reptiles; every approach of the whole earth was as though not as much as a needle's point remained, in which there was no rush of noxious creatures."

In chapter four of the Zad Sparam (the tenth verse) Aharman is said to cause disfigurement of the creatures Ahura Mazda, which also points to a material agent by necessary implication.

The explanation of this disfigurement is furnished in Shikand Gumanik Vijar (Chap. ii. 6-9) as follows:—

> "Being injured and injuring, however they occur, do not take place except from difference of nature and those of a different nature. Because in those of a like nature there exist similarity of will and unanimity, one towards the other, not injuring and being injured. And those of a different nature, on account of their opposing nature, are destroyers and injurers, one of the other, however they come together. Those of a like nature, on account of unanimity and similarity of nature, are lively, efficient, and mutually helping, when they come together" (SBE. vol. xxiv. 123).

What, then, becomes of the omnipotence of Ahura Mazda, if he is unable to keep off Aharman? The reply is (SBE. vol. xxiv. pp. 124-125):—

> ".....The evil deeds of Aharman are owing to the evil nature and evil will which are always his, as a fiend. The omnipotence of Auhar Mazd is that which is over all that is possible to be, and is limited thereby......If I say that the creator Auhar Mazd is able to keep Aharman back from the evil which is his perpetual nature, it is possible to change that nature which is demoniacal into a divine one; and that which is divine into a demoniacal one; and it is possible to make the dark light, and the light dark."

This is simply charming; omnipotence, certainly, does not include the doing of the impossible. Accordingly, Angra

Mainyu boasts of his indestructibility in the following remarkable words:—

> "All the gods together have not been able to smite me down in spite of myself, and Zarathushtra alone can reach me in spite of myself. He smites me with the Ahuna Vairya, as strong a weapon as a stone big as a house; he burns me with Asha-Vahishta, as if it were melting brass. He makes it better for me that I should leave this earth, he, Spitama Zarathushtra, the only one I who can daunt me" (SBE. vol. xxiii. pp. 274 and 275).

The Ahuna Vairya is the Parsi prayer and Asha-Vahishta a purificatory formula, so that what is meant is that the Enemy, whom the gods are power less to destroy, is actually vanquished by a Master Ascetic who has perfected himself ill holiness and piety.

The meeting of the two opposite forces takes place in neutral territory—a sort of "no man's land"—where the final battle is to be fought. This is because neither the real nature of spirit (the realm of Dharma Jnana) nor that of Matter (the abode of Evil) can be penetrated by any possibility, so that what is affected by thcir mingling or commingling is only the manifestation of attributes. Hence it is said of Auhar Mazd and Aharman that" between them was empty space, that is, what,they call 'air,' in which is now their meeting" (Bundahish, i. 4; SBE. vol. v. p. 4).

The combatants are the angels of light and the progeny of darkness, that is, fiends. The leader of the former is Auhar Mazd who is omniscient, but the leader of fiends is "unobservant and ignorant" (Bundahish, i. 19), and cannot foresee his future doom (Dinkart; ERE. vol. i. 237). Accordingly, Ahura Mazda says to the Evil One: "You are not omniscient and almighty, O evil spirit! so that it is not possible for thee to destroy me, and it is not possible for thee to force my creatures so that they will in not return to my possession" (Bundahish, i. 16). The final defeat of Aharman is to be brought about by man (ERE.! vol. i. 237).

Dharma-Jnana (Auhar Mazd), therefore, obtains, time from his blind and ignorant adversary for "the intermingling of the conflict" (Bundahish, i. 18). For, the final overthrow of evil not being possible till the appearance of the righteous man, Auhar Mazd, incapable of accomplishing the impossible, is powerless to obtain a victory over the hated rival. This is the period of the "intermingling of the conflict," during which the soul passes through the mineral, the vegetable, the animal and also through unsuitable human forms.

The principal angels[8] are:—

(1) Vohu Manah=Good Thought;

(2) Asha Vahishta=Perfect Righteousness;

(3) Khshathra Vairya=Wished-for Kingdom;

(4) Spenta Armaiti=Holy Harmony (piety);

(5) Haurvatat=Saving Health; and

(6) Ameretat=Immortality.

These are the six arch angels. The demons are their opposites. The chief of the fiends is of course, Aharman, whose place is filth and who does not think, nor speak, nor act for the welfare of the creatures of Auhar Mazd (Bundahish, xxviii. 1 and 2). Amongst others, the business of Akoman is that he "gave vile thoughts and discord"; Taromat is the produced of disobedience; Mitokht is the liar; Arask is malice; Akatash represents perversion; Az, greediness; Aeshm, wrath; and Nas causes pollution and contamination. And "with everyone of them are many demons and fiends co-operating......There are demons of rain, pain, and growing old......and bringers of stench, decay and vileness, who are many, very numerous, and very notorious; and a portion of all of them is mingled in the bodies of men, and their characteristics are glaring in mankind.......Various new demons arise from the various new sins the creatures may commit" (Ibid. chap. xxviii). Because the demons are produced and strengthened by evil thoughts, words and deeds, it is said: "commit no lustfulness; so that harm and regret may not reach thee from thine own actions" (Dina-i-Mainog-i Khird, ii. 23-24). The same idea runs through the following statements also:—

> "......and demon worship was porformed by thee, and demons and fiends were served (Ibid ii. 172-173).
>
> "The ceremonial worship which they perform in a fire-temple, when not done aright, does not reach unto the demons; but that which they perform in other places, when they do not perform it aright, does reach unto the demons; for there is no medium in worship, it reaches either unto the angels or unto the demons" (Shayasht-La-shayasht. ix. 5).

Angels are not created by our deeds, of course, because they are already in existence as the opposites of the evil tendencies of the soul, so that the destruction of the demoniacal tendencies is really the means of their appearance or manifestation, but not of their creation. For this reason they are regarded as the creations of *Dharma-Jnana* (Auhar Mazd), out of whose eternal splendour they arise. They are said to shower bounties and blessings on men, because prosperity is the result of such excellent qualities as "good thought," "holiness," and the like. The angels dwell in the Realm of Light, in the splendour of *Dharma-Jnana*, protected by the rampart of Understanding (Zad Sparam, v 1), built by the beneficent spirit, Auhar Mazd.

Of the other varieties of creation, everything represents some abstraction, pertaining to religion or its antithesis, irreligion. Death is spiritual extinction; corruption, the filth of disbelief, and cow, spiritual piety. The Iranians are the pious followers of Auhar Mazd. Armaiti is saintly piety, and the soul of the kine, the spirit of the pious, wailing in distress for the advent of the saviour. The same spirit of personification prevails in all the other departments of creation. This is very clearly stated in the nineteenth chapter of the Bundahish from which we need quote only the following striking passages:—

> "The conclusion is this, that, of all beasts and birds and

fishes, everyone is created in opposition to some noxious creature.......The cock is created in opposition to demons and wizards, co-operating with the dog; as it says in revelation, that of the creatures of the world, those which are co-operating with Srosh, in destroying the fiend, are the cock and the dog.......The dog is a destroyer of such a fiend as covetousness, among those which are in the nature of man and of animals (verses 30,33 and 34)......Dogs are created in opposition to the wolf species and for securing the protection of sheep (verse 27).....Auhar Mazd created nothing useless whatever, for all these are created for advantage; when one does not understand the reason of them, it is necessary to ask the Dastur (high priest), for his five dispositions are created in this way that he may continually destroy the fiend (verse 36)"

I do not suppose there is a *dastur* alive to-day who has the least idea of what the creations of Auhar Mazd mean; they all seem to have imbibed the poison of exotericism rather well, and cannot perceive aught but the fashionable "lofty monotheism" (see, for instance, The Teaching of Zoroastrianism by S. A. Kapadia, p. 17) in every nook and corner of their Holy Books! 'Revelation' according to their Scriptures, however, is "the omniscience and goodness of the unrivalled Auhar Mazd" (Bundahish, i. 2), and is concerned with the "explanation of both spirits together" (Ibid. verse 3). This is a clear indication that the allegorical text of the Scripture is readable only in the light of the scientific truth, the numerous phases of which are personified as angels, men, and the like. Scientific truth, therefore, is the real key to the opening of the rusty padlocks and other contrivances of mythology and mystic thought.

To revert to the termination of the divine scheme of creation, it is noticeable that resurrection itself has quite the scientific significance which is associated with the idea of redemption or *nirvana*, for it is said (Yasna, xix. 9):—

"And the more bountiful of the two spirits (Ahura) de-

> clared to me (Zara-thushtra) the entire creation of the pure, that which exists at present, that which is in the course of emerging into existence, and that which shall be with reference to the performance and realisation of the action of a life devoted to Mazda."

And this is proclaimed as a symbol to the learned (*Ibid.* verse 11). The individual character of the doctrine is taught even more clearly in Yasna thirtieth, the second verse of which reads:

> "Hear ye then with your ears: see ye the bright flame with (the eyes) of the Better Mind. It is for a decision as to religions man and man, each individually for himself. Before the great effort of the cause, awake ye (all) to our teaching!"

Verse 3 then exhorts men to make their choice not as evil doers.

> "Thus are the primeval spirits who as a pair (combining their opposite strivings) and (yet each) independent in his action, have been famed (of old). (They are) a better thing, they two and a worse, as to thought as to word and as to dced. And between these two let the wisely-acting choose aright. (Choose ye) not (as) the evil. doers."

Finally, it is said in the Zad Sparam (chap. v. 4):—

> "It is said in the Gathas, thus, 'So also both these spirits have approached together unto that which was the first creation—that is, both spirits have come to the body of Gayomard. Whatever is in life is so through this purpose of Auhar Mazd, that is: So that I may keep it alive; Whatever is in lifelessness is so through this purpose of the evil spirit, that is: So that I may utterly destroy it; and whatever is thus is so until the last in the world, so that they (both spirits) come also on to the rest of mankind. And on account of the ulter depravity of the wicked their destruction is fully seen, and so is the perfect meditation of him who is righteous the hope of the eternity of Auhar Mazd'" (SBE. val. v. 198).

Zarathushtra, therefore, is not a World-Redeemer, an abstraction of the same type as the Messiahs but in different faiths, Krishna, Christ, Tammuz and others.

The readjustment of things at the resurrection only means the purification of the soul-substance, poetically conceived as the "renovation of the world," For the soul-substance is to be renovated by being purged of every particle of matter through the elimination of all ideas of virtue and vice both. Godhood is above both good and evil, and consists in pure Self-Contemplation, but virtue is as much a cause of bondage as vice, the only difference between them being that while the bondage resulting from virtue is less unpleasant and more agreeable, that brought about by vice is intolerable and bitter.

To proceed with the final restoration at the resurrection, it is to be noted that it will not be a creation of that which had no existence whatsoever, like the attributes arising from the fusion of spirit and matter, that neither exist in pure spirit, nor in pure matter, but arise, as it were, miraculously, from nought. So it is said:—

> "Observe that when that which was not was then produced, why is it not possible, to produce again that which was? for at that time one will demand the bone from the spirit of earth; the blood from the water, the hair from, the plants, and the life from, firs, since they were delivered to them in the original creation" (Bundahish, xxx. 6).

The attributes mentioned, are the natural properties, of spirit which become vitiated by the defilement of matter, and remain unfunctioning during the condition of impurity.

The idea of Yima's *vara* explains this point fully. The legend of this *vara* is as follows: a great disaster was to come over the world; Ahura Mazda employed Yima, the paradise-king, to prepare an enclosure to hold cattle, beasts of burden, useful animals, men and women, of the best and most beautiful kinds, together with birds, and burning fires, and seeds of all kinds of trees,—all these in pairs without any blemish or token of the evil spirit. This *vara* is now hidden under ground, but will be opened in Hushetar's millennium, when men and animals will issue from it and arrange the world again, and there will be a time of fulness and prosperity (The Teachings of Zoroaster, by S. A. Kapadia, p. 30; ERE. vol. i. 201).

The idea is that the best attributes of the spirit are now lying hidden behind the impurities of matter; without performing their functions, but when the righteous Redeemer shall arise who shall dispel the impurities from his soul, these most excellent attributes, which are only hidden now, shall become manifest and the purity of Spirit as an Omniscient God, Full and Perfect in His own Self, shall be attained.

The last stage of the "Renovation of the world" is thus described in the Bundahish (chap. xxx) :—

> "Afterwards the fire and halo melt the metals of Shatvairo in the hills and mountains, and it remains on this earth like a river. Then all men will pass into that melted metal and become pure......Soshyans, with his assistants, performs a Yazishn ceremony in preparing the dead, and they slaughter the ox Hadhayos in that Yazishn: from the fat of that ox and the white Hom they prepare Hush, and give it to all men, and all men become immortal for ever and everlasting.....so they act now in the world, but there is no begetting of children....... Afterwards, Auhar Mazd seizes on the evil spirit, Vohuman on Akoman, Ashavahisht on Andar, Shatvaho on Savar, Spendarmad on Taromat who is Naunghas, Horvadad and Ameredad on Tairevand Zairich. True-speaking on what is Evil-speaking, Srosh on Aeshm. Then two fiends remain at large. Aharman and Az; Auharmazd comes to the world himself the Zota and Srosh and Raspi, and holds the Kusti in his hand: defeated by the Kusti formula the resources of the Evil spirit and Az act most impotently, and by the passage through which he rushed into the sky he runs back to gloom and darkness. Gochihar burns the serpent in the melted metal, and the stench and pollution which were in hell are burned in the metal, and it (hell) becomes

> quite pure. He (Auharmazd) sets the vault into which the evil spirit fled, in that metal; he brings the land of hell back for the enlargement of the world; the renovation arises in the universe by his will, and the world is immortal for ever and everlasting....This earth becomes an iceless slopeless plain; even the mountain whose summit is the support of the Chinvar bridge, they keep down, and it will not exist."

Such is the beautiful allegorical narrative of the events that are sure to take place in the experience of everyone to be redeemed. The drama is repeated each time that an impure soul attains to the purity of its true self. Then are all tendencies and traits and notions and ideas broken up and thrown into the melting pot of *vairagya*, with the result that all that is other-than-the-self is completely burnt and destroyed by the fire of *tapas*. The hole of desire through which the Evil Spirit rushes on the creatures of Ormazd is now closed for ever, and is covered over with the vault of desirelessness, the symbol and assurance of Divinity, that is of Omniscience, Infinite Power, All-blissfulness, Perfection and Immortality. The souls that reach *nirvana*, of course, neither marry nor are given in marriage; They wear no clothes, nor partake of food; nor is a shadow cast by them.

Our survey of Parsi-ism is now complete, and it entitles us to say that there is nought in its real teachings to disentitle it to a seat in the great Pandal of Wisdom where Rationalism presides over the congress of Faiths. It rather seems to me that the sublime allegories of Zoroastrianism have supplied the basic framework to several of the neighbouring creeds for their own mythologies. The doctrines of creation and deluge are the most striking parallels among others. Their explanation, too, is to be sought on the lines already laid down, not in an historical sense. Perhaps the day is not far off when all these mythologies will be made to yield their secrets. In the meanwhile the present state of our knowledge fully warrants the conclusion that they lend not the least support to the notion of creation which they are popularly supposed to teach. The fact is that the secrets embedded in these mythologies were so subtle and profound as to be almost wholly beyond the man in the street, and the Jews at least had actually forbidden their study, except with proper safeguards against error. "The work of creation," the Mishna taught, "should not be studied by a company of two, and the Chariot [metaphysics] not even in solitude, unless the student be sagacious and capable of drawing the right conclusions" (ERE. vol. iv. p. 245). The Hindus, too, prohibited the *Sudras* (esoterically, those not endowed with Brahmana intelligence) from reading the Vedas. In Zoroastrianism also it is said:—

> "Comprehending the sacred being is possible through undecayed understanding, fervent intellect, and decisive Wisdom" (Shikand-Gumanik Vijar, v.5 ; SSE. vol. xxiv p. 140).

Again, as to the method of comprehending the Sacred Being, it is said in the same book (chap. x. 33-37):—

> "Now it is necessary for every intelligent person to understand and to know thus much, that is from whom it is necessary for us to flee and to abstain, and with whom is the hope, and with whom the maintenance of our protection. The method for this acquisition is nothing else but to understand the sacred being in his nature, because......it is not only desirable to know his existence, but it is necessary to understand his nature and his will."

I shall now complete this short survey of the fundamental doctrines of Zoroastrianism before concluding this lecture. That its doctrines implied transmigration is evident from the general scheme of its teachings already outlined by me. We have also authority for the view that the soul is immortal by nature.

"The spirit of the body," says the Dadistan-i-Dinik (chap. xvii. 4), "on account of being the spiritual life for the heart in the body, is indestructible; so is the will which resides therein, even when they shall release it from its abode."

According to Shayast La-shayast (xvii. 7),

"The soul of him who commits sodomy will become a demon, and the suul of him who performs religious rites of apostasy will become a darting snake."

In chapter four of the Shikand-Gumanik Vijar the destiny of the soul is traced out in this way:

"Moreove, if the births of the worldly *existences* are mostly manifest through the occurrence of death therein, even then it is seen that death is not a complete dissolution of existence, but a necessity of going from place to place, from duty to duty. For, as the existence of all those creations is derived from the four elements, it is manifest to the sight that those worldly bodies of theirs are to be mingled again with the four elements. The spiritual parts, which are the rudimentary appliances of the life stimulating the body, are mingled with the soul—on account of the unity of nature they are not dispersed—and the soul is accountable for its own deeds. Its treasurers, also, unto whom its good works and offences are intrusted, advance there for a contest. When the treasurer of the good works is of greater strength, she presenes it, by her victory, from the hands of the accuser, and settles it for the great throne and the mutual delightfulness of the luminaries; and it is assisted eternally in virtuous progress. And when the treasurer of its offences is of greater strength, it is dragged through her victory, away from the hands of the helper, and is delivered up to the place of thirst and hunger and agonising abode of disease. And, even there, those feeble good works, which were practised by it in the worldly existence, are not useless to it, for, owing to this same reason, that hunger and thirst and punishment are inflicted or, it proportionately to the sin, and not lawlessly, because there is a watcher of the infliction of its punishment."

In the thirty-fifth chapter of the Dadistan-i-Dinik the important question is raised: "Does this world become quite without men, so that there is no bodily existence in it whatsoever, and then shall they produce the resurrection, or how is it?" This is answered as below:—

> "The reply is this, that this world, continuously from its immaturity even up to its pure renovation has never been and also will not be, without men; and in the evil spirit, the worthless, no stirring desire of this arises. And near to the time of the renovation, the bodily existences desist from eating, and live without food: and the offspring who are born from them are those of an immortal, for they possess durable and blood-exhausted bodies. Such are they who are the bodily existing men that are in the world when there are men, passed away, who arise again and live again."

In addition to these a great many authorities[9] are quoted in the Fountain-Head of Religion by Ganga Prasad which plainly teach metempsychosis without qualification or reserve. The Mazdakyahs, a sect of the Magi, openly professed belief in transmigration (see Haug's Essays on The Parsis, p. 15).

These authorities clearly point to the continuity of life after death, and to its transmigration into different conditions, till with the aid of the purifier (the Holy Ghost, i.e., *tapas*) it can effect its escape from subjection to death, when it rises up to the Holy Abode of the Blessed, as pure and purified Effulgence of Spirit, Holy, Immortal and Divine in all respects.

As for *tapas*, the weaklings of our day are all, more or less, eager to maintain that it is undesirable, and the Parsis are no exception to the rule, as is evident from the following from Mr. Kapadia's Teachings of Zoroaster (page 44):

> "Unlike other religions, it condemns rasting or total abstaining from food as a wicked and a foolish act, which injures and enervates the body."

This is, however, quite untenable in the light of our knowledge. The Dadistan-i-Dinik shows how individual effort must rise upto what is termed disquietude to eradicate sin.

> "....decrease or sin and the increase of good works, owing to good thoughts, good words, and good deeds, arise really from the effort and disquietude which come on by means of the religion the soul practises, and

> through the strength in effort, steadfastness of religion, and protection of soul which the faithful possess" (SBE. vol. xviii. 34).

The life of the body is to be offered as a sacrifice. It is said in Yasna xxxiii (verse 14):—

"Thus, as an offering, Zarathushtra gives the life of his very body" (SBE vol. xxxi p. 79).

Again, in Yasna xiv (verse 2) it is said:

> "And to you, O Ye Bountiful, Immortals! would I dedicate the flesh of my very body, and all the blessings of a prospered life" (SBE. vol. xxxi. p. 253).

What these passages teach is the old doctrine of mortifying the flesh and bodily lusts, though, of course, fasting alone is not the end in view.

> "With us the keeping of fast is this, that we keep fast from committing sin with our eyes, and tongue, and ears, and hands and feet."—(The Teaching of Zoroaster, p. 44).

I do not think that the tongue and the hands can be said to observe a fast when they are engaged in killing an innocent life or in devouring its flesh! It is also distinctly said that "near to the time of the renovation the bodily existences desist from eating, and live without food" (Dadistan-i-Dinik. chap. xxxv. 3 ; SBE. vol. xviii. p. 77).

FOOTNOTE

1. The Stoics, too, held that the will acting under the complete control of reason is the sole principle of virtue, and that all emotional part of our being is of the nature of disease (see Lecky's Hist. of European Morals Chap. ii.)
2. Cf." For elsewhere our rule of life is named 'The way'." Tertullion's Treatises (concerning Prayer) page.28.
3. Cf. 1 Cor. iii. 10-16 where the building symbolism is employed with charming effect by St. Paul

4. Cf. "The precept prohibiting the use of beans is one of the mysteries which the ancient Pythagorians never disclosed, and which modern ingenuity has in vain attempted to discover" (The Mysteries of Freemasonry by John Fellows, p. 198).

5. Cf. "Ceilings enriched with gold, and houses adorned with mosaics of costly marbles, will seem mean to you, now when you know that it is you yourself who are rather to be perfected you who are rather to be adorned, and that dwelling in which God has dwelt as in a temple, in which the Holy Spirit has begun to make His abode, is of more importance than all others. Let us embellish this house with the colours of innocence, let us enlighten it with the light of justice: this will never fall into decay with the wear of age, nor shall it be defiled by the tarnishing of the colours of its walls nor of its goold. Whatever is artificially beautified is perishing; and such things as contain not the reality of possession offord no abiding assurance to their possessors. But this remains in a beauty perpetually vivid in perfect honour, in permanent splendour. It can neither decay nor be destroyed; it can only be fashioned into greater perfection........"—Ante Nicene Christian Library vol. viii. (Cyprian) p. 13.

6. Cf. "Not to do my own proper will,
But to subdue my passions still;
The rules of masonry in hand to take
And daily progress therein to make."
(Mysteries of Freemasonry, 263).

7. To such an extent did the spirit of mystification sway the human heart that the very namas of sciences came to be employed as symbols of mystic thought. Thus, Grammar signified Purity of thought and speech; Rhetoric, Profundity of knowledge; Logic, Truth; Arithmetic, Union; Music, Harmony, and Astronomy—Faith (The Evidences of Free-Masonry from Ancient Hebrew Records by Rabbi Bro. J. H. M. Chumaceiro, p. 25).

I even suspect that Indian Astronomy (at least that branch of it which professes to foretell the future) is an allegorical representation of the department of Karma, so that of the eight kinds of Karmas enumerated in Jaina Books, seven, excepting the Mohaniya class, are represented by the seven planets including the sun and the moon, while the two types of the Mohaniya Karma (see p, 95 *ante*); namely, the faith-obstructing and the conduct-obstructing

Mohaniya, which darken and eclipse the faculties of *jnana* and *darshana* (knowledge and faith), are the Rahu and Ketu that originally constituted but one organism, and that are the causes of the solar and that eclipses, according to the Indian view.

8. It is worth noting that Philo, the most prominent Jewish philosopher and theologian of the first century A.D., regarded the angels as rational powers that accompanied God (Philo's contribution to Religion p. 199). It would seem that Angelology was developed to an extraordinary extent within Judaism a little before Philo's time, "perhaps chiefly under the influence of Babylon and Persia; and the stress laid upon the Holiness of God in the post-exilic community gave an impetus to a large number of personifications of the Divine" (Ibid. pp. 159-160.).
9. Two of the texts referred to read as follows:—
    1. "To reject the old frame and to assume a new body is inevitable" (Hoshang 14).
    2. "….he who….has done good deeds, is born as a king, minister, ruler or a rich man; so that he may reap the fruits of good deeds….Those griefs, troubles, and disease which befall kings during their enjoyments are due to the evil deeds of their previous birth……The lion, the tiger, the leopard, the panther, the wolf, and all other ferocious animals which cause injury to other animals…..were previously men possessed of authority and dignity; while those animals which are now killed by men were their ministers, servants and helpers, and did evil deeds under their instructions and with their help, and caused pain to harmless and innocent animals" (Nama Mihabad 67, 68, 69 and 71).

CHAPTER - VII

GOD

The subject of this evening's lecture is God or rather the idea of God, which has given rise to the greatest amount of misunderstanding among men. The most widely prevalent idea of Godhead to-day is that there is one Supreme Being who is the maker and ruler of the world and the arbiter of the destinies of living beings, judging and awarding the fruits of actions of men according to their deserts.

I now propose to examine this idea in its different bearings and aspects.

The very first question in connection with the notion of such a god is about the nature of the evidence that is adduced in proof of his existence and attributes. A thing is proved in one of the following three ways, namely, (1) by personal observation, (2) by the inferential process of the mind, or (3) by the testimony of reliable witnesses. Let us see by what kind of evidence is the popular idea of god sought to be proved. Now, our personal observation certainly does not prove it. Who could have seen himself or anyone else being created when he was not? As a matter of fact it is not possible even to see a god with the physical eye. There is no one who has actually perceived a pure Spirit, and God is said to be a pure Spirit. For a pure Spirit is not endowed with sensible qualities which alone are perceivable by the senses. It is idle to talk of private intuitions, since there is no kind of a god whose devotees have not claimed to know him through intuition. Besides, as stated in the second lecture, if vague convictions of men could be substituted for sound reason, philosophy and science might as well begin to pack off! The extreme absurdity of the intuitive theory is evident from the fact that these erratic flashes of native wit prove, on careful examination, to be of the nature of pure self-deluding assurances, born of a faith that is at once over-zealous and unreasoning.

With respect to testimony, also, it is evident that no one is entitled to speak from *personal* knowledge. For he who would give evidence of the existence of a pure Spirit must have seen Him himself; but this is impossible, as already seen. We are thus left with the scriptural text as the only kind of evidence that might be admissible, provided that the scripture which is supposed to prove the being of a Supreme Being proceed from an Omniscient God and also that it be a true record of what such a Teacher said on the point. Now, none of the scriptures that are deemed to prove the being of a creator, or providence, is or can be, the work of an Omniscient Teacher. They are mythological in nature, and betray their finite human origin at every turn. For the one simple reason that suffices to establish their human authorship. is to be found in the fact that their authors failed to see the amount of misunderstanding, hatred and bloodshed that was sure to flow from mythological conceptions passing current as real characters and figures of history. An Omniscient Teacher, instructing humanity for their good, must be presumed to have foreseen that the diguising of the basic principles of truth in mythological masks would make the Muham-madan, the Jew, the Christian, the Hindu and all others fly at one another's throat, so that he must be accused of having deliberately planned the pillage, vandalism and carnage that have been wrought in the world, in the name of religion and god. I am sure no theist will be willing to attribute to his god all this.

The true characteristics of the Word of an Omniscient Teacher are given in the *Ratna Karanda Shravakachara* as follows:

(1) It proceeds from a Tirthamkara, of whom there are only 24 in each cycle of time (of countless millions of years);

(2) It cannot be over-ridden in disputation;

(3) It cannot be falsified by perception, inference or testimony;

(4) It reveals the nature of things as they exist;

(5) It is helpful to all souls-human beings, animals, and all others; and

(6) It is potent enough to destroy all forms of falsehood.

The creed of Mercy and Truth (science) enunciated by omniscient 'lips' is the true Word of God; for mercy (and not sacrifice) is helpful to *all*, and scientific truth is alone endowed with the other qualifications enumerated under heads two to six. And the absolute accuracy of revealed truth is fully guaranteed by the omniscience of the teacher which is all-embracing in its scope. It is no use looking out for these attributes in mythological compilations; they are more likely to be met with in the scientific Siddhanta of Jainism. If the theists of the diverse creeds would but pause to ponder over the differences about the attributes, functions and doings of their respective Godhead, they would not be long in arriving at the conclusion that the god who is said to be the Father of Jesus cannot possibly be the same as the Allah of Islam or the Ishvara of the Hindus, who deny having any such thing as a son. Neither can the god of the Arabs, who claim to have had a direct revelation on the subject, he the same divinity whose followers deny the very fact of revelation in Arabia and Palestine. In these circumstances, it is idle to talk of revelation: what would be more profiting would be to work out the nature of the different Bibles and Gospels with a view to get at their real teachings, on the lines already laid down in these lectures. As a matter of fact, what has already been said is more than sufficient to disprove the allegation that certain scriptures teach the worship of a creator. Mythological in conception and expression, they cannot be accepted in their literal sense, that is historically, in respect of even a single particular.

There remains the inferential method to prove the existence of an all-wise creator and manager of the Universe. But as to this I would like you to read what Joseph McCabe who was an ordained clergyman of the Christian church till he separated himself from it has to say on the subject.

> "The men and women of our time," writes Mr. McCabe, "are not much interested in the God of nature. A cold intelligence, that fashions atoms and stars and flowers, and leaves men to their own imperfect devices, is not quite the God Christianity led them to expect. Where is the God who counts the hairs of our head, and marks the fall of sparrows, and loves men above all his works?
>
> "This is the gravest question raised by the war in connection with religion. The Rev. R. J. Campbell, who has made earnest efforts week by week to stem the rising tide of scepticism, complained that the war really raised no new issue at all. He could not, he said, understand why religious people were suddenly disturbed. Of course it has raised no new issue. What it has done is to enforce, to give a tragic and stupendous form to, questions that have long been in people's minds. The ordinary man or woman is, as I said, mildly interested in the God of nature. It is God as **Providence** that mailers. We should like to see a little of this vast intelligence devoted to helping the stumbling steps, sparing the bleeding feet, of man. We should like to see this supreme benevolence that feeds ravens making some mark in the human order, helping our halting wisdom to lessen the world old flow of tears and blood, guarding the innocent frum pain and privation, snatching the woman and child from the war-drunk brute—or, what would be simpler and better, preventing the birth of the brute or the germination of his impulses. Just this has always been the supreme difficulty of the theologian. He cannut show us any clear trace of the action of God in the human order He leaps occasionally at legends like that of the

angels at Mons, or the miracles of Lourdes, which do not survive enquiry, but he is, as a rule, pained to find that the human order is precisely that in which the finger of God cannot be clearly traced He murmurs that God works secretly, subtly, in the dim depth of the mind, that he has given men 'free wil' and must respect it; that perhaps the highest form of kindness is to let a man grow strong by himself. Behind all these nervous apologies is the blank perception that the God he sees so clearly in sunsets and roses and birds of paradise cannot be definitely traced anywhere in the life of man. Has anything happened in this generation, anywhere on earth, in which one can plausibly trace the finger of God? Is there any event in this whole long record of man's career in which we detect it? Where is the event that we cannot satisfactorily resolve into its natural causes? It is this doubt that the war has clinched. It was not as if men did not need assistance. What an agonising record is that of our race! Hundreds and thousands of years were spent by primitive man in stumbling through the horrors of savagery toward the threshold of civilisation. Then this civilisation was so imperfect, and retained so many barbaric idcas, that pain and misery were still the lot of millions. Even to-day we gaze almost helplessly upon the wars the diseases, the poverty, the crimes, the narrow minds and stunted natures which darken our life. And God, it seems, was busy gilding the sunset or putting pretty eyes in peacock's tails.....Religious writers say that God permitted the war on account of sin. The motive mailers little much 'permission' is still vindictive punishment of the crudest order. What would you think of the parent who would stand by and see his daughter grossly outraged, while fully able to prevent it? And would you be reconciled if the father proved to you that his daughter had offended his dignity in some way?"—(The Bankruptcy of Religion, pp 30-34).

I think Mr. McCabe leaves nothing for me to add against the notion of a Providence ruling over the world. I shall, therefore, now proceed to examine the idea of God as a creator.

Now, the argument by which Thelogy seeks to establish its proposition—that there is a world-maker—consists in an analogy between a watch and the world; you cannot have a watch without a watch-maker, neither can you have a world without a world-maker! This is all that there is of logic in the theologian's case; and this also is but very poor logic in itself; for analogy—is no argument, as every logician knows. We have seen in our second lecture that a *vyapti* (an universally true logical relationship) is needed to found a syllogism upon: It is certainly not an universal truth that all things require a maker. What about the food and drink that are converted in the human and the animal stomach into urine, faeces and filth? Is this the work of a god? There are other forms of filth which are made in the body. I shall never believe that a god gets into the human or animal stomach and intestines and there employs himelf in the manufacture, storage and of disposal of filth. Now if this 'dirty' work is not done by a god or goddess, but by the operation of different kinds of elements and things on one another, in other words, if bodily products be the result of purely physical and chemical processes going on in the stomach, the intestines, and the like, it is absolutely untrue to say that it is a rule in nature that everything must have a maker or manufacturer. The argument is also self-contradictory with respect to the maker of that supposed world-maker of ours; for, on the supposition that everything must have a maker, we would have to have a maker of that maker, and another maker of this maker's maker and so forth! There is no escape from this difficulty except by holding that the world maker is self-existent. But if nature could produce an 'unmade' maker, there is nothing surprising in its producing a world that is self-sufficient and capable of progress and evolution. This simply means that if a creator can be supposed to exist without having been created by anyone, it involves no violation of the canons of logic, or laws of thought, to posit a world which is eternal and indestructible.

We have seen that both the souls and the ultimate units of

matter, whether they be called atoms or anything else, are devoid of parts and indestructible. Neither could they have been manufactured in any way, for they contain no elements which might be said to have been put together. The case with spirits, which are termed souls in their impure state (notice the distinction between spirit, soul and body, drawn by St. Paul, in 1 Thessalonians, v. 23) is still more striking, for their supposed maker is also a pure Spirit. How can spirit be eternal in one case and a created article—a product *ex nihilo*, in the fullest sense of the phrase—in all others? I think this marks the limit of absurdity in metaphysics.

Whence the rewards and punishments for the deeds and misdeeds of individuals, then? Whence, indeed, if not from the very agency that is responsible for the punishment of him who sitting on the tree-trunk would strike at its root?

If I put my hand on fire, I can tell you precisely what the result of my folly would be long before it is to be judicially determined by a divine judge in heaven! Nature is all-powerful; she requires no judge, no constabulary and no prisons for her culprits. Her punishments are swift, sure and unrelenting. If we only know where to look for them, we shall find her 'judgments' unerring. The man who is cruel and selfish, who leads an unrighteous life, who tramples upon the feelings and susceptibilities of others, does not suspect that the recording angel of Destiny is noting all his misdeeds in the self-registering Ledger of Karma, that perpetually readjusts itself automatically. He has no idea that his purer human instincts are being gradually debased into evil tendencies and traits, and knows absolutly nothing of the terrible changes which are taking place in the constitution of the inner *Karmana sharira* (disposition in a rough way) that will drag him into unhappy surroundings and evil associations when this outer mortal coil shall have been shaken off. The man of piety and self-denial is, likewise, offected, literally, by his virtue. He generates forces that will lead to happy prosperous conditions, an attractive healthy body and exalted status, and, on the complete separation of his soul from matter, finally, also to *nirvana*. No judge or magistrate is needed for all this; the properties and functions of different substances suffice fully for the rewarding and punishment of souls. If the theologian would but pause to ask himself: how a god created the world or awarded punishments and rewards, he would perceive the untenability of the position taken up by him. For the God of theology is pure Effulgence of Spirit, and has no 'hands' with which to compound elements together and manufacture things, or condition the circumstances of men. Besides, Godhood is the perfection of holiness, and cannot be deemed to find it agreeable work to be constantly engaged in the formation of men and animals with his hands or otherwise in such unholy places as some of the wombs obviously must be. But there is just one more loop-hole of escape here left to exotericism, and that is the analogy of the soul's own activity. I now imagine him to say that as the soul moves its physical, bodily limbs, though it has no hands and feet itself, in the same way we should think of the actions of a creator. Even here the important fact is ignored that analogy is no argument! But even the analogy itself is not sound in this instance because it ignores the most striking feature of distinction between an unredeemed soul and God, which consists in this that the former is literally tied to the bars and levers of movement in the physical body, through two inner bodies of fine matter, while the latter is altogether *mukta*, *i.e.*, free from all kinds of ties and bonds and from all sorts of subtle and gross bodies. Because of its being thus tied to the nerves, and through them, to the muscles of the hands and legs, every movement of the soul is immediately communicated to the bodily limbs. A pure Spirit, such as the creator is said to be, is not tied to anything in this or in any other manner, and consequently cannot move anyone's hands or feet. Apart from this, assuming even for the sake of argument, that there is a creator who is tied to the world in the manner of an unredeemed soul, his movements will be always infructuous in the absence of a hand to grasp, to mix and to manufacture, so that he will be really able to make nothing.

We have seen that the attribute of holiness associated with God is utterly incompatible with the creative activity attributed to him. But is his perfection in respect of happiness[1] any the less incompatible with his constant engagement as a maker and creator? We know now that perfect happiness is possible only on perfection in renunciation, so that he who has not a spare moment to himself, from one end of eternity to the other, cannot possibly be regarded as happy. I think the case is well put in the Bhagvad Gita (v. 14-15) in this respect:

न कतृर्तवं न कर्मारणी लोकस्य सृजति प्रभुः।
न कर्म फल संयोगं स्वभावस्तु प्रवर्त्तते॥
नादत्ते कस्य चित् पापं न चैव सुत्कृतं विभुः।
आज्ञनेनावृतं ज्ञानं तेन मुह्यान्त जान्तवः॥

[Tr. Neither agency nor actions does the lord create for the world, nor does he bring about the union with the fruit of action: all these are caused by the nature of things! The Lord does not remove the sin of anyone; nor take away the merit of anyone's good works: Knowledge is enveloped by nescience, hence are mortals deluded!]

I have no time to pursue this theme any further in this lecture here; but there is just one argument which settles the whole point if anyone would but reflect on it dispassionately; and it is this that in respect of its properties and functions one spirit is like any other spirit, so that if creative activity be a function of one spirit it must also be a function of every other spirit. Every soul would then be endowed with creative activity, which is not the theologian's case by any means.

As for the religions that are deemed to subscribe to the theory of creation, we have already unravelled the Zoroastrian tenets in the preceding lecture, and found that its twin creators merely symbolise *Dharma-jnana* and Matter. The view of the ancient Egyptian Philosophers, that the Supreme Being who is infinitely perfect and happy was not the creator of the world, has also been described in connection with the unravelment of Masonic Symbolism. The Christian, the Muslim and the Jewish notions of creation are grounded upon a literal reading of the Book of Genesis in the O. T. of the Holy Bible. That this is a purely mythological document has been amply demonstrated in these lectures, and it may be added further that Moses Maimonides, a learned Jewish Biblical interpreter of the twelfth century, describes the account of creation as one of the profoundest mysteries which he regards himself under a religious obligation to guard from falling into the hands of the profane. Nevertheless he gives strong hints as to its proper interpretation, and says:—

> "The restoration of the Kingdom of Israel, its stability and permanence, is described as a creation of heaven and earth" (The Guide to the Perplexed, p. 207).

Israel,[2] of course, is another symbol for the soul (*vide* the Lost Language of Symbolism Vol. I.), so that the account of creation is really the account of the reclamation and recovery of the soul, with the resting on the completion of the work, i.e., the acquisition of Right Faith. This is well borne out by what Origen says of creation; that 'God never made anything mortar' (Original vol. ii. 218). According to an authoritative work, the "Minhat Kenaot" (referred to in the Jewish Encyclopaedia, vol. i.):—

> "From creation to revelation all is parable."

This view was fully accepted in the writings of the most thoughtful of the earliest Fathers of the Christian Church, *e.g.* Origen (see, in addition to the citation given, his Philocalia pages 16, 61 and 225), Clement (vol. ii. pp. 239, 339 and 476), and Hippolytus (vol. i. 399).

Certainly, the words 'Heavenly Father' in the mouth of Jesus do not signify a creator, and have no reference to the notion of a general or special creation of anything. That notion has been acquired from the outer husk of the Old Testament teaching, without any regard to its real significance. In Hinduism, too, the idea of Ishvara as the creator of the Universe is a coarsening of the real significance of the function of

Brahma, the creator. Life itself is the true creator, in reality, for every soul is the maker of its own body and conditions; but Life is, as such, only an aspect lof the essence of the soul. Brahma is not even a personification of Life, but of the *buddhi* (intellect) that is turned towards Life. Hence, Brahma's creation consists in the spiritual ideas with which he peoples the realm of the individual mind, and, as we have already seen, it is this creation that Vishnu (*Dharma*) preserves. Mr. K. N. Iyer has the following interesting note on the creation of Brahma in his Permament History of Bharatavarsha (see vol. i. p. 295):—

> "The creatian of Brahma......virtually means the destructian of all the worldly desires, and the consequent rising of a devotional tendency in man. Vishnu preserves and develops the *buddhi* created by Brahma and daes nat preserve any ather absurdities. Shiva is primarily the cause of Brahma's creation by his destroying the wordly desires, and lastly, he is the cause of final liberatian by annihilating the good effects of religiaus devatian and practice Brahma, Vishnu and Shiva.....exhaust the religious requirements for the final emancipatian of man,"

Similar conclusions are reached by the interpretation of the vision of St. John in the New Testament (see the Vision of St. John or Revelation Explained).

It is thus clear that in none of the religions which to-day hold to the belief in the ereation of the world is there anything like real support to be found for the notion.

I shall now cite some of the holy texts expressive of divine attributes from different scriptures.

(1) "I create evil" (Isaiah, xlv. 1).

(2) "Wherefore I gave them statutes that were not good, and judgments whereby they should not live" (Ezekiel, xx, 25).

(3) "It repented the Lard that lie had made man an earth and it grieved him at his heart" (Genesis, vi. 6).

(4) "I the Lord thy God am a jealous God, visiting the iniquity of the fathers upon the children unto the third and fourth generations of them that hate me" (Deut. v. 9).

(5) "Shall there be evil in a city, and the Lord have not done it" (Amos, iii. 6)?

(6) "He cast upon them the fierceness of his anger, wrath, and indignation, and trouble, by sending evil angels among them. He made a way to his anger; be spared not their soul from death, but gave their life over to the pestilence" (Psalm, lxxviii, 49-50).

The above are from the Holy Bible.

Turning to Al Qur'an, we find:

(1) "Whatever misfortune befallen you is sent you by God" (chap. xlii).

(2) "We have created for hell many of the jinns and men" (chap. xlv. 180).

(3) "He whom God shall cause to err shall have no direction" (chap. xiii. 33).

(4) "God misleadeth whom he will and whom he will he guideth" (chap. xvi. 95).

(5) "The word which has proceeded from me must necessarily be fulfilled when I said, Verily, I will fill hell with jinns and men altogether" (Sura Sijda).

The Hindu Scripture also has it:

"He makes whomsoever he wishes to lead up from these worlds, do good deeds; and makes him whom he wishes to lead down from these worlds, do bad deeds" (Kaush. UP. iii. 8; SSP. p, 212).

The Hindu Puranas even ascribe deception to their Godhead, such as his appearing in the form of a beautiful maiden at the churning of the Ocean, when he not only deceitfully prevented the *asuras* (demons) from drinking the nectar to which they were entitled according to their pact with the *devas* (god), but also immediately slew Rahu, who, perceiving the fraud, had managed to secure a little of the immortalising draught.

Such are a few of the attributes of Divinity according to the several scriptures quoted. I do not know if you have read Huxley's works, but in one of them he has some very pertinent observations to make on our subject. He writes (see" Science and Hebrew Tradition," p. 258):—

> "In my opinion it is not the quantity, but the quality, of persons among whom the attributes of divinity are distributed, which is the serious matter. If the divine might is associated with no higher ethical attributes than those which obtain among ordinary men; if the divine intelligence is supposed to be so imperfect that it cannot see the consequences of its own contrivances; if the supernal powers can become furiously angry with the creatures of their omnipotence, and in their senseless wrath, destroy the innocent along with the guilty; or if they can show themselves to be as easily placated by presents and gross flattery as any oriental or accidental despot; if, in short, they are only stronger than mortal men and no better, then, surely, it is time for us to look somewhat closely into their credentials, and to accept none but conclusive evidence of their existence."

I do not think it is necessary for me to labour the point any further; it is evident that the error in this instance also is rooted in the misinterpretation of the scriptures, which in the cases examined are all mythological, without a single exception. I shall presently explain what is the proper significance of ,the idea, but I want you to see in the first instance that is not a thing that can be given by anyone from without. The destruction of desire by a life of 'suffering,' and not the grace or favour of another, is the means of deliverance from bondage and transmigration. St. Paul teaches us:

> "The spirit itself beareth witness with our spirit that we are the children of God: and if children, then heirs of God, and joint-heirs with Christ, if so be that we suffer with him, that we may also be glorified together."—Romans viii. 16-17.

Again in 2 Timothy ii. 11-12 he writes :

> "If we be dead with him, we shall also live with him; if we suffer, we shall also reign with him."

In 2 Cor. iv. 10 he writes:

> "Always bearing about in the body the dying of the Lord Jesus, that the life also of Jesus might be made manifest in our mortal flesh."

It is the grace of the Messiah within which is implied in the doctrine of Grace, not the favour of a friend at Court. For well does Mahummad say in Al Qur'an:

> "Dread the day wherein one soul shall not make satisfaction for another soul; neither shall any intercession be accepted from them, nor shall any compensation be received, neither shall they be helped" (Sura Baqr).

> "No soul shall acquire any merits or demerits but for itself; and no burdened soul shall bear the burden of Another" (Sum Anam).

In the New Testament, too, Jesus says with reference to himself:—

(1) "If you love me, keep my commandments" (John "xiv. 15).

(2) "Why call ye me, Lord, Lord, and do not the things which I say" (Luke vi. 46).

(3) "And he that taketh not his cross, and followeth after me, is not worthy of me" (Matt. x. 38).

(4) "And I seek not mine own glory" (John viii. 50).

(5) "Except ye repent ye shall all likewise perish" (Luke xiii. 3).

(6) "The blessed are they that hear the word of God and keep it" (Luke xi. 28).

As for Hinduism, it has always taught that salvation was to be had by knowledge and works, but not by the favour or grace of another. Wherever you find grace referred to in this connection in the scriptural text, you will find it to bear reference to the indwelling divinity of the soul itself, though the true significancy of words is more likely to be concealed by the employment of a mystic and mystifying symbolism, as a setting.

In very truth, Omniscience, Immortality and Joy are the natural attributes of the soul itself; hence there can be no obtaining them from without. They have to be brought out from within by the removal of impurities, not to be acquired by purchase or otherwise from another. The bonds, even, that debar us from the realisation of these inborn, inherent perfections of ours are not destructible otherwise than by one's own exertion; for they can only be destroyed by perfect desirelessness and dispassion, which every soul must evolve out for itself.

I think I should explain, while I am still on the subject, that there are two kinds of souls, namely,

(i) those that shall obtain salvation sooner or later (the *bhavyas*), and

(ii) those that shall never obtain salvation (the *abhavyas*=a, not + *bhavyas*).

The latter are quite as good in all respects as the *bhavyas*, but, unfortunately, their *karmas* are such as will never make them accept the teaching of Truth. There are two kinds of souls in this class, namely, those to whom the Truth will be always disagreeable and who will therefore never be induced to accept it, and those to whom the true Teaching will not be disagreeable, but who will never get an opportunity for acquiring it. It is to the case of the *abhavyas* that such texts as the following bear reference:—

> "We have created for hell many of the jinns and men (Al Qur'an chap. xvi. 180).

They shall never have the light of Life, and, consequently, never find a way out of the *samsara* (cycle of transmigration). Yet no external god or creator is responsible for their eternal bondage. Their own *karmas* (evil deeds) stand in their way and debar them from the acquisition of the five *labdhis* (auspicious psychological changes) described in our third lecture. It is with the acquisition of these *labdhis* that the doctrine of grace is associated, for they cannot be acquired by study or argument or instruction: They are themselves necessary for the serenity of disposition and clarity of mind without which truth cannot be distinguished from untruth, or be acceptable to the soul. How, then, can they be acquired? By grace and grace alone; that is to say by the soul itself becoming invested by the element of grace. The grace of anyone else will not do; every soul must manifest that most auspicious of the divine attributes in its own being. And the only way for the acquisition of grace is the practising of the divine virtues of forgiveness and mercy. Here it is that the true value of the doctrine of *ahimsa* (non-injuring any form of life) is realised, for refraining from killing and maiming or otherwise injuring others is the true scope of forgiveness and mercy. Those who practise *ahimsa*, therefore, are alone entitled to obtain *nirvana*, for they shall speedily acquire the divine grace that shall put an end to their transmigration.

The doctrine of grace, thus, itself teaches a very different thing from what it is supposed to do. As for the idea of absorption in God, that is clearly a mystic teaching implying no more than the acquisition of the status and divinity of Godhood. For there can be no merger of two or more real entities into one another by any possibility. The analogy of the absorption of a drop in the sea is beside the point, and actually proves the opposite of that which it is intended to prove, since the sea is but a collection of drops, so that the additional drop only goes to increase the number of those already there.

Some say that it is the vision of Ishvara which they seek. These are also mystics, who have taken the metaphorical expression of their predecessors in a literal sense. For the vision or contact of another cannot possibly offord anything more than a passing sensation which is as different from true happiness as chalk from cheese. As a matter of fact, true joy is an attribute of the soul, and becomes an actuality of experience the moment one gives up the idea of extracting it from things outside one's own self. Therefore, so long as we try to extract it from objects external to our own self, so long as we expect to obtain it from an Ishvara or an Ishvara's vision, it cannot come into manifestation. And what are we to think of a being who promises to grant boons to his worshippers in lieu of their worship? Can he be full and perfect in himself? No, certainly not, else why *desire* to be worshipped? He cannot even be a true friend to his devotees, for all the favours that any outside agency can confer on the soul must fall under the class of epithymetic or sensual pleasure (that is to say, the, pleasure that is enjoyable or enjoyed through the senses), which is the forbidden fruit.

I think here also it is evident that the entire confusion has resulted from a misinterpretation of the language of the scriptnres. I shall now proceed to explain what the idea of God represents in mystic script.

The Persian word for God is khuda, which is a descriptive appellation, and means the self-existent. This, no doubt, bears reference to Spirit or Life that is its own source and eternal. The word Jehovah (more correctly, Jahweh) also literally means the Living Reality (see the Lost Jangnage of Symbolism, vol. 1. p. 302). This is in complete harmony with the nature of Life, which, as we have seen, is fully divine. Jehovah himself said:

> "That thou mayest love the Lord thy God, and that thou mayest cleave unto him: for he is thy life, and the length of thy days....." (Deut. xxx. 20).
>
> Jesus, too, says:
>
> "I am the resurrection and the life" (John xi. 25)
>
> St. Paul also refers to Christ "who is life" in his Epistle to the Colossians (chap. iii. 4).

The most significant name of God is "I am." This is common to Hinduism, Zoroastrianism, Judaism and Christianity.

योऽसावसौ पुरुषः सोऽहमस्मि

says the Isavasya-Upanishad (verse 16), which means

> "That yonder person who dwells in Asu (Life) is known by the name of Aham, 'I' (i.e., the supreme), and Asmi, 'I am' (the only standard of existence)."—SBU. (Isavasya-Upanishad).

Soham Asmi (I am that I am), is the text of the great ineffable name of God, according to Madhva (*Ibid*. Intro).

In the Hormuzd Yasht it is recorded:—

> "Then spake Zarathushtra: Tell me thou, O Pure Ahuramazda, the name which is thy greatest, best, fairest and which is the most, efficacious for prayer.
>
> "Thus answered Ahura Mazda: My first name is Ahmi (I am), and my twentieth is Ahmi yad Ahmi Mazdao (I am that I am Mazda)."—Haug's Essays on the Parsis, p. 195.

Ahura, as Dr. Speigel opines (see the Fountain-head Of Religion, p. 73), is identical with Jehovah, and means the Lord of Ahu (Sanskrit Asu=Life). As for Judaism, the Book of Exodus in the Old Testament of the Holy Bible records the following significant dialogue between Jahweh and Moses:

> "And Moses said unto God, Behold, when I come unto the children of Israel, and shall say unto them, The God of your fathers hath sent me unto you; and they shall say unto me, What is his name? What shall I say unto them?
>
> "And God said unto Moses, I AM THAT I AM: and he said Thus shalt thou say unto the childrem of Israel, I AM hath sent me unto you (Exodus iii. 13-14)

Lastly, Jesus also refers to I AM in the mysterious expression which Christians find it so difficult to explain:

> "Before Abraham was I am" (John viii. 58).

The context in which this is given is a disputation between Jesus and certain of the Jews. The former in his usual parabolic way declared:—

> "Your father Abraham rejoiced to see my day: and he saw it, and was glad."

What followed is thus described by John:—

> "Then said the Jews unto him, Thou art not yet fifty years old, and hast thou seen Abraham?
>
> "Jesns said unto them, Verily, verily, I say unto you, Before Ahraham was I am"(John viii. 56-58).

If you simply treat the term 'I AM' as they were intended to be treated, namely, as a noun, the name of God, that is Life, you will avoid the difficulty which others have felt in connection with this mysterious utterance. It would then simply read: 'I AM' was before Abraham.

And this is certainly very much to the point. Do you now perceive the nature of Divinity? His name is 'I AM' a most appropriate descriptive appellation of Life or Being which truly *is*. Suppose you were desirous of personifying Life as an anthropomorphic deity, and asked it to describe itself and to find for itself a name that was expressive of its characteristic function: do you think it could describe itself more accurately or in a better way than by saying 'I am he who is,' *i.e.*, 'I am that am,' or simply as 'I am?' I do not think it is possible to find a better expression than 'I am' as a name for Life. We thus come back, in this roundabout way, to the old scientific formula of Religion: with reference to the nature of the essence of being the *jivatman* (ordinary soul) is the same as the Paramatman (God).

Amongst the Muslim names of God also we find Al Haiy (The Living), Al Qaiyum (The Subsisting), As Samad (The Eternal), Al Awwal (The First) and Al Akhir (The Last). The last two of these names are the same as are given in the Book of Revelation in the Bible (chap. i. 8), where it is said:

> "I am Alpha and Omega, the beginning and the ending, saith the Lord, which is, and which was, and which is to come, the Almighty."

The same is recorded in the Book of Isaiah:

"I am the first, and I am the last, and beside me there is no God" (chap. xliv. 6).

This is repeated in several places (see Isaiah xlviii. 12 in particular). In Sura Zariyat it is said:

"I am in your individuality but you do not see:"

What else is there which is in our individuality and divine except Life itself?

The true interpretation of the text of John viii. 58, which must be quite clear by this time, is that the soul is immortal and has existed from all eternity in the past. Hence it existed also in the day of Abraham. Jesus might as well have used the language of the Bhagavad Gita in answering the Jews:

"Nor at any time was I not, nor thon, nor these princes or men, nor verily shall we ever csase to be" (Disc. ii. 12).

As regards the statement: "Abraham rejoiced to see my day, and he saw it and was glad," it is clear, especially with reference to the words "my day," that the allusion is to the glory appertaining to the status of a 'son of God,' but not to Jesus whose "day" could be seen by Abraham only if it were possible to annihilate the long centuries which separated them from each other. Where we go wrong is in trying to *idolize* a living or imaginary being—whether he be Krishna, Jesus or anyone else—instead of *idealising* the *Massiah*, or Jina (the Conqueror), as He is termed in Jainism. *Idealatry*, I repeat, is the path of Salvation; *idolatry* will only keep us entangled amongst stones! St. Paul claimed no higher merit even in the resurrection of Jesus. He distinctly says:—

"But if there be no resurrection of the dead, then is Christ not risen" (1. Cor xv. 13).

This is repeated a few verses later in a still more uncompromising spirit:

"For if the dead rise not, then is Christ not risen" (1 Cor. xv. 16).

The fact is that we have utterly deluded ourselves with

false notions about the personality of Jesus, and have therefore failed to understand the true teaching of Religion. To Paul's mind the resurrection of Jesus was a corollary from the fact of the "rising of the dead," not the basis for the inference of their rising. Christ is thus the Ideal of Life appearing in the mystic garb of the Jews, as much as Krishna is the same ideal in a Hindu setting. The original at the back of all these mythologies is the real Conqueror, the true *Jina* or *Tirthamkara*. The last of the Jinas is Paramatman Mahavira,[3] who realised the inherent Divinity and Perfection of Life in His own worshipful Self, and who taught the Path of Perfection, along lines of scientific thought, to others. He was preceded in this cycle of time by 23 other Holy Ones whose Worshipful Feet have left indelible impressions on the sands of time for us to walk on. The first of these Holy Paramatmans is Rishabha Deva, whose very name is the symbol of *dharma* in the oldest mythology (the Vedic) of the world. His distinguishing mark, the Bull, is also an emblem of *dharma* (religion).

तस्य भरतस्य पिता ऋषभः हेमाद्रेर्दक्षिरणं वर्षं महद्भारतं नाम शशास॥

—वराह पुरारणम्

ऋषभो मेरुदेब्याञ्च ऋषभाद्भरतो भवत्।
भरताद्भारतं वर्षं भरतात्सुमतिस्त्व भूत॥

—अग्नि पुरारणम्॥

The meaning of these texts is that Bharata is the son of Risbabha by Maru Devi. He ruled over Mabat-Bharata-Varsha to the south of the Himavat, and Bharata-varsha took its name from him. His son is named Sumati. In the Narada Purana also it is said: "O, king the Bharata-khanda originally took its name from Bharata son of Rishabha" (PHB. Vol. i. pp. 205, 207, 210 and 213). Mr. Iyer's comment on th is is as follows :

> "The name Rishabha constantly mentioned a referring to the father of Bharata, signifies Dharma usually described as a bull in the Puranas" (Ib.id. p. 213).

According to Srimad Bhagavata, Rishabha Deva was the son of Nabhiraja by Maru Devi, and Bharata was his son. This is in agreement with the Jaina tradition. Thus, all these works on Hindu mythology definitely show that in personifying Dharma for the requirements of their mythological teaching the minds of the *rishi*-composers of these ingenious symbols naturally went back to Rishabha Deva, as the first *Tirthamkara* and founder of *Dharma*. The Bull is the mark by which the images of Paramatman Rishabha are distinguished from those of the other *Tirthamkaras*, in the Jaina Temples, and it is therefore not at all surprising that it should also be associated with *Dharma*, in the symbolical language of Hindu mythology.

As implied in the passage from St. Paul, already quoted—"For if the dead rise not, then is Christ not risen" (1 Cor. xv. 16)—souls have been always obtaining resurrection from the dead and attaining *nirvana*; but the *Tirthamkaras* are only 24 in each cycle. They are the greatest of all living beings and attain to the most exalted Supreme Status on account of having evolved out the following auspicious characteristics, in the highest degree of excellence, in their previous life or lives:

(1) purest faith,

(2) devotion to the three fold *marga* (path) and to those who follow it,

(3) observance of vows,

(4) study,

(5) constant attachment to *dharma* and detachment from the world,

(6) renunciation, *i.e.*, possession-lessness,

(7) *tapascharana* (asceticism),

(8) *sadhu-samadhi* (self-contemplation),

(9) service of all beings, especially of the saints and true-believers,

(10) *idealatry* or devotion to the *Tirthamkara*,

(11) devotion to the *acharya* (head of saints),

(12) devotion to spiritual teachers (*upadhyayas*),

(13) devotion to scripture (*i.e.*, study of the scriptural text with respect and veneration for the Word of God),

(14) observance of rules of conduct prescribed by the scripture,

(15) the spreading of the Truth and living up to it oneself, and

(16) affection, like that of a cow for her calf, for all those who are pursuing the right *marga* (path).

The effect of the merit acquired by these *shubha* (auspicious) *karmas* is the obtainment of the highest status as a *Tirthamkara*. The *Tirthamkara* is a man who may say of himself, in the words of the prophetic author of the Apocalypse:

> "I am he that liveth, and was dead, and, behold, I am alive for ever more, Amen; and have the keys of hell and of death" (chap. i. 18).

Tirthamkara-hood is obtained on the manifestation of omniscience as a result of the destruction of the knowledge-obstructing 'busher' (*jnana-avarana*=a cover on knowledge) from the soul.

The *Tirthamkara* is free from (1) hunger, (2) thirst, (3) senility, (4) disease, (5) birth, (6) death, (7) fear, (8) pride, (9) attachment, (10) aversion, (11) delusion, (12) worry, (13) conceit, (14) hatred, (15) uneasiness, (16) sweat, (17) sleep and (18) surprise. *Devas* and men assemble to worship Him; His speech is like the "voice of many waters" (Rev. i. 15), that can be heard from a great distance and is termed *Jina-bani* (the Voice of God) or *Shruti* (Revelation). His countenance is resplendent like a thousand suns shining in one place! The living embodiment of mercy, He preaches *dharma* to the blessed amongst devas and men and others prior to his entering *nirvana*, when the complete separation of spirit from matter leaves Him as pure Effulgence of Paramatmanship, faultless, painless and *avidya*-less (ignoranceless), and endowed with Omniscience, Eternal Bliss, Immortaltty and *Veerya* (Infinite energy). As such, there is no further continuation of *Shruti* in the absence of matter, the medium of sound (speech). The *Tirthamkaras* and the other Holy Ones who have attained *nirvana* have no desire to be worshipped by men; nor do they undertake to grant boons for a sacritice or song. They are above the reach of desire and want. Their perfections are immeasurably greater than language can praise; Their virtues transcend all that can be described in words! Their worship is not idolatry but *idealatry*, they are models of perfection for us to copy and imitate and to walk in the footsteps of.

Such is the description of Divinity in the simple language of Religion, the Science of all sciences.

I can now imagine you asking the question, how is it that this pluralistic teaching about God is not to be found in other religions? But do not be surprised if I tell you in reply that you have not looked for it where you should have, and that this is the true basis of all religions, except of those that have sprung up, like mashrooms, in recent times, purely an the error-heap of others. These last-named religions are neither founded on revelatian, nor an a philosophic enquiry, nor even on anything like a true insight into the arcana of ancient dogma and myth. I shall not, therefore, refer to them in the course of these lectures; but leave you to form your own apinion about them. Only one observation I need make about them here, and that is that in same cases miracles are *supposed* to have been performed by their founders—a fact which in the minds of unthinking masses is generally associated with divinity or divine grace. You will excuse me if I cause any of you pain by saying that I frankly disbelieve these modern miracles. Some of them have been expased in warks written by Messrs. Maskelyne, Farquhar ('Modern Religious Movements'), Joseph McCabe ("Is Spiritualism Based an Fraud") and others.

But even assuming them to be true, which I think would be rather rash to say the least of it, miracles are alleged to have been performed by Hindus, Muhammadans, Jainas, Christians, and others, including savages and fetish-worshippers. Whom to believe, then? I think the true secret of wonder-working in all genuine cases lies in the development of certain 'mysterious' faculties of the soul, normally or abnormally brought about; but these are like athletics which have nothing to do with the beliefs or disbeliefs of men.

To revert to the pluralistic conception of Godhead, Hinduism, in almost all its phases, teaches the divinity of the soul, and is altogether pluralistic in form and belief, so that it is unnecessary to dwell upon it any longer. Amongst the rest, Allah, the Muslim name of God, which is in fact Al-ilah, is really pluralistic in sense. The Encyclopaedia of Religion and Ethics has the following significant comment to make on the word (vol. vi. p. 248):—

> "The word *Ilah* (identical with the *eloah* of Job)...... appears from its form to be originally a plural, and indeed, of the earlier semitic il (Heb. *el*)......Of *ilah* itself the Biblical elohim is a further plural, of which, curiously, there appears to be a trace in the Arabic vocative of Allah, *viz*, *illahumma*, which the native grammarians find the greatest difficulty in explaining."

The etymological significance of the word God is not quite clear, but according to the Imperial Dictionary it was applied in Old Norse or Icelandic, the oldest of the Scandinavian group of tongues, "to heathen deities (neuter and almost always plural), and afterwards changed to gild, to signify God." But if the etymology of the word is not quite traceable, the Bible itself leaves no doubt about the plurality of the Godhead. In the very first book of thc Old Testament Godhead is spoken of in the plural.

> "Behold the man has become as one of us" (Genesis, iii. 22).

The *italics*, no doubt, are mine; but not the words they emphasize. According to the fifth verse of the third chapter of the book of Genesis the serpent tempted Eve, saying "Ye shall be as gods." In the sixth verse of the 82nd Psalm it is said:

> "I have said, ye are gods; and all of you are children of the Most High."

In John x. 33-34 Jesus says directly with reference to this statement:

> "Is it not written in your laws, I said, ye are gods? If he called them gods unto whom the word of god came, and the scripture cannot be broken:
>
> "Say ye of him, whom the Father hath sanctified, and sent into the word, thou blasphemest, because I said, I am the son of God?"

In Exodus xxii, 28 it is forbidden to revile the gods—

> "Thou shalt not revile the gods, nor curse the ruler of thy people."

It is well-known that the ancient Jews had their teraphim who are thus described in the Imperial Dictionary:

> "Teraph. A Household deity or image reverenced by the ancient Hebrews. The teraphim seem to have been either wholly or in part of human form.....They appear to have been reverenced as household gods.....They are mentioned several times in the Old Testament."

Laban, Jacob's relation, possessed *images* of such 'household' deities which were carried away by stealth by Rachel, Jacob's wife (Genesis, xxxi. 19). Then came God to Laban in a dream (verse 24). Laban next day demanded from Jacob: "Wherefore hast thou stolen my gods?" (verse 30).

In Hosea (chap. iii. 1) we are told:—

> "For the children of Israel shall abide many days without a King, and without a prince, and without a sacrifice, and without an image, and without an ephod, and without teraphim."

But if the Books of the Old Testament only refer to Gods in the plural number in a general way, in the Jewish Apocrypha, much of which seems to have been lost, there is actually a concealed allusion to the four and twenty *Tirthamkaras* Themselves. In the Apocryphal Work known as the "Ladder of Jacob," it is said:

> ".....And the top of the ladder was a face as of a man, hewn out of fire. Now it had twelve steps upto the top of

> the ladder, and upon each step upto the top were two human faces on the right and the left-twenty-four faces seen to the breast, on the ladder."

The explanation of the mystery is thus given in the work quoted:

> "The ladder which thou sawest, having twelve steps having two human faces which changed their appearance-now this ladder is this age and the twenty-four faces are the kings of the lawless heathen of this age. Under these kings will be tried (thy children's children and the line of) thy sons."—The Lost Apocrypha of the Old Testament: The Ladder of Jacob, pp. 96, 98 and 99.

The allusion, though not complete in all respects, undoubtedly points, in the above account, to the four and twenty Tirthamkaras, who are described as the kings of the lawless heathen, under whom the line of Jacob will be judged. The significauce of these terms is as follows: the lawless heathen are the non-Israelites who have attained to Self-Realization (having risen above the law, whence the description lawless). The full significance of the term lawless will become clear at once, if a reference be made to the amusing, and at times also bitterly tantalising, controversy between the *zāhids* (strictly pious followers of ritualism, *i.e.*, of the dead letter of the law) and *rinds* (who have shaken themselves free from chilling observances) in Islam. The unbounded contempt in which the latter held their rivals will be evident from a single couplet of a Persian gnostic which runs as follows:

> Zahid-i gumgashta ka mujh rind se itna hai farq
> Woh kahe *Allah hu*, main kahun *Allah hun*?

Translated into English it reads: the difference between the *zāhid* who have lost his way and the free-thinking me, the *rind*, is only this: he says '*Allah hū*' (he is God); I say '*Allah hun*' (I am God)! Hence, those who have realized the Self are the lawless, and their four and twenty Kings are the twenty-four *Tirthamkaras*, under whom will be judged the children and descendants (followers) of Israel, that is to say, by whose standard will judge themselves all those who seek to attain to Spiritual Perfection.

This doctrinal identity is most strikingly illustrated in the case of the New Testament, whose last book, the Apocalypse, or Revelation, also refers to exactly the same numbers of Elders.[4]

The fourth, the fifth and the sixth chapters of the Apocalypse deal with the subject and run somewhat as follows:—

Chapter iv.

(1) A door was opened in heaven, and John, the divine, heard a voice: 'come up hither; I will show thee things which must be hereafter.'

(2) John was immediately in spirit, and beheld a throne set up in heaven, "and one sat on the throne.

(3) "And round about the throne were four and twenty seats; and upon the seats I saw four and twenty elders sitting clothed in white raiment; and they had on their heads crowns of gold.

(4) "And out of the throne proceeded listnings and thunderings and voices, and there were seven lamps of fire burning before the throne which are the seven spirits of God.

(5) "......and in the midst of the throne, and round about the throne, were four beasts full of eyes before and behind."

(6) The first beast was like a lion, the second like a calf, the third had the face as a man, and the fourth was like a flying eagle.

(7) Each of these beasts has six wings which are full of eyes, and they rest not day and night, but keep on saying, "Holy, holy, holy, Lord God Almighty, which was, and is, and is to come."

(8) "And when those beasts give glory and honour and

thanks to him that sat on the throne, who liveth for ever and ever,

(9) "The four and twenty elders fall down before him that sat on the throne, and worship him that liveth for ever and ever, and cast down their crowns before the throne, saying,

(10) "Thou art worthy, O Lord, to receive glory and honour and power; for thou hast created all things, and for thy pleasure they are and were created."

Chapter v.

(1) "And I saw in the right hand of him that sat on the throne a book written within and on the backside, and sealed with seven seals.

(2) "And I saw a strong angel proclaim with a loud voice, who is worthy to open the book, and to loose the seals thereof?

(3) "And no man.....was able to open the book, neither to look thereon.

(4) "And I wept much because no man was found worthy to open and to read the book, neither to look thereon.

(5) "And one of the elders said unto me, Weep not: behold, the Lion of the tribe of Juda......hath prevailed to open the book, and to loose the seven seals thereof.

(6) "And I beheld, and, lo, in the midst of the throne and of the four beasts and in the midst of the elders stood a lamb.

(7) "And he came and took the book out of the right hand of him that sat upon the throne."

(8-14) The Lamb is now hailed with rejoicings by a whole multitude, including the 24 Elders and the four beasts, and every living being gives him blessings, and wishes him honour, and glory and power.

Chapter vi.

The Lamb opens the seals of the book which is written inside and at the back and is sealed with seven seals and which he had taken from the right hand of 'him' that sat on the throne.

Such is the graphic account of that "which must be hereafter," which John, the Divine, has recorded in the Book of Apocalypse. But it is not to be supposed that John is here narrating a would-be scene in a would-be drama on a would-be Judgment Day in the future. Of what earthly use would it be to us if he did that? The Book of Revelation was not intended for our mystification, but as a partial lifting up of the veil which hung over the inner secrets of what was known as the "mysteries" portion of the secret doings at the divers lodges of mysticism.

The narrative is an account of the initiation of the "Lamb" in the Divine Court of Life and in the presence of the four and twenty *Tirthamkaras* or Treaching Gods, all robed in white and wearing crowns of gold.

The 'one' on the throne is Life itself, without which there would have been no court, no *jiva* to be saved, no initiation and no divinity. Thunder and lightnings are emblems of Life's explosiveness, since dead things move not of themselves. The four beasts with eyes in both directions are the four classes of living beings, that is those whose bodies are made of the four different elements of matter, the air-bodied, the fire-bodied, the water-bodied, and the earth-bodied, eyes being symbolical of perception, or knowledge, that is a function of Life, and the different beasts representing different elements of matter (see the Key of Knowledge). The six wings of each of these beasts have a reference to the descending and ascending arcs of time, called *avasarpini* and *utasarpini* which are divided into six *aras* (spokes) each, in which the four kinds of *jivas* (souls) undergo different kinds of experience, on account of the changes of conditions. The seven lamps of fire signify the seven *tattvas* (essentials) of Knowledge (see page *ante* 96), and also the burning up of the seven constituents of the lower nature, the senses, *manas* and intellect, symbolised by the seven tongues of Agni in Hindu symbology, and the " Lamb" is the symbol of excellent meekness, the soul (Jesus) must acquire before it is qualified to receive the "book written inside and at the back" from the hands of Life.

The unceasing glorification and praise of the Godhead on the part of the four beasts is expressive of the fact that Life is loved by and dear to all kinds of living beings. It is said in the Qur'an (chap. xxiv):—

> "Dost thou not perceive that all creatures both in heaven and earth praise God: and the birds also, extending their wings?"

Surely, the one thing which the birds can be deemed to praise, extending their wings, is Life whose joyous pulsation is dear to every living being, whether bird or beast or man! Firdosi well expresses this when he says:—

میازار مورے کہ دانہ کش است

کہ جان دارد و جان شیرین خوش است

[Tr. Hurt not the ant that carries the grain; for it has life, and sweet life is joyous!]

The part assigned to the 24 Elders is also emblematic of the relation between Life and Its most glorious manifestations, the *Tirthamkaras*.

The worshipping[5] of the one on the throne is the symbol of the recognition of the Divinity of Life that is common to all the Perfected Souls. Thus, while true divinity appertains to Life, the *Tirthamkaras* are the Teachers under whose instruction that divinity is to be developed; for they have attained to the loftiest heights of Perfection Themselves. A *Tirthamkara* is, accordingly, the most venerable and the most worshipful Teacher. He is called Father or Heavenly Father, not because He is the maker of anything or being, but on the same ground on which ordinary priests and preceptors are termed father. The doctrine of baptism, or the second birth, which is common to most of the Indian religions and Christianity is the root-doctrine of the idea of the fatherhood of the Teacher.

As said in the Key of Knowledge,

> "It will not surprise modern theology a little to be told that its error of regarding God as a maker is ultimately traceable to the notion of the second birth, which......is grounded on the doctrine of baptism, i.e., initiation into the secret science of the soul. If modern theologians would but reflect on the matter, they would not be slow to realise that the fatherhood of the clergy, which prevails in almost all the ancient religions of the world, Can have reference not to the physical body but to the initiation of the soul in the mysteries of the spiritual side of Life, poetically described as the birth of a man in spirit, or simply as the second birth. It is with the notion of the second birth that the idea of the fatherhood of the clergy is associated; for the ***guru***, (spiritual preceptor) who brings it about, and who is entitled, for that reason, to all the respect, if not to greater reverence, than what is due to the progenitor of one's physical person, is its cause or author, and must be described as 'father' to keep to the metaphor.
>
> "Now because the *Tirthamkara* (God) is the greatest and the most worshipful guru of all, nobody is better entitled than He to the title. This was the original idea; but when the true teaching of religion was lost sight of in the underground mazes of mythology, and the conception of divinity was replaced with erroneous notions of the latter-day theology, which insists on reading the mystery-language of its scriptures in a literal sense, the purity or the original conception of the ratherhood or God also came to be replaced by the coarse and undignified notion of a maker in the physical sense. That the clergy should have remained unaffected by the error affecting divinity, is not surprising under the circumstances, and is precisely what was to be expected; for they have never passed through the melting-pot or mythology to give rise to misunderstanding, though many

> people are now ignorant of the precise reason why they should be addressed as 'father,' and take the appellation as merely a term or respect" (chapter vi).

Thus, the real God for the soul is its own life or being, that is the soul-substance itself, which is the material cause (*upadana karana*) of the subsequent Godhood, to be evolved out under instructions from one who has already attained to Godhood, namely, a *Tirthamkara*, the outer Guide and God. This amounts to saying that there is only one real God for each soul—its own Self—which is similar in nature to but not identical with any other soul, whether Perfected, *i.e.*, a Saved One, or not. To this God it is enjoined to cling with all its might. This is the ground on which is founded the doctrine of absolute *unity* of God, and man is warned against associating any other with this God. If you reflect on the subject, you will see that there is no giver of Godhood, Immortality, Bliss and other attributes of Perfection outside the soul itself; for these are inherent in the soul's own nature and cannot be had from anyone else. Hence, the emphasis on the exclusive unity of the real God. As taught in the Qur'an (chapter xxii), whoever associates another with this God is like that which falleth from heaven. Besides this real God, there are two other kinds of Gods whose worship is prevalent in the world, namely the true Teachers or *Tirthamkaras*, who are to be *idealised* as models of Perfection for us to take pattern after, and the imaginary gods of mythology, which are pure personifications of the different aspects of life and of certain other abstractions. It is the worship of these mythological products of the human imagination that is forbidden and is the cause of all kinds of misunderstandings, bloodshed and superstition.

We shall consider the proper form of worship in our next lecture, but before concluding this one I must draw your attention to the fact that in Zoroastrianism also the conception of Ahura Mazda is pluralistic. Haug points out with reference to the word *ahuraonho* (see Essays on The Parsis, p. 199, footnote):—

"From this......one may clearly see that *ahura* is not a title confined to the Supreme Being, but can be applied to men also."

In Yasna xxviii. 9 it is said:—

"With these bounties, O Ahura, may we never provoke your wrath, O Mazdah and Right and Best thought......ye are they that are mightiest to advance desires and Dominion of Blessings" (Early Zoroastrianism, p. 346).

The same idea underlies the teaching in Yasna Ji. 20, which reads:

"Your blessings shall ye give us, all ye that are one in will; with whom Right, Good Thought, Piety, and Mazdah (are one), according to promise, giving your aid when worshipped with reverence."

It is even acknowledged that there were prior true religions which were worshipful.

"And we worship," says Yasna xvi. 3 (SBE. vol. xxxi pp. 255-256). "and we worship the former religions of the world devoted to righteousness......"

What is still more significant is that Zoroastrianism mentions the number of Ahuras as precisely four and twenty[6] (see Early Zoroastrianism by pp. 402 *et seq*).

FOOTNOTE

1. Cf. ".......How can we assume that a world full of evils is the creation of the Gods? What have we? Barren deserts, arid mountains, deadly marshes, uninhabitable arctic zones, regions scorched by the southern sun, briars and thorns, tempests, bailstones: and hurricanes, felocious beasts, diseases, premature deaths; do they not all abundantly prove that the Deity has no hand in the governance of things?....It is possible, nay, certain, that Gods exist; ali the nations of the earth agree to that. But those supremely happy beings, who are free from passion and

favouritism and all human weaknesses, enjoy absolute repose." Weber's Hist. of Philosophy, p. 137).

2. In the 9th volume of the Ante Nicene Christian Library (see p. 56) also the term Israel is explained as meaning the man who sees God.

3. It is interesting to note in this connection that the Indian festival of **Dipavali**, which, occurring in the beginning of winter marks the commemoration of the **nirvana** of Mahavira, has its reverberation in Egyptian Mythology, where it is associated with the Osirian celebrations. It is said in "In Search of Jesus Christ" (see chapter 19): It is not out of place to remark that as god of the dead, one item of the Osirian celebration in the middle of November was the illumination of all tbe houses to receive the souls of the dead—an all souls' day—exactly as we Indians do in this very season. Curious coincidence indeed!" Nay it is something more than a mere coincidence. The **Dipavali** festival consists in general public illuminations, as did the Osirian illumination. Mahavira, with whom it is connected, was a *Tirthamkara* which term is the equivalent of what would be a resurrection God in mystical thought; and Osiris is actually an allegorical rendering of a resurrection God! Mahavira attained **nirvana** on the 15th of the month of Kartik; which generally corresponds to November, and the Osirian illuminations took place in November too! These are, indeed, curious coincidences, if they be coincidences at all!

4. It should be noted that the Sanskrit *Jestham* (the elder) is also one of the epithets of a *Tirthamkara* in Jainism (see the "Brihat Svayambhu Stotram" and "Jaina Dharma" by Mr. Sheobarat Lal Varman, p. 51).

5. The adoration of the "Lamb" in the Apocalypse (chap. v. 8) similarly means the adoration of the supreme status, object of worship being not any particular individual, whether God or man, but the attributes of Divinity, as found in the Highest Manifestation of Life Divine. For wise men 'worship'. not individuals, to be allowed to pick up crumbs from their tables, but the supreme status, that

is to say the attributes of Perfection in 'Paramatmans' (Gods) which they aspire to develop in their own soul.

6. Cf. "….Mayst thou (O Man!) rise up there……along the path made by the Gods, the watery way they opened" (Vendidad, Forgard xxi. iii-c; SBE vol. iv. p. 227). It is interesting to note that the etymological significance of the word **tirthamkara** is the finder of a fordable channel across the sea (of **samsara**—the state of transmigration).

CHAPTER - VIII

RITUAL

In this lecture we shall endeavour to enquire into the different forms of worship which have prevailed amongst men. These may be summed up under the following heads;

(1) Prayer,

(2) Sacrifice,

(3) Pilgrimage,

(4) Meditation,

(5) Purification, and

(6) *Tapascharana* (asceticism).

We shall take these up one by one to understand their real significance. To begin with prayer, which, in the current sense, is only a begging for favours and boons from a superhuman being, it is evident now that there can be no such thing as a prayer-bureau in nature. The stern realities and horrid facts of the last European war prove only too eloquently that there was none to listen to the wail and lament of the starving, suffering, and heart-broken peoples. Men of every religion which taught prayer constantly prayed for years, from day to day. Hindus, Muhammadans, Buddhists, Christians, Jews and others joined in begging for the cessation of the conflict, or at least for the lessening of suffering and pain, but all in vain ! And, we are still suffering from its terrible effects even to-day. Surely, it is a pure force if this is all the result that prayer has to show! But the fact is that prayer was never intended to be used in this way.

Prayer is analysable into the following factors, namely:

(i) whom to ask from?

(ii) who is to ask?

(iii) what is to be asked? and

(iv) how to ask?

As to the first of these points, we have already seen that the *Tirthamkara* are only Teachers, but not the givers of boons or grantors of prayer, while the mythological deities are purely imaginary. There is no other god to grant a prayer except the one that is within, and it is this inner Divinity that is the real grantor of wishes. For the rule with Life is that it is affected by its beliefs, so that whatever it believes it becomes. For this reason it is that in the Bible the teacher tells the disciples:—

> 'Therefore I say unto you, What things soever ye desire. when ye pray, believe that ye receive them, and ye shall have them.'—Mark xi, 24.

The element of belief which is altogether out of place with reference to an external deity, is fully in keeping with the nature of the divinity of the soul that becomes a quickening spirit by self-consciousness. Hence, the greater the clinging to this in-dwelling God, the greater the manifestation of Divinity and the power to work miracles. Accordingly in the Bible we find Jesus saying with reference to his miracles:

> "Verily, I say unto you, He that believeth on me, the works that I do shall he do also; and greater works than these shall he do, because I go unto my Father" (John xiv, 12).

Power is developed by fasting and 'prayer,' as was explained when the disciples, having failed to exorcise an evil spirit (which meant the eradication of an evil tendency), demanded an explanation of their failure. It was then said:—

> "This kind can come forth by nothing, but by prayer and fasting" (Mark ix. 29).

But the most significant of these stray passages is the one recorded in Mark vi. 5 and 6, with reference to the miraculous powers of Jesus when in his own country:

> "And be could there do no mighty work, save that he laid his hand upon a few sick folk, and healed them.
>
> "And he marvelled because of their unbelief."

When performing a healing miracle, Jesus never failed, according to the Bible, to ask the patient if he believed, and after his recovery, to tell him that his faith had made him whole. This shows that there is a law governing miracles which is quite independent of personality and status. It, no doubt, happens at times that we get what we pray for; but this is not confined to any particular class or community of men, and even worshippers of such things as dead men's graves, stones and trees have had their prayers 'granted' at times! All this is really co-incidence, which means that the event prayed for was bound to happen, and would have happened, whether anyone prayed for it or not, and that its synchronism with prayer could not be attributed to interference on the part of a prayer granting agency in any sense. There are many coincidences always occurring in nature which even the, most unreasoning deism would refuse to regard as evidence of a divine response to prayer, *e.g.*, the death of an enemy or his being overtaken by calamity. But if we are debarred from regarding these dark occurrences as response to prayer, because of their tendency to leave a stain on the honour and goodness of their perpetrators, what is our warrant for ascribing any other to the agency of a god?

So much for the first point; as for the second which is covered by the question, who is to ask or pray? I think you will agree with me that the real grantor of wishes being the inner God, only he who is a 'devotee' of His is entitled to pray to Him. As for others who do not do His will, they are hypocrites and workers in iniquity; they know not their God, and cannot have their wants attended to. The Book of Proverbs (in The Old Testament of the Holy Bible) points out the attitude of Life towards them in striking terms (chap. i. 28 and 29):— .

> "They shall call upon me, but I will not answer; they shall find me early, but they shall not find me.

"For that they hated knowledge, and did not choose the fear of the Lord"

Again it is said:

> "The Lord is for from the wicked, but he heareth the prayer of the righteous" (Proverbs xv. 29).

The wicked has his eyes turned outwards in the direction of the world of desire and lust, while the Realm of Life lies inwards. On the other hand, the righteous man is the doer of the right thing, and the right thing is the will of the Lord, that is to say, what is helpful to, i.e., pleases Life. Hence is the Lord for from the wicked, but he heareth the prayer of the righteous!

Again he who will pray to Life must be endowed with Right Faith, that is to say, he must believe in the divinity of Life, for it is said:

> "He that turneth away his ear from hearing the law, even his prayer shall be abomination" (Proverbs xxviii. 9).

The devotee should also be free from *himsa* (causing i.njury to living beings):—

> "And when ye spread forth your hands, I will hide mine eyes from you; yea, when ye make many prayers, I will not hear. Your hands are full of blood" (Isaiah i, 10).

Judaism further points out: "Good works are a prayer acceptable to the Lord" (The Lost Apocrypha of the Old Testament p. 91).

Right Faith, Right Knowledge and Right Conduct are, then, indispensable for prayer; it is vain for anyone else to pray.

The third point is: what is to be asked for in prayer? This has practically been already answered under the second head; there should be nothing against Law (*Dharma*), and nothing that would be incompatible with Right Faith. The faithful should only attend to the business of the 'father' (Luke ii. 49). This is the only thing we can ask from Life.

As Bias of Priene points out:—

> "Despise all those things that you will not need when you are released from the body, but those things that you will need then, discipline yourself to attain and in-

> voke the gods to help you" (Fornell's Higher Aspects of Greek Religion p. 142, quoted from 'In Search of Jesus Christ' p. 80).

The beauty of the Prayer which Socrates offered extorts our admiration:—

> "O beloved Pan and the other Gods who dwell here, grant to me that I be beautiful within, and that all I have of the external things be harmony with that which is inward. May I only deem the wise to be rich, and may my possessions be such as no other than the right-minded would bear or hold" ('The Greek Ethical Thought,' by Hilda D. Oakeley, quoted from 'In Search of jesus' p. 80).

To beg for wealth, children, worldly pomp, destruction of those we hate, etc., is forbidden. They only engender evil *karma*, and put you away from God. Such, indeed, would appear to be the teaching of the Bible which makes Jesus say:—

> "No man can serve two masters; for either he will hate the one, and love the other or either he will hold to the one and despise the other. Ye cannot serve God and Mammon.
>
> "Therefore I say unto you, Take no thought for your life, what ye shall eat, or what ye shall drink: nor yet for your body, what ye shall put on. Is not the life more than meat, and the body than raiment ?"—Matt. vi 24 and 25.

According to Tertullion (see Tertullion's Treatises: concerning Prayer, p. 29), "From every possible clouding of the spirit the purpose of prayer ought to be free, since that purpose proceeds from a spirit like unto that spirit to which it is directed." The reason is that "He seeks worshippers of a like kind" (Ibid. p. 43).

The form of the prayer actually taught in the New Testament is full of hidden meaning. This is how it reads (Matt. vi. 9-13):—

> 9. "Our Father which art in heaven, Hallowed be thy name.

10. "Thy kingdom come. Thy will be done in earth, as it is done in heaven.
11. "Give us this day our daily bread.
12. "And forgive us our debts (sins), as we forgive our debtors.
13. "And lead us not into temptation, but deliver us from evil: for thine is the kingdom, and the power, and the glory, for ever, Amen."

This is surely not prayer, but a combination of

(i) praise for the Lord (Life),

(ii) an expectancy of the coming of His kingdom, together with a longing for a different order of things on earth, like it is in heaven;

(iii) a request for just one's daily bread, *i.e.*, an implied disclaimer of the wealth and pomp that might be possessed by the devotee;

(iv) repentance for sins; and

(v) a sense of horror for future failings, coupled with a desire for deliverance from evil.

Such is the analysis of the Lord's Prayer[1] as taught in the Christian creed. This is, however, nothing but simply another version of the Jaina *samayika* (daily meditation) which was taught by Paramatman Mahavira to his disciples long before the birth of Christianity. Here are the component parts of the *samayika*, as described in Jaina Books:—

(i) repentance for past faults,

(ii) resolving to refrain from sinning in the future,

(iii) renunciation of personal likes and dislikes,

(iv) praise of the divine attributes of the Holy *Tirthamkaras*, who are models of perfection for us to copy.

(v) adoration of any particular *Tirthamkara*, whose biography is to be taken as furnishing inspiration for our own soul, the Perfect One having risen to the supreme status of Divinity from the ordinary position of a sinful soul, and

(vi) withdrawal of attention from the body, and its being directed towards the soul.

Of these points the first two aim at the elimination of sin, the third is directed at the development of the spirit of dispassion, the fourth, at impressing the mind with the divinity of Life and the heights of glory to which a soul may attain, the fifth, at securing speedy deliverance from evil by following in the footsteps of a Living Example, and the sixth, at the correction of the error of the body being taken for the man as well as the subjugation of the flesh.

Not altogether uninteresting is Tertullion's interpretation of the Lord's prayer. He says:—

> "By a figurative interpretation as flesh and spirit, we have 'earth' and 'heaven'. And yet even if the petition is to be understood in its plain sense, nevertheless it has the same meaning, that in us God's will may be done on earth, and that, of course, it may be done in heaven also. That else does God will but that we should walk according to His training? We ask, therefore, that He supply us with the nature and power of His will, that we may be safe both in heaven and on earth, because the chief purpose of His will is the salvation of those whom he has adorted" (Tertullion's Treatises: Concerning Prayer, p. 23).

Then, with reference to the Kingdom of God, he says:—

> "It means in us, of course" (Ibid. 24)

Why are we seeking to enter into it? is thus explained:—

> "We are eager to enter into our kingdom: we do not want to serve too long. Even if the request for the coming of the kingdom had not been prescribed in the prayer, we would of our own accord have proffered that petition in our haste to embrace our hope."—Ibid. 24.

I ought to say while I am still on the subject that the Biblical idea of the kingdom of God, which the devotee longs to behold, is nothing other than that of a manifestation of the Godhood of Life in his own self. This is how it is described in the Bible:

> "The kingdom of God cometh not with observation; neither shall they say, lo here! or, lo there, for behold, the kingdom of God is within you" (Luke xvii. 20-21),

Now, what is within us is just simply Life which is divine, so that the words 'thy kingdom come' in the Lord's prayer actually imply a fervent longing on the worshipper's part, for his own spiritual perfection.

That Christianity is altogether opposed to prayer will become clear if you consider what things you can pray for and what the teaching of the gospels is as to them. Here is a list of the things one can ordinarily pray for, together with what the teacher would have said as to each of them, if he were asked for the gift.

Objects of prayer.	*Biblical teaching.*
1. Wealth...	1. You cannot love God and Mammon Go sell off all ye possess, give it away in charity, and come and follow 'me.' Lay not up treasures for yourself on earth, etc.
2. Life and health.	2. If anyone come after 'me' and hate not his life he cannot be my disciple. He who shall save his life shall lose it.
3. Home	3. Foxes have holes and the birds of the air nests, but the son of man hath not where to lay his head.
4. Marriage	4. Blessed are the eunuchs who have made themselves so for the kingdom of heaven.
5. Love of the family	5. If any come after 'me' and hate not

and their well-being.	his wife and father and mother and sister, etc., etc., he is not worthy of 'me'.
6. Leave to give a decent burial to relations and friends.	6. Leave the dead to bury their dead; come thou and follow 'me'.
7. Dresses	7. Copy the lilies of the valley; they need no dresses.
8. Food	8. Woe unto you that are full, for ye shall hunger I The workman is worthy of his meat. Follow the sparrows: they till not nor sow!
9. Knowledge happiness.	9. But these are not grantable by anyone, whether god or man. Study is required for knowledge and dispassion for joy.

You will also surely remember what is said about works: 'Why call ye me Lord, Lord, and do not the things that I say!' Thus Christianity was not meant to foster prayer in any sense. As a matter of fact Jesus never taught any prayer to his followers until they happened to ask him: "Lord! teach us how to pray." What he then taught was not prayer but a formula for meditation and contemplation, which is a very different thing.

I shall now take you through the Muslim form of prayer, omitting those parts of it that merely refer to the personality of their prophet.

> "I have purposed to offer up to God only, with a sincere heart.....prayers."
>
> "God is Great!
>
> "Holiness to Thee, O God!
>
> "And praise be to thee!
>
> Great is thy name!
>
> Great is Thy Greatness!

There is no deity but thee!

"I seek refuge from God from cursed Satan.

"In the name of God, the compassionate, the merciful.

"Praise be to God, Lord of all the worlds!

The compassionate, the merciful!

King of the day of reckoning!

Thee only do we worship, and to thee only do we cry for help

Guide thou us in the straight path,

The path of those to whom thou hast been gracious;

With whom thou art not angry, And who go not astray.—Amen."

"Say: He is God alone:

God the eternal!

He begetteth not,

And is not begotten;

And there is none like unto him,

"God is great!

"I extol the holiness of my Lord, the Great!

"I extol the holiness of my Lord, the Great!

"God hears him who praises Him.

"O Lord Thou art praised.

"God is Great!

"I extol the holiness of my Lord, the Most High!

"I extol the holiness of my Lord, the Most High!

"I rise and sit by the power of God!

"God is Great!

"I extol the holiness of my Lord, the Most High!

"I extol the holiness of my Lord, the Most High!

"I extol the holiness of my Lord, the Most High!

"I seek forgiveness from God, My Lord, and I repent

before Him!

"God is Great !

"The adorations of the tongue are for God, and also the adorations of the body, and alms-giving!

"Peace be on thee,O Prophet, with the mercy of God and His blessings!

"Peace be upon us and upon God's righteous servants!

"I testify that there is no deity but God.

"O God, thou art to be praised and thou art great!

"O God, our Lord, give us the blessings of this Life, and also the blessings of life everlasting.

Save us from the torments of fire.

"The peace and mercy of God be with you."

"The peace and mercy of God be with you."

—Huge's Dictionary of Islam.

Here also we have praise, repentance, fear of evil, the longing to tread the 'path' of those to whom *Life* has been gracious and who go not astray, and insistence on the unity of Life, on the attribute of holiness, and on the employment of speech and body in the praises of the Lord and of the purse in alms-giving.

According to the Sufis, "salat (Persian, namaz=prayer) is derived from waslat, adhesion, approaohing; the exoterios understand by this 'to adhere' to certain, particular ordinances in prayer'; and the esoterics 'the adhesion of the lover to the beloved'. Shibli said 'wadu (ablution before salat) is separation and salat is adhesion'. *Mon lam van fasala lam yattasal*. 'He who did not separate, did not adhere" (The Secret of Ana'l Haqq, by Khaja Khan, p. 88). Here also it is clear that what was intended was the renunciation of egoity. As a poet has put it:

نماز عاشقان ترک وجود است
نماز زاهدان قد و سجود است

[Tr. The namaz of lovers is relinquishment of self; That of the devotee is sitting and prostration!]

"This namaz is the ascension of the moumin [true believer]—who after emptying himself of his self, reaches his beloved.....At this stage one says his prayers to self" (The Secret of Ana'l Haqq, p. 89).

The Buddhist prayer is likewise a combination of an expression and an inspiration—expression of belief and inspiration of ideal and zeal. As an expression of faith, Buddhist prayer pays homage to Buddha, to his truth and community, mostly in adoration and exultation, which serve, at the same time, as a confession of faith. As an inspiration of ideal aspiration it takes the form of a solemn vow to commit oneself to efforts in moral perfection (ERE. vol. x. page 167).

As compared with this, the Hindu *Gayatri* is simplicity itself: "We meditate on the excellent glory of that Sun-God; may he draw our intellect towards himself." It is a prayer for enlightenment and knowledge to the Sun, the worship of the Sun signifying merely the adoration of the internal *atman* (soul). For it is said in the Maitrayanopanishad:

> "The sun outside is the objective Atman and prana (life) is the internal 'Atman': The workings of the one are compared to those of the other Therefore meditate upon the sun as one and apply to the atman" (PHB vol. 1. p. ,473).

The Stoic's prayer may be compared with the Hindu supplication:

> "Do thou, Zeus, giver of every good thing wrapt in cloud and bright lightnings, save mankind from woeful ignorance; do thou, Father, dispel it from the soul" ('The Stoic Creed' by W. L. Davidson 236, quoted from 'In Search of Jesus' 80)

The Parsi prayer has been already given in the first lecture, and reads:—

"As the Ahu is to be chosen.

"So (let) the Ratu (be) from every legal fitness,

A creator of mental goodness,

And of life's actions done for Mazda;

And the kingdom (be) to Ahura,

Whom (the Ahu, or the Ratu) He has appointed as nourisher to the pure." -ERE. i. 238.

Haug's rendering of this is even more lucid: he translates it thus:—

> "As a heavenly Lord is to be chosen, so is an earthly master (spiritual guide) for the sake of rightoeusness, (to be) giver of good thoughts of the actions of life towards Mazda, and the dominion is for the Lord (Ahura) whom he (Mazda) has given, as a protector for the poor" (Haug's Essays On The Parsis page 141, Footnote).

Here also there is no question of begging for boons, but only of the merits or qualifications of the heavenly Lord or Guide and of the earthly spiritual preceptor.

It is thus evident that the term prayer is a misnomer with reference to these so-called prayer formulas and texts, and that it was never understood in the ancient days to be a supplication to any external deity for boons.

As regards the fourth point, namely, how to pray? it is clear that the daily meditation must combine all those elements which are necessary for the increase of faith, merit and dispassion. Now, faith increases by impressing the mind with the divinity of the soul and by a reading, with respect and reverence, of the lives of those who have attained to divinity. Merit is obtained by refraining from sin, that is, by confession and repentance: and dispassion is acquired by the elimination of *raga* (attachment) and *dvesha* (aversion) and by, the mortification of the flesh.' All these points are kept in view in the *Jaina Samayika*, which for this reason, is the most excellent form of meditation. I need not dwell upon the subject any longer but may aptly close it with the recitation of the *Samayika Patha* by Saint Amitagati, which is really a beautiful composition from a literary point of view also. An English translation of it was published by Mr. Ajit Prasad Jain in 1915 and I have departed from it but little.

The Samayika-patha :-

सत्त्वेषु मैत्रीं गणिषु प्रमोदं,
क्लिष्टेषु जीवेषु कृपापरत्वम्।
माध्यस्थभावं विपरोतवृत्तौ,
सदा ममात्मा विदधातु देव॥१॥

O Lord [Life]! make myself such that I may I always have love for all beings, pleasure in the company of those endowed with excellent qualities, sympathy for those in pain, and tolerance for those preversely inclined!

शरीरतः कर्त्तुमनन्तशक्तिं,
विभिन्नमात्मानम मस्तदोषम्।
जिनेन्द्र कोषादिव खड्गयष्टिं,
तव प्रसादेन ममास्तु शक्ति॥२॥

May Thy Grace enable me, O Jinendra! to separate, like the sword from its scabbard, the Self, which is faultless and possessed of infinite power, from the body!

दुःखे सुखे बैरिणि बन्धुवर्गे,
योगे वियोगे भवने वने वा।
निराकृताशेषममत्वबुद्धेः,
समं मनो मे ऽस्तु सदापिनाथ॥३॥

May my mind, 0 Lord! be always at equilibrium, with the sense of attachment completely destroyed, in pleasure and pain, among friends and foes, in gain and in loss, at home and abroad!

मुनिश! लीनाविवकीलिताविव,
स्थिरौनिषाताविवविम्बिताविव।
पादौ त्वदीयौ मम तिष्ठतां सदा,
तमोधुनानौ हृदि दीपकाविव॥४॥

O Revered of all Saints! may Thy feet be ever enshrined in

my heart as a light that destroys all darkness, and there be engraved, and impressed and fixed, and imaged and unified with it!

एकेन्द्रियाद्या यदि देव देहिनः,

प्रमादतः संवरता इतस्ततः।

क्षता विंभिन्नामिलितानिपीड़िता,

तदस्तु मिथ्या दुरनुष्ठितं तदा॥५॥

O Lord! if I have, by the carelessness of my movements, destroyed, cut asunder, brought in (incompatible) connection, or otherwise injured, any organism endowed with one or more senses, may such wrong action of mine be annulled!

विमुक्तिमार्गप्रतिकूलवर्त्तिन।

मया कषायाक्षवशेन दुर्धया।

चारित्र शुद्धेर्यदकारि लोपनं,

तदस्तु मिथ्यामम दुष्कृतंप्रभो॥६॥

Moving away from the path of salvation, if I have, in consequence of being overpowered by passions and lusts, perversely omitted to observe the rules of proper conduct, may such failings of mine, O Master! be set at nought!

विनिन्दनालोचनगर्हणैरहं,

मनोवचः कायकषायनिर्मितम्।

निहन्म पापं भवदुःखकारणं,

भिषग्विषंमत्रगुणैरिवाखिलम्॥७

Just as the physician destroys the evil effect of poison by the power of incantations, so by self-analysis, self-censure and repentance, I destroy sin, from which all ills in the cosmos proceed, whether it be committed through the mind, speech or body, or through passion!

अतिक्रमं यं विमतेर्व्यतिक्रमं,

जिनातिचारं सुचरित्रकर्म्मणः।

व्यधादनाचारमपि प्रमादतः,

प्रतिक्रमं तस्य करोमि शुद्धये॥८॥

O World-Victor! I purify myself by per-forming expurgation for all foolish deviations from rectitude due to indifference, whether it amount to *atikarma*, *vyatikarma*, *atichara* or *anachara*!

क्षतिं मनः शुद्धिविधेरतिक्रम,
व्यतिक्रमं शीलवृतेर्विलंघनम्।
प्रभोऽतिचारं विषयेषु वर्त्तनं,
वदन्त्यनाचारमिहातिसक्तिताम्॥९॥

A*tikarma* is the defiling of the purity of the mind; *vyatikarma* is the violation of the moral vows; *atichara*, 0 Lord! is indulgence in sensual desires, and *anachara* is defined as excessive attachment to things!

यदर्थमात्रापदवाक्यहीनं,
मया प्रमादाद्यदि किञ्चनोक्तम्।
तन्मे क्षमित्वाविद धातु देवी,
सरस्वती केवलबोधलब्धिम्॥१०॥

O Goddess Saraswati [*Jina-bani i.e.*, the Word of God]! pray excuse me if, through inattention, I have uttered anything wanting in meaning, spelling, word, or sense, and grant me the boon of knowledge absolute!

बोधिः समाधिः परिणामशुद्धिः,
स्वात्मोपलब्धिः शिवसौख्यसिद्धिः
चिन्तामणिं चिन्तितवस्तुदाने,
त्वां वंद्यमानस्यममास्तुदेवी॥११॥

O Goddess, Thou art like the Jewel Chintamani in granting all desired objects; may I, by worshipping Thee, obtain wisdom, control of mind, purity of thought, realisation of my own-self, and perfect happiness everlasting!

यः स्मर्य्यते सव्वमुनीन्द्रवृन्दैः,
यः स्तुयते सर्वनरामरेन्द्रौः।
यी गीयते वेदपुराणशास्त्रैः,
सदेवदेवा हृदये समास्ताम्॥१२॥

May that Lord of Lords be enshrined in my heart, who is an object of contemplation for groups of ascetic saints, who is adored by all the Monarchs and Lords of the celestials, and whose praises are sung by the Vedas, Puranas and Scriptures!

यां दर्शनज्ञान सुखस्वभावः,
समस्तसंसारविकारव ह्यः।
समाधिगम्यः परमात्मसंज्ञः,
स देवदेवोहृदये ममास्ताम्॥२३॥

May that Lord of Lords be enshrined in my heart, whose nature is Knowledge, Wisdom, and Happiness, who is free from all kinds of imperfections that abound in the world, who is reached through *samadhi* (pure unruffled self-contemplation), and who is termed the Most High!

निषूदतेयो भवदुःखजालं,
निरीक्षते यो जगदन्तरालं!
योऽन्तर्गतो योगिनिरीक्षणीयः,
सदेवदेवोहृदये ममास्ताम्॥१४॥

May that Lord of Lords be enshrined in my heart, who destroys all the trammels of the world, who sees all that is innermost in the Universe, who can be realized by the inner self and who is perceived by His devotees!

विमुक्तिमार्गप्रतिपादको यी,
यो जन्ममृत्युव्यसना दिव्यतीतः।
त्रिलोकलोकी बिकलोऽकलङ्कः,
स देवदेवो हृदये ममास्ताम्॥१५॥

May that Lord of Lords be enshrined in my heart, who has shown the path of salvation, who has passed beyond Birth and Death (that proceed from sin), who sees the three worlds and who is bodiless and faultless!

कोढ़ीकृताशेषशरीरिवर्गः,
गगादयो यस्य न सन्तिदोषाः।
निरिन्द्रियो ज्ञानमयोऽनपायः,
स देवदेवो हृदये ममास्ताम्॥१६॥

May that Lord of Lords be enshrined in my heart who is free from all kinds of passions and faults which are found in embodied beings, who is wisdom personified and is above the senses and Eternal!

यो व्योपको विश्वजनीनवृत्तेः,
सिद्धी विबुद्धो धुतकर्मबन्धः।
ध्यातो धुनीते सकलं विकारं,
स देवदेवी हृदये ममास्ताम्॥१७॥

May that Lord of Lords be enshrined in my heart, who, being the source of universal good, is all-pervading, perfect and all-knowing, who is the destroyer of bonds of *karma*, and by turning to whom all forms of evil are annihilated there and then!

न स्पृश्यते कर्मकलङ्कदोषैः,
यो ध्वान्तसंघैरिव तिग्मरश्मिः।
निरञ्जनं नित्यमनेकमेकं,
तं देवप्राप्तं शरणं प्रपद्य॥१८॥

I seek, shelter in th at Supreme Lord, who cannot be touched by the contamination of *karmic* filth, just as clouds of darkness cannot affect the strong-rayed Sun, and who is stainless, eternal, one, and many!

विभासते यत्र मरीचिमाली,
न विद्य माने भुवनावभासी।
स्वात्मस्थितं बोधमयप्रकाशं,
तं देवमाप्तं शरणं प्रपद्ये॥१९॥

I seek shelter in that Supreme Lord, who, centred in His own self, diffuses the Light of Wisdom and illumines the universe in a way that the sun cannot!

विलोक्यमाने सति यत्र विश्वं,
विलोक्यते स्पष्टमिद विविक्तम्।
शुद्धं शिवं शान्तमनाद्यनन्तं,
तंदेवमाप्तं शरणं प्रपद्ये॥२०॥

I seek shelter in that Supreme Lord, by seeing whom all the universe is distinctly and clearly seen, who is Pure, Blissful, Ever-Tranquil, and without a beginning and without an end!

येनक्षता मन्मथमानमूर्च्छा,

विषादनिद्राभयशोक चिन्ताः।

क्षयाऽनलेनेव तरुप्रपञ्च,

स्तं देवमाप्तं शरणं प्रपद्ये॥२१॥

I seek shelter in that Supreme Lord, who has annihilated desire, pride, delusion, anguish, sleep, fear, sorrow and anxiety, like a wild fire that burns up a whole forest!

न संस्तरोऽश्मा न तृणं न मेदनी,

विधानतो नोफलको विनिर्मितम्।

यतो निरस्ताक्षकषायविद्विषः,

सुधीभिरात्मैव सुनिर्मलो मतः॥२२॥

Neither a cushion of grass, nor a wooden plank, neither a slab of stone, nor even a seat on the ground is essential for the purpose of meditation; the Atman himself which has subdued his foes—passions and lusts—has been described by the wise as the pure seat!

नसंस्तरो भद्र समाधिसाधनं,

न लोक पूजा न च संघमेलनम्।

थतस्ततोऽध्यामरतो भवानिशं,

विमुच्य सर्व्वामपि बाह्यवासनाम्॥२३॥

No seat, my good friend is needed for communion with God; neither are joint worship of assemblies of men, nor group meetings required for the purpose; renounce thou all desire for the not-self, and engage thyself constantly in thine own self, in every possible way!

न सन्ति बाह्या मम केचनार्था,

भवामि तेषां न कदाचन हम्।

इत्थं विनिश्चित्य विमुच्य बाह्यं,

स्वस्थः सदात्वं भवभद्रामुक्त्ये॥२४॥

"None of these objects outside me is mine; may I never be theirs."—Determine this in thy mind, and break thy connection with the not-self; and O good friend! if thou wishest to secure Deliverance, thou shouldst always remain centred in Thyself!

आत्मानमात्मन्यविलोक्यामान-

स्त्वं दर्शनज्ञानमयो विशुद्धः।

एकाग्रचितः खलु यत्र तत्र,

स्थितीपिसाधुर्लभते समाधिम्॥२५॥

Thou, who seest Thyself in Thyself, art pure and possessed of (infinite) perception and wisdom: the sage who can concentrate his mind attains communion howsoever situated!

एकः सदा शाश्वति को ममात्मा,

विनिर्मलः साधिगमस्वभावः।

बहिर्भवाः सन्त्यपरे समस्ता,

नश शिवतःकर्मभवाःस्वकीयाः॥२६॥

My self is ever One, Eternal, Pure, and All-knowing in essence; all the other objects are outside me, not eternal, and are connected with me through my own *karmas*!

यस्यास्ति नैक्यं वपुषापि सार्द्धं,

तस्यास्ति कि पुत्रकलत्रमित्रैः।

पृथक्कृते चर्मणि रोम कूपाः,

कुतो हि तिष्ठन्ति शरीरमध्ये॥२७॥

How can he, who is not one even with his own body, be connected with his son, wife, or friends? If the skin be removed from the body, where would the pores abide!

संयोगता दुःखमने कभेदं,

यतोऽश्नुते जन्म वने शरीरी।

तत स्त्रिधासो परिवर्जनीयो,

यियासुना निवृत्तिमात्मनीनाम्॥२८॥

The Self, encased in the body, undergoes various kinds

of sufferings, because of the bodily connection; therefore, he who desires Deliverance should avoid this corporeal contact through mind; speech and action!

सर्व निराकृत्य विकल्पजालं,

संसारकान्तार निपातहे तुम।

विविक्तमात्मानम बेक्ष्यमाणे,

निलोयसे त्वं परमात्मतत्त्वे॥२९॥

Liberate thyself from the trammels of doubt through which thou art lost in this World-forest. Realize thyself as separate and absorbed in contemplation of the Highest Self!

स्वयं कृतं कर्म यदात्मना पुरा

फलं तदीयं लभते शुभाशुभम्।

परेणं दत्तं यदि लभ्यते स्फूटं

स्वयंकृतंकर्मनिरर्थकं तदा॥३०॥

Whatever *karmas* you have performed previously, you experience their consequenees, whether good or evil. If what you experience is caused by another's *karmas* then the *karmas* you performed have clearly been of no effect!

निजार्जितं कर्म विहाय देहिनो,

न कोपि कस्यापि ददाति किंचन।

विचारयन्नेवमंनन्यमानसः,

परोददातीतिविमुञ्चशेमुषीम्॥३१॥

"Leaving aside the accumulated *karmas* of the dweller in the body, no one gives anything to any one."—Think of this wlth a concentrated mind, and give up the idea that there is another who gives.

यैः परमात्माऽमितगतिवन्द्यः,

सर्वविविक्ता भृशमनवद्यः।

शश्वदधीते मनसि, लभन्ते,

मुक्तिनिकेतं विभववरंते॥३२॥

Such persons as those who always meditate upon the

Highest Self who is revered by Amitgati, who is distinct from every thing, and who is worthy of high praise, attain the supreme bliss which abides in Salvation!

I now pass on to a consideration of the doctrine of sacrifice which still prevails in many religions. I have no time here to trace the origin of this cruel practice, but we shall see that it is one of those doctrines which have been grossly misunderstood by men. It is not necessary to dwell on the subject at any great length; a few extracts from the Scriptures of those very creeds which practise it will suffice to remove the delusion.

The following passages in the Old Testament have a direct bearing on the interpretation of the sacrificial texts.

1. "Hath the Lord as great delight in burnt offering and sacrifices as in obeying the voice of the Lord? Behold, to obey in better than sacrifice, and to hearken than the fat of rams" (1 Sam. xv. 22).
2. "I will take no bullock ant of thy house, nor he-goats out of thy folds. For every beast of the forest is mine, and the cattle upon a thousand hills. If I were hungry I would not tell thee: for the world is mine and the fulness thereof. Will I eat the flesh of bulls, or drink the blood of goats? Offer unto God thanksgiving; and pay thy vows unto the Most High" (Ps. L 9-15).
3. "O Lord, Open thou my lips; and my mouth shall shew forth thy praise. For thou desirest not sacrifice, else would I give it: thou delightest not in burnt offerings" (Ps. li 15 and 16).
4. "To what purpose is the multitude of your sacrifices unto me? saith the Lord: I am full of burnt offerings of rams, and the fat of fed beasts; and I delight not in the blood of bullocks, or of lambs, or of he-goats......Bring no more vain oblations; incense is an abomination unto me; the new moons and sabbaths, the calling of assemblies, I cannot sway with; it is iniquity even the solemn meeting. Your

new moons and your appointed feasts my soul hateth; they are a trouble unto me; I am weary to bear them and when you spread forth your hands, I will hide mine eyes from you: yea, when ye make many prayers I will not hear: your hands are full of blood" (Isaiah i. 11-15).

5. "He that killeth an ox is as if he slew a man, he that sacrificeth a lamb, as if he cut off a dog's neck; he that offereth an oblation, as if he offered swine's blood; he that burneth incense, as if he blessed an idol. Yea, they have chosen their own ways, and their boul delighteth in their abominations " (Isaiah, Ixvi. 3).
6. "I desired mercy and not sacrifice, and the knowledge of God more than burnt offerings" (Hosea vi. 6).
7. "To what purpose there cometh to me incense from Sheba, and the sweet cane from a far country? your burnt offerings are not acceptable, nor your sacrifices sweet unto me" (Jeremiah vi. 20).
8. "They sacrifice flesh for the sacrifice of my offerings, and eat it, but the Lord accepteth them not: now will he remember their iniquity, and vist their sins; they shall return to Egypt" (bondage).—Hosea viii. 13.
9. "I hate, I despise your feast days, and I will not smell in your solemn assemblies. Though ye offer me burnt offerings, and your meat offerings, I will not accept them: neither will I regard the peace offerings of your fat beasts" (Amos v. 21 and 22).
10. "Put your burnt offerings into your sacrifices, and eat flesh. For I spake not unto your fathers, nor commanded them in the day that I brought them out of the land of Egypt, concerning burnt offerings or sacrifices: but this thing commanded I them, saying: Obey my voice, and I will be your God, and ye shall be my people: and walk ye in all the ways that I have, commanded you, that it may be well unto you" (Jeremiah vii 21-23).

11. "Sacrifice and offering thou didst not desire; mine ears bath thou opened: burnt offerings and sin offerings hast thou not required" (Ps. xl. 6).
12. "I will praise the name of God with a song, and will magnify him with thanksgiving. This shall please the Lord better than an ox or bullock that bath horns and hoofs" (Ps. lxix. 30 and 31).
13. "The sacrifices of God are a broken spirit; a broken and a contrite heart, O God, thou wilt not despise" (Ps. Ii. 71).
14. "Wherewith shall I come before the Lord and bow myself before the High God? shall I come before him with burnt offerings, with calves of a year old? Will the Lord be pleased with thousands of rams, or with ten thousands of rivers of oil? shall I; give my firstborn for my transgression, the fruit of my body for the sin of my soul? He hath showed thee, O man, what is good; and what doth the Lord require of thee, but to do justly, and to love mercy, and to walk humbly with the God."—[Micab, vi. 6-8].

These are all from the Old Testament itself, and they leave no doubt in the mind that the grossest error has been made in the matter of sacrificial ritual by reading the text in the literal sense, which was never intended to be so read by anyone. Christianity saw the fatal error and a bolished sacrifice. "I will have mercy and not sacrifice" (Matt. ix. 13)—is the message of love, in the New Testament.

According to Zoroastrianism also meat offerings are condemned. It is said in Shayast La-Shayast xi. (5): "There have been those who may have spoken about protection, and there have been those who may have done so about meat-offerings; whoever has spoken about protection is such as has spoken well, and whoever has spoken about meat offerings has not spoken every thing which is noteworthy" (SBE. vol. pp. 337-338).

It is also said in the same work (chap. x. 34; SBE. vol. v. p. 332):—

> "The rule is this, that meat, when there is stench or decomposition not even originating with it, is not to be prayed over."

To turn to Islam, there is no doubt that Muhammad understood the real significance of the doctrine of sacrifice, but he feared to kindle the ire of his countrymen. Accordingly, he merely contented himself by pointing out the symbolic nature of sacrifice, but did not forbid it openly, as Christians had done before him. It is said in Al Qur'an Chapter xxii:—

> "The camels slain for sacrifice have we appointed for you as symbols of your obedience unto God. Their flesh is not accepted of God, neither their blood, but your piety is accepted of him."

It is impossible for language to be more clear or emphatic! But, alas! it fell dead on the Arab ears, as the earlier prophetic speech had fallen on the Jewish ears. Wonderful is man even in his stupidity! He imagines even the Holiest of the Holy bending low to eat the flesh and drink the blood of fed beasts! We shall deal with the cow sacrifice[2] of Islam later on.

Turning to Hinduism, we find the same allegorical explanation of the sacrificial text as in the other creeds examined by us.

1. "The sacrificer is himself the victim. It (the sacrifice) takes the very sacrificer himself to heaven" (Tait. Br. ii. 2. 8. 2.)
2. "The secrifice is the representation of the man himself" (SBE. xii. p. 78 note).
3. "The sacrificer is indead the sacrifice" (Tait. Br. 1. 1. 2. 8).
4. "Now the sacrifice is the man" (Sat. Brab. 1. 3. 2. 8=SBE. xii. 173).

In the symbolical speech of the Hindus,

> "The ten senses are the sacrificers, their objects are the sacrificial stuffs, and burning their stuffs away is the sacrifice. The ten senses, or the Devas, are the ten fire.

> Chitta [mind] is the sacrificial ladle and the sacred knowledge is the wealth utilised..... Tamas is smoke and Rajas its ashes.
>
> "The secret of yoga-yegna is this. There are four sacrificers to be known. The five senses, mind and intellect make up the seven causes of Karmas. Their actions constitute the Karma. The Ego-underlying these is the doer or Karma. When one is attacped to these seven, the good and bad offect him, otherwise they become the real sources for moksha or emancipation" (PH B. vol. ii pp. 638 and 639, and for the original Sanskrit texts. pp. 634 to 636).

According to the Chhandogya Upanishad (chap. iii. 174). "Austerity, charity, simplicity, *ahimsa* and truthfulness form his fee (let the aspirant acquire these by self-sacrifice)."

It was, thus, the sacrifice of desires[3] that *yajna* signified, not the cruel slaughtering of poor helpless dumb animals whose blood could only go to form a hard encrustation of evil *karma* about the sacrificer's own soul, dragging it in the end into conditions of existence which one simply shudders to think of. It is dreadful to think of the countless millions of horses, cows, buffaloes, bullocks and goats that have paid with their lives for human perversity! The horse that was to be sacrificed is the mind; the cow, the lower or sensual ego, in the sense of نفس (lit. breath); buffalo, ignorance; bullock, stupidity or stiff-neckedness; and he-goat, carnal lust. Of these, the cow has been the source of a great deal of bloodshed in recent times in India. Yet the cow is a mere symbol for the senses, or, in general, sensuality or *nafs*, as it is termed in Islam. In Muslim symbology *nafs* (نفس) is also represented by the dog,[4] which is the most unclean of animals; for the dog is known to eat up all kinds of things, clean and unclean both, and applies his nose to anything directly he sees it, while *nafs* (the desiring mind) is no better. *Sag-i-dunia* (dog of the world) is the contemptuous expression of saints for those entangled in the world, on account of their sensual *nafs-parasti* (lit. sense-worship, hence the pursuit of lusts). It is this lustful *nafs* that is symbolised by cow for the purpose of sacrificial teaching. The occasion of the sacrifice is thus related in the Qur'an (chap. ii):—

1. "And when Moses said unto his people, verily God commands you to sacrifice a cow, they answered, *Dost thou make a jest of us* ?

2. "Moses said, God forbid that I should be one of the foolish.

   "They said, Pray for us unto thy Lord, that he would show us *what it is*.

3. "Moses answered, He saith, *it is a cow neither old not young, of a middle age between that*: do ye therefore that which ye are commanded

4. "They said, Pray for us unto thy Lord, that he would show us *what colour she is of.*

5. Moses answered, He saith, *she is a red cow, intensely red, her colour rejoiceth the beholders.*

6. "They said, Pray for us unto thy Lord, that he would show us *what it is*; verily cows are alike to us, and we, if God please, will be directed.

7. "Moses answered. He saith, *she is a cow not broken to plough the earth, or water the field, a sound one; there is no blemish in her*.

8. "They said, now *thou hast brought the truth.*

9. "Then they sacrificed her, *yet they were near not doing it*.

10. "And when *ye slew a man and contended among*
11. *yourselves concerning him*, God brought forth to light that which ye concealed.
12. "For we said, *Strike the dead body with part of the*
13. *sacrificed cow: so God raised the dead to life, and*
14. *showeth you his signs, that peradventure ye may*
15. *understand.*"

Such is the legend of the sacrifice of the red heifer, and it is a truly remarkable story, ingenious, well-conceived and mystic to its core. I have italicised the most remarkable portions of it, and numbered them on the margin.

(1) Our item No.1 is a surprise. The God with whom the Jews are familiar wants the sacrifice of a cow, yet is his command received with levity and surprise—'Dost thou make a jest of us?' Neither God nor Moses is, however, angered by this levity. Moses is quite serious—'God forbid that I should jest with you in this matter?,

(2) The Jews now ask, "*What it is*?" This is sufficiently significant by itself—What do you mean by a cow-sacrifice? God is the protector of life, and you say that he wants a sacrifice! Surely, this is a riddle: What does it mean? What is it?

(3) 'It is a cow that is neither young nor old, but of a middle age between that.'

(4) 'Tell us its colour,' they ask again.

(5) 'Red, intensely red, the delight of the beholders!'—answered Moses.

(6) 'They still ask, '*What is it*, for cows are alike to us

(7) 'It is a cow that is not broken to plough the earth or water the field, a sound one, with no blemish in her'—replies Moses.

(8) As last the interlocutors are satisfied—"Now hast thou brought the truth." Moses has obtained pass marks!

(9) The cow is now sacrificed, yet the levity of the people is not at an end! They are yet near not doing it!

(10) The "they" of Moses' time now becomes "ye" and "yourselves."

(11) 'Ye slew a man and contended among yourselves coneerning him' (whether it was not all a delusion, the man and the deed?).

(12) The dead is stricken with part of the victim's body.

(13) He is raised to life by God.

(14) This is a sign.

(15) Peradventure 'ye may understand!'

I think it is impossible for language to be more pointed than it is here. The purport is plain, let him who has ears to hear and eyes to see perceive the truth. The cow that is neither old nor young, that is not broken to plough the earth or water the field, that is sound, without a blemish,[5] of an intensely red colour and the delight of the beholder, is the *nafs* that is rooted in the *bahiratman*, composed of the intensely red blood and the flesh made from it. Its colour is the delight of the beholder, because no colour can rejoice a beholder more than the glowing animation of life in living flesh. This idea is so well expressed in Chinese mysticism that I shall merely content myself by quoting from it (SBE. vol. xxxix. p. 230):

> "*Kung-ni* said Once when I was sent on a mission to *Khu*, I saw some pigs sucking at their dead mother. After a little they looked with rapid glances, when they all left her, and ran away. They felt that she did not see them; and that she was no longer like themselves. What they had loved in their mother was not her bodily figure, but what had given animation to her figure."

As for the colour of the heifer, I may say that the literal translation of the Arabic word used in the text is yellow, but this does not make any difference, for red[6] is the colour of the soul (in the sense of *nafs*=the *bahiratman*) and yellow, of the *qulb* (the scat of emotions, hence, the heart), according to Muslim mysticism (see "Studies in Tasawwuf, by Khaja Khan, p. 81). Thus, it is the sacrifice of the lower ego (the *bahiratman*) that is intended in either case.

The derivation of the English word sacrifice, I am happy to note, is singularly accurate, and directly points to the true sense of a sacrifice (Latin *sacrificium* from *sacer*, holy and *facere*, to make). It is, thus, the doing of an act that is calculated to make us *holy*. This most certainly can never be the shedding of the blood of an innocent victim; for blood washes away not the impurities of passions and lusts, but actually hardens the tender human nature which is a very necessary qualification for salvation. And even if it were possible to maintain, which it is not in the light of our knowledge to-day, that by the sacrificial blood some supernal power could be induced to forgive or condone the sins of a villain, it is clear that that would not convert the evil-doer into a saint. An internal change on the part of the sinner himself is needed to make him *holy*. The true etymological significance of the word holy itself is very instructive. It is derived from the Anglo-Saxon *hal* (Old German and Icelandic, *heil*, and Gothic *hails*), meaning *whole*, sound or safe. There is, thus, no question of condonation or forgiveness of sins, but of making whole, of removing unsoundness, of eradicating 'disease.' It is the sacrificing of the *bahiratman*, in symbolic thought, the *purushamedha* of the ancient Hindus, which alone has the effect of making us *holy*. As the unholy traits and tendencies constituting this ill-omened factor of evil are eradicated and destroyed from the heart, divine grace is set free, to manifest itself in the life of their destroyer, till finally, on the destruction of all the forces of sin and evil, the perfection of Divinity is enjoyed by the *jiva* (soul), now become perfectly *whole* and *holy* by the very act or fact of ridding himself of these agents of defilement and corruption.

The substance of the accusation—when ye slew[7] a man (according to the letter of the text, it should be when ye slew a soul)—is that the real man has been smothered by the apparent ego, the *bahiratman*, of the soul-less humanity, who regard Life as the product of matter, and themselves as no other than the physical body. They have killed the soul, as it were, and then contend among themselves, concerning it—whether it exist? whether it be not the product of matter? and so forth. God (Life) now astonishes you with a miracle. He asks you to touch what you regard as a dead carcass with a part of the sacrificed cow, when lo! and behold! a quickening Spirit immediately springs into life to name the *bahiratman* as His slayer!

Such is the magical effect of the sacrifice. No sooner is the soul *touched* (characterised) by the dead *nafs* than is it electrified into Life. This is how the dead are raised to life! *Peradventure ye may understand*.

Perhaps it will not be quite uninteresting to give the whole story of this red heifer. It is thus related In Sale's Koran (see pp. 8 and 9):

> "A certain *man* at his *death* left *his son*, then a *child*, a cow calf, which *wandered* in *the desert till he came of age*; at which time his, mother told him *the heifer was his*, and bid him fetch her, and selt her for *three pieces of gold*. When the young man came to the *market* with his heifer, *an angel* in the shape of a man accosted him, and bid him six pieces of gold for her, but he would not take the money till he had asked his mother's consent; which when he had obtained, he returned to the market place, and met the angel, ,who now offered him twice as much for the heifer, *provided he would say nothing of it to his* mother, but the young man refusing went and acquainted her with the additional offer. The woman *perceiving it was an angel*, bid ber son go back and ask him what must be done with the heifer, whereupon the angel told the young man that in a little time the children of Israel would buy that heifer of him at any price. And soon after it happened that an Israelite, named Hawmiel, was killed by a relation of his, who, to prevent discovery, *conveyed the body to a place considerbly distant from that where the fact was committed. The friends of the slain man accused* some other persons of the murder before Moses, but they *denying the fact*, and *there being no evidence to convict* them, God commanded *a cow, of such and such particular marks, to be killed*, but *there being no other which answered the description except the orphan's heifer*, they were obliged to buy her for as much gold as her hide would hold; according to some, for her full weight in gold, and, as

> ethers say, for ten times as much. This heifer they sacrificed and the dead body being, by divine direction, struck with a part of it, revived, and standing up, named the person who had killed him, *after which it immediately fell down dead again.*"

This is the legend, which, according to Sale, "seems to be borrowed from the red heifer, which was ordered by Jewish law to be burnt, and the ashes kep for purifying those who happened to touch a dead corpse; and from the heifer directed to be slain for the expiatin of an uncertain murder" (*ibid.* p. 9 footnote). The general opinion about the differences between the Bible and the Qur'an, of course, is that Muhammad knew little or nothing of the Jewish history and tradition and that the Qur'an contains only half distorted half-understood tenets of Judaism. It is true, no doubt, that the Qur'an is not an original work and much of what it contains was taken from the earlier creeds as Tisdall has fully shown; but that Book itself never made any secret of it and openly said:

> "Every age hath its book of revelation [Chap. xiii]......The Koran is not a new invented fiction, but a confirmation of those scriptures which have been revealed before it [Chap. xii].....There has been no nation but a preacher hath in past times been conversant among them [Chap. iii. 35].....I swear by the instructive Koran that thou art one of the messengers of God sent to show the right way" [Chap. iv. 361.]

Modern critics unfortunately know nothing of religion, and like the exoterics themselves display gross ignorance in understanding the mystery language of Mysticism. The story of the red heifer is not a narrative of facts that could be borrowed or twisted out of shape; it is the heritage of the whole race, and belongs as much to you and me as to Muhammad and the Israelites. No one has a right to object to your embellishing it still further, provided you have the capacity to do so; but otherwise you must hand it down to posterity as you received it, without change or alteration.

As regards the elucidation of the further details of the

legend the man[8] who left a son and a heifer at his death is Spirit whose death signifies its impurity.[9] The soul is the son of Spirit and the owner of the heifer of *nafs*. This is the doctrine of Sonship[10] once more in disguise. Before Muhammad, Christianity had preached it to the world, and before it had Hosea declared; "Ye are the sons of the living God" (Hosea i. 10). And Hosea had no delusions about this, for we also have it from him:—

> "Yet I am the Lord thy God, from the land of Egypt, and thou shalt know no God but me for there is no saviour beside me" (chap. xiii. 4).

St. Paul, too, maintained that as many as were led by the spirit of God were the sons of God (Romans viii. 14). In Hinduism also the curse of Savitri on Indra, i.e., Life personified, was that he was to lose his city and station and to be bound in chains. This was modified by Gayatri to the effect that his son would be his liberator. The doctrine of 'sonship' did not, it is obvious, originate with Christianity which regards its founder both as man (John viii. 40 and Luke iii. 23) and Son of God. The element of confusion that is likely to arise from such conflicting descriptions can be easily avoided with reference to *Naya-Vada* (discrimination of standpoints). For according to the body, the man is the son of a particular person; but from the point of view of the soul, he is the child of Life itself. Hence, the mystifying references to a Self-conscious Soul, who is now described as a man and now as a Son of God. The mystery of the co-existence of the Father and the Son in the Holy Trinity also finds an easy solution now. In so far as the Perfected Soul is the manifestation of the divinity of Life, he is the Son[11] of Life; but in so for as He is the very soul-substance itself that existed in the condition of impurity previously, and in fact eternally, he is coeval with Life itself, hence contemporaneous with the 'Father'! We can now understand why in the formulary, or creed, propounded by the Council of Nicea such vehement bitterness was shown in insisting upon the co-eternity of the 'Father' and the 'Son' (see The Conflict Between

Religion and Science, by J. W. Draper chap ii.): "The Holy Catholic and Apostolic Church anathematizes those who say that there was a time when the Son of God was not, and that before he was begotten he was not, and that he was made out of nothing or out of another substance, or essence, and is created, or changeable, or alterable."

The son who is to offer *shrāddha* for the salvation of his parent in Hinduism is also a representation of the soul that is seeking emancipation. The parent is the purity of the soul-substance, which is now (spiritually) dead and in hell (allegorically, the state of bondage, *vide* the Key of Knowledge). The *shraddha* is the *shraddhana* (faith) supported by and fed on know ledge, which will revive the 'dead' spirit, and enable it to attain to *nirvana*. The dead pitris (ancestors) are the divine qualities which are now un-functioning, and which are to be revived by knowledge and faith. The feasting of *Brahmanas* (literally, the Knowers of Brahman, i.e., Divinity) is, naturally, intended to afford an opportunity for the acquisition of Right Faith and Knowledge.

To revert to the heifer-myth, the desert in which the heifer wanders during the infancy of the 'son' is the dreary realm of transmigration where the heifer of *nafs* may be said to wander about unchecked, till *manhood* be reached. This refers to the advantage of the human birth which is generally the starting point for the journey to *nirvana*. Here an opportunity is offered for the subjugation of the wandering heifer with knowledge and *tapas*. The term desert is to be compared with the Garden of Eden where man was placed before the fall.

The orphanage of the son is indicative of the nature of life which has no outside patron or protector. It is taught in the book of Psalms (Ps. xlix. 7):

"None of them can by any means redeem his brother,
nor give to God a ransom for him."

The Prophet of Islam, too, taught:

"Dread the day wherein one soul shall not make satisfaction for another soul; neither shall any intercession be accepted from them nor shall any compensation be received, neither shall they be helped" (Sura Baqr).

And in the Jaina Scriptures the friendlessness of the unemancipated soul is actually appointed a subject for meditation. This is how this particular form of meditation runs:—

"None can help the *jiva* (soul) in his trouble; he alone has to bear his pain and suffering; friends, relations, wife and children are powerless to combat suffering and disease; *dharma* (religion) is the only protector of the helpless"—(The Practical Dharma p. 53).

It is this want of a protector that is likened to the condition of orphanage. The mother referred to is the understanding which at first arrives at a low estimate of the *nafs*. The market is the world of strife and bustle where men go to earn money or to affer their 'goods' for sale. Here the worldly man goes out to sell, offer his labour for three pieces of gold, to be explained anon. The angel in human guise is the effect of meritorious deeds in the past lives, appearing as a good counsellor. The insistence on the consultation of the understanding (the mother) is an indication of wisdom, that avoids doing things rashly. The refusal of a more tempting offer still is an indication of self-restraint. The Israelite killed is the soul that is slain by its relation, the *bahiratman*—'he who shall find his life shall lose it etc.' (Matt. x. 39) The denial of the soul is its slaying. 'The discovery of the deed is prevented by the body being conveyed to a place considerably distant from that where the fact took place'—this signifies the wholesale constitutional changes that are implied in rebirth (transmigration).

The friends of the slain man who accuse the *bahiratman* of having murdered the soul are the attributes of pure discrimination, judgment and the like which have come to suspect the real nature of the 'usurper.' The accused persons (materialism or the materialists) deny that there was a soul to be murdered. The evidence is not sufficient to convict the unrepentant *bahiratman*. This means that speculative intellec-tualism (as the mystics know of) is seldom sufficient to *convince* an unwilling disputant.[12] A practical test is caned for under the circumstances. 'Strike the "dead" with a part of the burnt *nafs*.' It is done; and lo! a complete miracle is wrought!

The cow that was worth three pieces of gold when alive is of inestimable value now that it is dead! It is literally worth its weight in gold.

The three pieces of gold for which living *nafs* was to be sold represent ample means for procuring (1) necessaries, (2) comforts and (3) luxuries of life. For these men barter their souls.

The description of the cow is not answered by any other cow than the orphan's; for *nafs* is really not a member of the bovine class. The bodily man regards himself as entirely composed of flesh and blood, whence the colour of the orphan's cow, red, intensely red. We have it in the fifth book of Moses that blood is life (Deut. xii. 23).

Nafs is also neither young nor old, but common to both, youth and old age.

An ordinary cow could not surely help growing old between the death of the orphan's father and the attainment of manhood by him who was but a child at the time. And who would have paid three pieces of gold for an untamed useless cow that had wandered all its days in a desert?

The description, that it is not broken to plough the earth or water the field, is also very suggestive, showing that one need not look for the object (to be sacrificed) among the cattle that are employed in the plough or for the irrigation of fields.

The falling dead of the body ofter the 'miracle' is probably intended to signify the escape of the soul from its long-continued captivity, when the body is left behind and the Spirit soars away upwards to *nirvana*.

*Cf. (The Sufi's challenge) :—

لب به بندو چشم بندو گوش بند

گر نه بینی سر حق برما بخند

Such is the sublime teaching embedded in the legend of

the sacrifice of the red heifer, which, unfortunately, has been understood in quite an opposite sense. Indeed the entire doctrine of sacrifice has been grossly misunderstood by men who have been doing themselves incalculable harm instead of good. I need only add about this heifer legend that it contains, within the small dimensions of a solitary pictogram, the highly condensed essence of the entire religious and philosophical lore, and estimates, most accurately, the value of *nafs* with reference to three kinds of ideals, material, heavenly and divine. Its temporary control enables man to eke out his living in this life, by manual labour or otherwise (three pieces of gold); by curbing it regularly heavenly pleasures are enjoyed in the next rebirth (six pieces of gold); but if it be destroyed totally, it immediately leads to Godhood, which means eternal Life and Joy and Immortality (its full weight in gold) !

According to Methodius also, who flourished about 1,700 years ago, the sacrifice of the heifer signified the curbing of desires. This is what he said on the subject:

> "Therefore also God commands Abraham. 'Take me an heifer of three years old, and a ram of three years old, and a turtle dove and a young pigeon' which is admirably said: for remark, that concerning those things, He also gives this command, Bring them Me and keep them free from the yoke, even the soul uninjured, like a heifer, and your flesh, and your reason; the last like a goat, since he traverses lofty and precipitous places, and the other like a ram, that he may in nowise skip away, and fall and slip off from the right way. For this shalt thou be perfect and blameless, O Abraham, when thou hast offered to me thy soul, and thy senses, and thy mind, which He mentioned under the symbol of the heifer, the goat and the ram three years old, as though they represented the pure knowledge of Trinity"—The Writings of Methodius (Ante-Nicene Christian Library, vol. xiv p. 44.)

Thus, the soul that is rid of the desiring nature is the offering. Tertullian says of such a victim:

"This is the victim, dedicated with our whole heart, fed on faith, cared for with truth unblemished in innocence, clean in purity, an offering of love garlanded, that we ought to escort to God's altar, in company with a procession of good works, midst psalms and hymns, and it will obtain all things for us from God."

The proper import of the term unblemished with reference to a sacrifice is well brought out by Philo, who is the leading authority on Jewish symbolism. He says (see Yonge's Philo Judams vol. iii. p. 212):

"And the accuracy and minuteness of the investigation is directed not so much on account of the victims themselves, as in order that those who offer them should be irreproachable; for God designed to teach the Jews by these figures, whenever they went up to the altars.....never to bring with them any weakness or evil passion in their soul, hut to endeavour to make it wholly and entirely bright and clean, without any blemish, so that God might not turn away with aversion from the sight of it."

We have it again from Philo:

"So that the real object taken care of is not the condition of the victims sacrificed in order that they may have no blemish, but that of the sacrificers that they may not be defiled by any unlawful passion." —Ibid. p. 230.

And he also tells us (*Ibid*. 235):

"The altar of God is the grateful soul of the wise man.....On this altar the sacred fire is continually kept burning, preserved with care and unextinguishable......"

At page 249 of the work quoted from we have it again:

"Accordingly, the man who is about to offer a sacrifice ought to examine and see, not whether the victim is without blemish, but whether his mind is sound, and entire and perfect."

The true meaning of Jewish sacrifices has already been shown to be esoteric. We learn from Philo a great deal of useful knowledge on the subject, "Pass Over" signified the passing over to God; wheaten flour is mind purified by instruction; the purpose of the injunction requiring the 'cutting up of the burnt offering joint by joint' is to make the soul naked of false opinions; to examine things separately with accuracy.

> "It is enjoined therfore that sacrificers, when they have flayed the burnt offering, shall cut it up joint by joint, in order in tbe first place that the soul may appear naked without any coverings, such as are made by empty and false opinions, and in the second place that it may be able to receive suitable divisions, for virtue is a whole and one, which is divided into corresponding species, such as prudence and temperance, justice and courage, that we, knowing the differences of each of these qualities, may submit to a voluntary service of them both in their entirety and in particulars."—Yonge's Philo Judreus vol.-ii. p. 226.

To revert to the legend of the cow sacrifice: Jalal-ud-din Rumi, the leading Muslim philosopher and saint whose poetical composition, entitled the Masnavi, has attained to a well-deserved world-wide fame, has also preserved the true significancy of the allegory. He says:

گاؤ کشتن هست از شرط طریق

تا شود از زخم دمش جان مفیق

گاؤ نفس خویش را زو تر بکش

تا شود روح خفي زنده بهش

Translated into English these verses read:

(1) The killing of the cow is enjoined in the Law so that life (soul) may be brought to sensibility with the wound of its tail!

(2) Kill the cow of thine *nafs*(نفس)that the soul that is insensible (or hidden) may come to life and light (knowledge)!

I now pass on to a consideration of the third item on the list of means for salvation, namely, pilgrimage. Now, pilgrimage is made to a place with a view to develop the germ of spirituality in the soul, and its efficacy depends on the accompanying mental attitude and the spirit of renunciation (*vairngya*), which are best developed outside the atmosphere of worldly bustle and home life. Junayd, a Muhammadan saint, well brings out the purport of pilgrimage in the course of his conversation with a man who has just returned from Mecca.

"From the hour when you first journeyed from your home have you also been journeying away from all sins?" He said "No!" "Then," said Junayd, "you have made no journey. At every stage where you halted for the night did you traverse a station on the way to God?" "No,' he replied. "Then," said Junayd, "You have not trodden the road, stage by stage. When you put on the pilgrim's garb at the proper place, did you discard the qualities of human nature as you cast off your clothes?" "No." "Then you have not put on the pilgrim's garb. When you stood at 'Arafat,' did you stand one moment in contemplation of God?" "No." "Then you have not stood at Arafat. When you went to Muzdalifa and achieved your desire, did you renounce all sensual desires?" "No." "Then you have not gone to Muzdalifa. When you circumambulated the Ka'ba, did you behold the immaterial beauty of God in the abode of purification?" "No." "Then you have not circumambulated the Ka'ba. When you ran between Safa and Marwa, did you attain to purity (Safa) and virtue (Muruwwat)?" "No." "Then you have not run. When you came to Mina, did all your wishes (muna) cease?" "No." "Then you have not yet visited Mina. When you reached the slaughter-place and offered sacrifice, did you sacrifice the objects of worldly desire?" "No." "Then you have not sacrificed. When you threw the pebbles, did you throw away whatever sensual thoughts were accompanying you?" "No." "Then you have not yet thrown the pebbles and you have not yet performed the pilgrimage."—(The Mystics of Islam, pp. 91 and 92).

The best place of pilgrimage, no doubt, is where the associations are the most ennobling and elevating, that is to say, which is associated with the Great Ones, the *Tirthamkaras*. Thither should the pious flock, for excellence in faith, renunciation and merit. There is little or no good in visiting such places as are associated with allegorical gods and goddesses.

I shall now briefly touch upon the subject of meditation which consists in the withdrawal of the mind from the world and in its becoming engaged in self-contemplation. The object is not merely to remain engaged in metaphysical speculation, but to realise the inner meaning of Life by directly feeling its pulsation in one's own self. Every movement, every tremour, every breath of this mysterious substance, must, therefore, be brought under personal observation and minutely analysed. But this can only be done by keeping the attention fixed steadily on the soul, exclusive of everything else. The mind is, however, so constituted that it will attend to anything but the soul, if left to itself; and even when deliberate effort is made to bring it under some sort of control, it is inclined to break loose on the very first shadow of an excuse-bodily discomfort, sensual excitement and the like-that might present itself. For this reason, the curbing of passions and desires and the mortifying and subjugation of the flesh are absolutely essential as necessary preliminary steps to meditation. A well-regulated life, with pure wholesome food, is, therfore, absolutely necessary, if real progress is to be made on the path. The use of meat and wine is forbidden, as they tend to disturb mental equanimity, excite the passions and coarsen those finer "threads" and nervous filaments which connect the soul with the mind, preventing thereby the turning of attention inwards, in the direction of the Self. Well does Isaiah say:

> "But they also have erred through wine, and through strong drink are out of the way; the priest and the prophet have erred through strong drink, they are swallowed up of wine, they are out of the way through strong drink; they err in vision, they stumble in judgment. For all tables are full of vomit and filthiness, so that there is no place clean" (Chap. xxviii. 7-8).

These are the external accessories to meditaion. The internal helpful causes are certain thought-forms which have been found to be highly useful as aids to self-realisation. Of these a very simple form is to imagine a pure Effulgent Divinity, a partless embodiment of pure Intelligence, pure Happiness and Peace, seated within the physical body. This is to be visualised by partly closing the eyes and by fixing the attention on the "inside". If it be found necessary to employ words with reference to this Divine Embodiment of pure Knowledge and Joy! it should only be meditated upon, with the aid of such words as are descriptive of the true nature of the soul—*Om, Sonam Arhan, Siddha, Paramatman, Niranjan*-pure), and the like. The following *shloka* is specially recommended;

एकोऽहं निरमलः शुद्धो ज्ञान दर्शन लक्षणः।

शोषा मे बाहिरा भावा सर्वे संयोग लक्षणः॥

This is to the effect that I am One; I am free from impurities; I am divine; I am pure; I am invested with the attributes of knowledge and perception; all else is outside me; is not me; and is the product of *karmas*! In this way should one meditate on one's own Self. As the power of steady meditation increases, a time comes when there is a coalescence of the subject and the object of contemplation, when he who contemplates finds himself merged in the being whom he contemplates upon; when the apparent is absorbed in the real. The Lover and the Beloved here become one; the devotee now realises his oneness with his God (Atman Dharma, pp. 27-29). What is meant is the merger of the potential (the unmanifest actual) in the *ideal*, the stamping of the purified substance of being with the impress of Divinity, the transformation of the *jivatman* into *Paramatman*, i.e., God. This is termed *entering into life*, and is a process so full of life and joy that those who have experienced its thrilling ecstasy even for the brief space of a second have been filled with it.

Such, briefly, is the description of meditation which is the most potent means of Self-realisation.

The remaining two items, namely, purification and *tapas* have already been sufficiently dealt with in these lectures. But it is well to know that purification and tallas are concerned almost exclusively with the riddance of the internal filth, not exclusively with the washing of the outer carcass or with bodily distortions and poses. Physical posture, fasting and the like are, no doubt, necessary for progress on the path, but they are only accessories to Self-contemplation, which is the direct cause of liberation. For without the controlling of the mind, speech and the body it is not possible to enjoy anything like steadiness in *dhyana* (meditation or contemplation) ; but without the *dhyana* itself what purpose shall be served by simple bodily mortification and self-torture? Neither Raja Yoga (union through the mind) nor Hatha Yoga (the path of physical austerity) is calculated to lead to satisfactory results for this reason. Even *Jnana* Yoga (the path of know-ledge) is not the right method by itself. 'fhe proper path consists in the union of Right Faith, Right Knowledge and Right Conduct, as defined,. in an earlier lecture. Bhakti Yoga (devotion) is certainly a very useful ally on the path, if rightly employed.

The object of devotion is, however, not a mythological god or goddess, but one's own soul primarily, though so long as perfection is not attained, one must *idealise* and be devoted to the *Tirthamkaras* than whom there can be no greater Teacher. As the Qur'an pointedly asks (Sura Baqr, verse 132):

> "The baptism of God! and who is better than God at baptising?

The life of Jesus is an epitome, in charming allegory, of the life of a *Tirthamkara*. It is the highest *ideal*, in Jewish thought and with all its Jewish imperfections, of Life Triumphant, of a Divine Sonship of Pure Spirit, of Divinity made manifest in man. Verily,

> "I say unto you that in this place is one greater than the temple."

Accordingly, the Message of Truth on the Victory-Banner of Gods is the Gospel of Life and Joy, composed in three of the sweetest of words-*ahimsa paramo dharmah* (non-injuring is the highest religion), that hold out a promise of Life to all beings, and to him who follows it in daily living, of Life Eternal as a Paramatman (God)!

FOOTNOTE

1. It would seem that the true purport of the Lord's Prayer, too, used to be kept secret from the generality of men, and was to be revealed to approved candidates alone:—

   "As those who were admitted to the inner sight of the mysteries had a formula or password, so the catechumens had a formula which was only entrusted to them in the last days of their catechumenate—the baptismal formula itself and the Lord's prayer In the Western rites the 'traditio symboli' occupies an important place in the whole ceremony. There was a special rite for it. It took place a week or ten days before the great office of Baptism on Easter-eve. Otherwise the Lord's prayer and the creed were kept secret and kept so as mysteries; and to the present day the technical name of the creed is a Greek word meaning password" (The Influence of Greek Ideas and u.sages On The Christian Church, p. 298)

2. According to Sir Syed Ahmed Khan:—

   "There is no religious foundation for the killing of animals in sacrifice at the Hajj to be traced in the Qur'an. Mecca is situated in a desert, destitute of animal life, it was difficult to procure food for man in such a place. For this reason people carried animals for food to places.....known as Budan and Khulayed. Those who did not carry them, had to purchase them at Mecca, kill them there and feed themselves and others. This alone appears to be the foundation of sacrifice in the Qur'an. In those days an untold number of animals was killed and left to be devoured by kites and jackals; this has no origin in the. religion of Islam" (Studies in Tasawwuf," pp. 104-105).

3. Further confirmation, by no means unexpected, of the above conclusion comes from a Jewish document more than two thousand years old:—

   ".......So, then all that is said concerning.....animals relates to righteousness and righteous dealings between man and man.....For he that presents the sacrifice makes an offering of his own soul and all its affections" (The Letter of Aristeas, p. 57).

4. Cf. " Jerusalem means the **sight of peace**, when......the **dogs** of the outside sense will be hushed" (The Message of Philo by K. S.Gnthrie, p. 50).

5. Cf. "You will discover that all this minuteness in reference to the animals shadows forth by means of symbols the improvement of your character. For the law does not exist for irrational creatures but for those possessing mind and reason, so that its concern is not for sacrificial animals, to provide that they be without blemish, but for those who offer the sacrifices, that they be not disquieted by reason of any passion. "—Philo quoted by H. A. A. Kennedy in Philo's Contribution To Religion, p 42.
6. Cf. 'The red colour of the cow.....suggests the colour of blood' (ERE. xi. 36).
7. Shaykh Ibrahim Gazur-i-Ilahi relates a story of a certain Fakir who entered the cloister of Junayid, wrapped in a black blanket. Junayid asked him the reason for his mourning. He said, "My God is dead!" On being asked to explain himself, he said, "Not knowing that my *nafs* [soul] was manifestation of God, I have killed it. and therefore I am in mourning for it."—("Studies in. Tasawwuf." p. 29).
8. It is interesting to note that 'purusha' (literally, the male) is the term used in Sankhyan Metaphysics for the Soul.
9. The idea of death in the caile of Spirit is that of the loss of Self-Knowledge which is due to the contact of matter. This is also the sense in which Jesus rebuked the disciple who wanted leave to bury the dead: "Fol1ow me and let the dead bury their dead". (Matt. viii. 22).

   This certainly meant that the burial of the dead was to be left to those who though alive physically were dead in spirit, in other words, to those who knew not themselves as spirits. The raising of the dead, or the resurrection from the dead, we also know now, means the conquest of death, and not the raising of the dead in the literal sense of the expression. According to the Sufis, "*fana* (annihilation or death)' is the non-recognizance of one's attributes as one's own but *baqa* (eternal life) is the recognition of the same as the attributes of God." (Studies in Tasawwuf, p. 71), According to Clement, the dead are those "who have fallen away from the dogmas and have placed the mind in subjection to carnal passions" (Clement's Writings vol vii p. 255). In the Ante-Nicene Library (vol. ix. pp. 75.76) the term is v. 6 it is applied to those who have not the spirit of God themselves. In 1 Timothy pointed out: "But she that liveth in pleasure is dead ;while she liveth.'

10. In the Masonic tradition (Lecture x) the Master Builder, Hiram Abif, is described as a widow's son, because Righi Conduct [the Architect of the Soul's Divinity, hence the Master Builder] has its origin in a soul whose pure spiritual nature is 'dead.' Bereft of her natural purity, the soul is likened, on account of the bereavement, to a widow, and the Master Builder whose " birth" takes place at a time when the soul is thus bereft of her spiritual nature, naturally becomes a widow's son

11. The purified self, the son of Life, is born of vairagy a, personified as Shiva ; and the process of generation is emhlemed by the copulative union of the *lingum* and *yoni* which are to be seen in Hindu temples dedicated to the god named The act of copulation itself is, on account of the idea of the pleasure associated with it, also symbolical of ananda (happiness), which accrues to the soul from its union with *vairagya* (renunciation).

12. Cf. (The Sufi's challenge):—

[Tr. Close the lips, shut the eyes, stop the ears; if thou. dost not then perceive the mystery of Truth, thou mayest taugh at us!]

CHAPTER - IX

SUMMARY AND CONCLUSIONS

Our labours are now about to be ended, this being the last of the lectures that I have to deliver before you. We have seen how different religion has proved from what we had taken it to mean, and how it really was the same teaching, the same principle, the same doctrine the same tenet under different names and forms and formulas. Systems as hostile as hinduism, that sanctified the cow, and Muhammadanism that enjoined its sacrifice, theologies so wide apart as Christianity that insisted on a belief in the existence of a son of God, and Judaism and others that denied that their God had a wife or son, have been found to be real brothers, descendants of the same Parent—the Scientific Truth—though unknown to and un-recognised by one another, owing to the differences of robes and masks they have been wearing and aiso of the parts they have been playing on the mythological stage from hoary antiquity. For say what men may to the contrary, scientific truth must have existed in the world before people could have set out to build their pantheons on its principles. Allegory cannot precede fact; it is the fact that precedes allegory.

But you might ask where is that real wisdom, where the scientific foundation, now which assuredly existed at the time of the framing of these mythologies?

How is it that we have only the mythologies left to us and not the scientific truth? The answer is that the allegorisers were not the pioneers themselves but highly-gifted Artists, who came

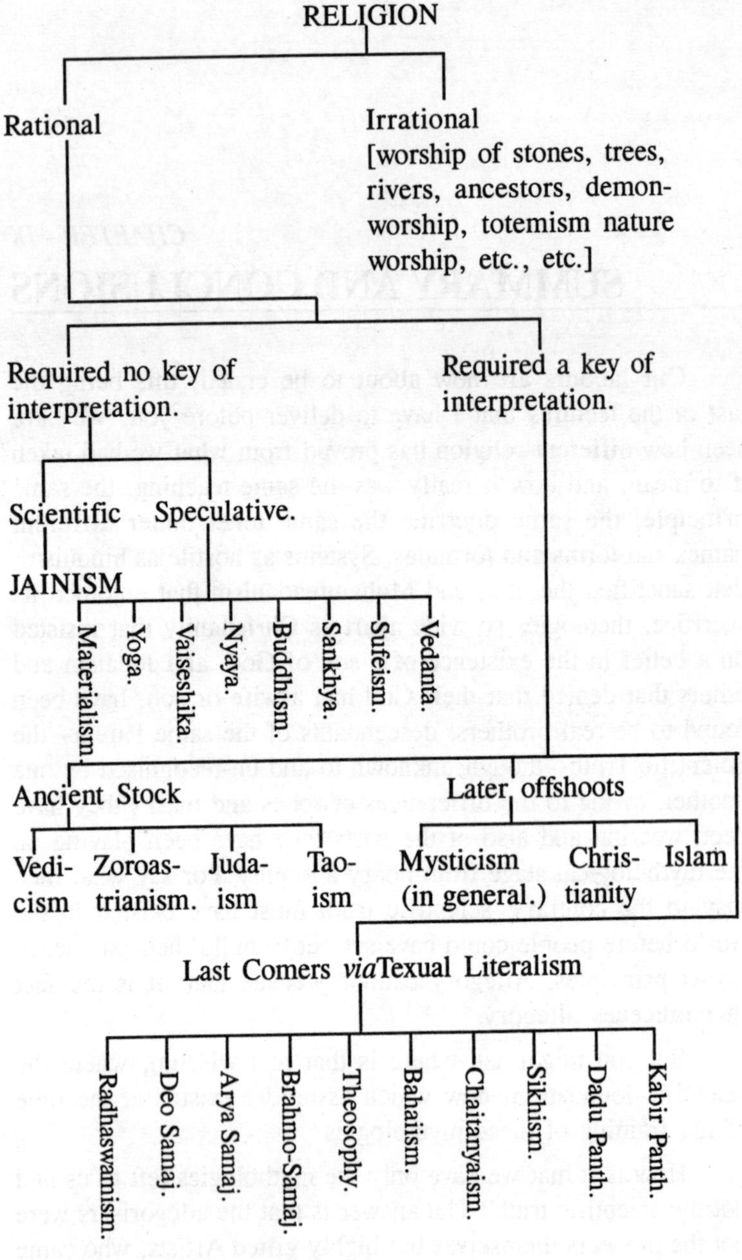
RELIGION
Rational
Irrational [worship of stones, trees, rivers, ancestors, demon-worship, totemism nature worship, etc., etc.]
Required no key of interpretation.
Required a key of interpretation.
Scientific
Speculative.
JAINISM
Materialism.
Yoga.
Vaiseshika.
Nyaya.
Buddhism.
Sankhya.
Sufeism.
Vedanta.
Ancient Stock
Later offshoots
Vedi-cism
Zoroas-trianism.
Juda-ism
Tao-ism
Mysticism (in general.)
Chris-tianity
Islam
Last Comers *via*Texual Literalism
Radhaswamism.
Deo Samaj.
Arya Samaj.
Brahmo-Samaj.
Theosophy.
Bahaiism.
Chaitanyaism.
Sikhism.
Dadu Panth.
Kabir Panth.

afterwards. They were not builders and they dug not their foundations themselves, but were content to embellish and decorate the Edifice of Truth raised by their Predecessors. Where is the scientific truth to be found? Who are these predecessors of the allegory men? Let us classify religions in a tabulated way to understand the narrative of the past. The following arrangement is justified by the conclusions established in the course of these lectures.

The position of Jainism is clear from the contents of our third lecture, which has been the basis of comparison and the means of reconcilation diverse faiths examined by us. As a matter of fact, the Creed of the *Tirthamkaras* furnishes the only platform where all other creeds may meet and be reconciled to one another. This "Confluence of Opposites," as the reconciliation of the apparently conflicting religions may be termed, is not possible else where, not because they have no place for a gathering of men, nor because they are all characterized by intolerance, nor because they do not desire to be reconciled, but because they are the followers of *Ekanta-Vada* (one-sided absolutism), the irreconcilable antithesis of *Anekanta-Vada* (many-sidedness or relativity of thought). The difference in the two views lies in this that while a non-Jaina would insist on the truth of his own faith, and would absolutely deny the validity of an opposite view, the Jaina would actually go out in search of the point of view (if any there be) from which the opposite view might be maintained. You have before you, in these lectures, the result of the Jaina research in the domain of religion. I need not tell you what conclusion it points to. There is a very happy agreement, as we have seen, amongst all religions, on the points established in the *Jaina Siddhanta*, every other ancient creed vying, as it were, with its compeers in offering its quota for the glorification of the Scientific Truth. This in itself, I am sure, is ample reward for the labour involved in studying the stand-points of others. As for our own satisfaction, we have the highest guarantee in the agreement between (*i*) science, (*ii*) reason and (*iii*) testimony; and, as stated in the second lecture, where these three combinedly agreed on any point, the matter was put absolutely beyond doubt and dispute for ever. We have before us (*i*) the truth as taught by the Perfect Ones, the *Tirthamkaras*, who attained to Godhood with its aid [Testimony of Gods], (*ii*) the confirmation of the Word of Law by a scientific study of nature [Science], (*iii*) the agreement of reason ofter the most searching enquiry [Logic]; and the most important of all (*iv*) actual corroboration furnished by every other ancient religion, without a single exception, showing, in the clearest possible manner, the concurrence of the entire human race in the past, as to the reality and practicability of the method!

The next question is, why are there no Omniscient Teachers to-day amongst us to settle our disputes? The reply is that these are very bad times, with worse to come in the future. The humanity of this age is not qualified for practising asceticism. You cannot have omniscience except as the culmination of a very high order of asceticism. Hence, when you have no true ascetics, you can have no omniscient Teachers either. These are, indeed, very bad times that we are passing through. None of the residents of our part of the world can obtain *moksha* in this age from this region. Worse times are to come. The whole of this evil period is of 42,000 years of which about 2500 have already passed. For this period the prophecy is that *nirvana* shall not be attainable then. There is a covert reference to this in the New Testament Scripture also:

> "....When heaven was shut up three years and six months, when great famine was throughout all the land" (Luke, iv. 25).

The number of months in 3 years and a half corresponds to 42 millenniums, taking a month as equivalent to a thousand years. Be that as it may, it is evident that there has been great deterioration amongst men during the last 2500 years in respect of—

(i) faith, that has been almost wholly replaced by either a pure soul-less materialism or by fantastical Literalism of mythological lore;

(ii) morality, which is daily growing lax, with deception, trickery and treachery becoming the prevailing traits amongst men;

(iii) leisure and ease, which are fast disappearing with the rise in the cost of living ;

(iv) intellectualism, the most highly lauded of which in our day has just settled down to the belief that the founders of our religions were primitive men, and but little better, in point of culture and accomplishment, than mere babes;

(v) science, which has finally consoled itself with the belief that there is to be an eternal peaceful end in the grave, there being happily no soul to worry one with its future destiny;

(vi) physical strength, which has deteriorated in some places quite appreciably, and which must further deteriorate as an inevitable result of privations, pestilence and perennial wars;

(vii) peace of mind, which is almost impossible without Religion, and which, in many cases, is being throttled by the high-pressure' speed of modern civilization.

These deteriorations are most pronounced in India and in certain other parts of Asia, but the turn of others is coming. The European Mahabharata has already laid the foundation of suffering and distress in the West, and the trend of the civilization of our times, with its soul-less politics and aspirations that do not admit of anyone living for long in peace, may be depended upon to complete the work of ruin in due course of time. One of the prophecies of religion is that there would be no fire left after 18500 years hence, and it is significant that coal is diminishing fast! Our outlook is sad, indeed; but I am not here to regale you with prophecies. These are bad times undoubtedly, and worse are still in store, though we may fairly expect an occasional arresting of the downward movement from time to time. This is the reason why there are no Tirthamakaras in our midst to-day, and why there will be none for some time to come. The next Tirthamkara will appear when a better order of things has been re-established after a certain time (about 81,500 years hence), according to the Jaina Scriptures.

The origin of Religion in a world that is eternal is out of the question. Whenever a *Tirthamkara* arises He re-establishes the Scientific Truths about the nature of Life, and these Truths are collectively termed Religion. The word of Instruction of the *Tirthamkara* is called *Shruti*, as distinguished from *Smriti* (memory, or what is worked out by the mind with the aid of memory). *Apta-vachanam* (the word of a Professor, hence *Tirthamkara*) is descriptive, in a scientific way, of the exact nature of things, as they exist in nature; but it is not argumentative. The real characteristics of true *Shruti* have been described by me ere this: they all bear nut its scientific nature. To-day men have the most fanciful notions concerning revelation, some say that it takes place only once before creation; some, that it proceeds from a Godhead in the high heavens; some, that it should be unintelligible in the nature of things, being the word of an infinite God. But all this is pure imagination The character of true *Shruti* is thus described in the Permanent History of Bharatvarsha, with which you have already become familiar:

> "Shruti Pramana is one of the six varieties of proofs classified in Sanskrit Logic, such as direct perception, etc. The instruction from an Apta or Professor of a practical subject with which he is practically acquainted, is described as shabda or Shruti Pramana, The instructions received from him furnish only a theoretical knowledge which has afterwards to be converted intro practical knowledge, by actual experiment or experience, in order to attain to the level of the professor's knowledge......The word Rishi denotes a person who has obtained the real knowledge by direct personal experience, and his description of such experience is first graped by Shruti or hearing by his scholars who have afterwards to practise for themselves and become Rishis or Seers like their Master" (vol. i. pp. 28 and 29).

Of course, the greatest Professor of Religion is the *Tirthamkara*, who rises to Godhood and Omniscience, than which, respectively, no status is more exalted and worshipful and knowledge, more perfect. The Word of the Master is spread far and wide by men; and is preserved in Scripture composed in different ways, according to the abilities and tastes of its composers.

In the present cycle what seems to have happened is this that a class of poets busied themselves with the Word of Truth, and built elegant fanciful myths round it. These were highly appreciated and proved so attractive for their hidden charm that men of all classes and countries vied with one another to secure the highest excellence, with the result that the Word of Law was literally smothered under the prolific productions of human imagination and poetic fancy, and came, after a time, to be lost to view.

After a time temples and pagodas sprang up exhibiting representations of these mythological conceptions of the mind, and the outer rabble were invited to visit, and later even encouraged to worship the man-made deities thus installed as objects of meditation and veneration. The outer rabble then had their turn. For with the inculcation of this impious form of worship, which was generally also a source of income to the priestly class, there sprang up a sharp division between those who held the secret, the esoterics, and the vulgar laity, the exoterics, who fed the former. The element of greed upon which the relation between the teacher and the taught rested was also not unproductive of evil result. As men are not born with an understanding of the secret significancy of allegorical myths, ofter the lapse of some time the masses came to firmly believe in the exoteric faith which alone was known to them, and intolerance for an opposite view, which later on, even led to bitter feuds and hatreds, begar to be practised by them. The number of esoterics dwindled, as was inevitable, side by side, till at last matters came to such a pass that no esoteric dared openly preach the truth to the outside rabble at large. It was then that the wisdom of secret initiation came to be recognised by the 'divines,' and many institutions and lodges were established for the purpose. They went by different names in different countries, but all aimed at the same thing—the resurrection of Life, the Son, or the Son of God, from the dead.

By this time the estrangement between those who followed the word of the *Tirthamkara* in its plain undisguised form, and the esoterics themselves, fostered, as it was, on the part of the latter, to keep up appearances before their vulgar clientele, had become quite pronounced. Matters went on like this till at last the branch finally set itself up in opposition to the Tree, and is now vociferously engaged in denying its relationship with the Source, calling it now atheistic, now indefinite, now *anti-Dharma* (the destroyer of Dharma). The 'last-comers' in our enumeration of religions are those who have come either as reformers of existing creeds or who have endeavoured to strike out into paths that run parallel to the ancient tracks but little. They have had no revelation, and their knowledge is derived mostly from the misunderstood word of some ancient scripture to which they have attached themselves. In short, they may be said to have just rushed up to the platform through the half-lit passage of Textual literalism, and are now waxing eloquent on their notions concerning the shadows they passed by in that dim uncanny light. Here and there we, no doubt, come across gleams of real insight in some of their works; but that is only where a reformer lingered a bit over some particular shadow in the course of his rush through the region of mythology and myth.

To turn now to the relation of the different creeds among themselves, Religion may be described as a Central Pagoda set on a hill-top, in the heart of a beautiful city, where the Effulgence of Pure Intelligence presides in its Eternal Splendour. This is the Holy *Jina-Bani* (Revelation) that proceeds from the *Tirthamkara* whose Worshipful Image is installed in the sanctuary to guide and inspire mankind in the Right Path. The Light of Intellectualism is here so powerful that only a few worshippers can approach the Sanctuary without blinking. But there are covered passages from different parts of the city which lead to an underground maze of courts over the walls of which are painted many beautiful figures of gods and men done in life-like perfection. Each tribe has its own court in the maze; there are the Vedic Court, the Jewish Court, the Parsi Court, the Arabian Court and many other Courts raised by different peoples some of whom have now entirely passed away. All these courts are built round the base of the Sanctuary where the Goddess *Jina-bani* presides over the IMAGE OF TRUTH; and the sculptures and the paintings on their walls are so arranged that they exactly fit into niches carved out in the wall of the Sanctuary itself by the Sculptors and Artists of old. And so excellent is their workmanship and so cunning the skill of the Sculptor that you do not preceive them as images made by human hand, but as living gods and men and animals, engaged in the fun and frolic of the Immortals. Here you have Ganesha presiding over the entrance to the Hindu Court, where you may still see Indra embracing a Brahmana's wife, marked with ugly spots that are turning into eyes at Brahma's intervention. In the Hebrew Court you see your Garden of Eden, with its two famous trees, and the tragedy of the fall being enacted in all its grim detail. Yonder in the Court of the New Faith you find John baptising at the forbidden Jordon, a Divine Soul raising the dead and crucifying the fleshly *bahiratman* in the place of the skull; and in 'Araby' you have Muhammadans and Jews joining in the celebrations over the sacrificial cow. But there is no passage from here into the Sanctuary, except through certain hidden doorways which are so completely concealed by the Artist's work as to be altogether unperceivable except with subtler vision. The whole of this maze of courts is plunged in total darkness, except for the thin coloured light from within the Sanctum Sanctorum that is illumining the wonderful images and pictograms themselves. There was a key which every one of the old Artists possessed, but it had been lost long before the commencement of the A. D. era, though it was reconstructed again at the time. Some 1300 years ago this key was again fitted into some of the locks, but since then it is to be doubted if anyone has ever possessed it or opened any of the locked doors till now. To-day you have had that key placed in your hands. As you see, it is not a key of iron or brass or even of a precious metal, like silver or gold, but the KEY OF KNOWLEDGE that illumines itself and its surroundings. Its supernal phosphorescence enables its possessor to perceive the hidden bars and locks that bar the way to the Inner Court of Life and Light. It is this Key of Knowledge for the loss of which the teacher in the New Testament upbraided the Doctors of Law:—

> "Woe unto you, lawyers! for ye have taken away the key of knowledge: ye entered not in yourselves, and them that were entering in ye hindered. " (Luke, xi. 52).

It is this very Key of Knowledge that has been reconstructed now and placed in your hands, and I trust you will not suffer it to be lost again.

There is one striking feature about this business of reconstruction of the Key of Knowledge: it was lost by Lawyers originally and it is a lawyer who is restoring it now!

I hope I have given you a true picture of the Temple of Unity and Union as it should be, for I should be sorry to tread upon anyone's susceptibilities. We must not, however, allow hysterical sentiment to interfere with scientific work; and if anyone feels aggrieved with my results, I can only assure him of my sincerity of purpose. All further talk is necessarily forbidden by the scientific nature of the research. There is real sweetness in the reflection that Scientific Truth was known to the whole of the human race at one time in the past, and I certainly was not the exclusive property of the Jainas of to-day. Nay, it is riot unlikely that the Jainas of to-day are the descendants of men that took up the torch only in recent historical times and that have been thwarted by ill-luck from carrying it round the world. Your ancestors, then, are as likely to have been the custodians of Knowledge Divine in the remote past as mine, so that you are no strangers to Truth!

The dates of the appearance of various Religions cannot, of course, be determined at this time, but the order of their appearance is easily perceivable to a great extent. Religion started as a Science of Salvation with the Jains in India. Outside India no one has ever claimed to have obtained Salvation, and certainly elsewhere Religion has never worn the scientific aspect it wears in Jainism. (See my "Rishabha Deva" and the "Vision of St. John"). Then came the Allegorists. They were also Jains, naturally. Their style was copied by the outsiders. The descendants of the Aryan Allegorists of India are to-day known as Hindus. The Rigveda is most probably the oldest allegorical Scripture of the world. It was certainly composed, in parts at least, that is, certain of its personifications, if not its language, were composed, before the advent of the 22nd *Tirthamkara*, Nemi Nath. Then arose the Sect which popularized sanguinary sacrifices. They misinterpreted the allegorical text, and began to sacrifice animal lives. After some hundreds, or perhaps thousands of years, a wave of reaction set in against animal sacrifice. This view is supported by the Hindu and the Jaina Books and the reaction to the sacrificial cult is easily traceable even in the Upanishads. (See the "Mahabharata" and my "Key of Knowledge"). The Mahabharata itself was composed after the institution of animal sacrifices; the Ramayana is more recent.

After the 22nd *Tirthamkara*, scientific Religion seems to have almost disappeared for a time, but the 23rd *Tirthamkara* appeared in the ninth century B.C. In His time a considerable stir appears to have been caused in Indian metaphysical thought. Probably the six schools of Hindu Philosophy originated during His life and became fixed in their present forms some hundred or two hundred years afterwards. It is not possible to determine the order of their appearance, because they all refer to, and at times also contradict, one another. But the system of Kapila seems to be a modified copy or reproduction of a somewhat similar but older exposition that was also known as Sankhya, and was advanced as an explanation of the world-process by Marichi *rishi* (really the soul of the 24th *Tirthamkara* in its incarnation as the grandson of Rishabha Deva, the founder of Jainism). The Religions of the Parsees, the Jews and of Lao Tse in China were, very probably, founded about this time or a little earlier.

The seed of Christianity was taken from India in the sixth century B.C. (See my "Jainism, Christianity and Science" and the "Vision of St. John"); but the Gospels were written some centuries later. Buddhism started in the life-time of the last *Tirthamkara* as a compromise between the caste exclusiveness of the Hindus and the rigid, disciplinary asceticism of the Jains. Buddha was certainly not born in the Religion be founded. He became a disciple of various teachers, including the Jains, in the beginning of his life, and then struck out into a new path.

The different systems of Mysticism in different countries arose in the way I have described in the course of this lecture, and are naturally posterior to the main Creeds.

The origin and the dates of the other Religions which have arisen within the last two thousand years are well known and need not be recapitulated here.

As for the practical value of the results achieved by ourselves in the course of the present investigation, I may be pardoned if I claim to place them at a height that has never even been regarded as possible of attainment thus for. This is the point where lasting concord, unbreakable peace, abiding goodwill dwell, where reconciliation itself, shorn of ugly memories of hatred and distrust, merges in fraternal regard and affectionate esteem that is to endure for ever and ever more! I am sure you will not disagree with me when

I claim the following results as having been attained by us:—

(1) all whole scriptures have been explained, or at least have been shown to be explainable *leaving no unintelligible residue, to clash with the established truth*;

(2) all inconsistencies and differences have been harmonized or at least shown to be capable of being harmonized, between different scriptures and the

different books, or parts of books, of the same creed;

(3) the opposition of scientific rationalism has been demolished; and

(4) a consistent, honourable and practical doctrine has been established, which aims at and is intended to secure the highest benefits for men, and the grace and joy of life for all living beings, including those in the lower grades of existence;

(5) and last, but by no means the least of all, a lasting and abiding agreement, which is the real guarantee of eternal friendship, has been established, without denying, or in any way restricting, the legitimate scope, aspiration and function of any of the parties.

And now a word about putting the ideal of Life into practice. Religion is, of course, of no avail unless it is put into practice. Mere theory is useless, though it is absolutely true that Faith once acquired must inevitably lead to *nirvana*, because it is a psychological law that *belief* never fails to translate itself into action sooner or later.

Now, if you look around you, you will find the world only too full of trouble and misery and discontent all over. There is desolation everywhere and hearts of men are pierced with grief and aching with pain. The havoc wrought is not due to any other cause, but has been brought about by the human hand itself. Our insatiable lust for dominion and gold is mainly responsible for all our calamities and suffering. We falsify our engagements; we violate our promises, solemnly made, and we trample on our treaties when they no longer serve our purpose! Yet we are ever ready to talk of Equity and Law and are never abashed to proclaim that we are walking in the appointed path of Duty and *Dharma*! Poor, wretched purblind man in his conceit he would not only deceive himself and his neighbour, but would also cheat the Law if he only knew how to throw dust into the eyes of Nature! The very first thing a man should do is that he should be honest with himself. All these hypocritical ideas and grabbing ideals should be replaced with the true conceptions of Life. For, as it is said in the Bible,

> "......what is a man profited, if he shall gain the whole world, and lose his own soul? or what shall a man give in exchange for his soul?" Matt. xvi. 26.

'Live and let live,' is the true motto for a truly religious life, with the emphasis placed on the second part. For if you are killed in the endeavour to make another live, your reward is life more full and abundant in the next incarnation, but should you be so unfortunate as, to sacrifice another's life, so that you might prolong your days on earth, there are only suffering and pain in store for you in the hereofter. Have you not read in the Bible?—

> "Go ye and learn what that meaneth, I will have mercy, and not sacrifice" (Matt. x. 13).

This is again repeated in Matt. xii. 7:—

> "But if ye had known what this meaneth, I will have mercy and not sacrifice."

Does it not strike you that if the taking of life be cruel and call for the exercise of mercy when done in the name of a god or goddess, does it cease to be cruel when done in the name of one's own palate or tongue?

As 'tolstoy says, "*if a man's aspirations towards a righteous life are serious his first act of abstinence will be abstinence from animal food, because not to mention excitement of the passion produced by such food, its use is plainly immoral, as it requires an act contrary to moral feeling-i.e., killing-and is called forth only by greed.*" He who deceives himself in the matter of animal food, will be deceiving himself in all other things. Life is dear and joyous to all, and he who destroys it for a momentary gratification of his palate, is certainly not fit to be admitted.in the Realm of Mercy and Love that are the two most prominent attributes of Divinity. With unmerciful instincts in full operation, the fusion of spirit and matter takes the very worst forms and drags one into the most undesirable surroundings and conditions in the next rebirth. It is possible for us now that we have the light of reason to guide us to reform ourselves, but it will not always be so if we fall into lower grades of life in the future.

In the 14th chapter of his Epistle to Romans St. Paul, too, condemns the practice of eating flesh, though unfortunately he does so in mystic style, which has to be unravelled first, before its sense can be understood. In the 17th verse he says:—

> "For the kingdom of God is not meat and drink; but right-eousness, and peace, and joy in the Holy Ghost."

Verse 20th then reads ;-

> "For meat destroy not the work or God. All things indeed are pure; but it is evil for that man who eateth with offence."

And the 21st verse points out;

> "It is good neither to eat flesh, nor to drink wine, nor anything whereby thy brother stumbleth, or is offended, or is made weak."

Finally, it is said in the 22nd and the 23rd verses:—

> "Hast thou faith I have it to thyself before God. Happy is he that condemneth not himself In that thing which he alloweth.
>
> "And he that doubteth is damned if he eat because he eateth not of faith: for whatsoever is not of faith is sin."

As already observed, the whole of this exhortation is couched in mystic style, which was probably adopted to keep the weaklings in faith from leaving the 'fold.' Its purport can, however, be easily reached if it is kept in mind that the brother referred to in the twenty-first verse, who will be destroyed, is the inner Self who is metaphorically described as the brother of the outer ego. The Inner Self is truly the one for whom Christ may be said to have died, as the 15th verse proclaims:—

> ".....Destroy him not with thy meat for whom Christ died."

The literal reading of the text will be meaningless and absurd; for a man's brother is not destroyed if he eat flesh. The hidden identity is reluctantly revealed in the 21st verse where it is said:—

> "Happy is he that condemneth not *himself* in that thing which he alloweth."

As to whether flesh can be said to be inherently impure, more than anything else that is eaten, St. Paul's line of thought is that there is nothing unclean of itself (verses 14 and 20). Certainly, grains, cereals, vegetables and also flesh are all made of the same material, in their ultimate analysis. But "to him that esteemet.h anything to be unclean, to him it is unclean" (verse 14). The test is that one should not eat "with offence" (verse 20), that is to say by causing pain to a living being. Even doubt is sufficient to lead to damnation, as the last verse shows; for he who would eat things which his own conscience does not clearly tell him are proper to be eaten cannot be deemed to have attained to spiritual purity. Hence, meat which is the cause of the weakening and 'destruction' of the inner Self, and which causes him to stumble, is forbidden from the higher standpoint, to the man who would like to benefit himself by the example of the Teacher.

To put it still more clearly, the question may be looked at from two different points of view, the material and the spiritual. The worldly man only asks the question: Is flesh unclean? does it make the man who takes it unclean? But the religious point of view is different; for Religion is intended for the welfare of the soul, and enables it to attain to divine Freedom and Perfection. It is from this point of view that flesh is forbidden as destructive of the inner Self:

> "Destroy him not with thy meat, for whom Christ died."

When the lust for flesh is lessened, we shall acquire a clearer outlook in politics, and the relations of nations, communities and states will then be adjusted and regulated by the rules of Mercy and Love.

It is well to know that there are four kinds of ideals in life which are termed

(*i*) *dharma* (religion or virtue),

(*ii*) *artha* (wealth),

(*iii*) *kama* (pleasure), and

(*iv*) *moksha* (salvation).

Of these, the first three are meant for the house-holder, and the last for the *sadhu* (saint) who has renounced the world. The rule of wisdom governing the house-holder's ideals is that pleasure (*kama*) is the lowest of all ideals,—and must be subordinated to *artha* (wealth), which in its turn, must be controlled by *Dharma*. For if you spend the time that should be devoted to the acquisition of wealth in reckless Bacchanalian revelry, you will soon find yourself reduced to beggary, while wealth acquired without a due regard to the rules of Religion can only lead to unhappy results in the end. Therefore,

> "......seek ye first the kingdom of God and his righteousness and all these things shall be added unto you" (Matt. vi. 33).

The *sadhu*, who has renounced the world, can, of course, have no other ideal in life than salvation. He, therefore, seeks neither pleasure, nor wealth nor even virtue, but becomes engaged in pure self-contemplation, to destroy his *karmas*. It should be stated that virtue is a cause of bondage as much as vice, the difference being that the bondage resulting from the former is pleasant—birth in a high family, happy surroundings, and the like-while vice gives rise to undesirable circumstances and conditions.

The *sadhu*, therefore, avoids both virtue and vice by becoming engaged in pure self-contemplation, which destroys the root of bondage—*raga* (attachment) and *dvesha* (aversion)—in no time.

I think I must stop now. I have said sufficient to enable you to get along without stumbling over the objects lying awry in the half-lit region of mythology. You must now take the spade in your own hand, and carry on the work of investigation in other places and beyond the limits which it has been possible for me to reach. I must, however, warn you against rash conclusions that have brought nothing but discredit on the true method in the past. As Forrar says (see "The History of Interpretation", p. 13):—

> "The arbitrariness of allegory served to establish the importance of the historical sense."

This is quite true, though Farrar himself was in no way near an understanding of the true purport of the books of the Old and the New Testaments, for lack of real scientific knowledge. You should cultivate the habit of patient research and thoughtfulness, and avoid hasty identifications. Above all remember that mythology is not a science to be encouraged, though its elucidation is now necessary to reconcile us to one another. For the real aspirant who wishes to know the Truth, the scientific path alone is indicated. He must follow the advice given by St. Paul to Timothy which was intended to strike at the very root of the historical sense:—

> "Neither give heed to fables and endless genealogies, which minister questions, rather than godly edifying which is in faith; so do" (1 Tim. i. 4).

This is repeated again in 1 Tim. iv. 7 where it is said:—

> "But refuse profane and old wives' fables, and exercise thyself rather unto godliness."

For St. Paul knew full well that the effect of preaching in the mystifying phraseology of the scripture was sure to be disastrous, and he said so in so many words (2 Tim. iv. 3 and 4):—

> "For the time will come when they will not endure sound doctrines.....and they shall turn away their ears from the truth, and shall be turned into fables."

Without a doubt, the seeker after the real Truth will find it much safer to keep away, at a respectable distance, from the winding by-paths and twists of mythology than to run the risk of losing himself in their labyrinthine mazes and unillumined crypts. In short, mythology is to be approached in the spirit of an explorer, never as a devotee; and the explorer's qualification —scientific knowledge of the department of Life whose various aspects lie petrified in the now-crumbling pantheons of the world—is as essential to successful work as is a spirit of sympathy for the views of the Architects whose hands were engaged in the shaping of the diverse gods and goddesses.

And now a word about the modern theories of evolution that proceed upon the assumption that mankind has evolved from a lower into a higher state, especially with respect to intellectualism and religion.

Well, I have only to say as to this that you have seen for yourselves whether we are wiser to-day than the ancients at whose primitive 'simplicity' it has become a fashion with the learned of our day to laugh in and out of season. Judge for yourselves whether you knew the truth or the ancients, and in case you come to the conclusion that your ideas about the wisdom and worth of the ancients were wrong then modify your notions of evolution and other erroneous views accordingly. I have not much time at my disposal now, nor do I possess the necessary qualifications to speak on the subject; but I will say this that our theories and notions about evolution and other kindred subjects are not based on any general or special revelation which cannot be altered; they are purely provisional hypotheses, hastily formed and intended only, as all provisional hypotheses are, to serve as working bases for further research. No true scientist will ever venture beyond this, but it is, reserved for the indifferent thinkers outside the region of science to shout themselves hoarse on the irrefutability of opinions thus hurriedly formed on insufficient basis! The hidden wisdom of the ancients is there to knock on the head all such speculations of the moderns who are even today almost wholly ignorant of this very secret Science of the soul. Hence, he who would form a theory of the intellectual infancy of the entire human race in the past would have first to account for this wealth of misunderstood wisdom which he has inherited from the remotest ancestor of his in the shape of fables and myths.

The fact is that knowledge is not a monopoly of any particular period, much less of the presentage. The ancients were better qualified for it by their simple living and high thinking; though in the very nature of things pure divine knowledge must always be confined to but a few assiduous men. Those outside the zone of this divine illumination must necessarily comprise all shades and grades of opinion from absolute savagery upward, and these would both copy and invent according to their lights and inclinations. Many of the ancient myths and rites, especially those centred in human sacrifice appear to be purely barbarous in origin, yet they might be no more than unhappy copies from symbolic originals. At the same time it is a fact that barbarism is at least as old as enlightenment, and the very attempt to spiritualise the sacrificial cult points to the humanising effect of Religion on a savage and barbarous horde. Certainly, the composers of the myths and rituals associated with human or animal sacrifice could not well have been truly pious vegetarians, who were not likely to have recourse to a symbolism that must have been revolting to their natural instincts and the merciful bend of the mind. The full development of Hindu thought has been traced out by me ere this elsewhere and probably the other systems will have to be worked out in the same way. Every case must, however, be dealt with on its own merits, as no hard and fast rules can be laid down which will govern all cases indiscriminately. I think I have said enough on the subject in these few words.

I shall now sum up the purport of religion which we have been studying for these past few weeks, in words that have been put in the mouth of Life itself:—

> "I call heaven and earth to record this day against you, that I have set before you life and death, blessing and cursing: therefore, choose life, that both thou and thy seed may live" (Deuteronomy xxx. 19).

In other words, "Life is God, and I am He," is the watchword in Religion, and you shall certainly not go astray if you endeavour, in every possible way, to make your abode in your Life which is your true work.

And now, before we part, let us join in praying to Life for its Divine Gifts of Love and Mercy and *Vairagya*, and in wishing Peace and Happiness to all living beings, including every manifestation of Life divine, howsoever lowly placed in the order of being to-day.

जिसने राग द्वेष कामादिक जीते सब जग जान लिया,
सब जीवों को मोक्ष मार्ग का, निस्पृह हो, उपदेश दिया।
बुद्ध, वीर, जिन, हरि, हर, ब्रह्मा, या उसको, स्वाधीन कहो।
भक्ति भाव से प्रेरित हो यह चित्त उसी में लीन रहो॥१॥[1]

His passions who has overcome,
All Nature's secrets who has known,
Salvation's Path to every soul,
Without a motive, who has shown:
Buddha, Vir[2], Jina,[3] Hari, Har, Brahma,
Or the Self Him you may call:
His attainments may, with devotion deep,
My mind eternally extol!

विषयों की आशा नहि जिनके, साम्य-भाव धन रखते हैं,
निज-पर के हित-साधन में जो निश दिन तत्पर रहते हैं।
स्वार्थ त्याग की कठिन तपस्या बिना खेद जो सहते हैं,
ऐसे ज्ञानी साधु जगत के दुःख समूह को हरते हैं॥२॥

Pleasures of life who ever despise,
Equanimity's wealth who seek,
Devoted ever to uplift and raise
Themselves and others in every way;
Onward who press on the thorny Path
Of self-denial, undismayed,
Such saintly sages do relieve
The pain and misery of the World!

रहे सदा सत्सङ्ग उन्हीं का ध्यान उन्हीं का नित्य रहे,
उनकी जैसी चर्य्या में यह चित्त सदा अनुरक्त रहे।
नहीं सताऊँ किसी जीव को झूठ कभी नहीं कहा करूँ।
परधन वनिता पर न लुभाऊँ संतोषामृत पिया करूँ॥३॥

Their company may I ever enjoy;
Their thought may life's inspiration be;
The Path illumined by their Feet
I wish to tread reverently!
Untruth I vow never to utter;
Pain to no one may I cause;
Coveting neighbour's wealth nor wife,
Contentment's nectar may I quaff!

अहङ्कार का भाव न रक्खूं नहीं किसी पर क्रोध करूँ,
देख दूसरों की बढ़ती को कभी न ईर्षा भाव धरूँ।
रहे भावना ऐसी मेरी सरल-सत्य व्यवहार करूँ,
बने जहाँ तक इस जीवन में औरों का उपहार करूँ॥४॥

May pride never puff me up;
Nor anger seize me ever;
The sight of another's luck may not,
Make me envious with his lot!
Fair and square my dealings be,
In all things big and small ;
The joy of life for me may lie
In making everyone happy!

मैत्री भाव जगत में मेरा सब जीवों से नित्य रहे,
दीन दुःखी जीवों पर मेरे उर से करुणा स्रोत बहे।
दुर्जन-क्रूर-कुमार्गा रतों पर क्षोभ नहीं मुझको आवे,
साम्य भाव रक्खूँ मैं उन पर ऐसी परिणति हो जावे॥५॥

Love for all I long to cherish;
Compassion for those distressed;
With toleration, I would regard,
The vicious, the vile, and the perverse men!

गुणी जनों को देख हृदय में मेरे प्रेम उमड़ आवे,
बने जहाँ तक उनकी सेवा करके यह मन सुख पावे।
होऊँ नहीं कृतघ्न कभी मैं द्रोह न मेरे उर आवे,
गुण-ग्रहण का भाव रहे नितदृष्टि न दोषों पर जावे॥६॥

May Life in Service find its Joy!
May I the virtuous ever adore;
May malice enter not my heart;
Ingratitude I wish to shun;
Adoring virtue, blind to faults.

कोई बुरा कहो या अच्छा, लक्ष्मी आवे या जावे,
लाखों वर्षों तक जीऊं, या मृत्यु आज ही आजावे।
अथवा कोई कैसे ही भय या लालच देने आवे,
तो भी न्याय मार्ग से मेरा कभी न पग डिगने पावे॥७॥

Let men applaud me or upbraid,
Let wealth come or depart;
Whether I live for many long decades,
Or death come just this day;
Threats of evil, however strong,
Seducements, corrupting with pelf—
May none of these, at any time,
Swerve me from the noble Path!

होकर सुख मे मग्न न फूले, दुःख में कभी न घबरावे,
पर्वत नदी स्मशान भयानक अटवी से नहीं भय खावे।
रहे अडोल अकम्प निरन्तर, मन दृढ़तर बन जावे,
इष्ट वियोग अनिष्ट योग में सहन शीलता दिखलावे॥८॥

Let pleasure never turn my head;
May pain disturb me never!
Nature's awesome loneliness
May never make me shiver!
Unmoved, unmoving may I remain
In hill or wood or dell,
Displaying noble moral worth
In good or bad environment!

सुखी रहें सब जीव जगत के, कोई कभी न घबरावे,
वैर-पाप अभिमान छोड़ जग, नित्य नये मङ्गल गावे।
घर घर चर्चा रहे धर्म की, दुष्कृत दुष्कर हो जावें,
ज्ञान-चरित उन्नत कर अपना, मनुज जन्म फल सब पावें॥९॥

May happiness be the lot of all ;
May distress come near none;
Giving up hatred sin and pride,
May men chant hymns of joy all day!
May Dharma be practised in every home;
May evil cease to be easily-wrought:
Increasing in wisdom and merit may all,
Realise the purpose of life-Moksha !

ईति भीति व्यापे नहीं जग में वृष्टि समय पर हुआ करे,
धर्मनिष्ठ होकर, राजा भी न्याय प्रजा का किया करे।
रोग मरी दुर्भिक्ष न फैलै, प्रजा शान्त से जिया करे,
परम अहिंसा धर्म जगत मे फैल, सर्वहित किया करे॥१०॥

May distress and terror no longer exist;
May rains descend in good time;
The King may, too imbued with Dharma,
With even justice rule over men!
May plagues, disease and famines cease;
May people live in peace;
May the exalted *ahimsa dharma* prevail;
And the Gospel of Mercy become
The source of good to all!

फैले प्रेम परस्पर जग में, मोह दूर पर रहा करैं,
अप्रिय-कटुक-कठोर शब्द नहि कोई मुख से कहा करैं।
बन कर सब युग बीर हृदय से देशोन्नति रत रहा करैं,
वस्तु स्वरूप विचार, खुशी से सब दुख संकट सहा करैं॥११॥

May mutual love prevail in the world;
May delusion dwell at a distance!
May no one ever utter offensive speech,
Or harsh, unpleasant words with his tongue!

May men, made heroes, O Jugal Kishore!
Whole-heartedly work in their country's cause!
May all understand the Laws of Truth,
And joyfully, sorrow and suffering endure!
- Amen!
Om; Peace: Shanti! Shanti!! Shanti!!!

FOOTNOTES

1. Composed by Pt. Jugal Kishore with whose kind permission it has been given here with translation.
2. Mahavira.
3. Conqueror.

INDEX

B

C

D

E

L

M

T

Z

✦✦✦